the FOOD of MOROCCO

Also by Paula Wolfert

Mediterranean Clay Pot Cooking

The Cooking of Southwest France

The Slow Mediterranean Kitchen

Mediterranean Cooking

The Cooking of the Eastern Mediterranean

Mediterranean Grains and Greens

Paula Wolfert's World of Food

Couscous and Other Good Food from Morocco

Paula Wolfert

Photographs by Quentin Bacon

Drawings by Mark Marthaler

the
FOOD of
MOROCCO

ecco
ANNIVERSARY
40

An Imprint of HarperCollins Publishers

The selection from *The Voices of Marrakesh* by Elias Canetti on page 111 is reprinted by arrangement with Carl Hanser Verlag, Zurich, 1968, c/o Joan Daves Agency as agent for the proprietor. Copyright © 1968 by Carl Hanser Verlag Munchen by arrangement with Elias Canetti, Zurich, 1967, 1995.

Winter Squash with Caramelized Onions and Moroccan Dessert "Truffles" with Dates, Almonds, and Apples (Haroset) are from Joan Nathan's *Quiches, Kugels, and Couscous: My Search for Jewish Cooking in France* (New York: Knopf, 2010). Reprinted with permission.

Portions of this book have appeared in somewhat different form in *Food & Wine* magazine, *Saveur* magazine, and *Metropolitan Home*.

HarperCollins books may be purchased for educational, business, or sales promotional use. For information please write: Special Markets Department, HarperCollins Publishers, 10 East 53rd Street, New York, NY 10022.

FIRST EDITION

Designed by MILK Design Group

Library of Congress Cataloging-in-Publication Data has been applied for.

ISBN 978-0-06-195755-0

11   12   13   14   15   INDD/QGT   10   9   8   7   6   5   4   3   2   1

1

INTRODUCTION

❧ page 3 ❧

2

THE ESSENTIALS OF MOROCCAN COOKING

❧ page 13 ❧

3

SALADS

❧ page 53 ❧

4

BREADS AND PASTRIES

❧ page 97 ❧

5

EGGS, BUTTER,
BUTTERMILK, AND CHEESE

❧ page 151 ❧

6

SOUPS

❧ page 169 ❧

7

COUSCOUS

❧ page 195 ❧

8

FISH

❧ page 239 ❧

9

POULTRY

❧ page 269 ❧

10

MEATS

❧ page 335 ❧

11

BEAN AND VEGETABLE DISHES

❧ page 411 ❧

12

DESSERTS

❧ page 439 ❧

13

BEVERAGES

❧ page 489 ❧

ACKNOWLEDGMENTS page 500
SOURCES page 502
BIBLIOGRAPHY page 506
INDEX page 507

chapter one

INTRODUCTION

❈

"If one loses one's way in Morocco, civilization
vanishes as though it were a magic carpet rolled up
by a Djinn . . . it is a good thing to begin with such
a mishap, not only because it develops the fatalism
necessary to the enjoyment of Africa, but because
it lets one at once into the mysterious heart of the
country: a country so deeply conditioned by its
miles and miles of uncitied wilderness that
until one has known the wilderness, one
cannot begin to understand the cities."

—*edith wharton*

❈

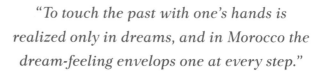

"To touch the past with one's hands is realized only in dreams, and in Morocco the dream-feeling envelops one at every step."

Edith Wharton wrote those words more than ninety years ago. And fifty years ago, when I first set foot in Morocco, there could not have been a better description of what I felt. I came as a nineteen-year-old beatnik. I had read the amazing novels and stories of Paul Bowles set in Morocco—lingered over his fine renditions of labyrinthine medinas and inscrutable utterances, not to mention his frightening dramatizations of the mysteries and adventures that may befall the stranger around every corner. I had come to an exotic land in search of "The Other." I was, I thought, prepared for most anything.

I soon discovered that it was I who was actually "the other." And as I explored, made my way through the narrow streets of the medina of Tangier, it was not the kind of adventures described by Bowles that befell me, but something else I was not prepared for: the seductions of Moroccan cuisine. These seductions did not creep up on me slowly, but hit me square in the face almost at once. The sharp scent of cumin on the air. Passing by a community oven and catching the scent of anise and freshly baking bread. The street smells of grilling skewered meats. Whiffs of pungently spiced fried fresh sardines. The unique aroma of chickpea flour being slowly baked with olive oil and eggs to make a glistening flan in a wood-fired oven. And at dusk, during the month of Ramadan, the surprise of watching as a voluptuous thick soup fragrantly seasoned with sweet spices was portioned out to people standing in line in the Grand Socco, the central marketplace, after the cannon in the Port of Tangier had been fired to mark the end of that day's fast.

Soon, at the homes of Moroccan friends, I tasted the more refined dishes: a pyramid of light, airy couscous topped with caramelized onions, raisins, and almonds; a *bastila*, pastry stuffed with dark pigeon meat, eggs, spices, and ground almonds and fried crisp; chickens prepared a half dozen different ways with preserved lemons and olives. The cuisine that was revealed changed my life. I became obsessed with learning everything I could about it. And the more deeply I explored, the more intensely I came to feel that this was the cuisine for me.

This book is a distillation of everything I know about Moroccan cuisine, everything I have learned about it during my fifty-year love affair with that country and its food. I have spent my professional life exploring the cuisines of the Mediterranean, and my fieldwork has taken me from

Spain to Turkey, from France to Tunisia, and to most every country and island in between. But always I have found myself coming back to Morocco, haunted by the tastes and aromas of the inimitable food that enveloped me through my early sojourns in Tangier.

I have written about this cuisine before, and I stand by my earlier book, still in print after more than thirty-five years. In that work, I presented Moroccan cooking as a prism through which to view an exotic foreign land, a gateway through which one could enter its culture. This book is different. I know so much more now, understand the cuisine so much better. I have added more than a hundred previously uncollected recipes to the earlier ones and placed a greater emphasis on the whys and wherefores of Moroccan cooking techniques.

Please note that I refer to "previously uncollected," not to "new." This is because, with only two exceptions, you will find no new recipes here in the sense that contemporary Moroccan chefs use the word. There has been a movement among them to rethink their national cuisine, to reconceive it and create new dishes. I respect their efforts, but I do not deal in invented dishes. My interest has always been in the real food that real people prepare and eat. The main task for me has always been to uncover these old dishes and figure out ways to reproduce them as authentically as possible in a modern American kitchen.

Morocco is a large country; its spell is great, its magic huge, its cuisine diverse. I make no claim to have uncovered all its culinary glories. What I bring to you here are simply my favorites, the dishes I like best and continue to cook. Because this is a personal collection, I can't guarantee you'll like every single one of my choices. My best advice is to look through the recipes, pick out ones you think you will like, and then immerse yourself in those.

Fifty years ago, I found the Morocco of Edith Wharton and Paul Bowles, but today I find a very different place. When I first visited, only ten percent of the population lived in cities. Today it's closer to eighty percent. This has brought huge changes. During the seven years that I lived in Morocco, for example, we always prepared our own bread dough at home, then sent it off to the neighborhood wood-fired oven to be baked. People today are busy. Many no longer have time to knead bread dough or prowl the souks in search of ingredients and special spice mixtures. In Casablanca, many middle-class women purchase their food at supermarkets and prepare their tagines in pressure cookers. These are practical solutions, and I understand them. But meals prepared this way lack the full flavor and special seductive quality of Moroccan food at its best.

The American culinary scene has changed greatly too. When I first wrote about Moroccan cooking, earthenware tagines were not available here. Now they are easy to acquire. We have food processors and electric spice grinders and wonderful raw ingredients. Before, grocers would shake

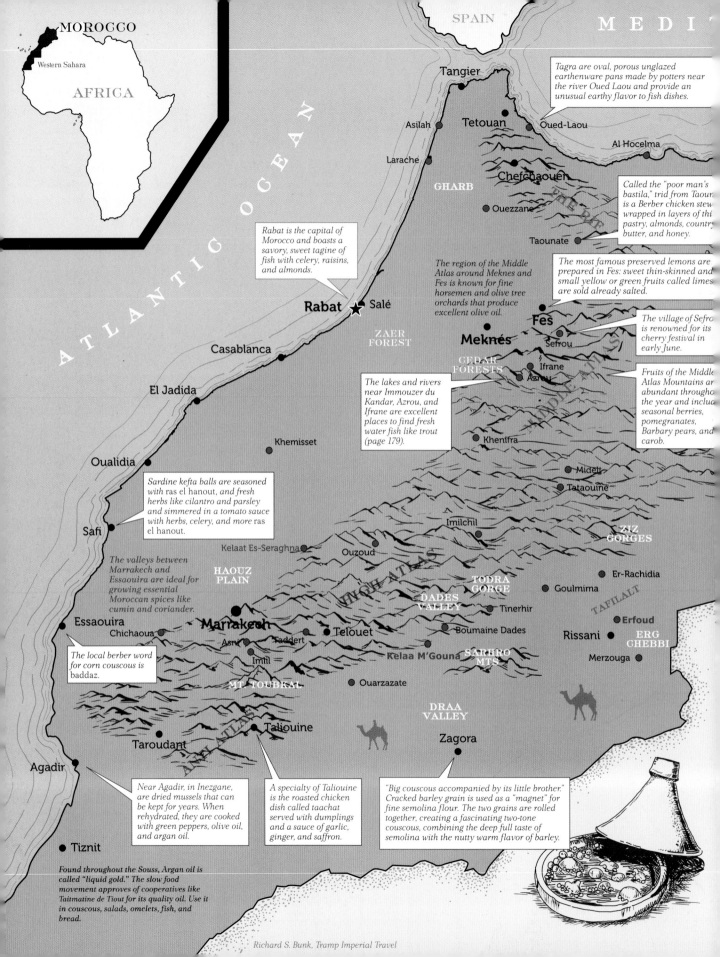

MOROCCO

Western Sahara

AFRICA

SPAIN

MEDIT'

ATLANTIC OCEAN

Tangier

Asilah

Larache

Tetouan

Oued-Laou

Al Hocelma

Chefchaouen

GHARB

Ouezzane

Taounate

Tagra are oval, porous unglazed earthenware pans made by potters near the river Oued Laou and provide an unusual earthy flavor to fish dishes.

Called the "poor man's bastila," trid from Taour is a Berber chicken stew wrapped in layers of thi pastry, almonds, country butter, and honey.

Rabat is the capital of Morocco and boasts a savory, sweet tagine of fish with celery, raisins, and almonds.

The region of the Middle Atlas around Meknes and Fes is known for fine horsemen and olive tree orchards that produce excellent olive oil.

The most famous preserved lemons are prepared in Fes: sweet thin-skinned and small yellow or green fruits called limes are sold already salted.

Rabat

Salé

Casablanca

ZAER FOREST

Meknés

Fes

Sefrou

CEDAR FORESTS

Ifrane

Azrou

The village of Sefro is renowned for its cherry festival in early June.

El Jadida

The lakes and rivers near Immouzer du Kandar, Azrou, and Ifrane are excellent places to find fresh water fish like trout (page 179).

Khenifra

Fruits of the Middle Atlas Mountains ar abundant throughou the year and includ seasonal berries, pomegranates, Barbary pears, and carob.

Khemisset

Oualidia

Midelt

Tataouine

Imilchil

ZIZ GORGES

Sardine kefta balls are seasoned with ras el hanout, and fresh herbs like cilantro and parsley and simmered in a tomato sauce with herbs, celery, and more ras el hanout.

Safi

Kelaat Es-Seraghna

Ouzoud

Er-Rachidia

Goulmima

TODRA GORGE

TAFILALT

The valleys between Marrakech and Essaouira are ideal for growing essential Moroccan spices like cumin and coriander.

HAOUZ PLAIN

HIGH ATLAS

DADES VALLEY

Tinerhir

Erfoud

Essaouira

Chichaoua

Marrakech

Telouet

Boumaine Dades

Rissani

ERG CHEBBI

Asni

Taddert

Kelaa M'Gouna

SARHRO MTS

Merzouga

The local berber word for corn couscous is baddaz.

Imlil

MT. TOUBKAL

Ouarzazate

ANTI ATLAS

DRAA VALLEY

Taliouine

Taroudant

Zagora

Agadir

Near Agadir, in Inezgane, are dried mussels that can be kept for years. When rehydrated, they are cooked with green peppers, olive oil, and argan oil.

A specialty of Taliouine is the roasted chicken dish called taachat served with dumplings and a sauce of garlic, ginger, and saffron.

"Big couscous accompanied by its little brother." Cracked barley grain is used as a "magnet" for fine semolina flour. The two grains are rolled together, creating a fascinating two-tone couscous, combining the deep full taste of semolina with the nutty warm flavor of barley.

Tiznit

Found throughout the Souss, Argan oil is called "liquid gold." The slow food movement approves of cooperatives like Taitmatine de Tiout for its quality oil. Use it in couscous, salads, omelets, fish, and bread.

Richard S. Bunk, Tramp Imperial Travel

elilla

Saidia

Oujda

ALGERIA

...s and tagines with ...oukes—small pasta ...alls steamed like ...cous.

Figuig

TANGIER
TANGIER: *Kalinté*, a chickpea flan dusted with cumin, Tangier's premier street food (page 113).
TANGIER: Fish tagine with wild cardoons, or artichokes.

CHEFCHAOUEN, TETOUAN & THE RIF MOUNTAINS
CHEFCHAOUEN: *Klila*, aged goat cheese and mountain honey, to flavor pasta soup (page 165).
CHEFCHAOUEN: Street carts with candied and roasted nuts.
OUDJA: "Thousand hole" semolina pancake called *khringo* (page 455).
OUDJA: *Babbouka*, stuffed lamb tripe.
RIF MOUNTAINS: *Byssara*, soupy fava puree eaten with scallions (page 436).
RIF MOUNTAINS: *Mengoub*, dried fava with meat confit (page 436).
RIF MOUNTAINS: *Seffa* couscous, a dessert moistened with lavender tea.
TETOUAN: Shredded pastry with almonds called *ktaif* (page 486).
TETOUAN: Sephardic *haroset* (page 452).

MIDDLE ATLAS, THE GHARB, FES & MEKNÉS
MIDDLE ATLAS: Hyayna and Taounate region famous for Arabian horse breeding, red couscous with spring greens, and harcha bread (page 116).
MIDDLE ATLAS: *Baqqula*, cooked salad of leafy greens. A savory winter dish in Fes (page 81).
MEKNES: Cafés serving perfumed coffee with cardamom, cinnamon, cumin, and ginger.
MEKNES: Major wine growing region.
THE GHARB: Eucalyptus, thyme, and orange blossom honey production.
FES: Excellent snail soup prepared by Hasnaoui, just past the Bou Inania Madrasa.
FES: *Tagine qamamma*, lamb layered with onion, tomatoes, and raisins (page 381).
SEFROU: The Jewish spirit, *mahia*, made from figs or cherries.

RABAT, SALÉ & CASABLANCA
RABAT & SALÉ are both credited with creating "khliî express" or meat confit (page 44).
CASABLANCA'S "Marché Central" sells camel meat. Look for the camel's head on display.
CASABLANCA'S Milk bars called *mahlabas* serve smoothies made with avocado, dates, almonds, and orange flower water (page 493).

EL JADIDA, SAFI, ESSAOUIRA & AGADIR
SAFI: Famous for pottery, fish, and shellfish dishes.
ESSAOUIRA: *Merk hzina* is Morocco's most refreshing and simple summer salad (page 58).
ESSAOUIRA & EL JADIDA: Corn couscous with shellfish (page 233).
AGADIR: Argan oil, also called "liquid gold," used in couscous, salads, omelets, fish dishes, and the famous dip, *amlou* (page 27).
OUALIDIA: Oyster farms (Oyster Farm #7 is famous) and wonderful shellfish, including mussels and sea urchins.
CHICHAOUA: Spice fields and the world's best cumin. Fresh toasting and grinding of whole cumin seeds is what gives Moroccan dishes their unique aromatic and vibrant finish. And, you don't need to toast these because they are much stronger in flavor.

MARRAKECH, PROVINCE OF HAOUZ, OURIKA VALLEY & THE HIGH ATLAS
MARRAKECH: *Mechoui and tangia*. You can find them just off the Djemaa el Fna, near Djam Kharbouch, or just ask for the "olive market."
MARRAKECH: Rabbit tagine at the Restaurant Tiznit just off Rue du Bank.
MARRAKECH: A great but little known specialty of Marrakech is chicken cooked with nigella seeds (page 298).
MARRAKECH: Djemaa el Fna stalls selling sweets, tagines, kebabs, snail soup, and more.
MARRAKECH: Old Jewish quarter, the Mellah, has some of the best spice dealers.
PROVINCE OF HAOUZ: Barley shoot couscous is considered the most delicious in Morocco. Immature barley is grilled in a pan with wild thyme. It is then cracked, sieved, steamed, buttered, and served with cold buttermilk (page 220).
THE HIGH ATLAS: Telouet on the route of the Tizi-n-Tichka; bread baked on stones; and figs picked green and added to couscous.
PROVINCE OF HAOUZ: Berber village specialty called *tagoula* made from slow-cooked, crushed barley grits enriched with argan oil, and served hot to "warm the body and the soul."
KELAAT ES-SERAGHNA: North of Marrakech, an omelet-like pancake stuffed with meat confit, tomato, and onion (page tk).
TADDERT: A stopping point for travelers on the Tizi-n-Tichka road, Taddert has grills, cafés, and shops that almost never close.

SOUTHERN MOROCCO
TALIOUINE: Center of Morocco's great saffron fields. Saffron green tea is prepared like mint tea and is a popular beverage.
TAROUDANT: Couscous with green figs and a southern version of *tangia* with calve's feet.
RISSANI: *Zegzaw*, a type of broccolini that flavors delicious soups and couscous (page 222).
TAFILALT: Specialties include bread stuffed with beef, onions, spices, and hard-cooked eggs.
ZAGORA: Date juice thinned with milk and water, simmered with rose petals, thyme, henna, and nutmeg.
FIGUIG: White truffles. You can buy them at the market at Tatouine.
TIZNIT: Tagine of lamb with raisins and almonds (page 371).

"The argan trees are everywhere, thousands of them, squat and thorny, anchored to the rocks that lie beneath in their dubious shade. They flourish where nothing else can live, not even weeds or cacti. Their scaly bark looks like crocodile hide and feels like iron. Where the argan grows, the goats have a good life. The trunk is short and the branches begin to proliferate only a few feet from the ground. This suits the goats perfectly; they climb from branch to branch eating both the leaves and the greasy, bitter, olive-like fruit. Subsequently their excrement is collected, and the argan pits in it are pressed to make a thick cooking oil."

—*paul bowles*

"There have been many attempts to divide Morocco into convenient sections for discussion, but most of them appear unnecessarily complex; it is easier to consider an inner Morocco and an outer Morocco, the two being divided by the whole mass of the Atlas Mountains, running from the southwest to the northeast of the country, and the Rif Mountains, which turn at right angles to these and form the Mediterranean wall."

—*gavin maxwell*

their heads when I asked for certain spices; today I usually hear, "Yes, we carry that!" Organic food and farmers' markets are found most everywhere. Great food products are easily obtainable. You can even buy preserved lemons at some markets. And if you can't find what you're looking for, there are superb mail-order sources for most everything you need.

A few words about tagines (I'm referring now to the elegant two-part vessel with the conical top in which Moroccan stews, also called tagines, are cooked). Must you acquire one? No, you don't have to—but you really should. A tagine will make it possible to cook Moroccan food the authentic way and present your dishes beautifully at table, and the results will greatly reward you. To put the question another way, would you even consider embarking on an exploration of Chinese food without purchasing a wok? I hope to demonstrate in this book that the tagine is an ingenious device in which a huge category of Moroccan dishes are best prepared. In my earlier book, I instructed readers to use enameled cast-iron pots. No longer! Working on my last two books, *The Slow Mediterranean Kitchen* and *Mediterranean Clay Pot Cooking*, convinced me once and for all that the vast majority of Moroccan dishes are best cooked slowly in earthenware. For reasons having to do with the recycling of moisture due to the conical shape of the lid and the final flavor-rich toasting once most of that moisture has been cooked off or absorbed, tagines make it possible to achieve a succulence and depth of flavor obtainable no other way. They are, you see, not merely stew pots, but become, in the later stages of cooking, portable ovens (a process explained in detail later in this book).

Moroccan food preparation is a "bottom-up" cooking style, conducted almost entirely on the stovetop. Yes, some stews are finished off in the oven or beneath the broiler, but in most cases, those are concessions to our modern kitchens, since we don't generally cook over charcoal braziers.

Another process emphasized here is steaming. The most obvious examples are the steaming of grains such as semolina, barley, and corn to make wonderful light couscous. But vegetables, fruits, meats, and poultry are also steamed to achieve succulence, taste, and aroma; maintain texture; and preserve nutrients. Often these ingredients, having been steamed, are finished by being caramelized in a skillet. Tagine cooking also involves steaming, which begins when the grated onions and/or a marinade generate moisture that instills a special silken quality to meat and vegetables that no other method (including sous-vide cooking) can rightly duplicate. And in a much shorter time!

In my earlier book, I recommended the use of fillo pastry, since authentic Moroccan *warqa* pastry is so difficult to make. Fillo is acceptable, but *warqa* is better, stronger, and thinner, and it bakes up crispier and flakier. Recently, after long experimentation and assimilating the advice of several Moroccan cooks, I developed an easy way to make this pastry using a paintbrush. If you follow my *warqa* recipes, your *bastilas* and other pastry dishes will be especially delicious, with an authentic Moroccan texture and taste.

I've also learned to place greater emphasis on the Moroccan pantry, not just preserved lemons, an essential ingredient (and very easy to put up), but also preserved meat, which I call "meat confit," and a rich tomato sauce, which I call "Tomato Magic," both used as condiments to enrich the flavor of your dishes. Many of my newly collected dishes come from the Berber, as opposed to the Arab, culinary culture, where these and other condiments are used to great effect.

In my earlier book, I made the point that great national cuisines depend on four factors: abundance of fine ingredients; variety and confluence of cultural influences; a great civilization; and a refined palace life. Morocco has been blessed with all four. And, indeed, the country has produced dishes of great refinement, and you will find recipes for many such dishes here. In truth, I can never decide which I prefer: the fabulous urban couscous dishes, *bastilas*, and complex dessert pastries, or the slow-cooked tagines of the Moroccan countryside. In fact, I like it all: the food of the palaces and the food of peasants and fishermen, made of simple ingredients and simply prepared. Moroccan food is wonderfully diverse, and therein lies its glory.

Moroccans put much store in what they call *baraka*, which means good fortune. And in culinary terms, *baraka* can also refer to an ability to start cooking with very little in the way of ingredients and yet feed many people from the food pot. With this book, I welcome you to the wonderful world of Moroccan cooking and wish you good fortune as you make, eat, and discover this amazing food.

chapter two

THE ESSENTIALS OF MOROCCAN COOKING

❊

"We shall never apprehend all the subtleties
of Morocco, any more than we shall eventually
succeed in understanding its profound reality.
Too many things there are different from
what seems to us natural, logical, and
commonsensical."

—*alain d'hooghe*

❊

THE ESSENTIALS OF MOROCCAN COOKING

MOROCCAN TAGINES
{ page 18 }

PRESERVED LEMONS
{ page 20 }

OLIVES
{ page 22 }

ARGAN OIL AND AMLOU
{ pages 26 and 27 }

SPICES AND SPICE MIXTURES
{ page 28 }

RAS EL HANOUT
{ page 32 }

"FAUX" RAS EL HANOUT #1 AND #2
{ page 36 }

LA KAMA SPICE MIXTURE
{ page 37 }

HARISSA SAUCE
{ page 39 }

HERBS AND AROMATICS
{ page 40 }

TOMATO MAGIC
{ page 41 }

HONEY AND FRAGRANT WATERS
{ page 42 }

MOROCCAN PRESERVED MEAT
{ page 43 }

"EXPRESS" MEAT CONFIT
{ page 44 }

TEN TIPS FOR PREPARING MOROCCAN FOOD
{ page 48 }

The Moroccan larder is a wondrous place, stocked with cereals and beans, dried and spiced meats, marinated olives, nuts, oil-preserved vegetables, dried fruits, and all kinds of spices and spice mixes to add to meat, fish, poultry, and vegetables to flavor them and liven them up. Most Moroccan larder items don't take up much room, nor are they difficult to make, and since many of them are preserved, they actually benefit from the passage of time. I think of the stocking of my larder as a gift to myself.

Though an absolutely delicious chicken with lemons and olives should, ideally, be made with Moroccan chickens raised in the Moroccan style and butchered the Moroccan way, and garnished with Moroccan olives and preserved Moroccan *doqq* (a fragrant lemon especially amenable to salt preservation), today, more than ever, we can make a great version of this dish with materials readily available in the United States: an air-chilled organic chicken; homemade preserved lemons; red (midway) or ripe green olives; and the finest and freshest spices now readily available in high-quality supermarkets and gourmet shops and online (see Sources). The trick, of course, is to shop carefully, frequent local farmers' markets, buy always for quality, and purchase organically raised meats, poultry, fruits, and vegetables.

Moroccan ingredients are fairly simple. My recipes do not require expensive materials. Great Moroccan food is made from modest products: grains, chickens, inexpensive cuts of lamb, beans, fresh vegetables, dried and fresh fruits, nuts, spices, herbs and aromatics, fragrant waters, olives, and olive oil. This chapter deals with all of these, and also includes recipes for such basic components as preserved lemons, an argan oil–almond honey, spice mixtures, tomato paste, "not-too-hot" harissa sauce, "saffron water," and preserved meat that's used as a condiment.

MOROCCAN TAGINES

Earthenware tagines have a wonderful ability to coddle food, bring out bright natural flavors and aromas, and produce an unctuous tenderness. According to some writers, earthenware will also impart *goût de terroir*, a "taste of the earth."

Unglazed earthenware pots, including those made from micaceous clay, should be seasoned before use. To season a new unglazed tagine: Rub the pot with a clove of cut garlic. Fill the shallow bottom dish with water or milk, place it in a cold oven, and set the temperature to 350°F. Bake the pot for 30 minutes, then turn off the heat and let it cool in the slowly receding heat, 2 to 3 hours. Drain off the liquid, wash the pot, dry it well, and rub with olive oil.

If you'd like to simulate the patina of an antique tagine, you can burnish the pot by rubbing it inside and out with a mixture of ½ cup olive oil and ¾ cup wood ash from the fireplace. Place in a cold oven, set the temperature to 250°F, and bake for 2 to 3 hours. Turn off the heat and let the pot cool in the oven. Repeat, if desired, for deeper browning.

To season a new partially glazed tagine: Soak the bottom dish in water to cover for 12 hours. Drain the dish, wipe it dry, and rub with a cut clove of garlic. Fill the dish again with water to ½ inch below the rim and add ⅓ cup vinegar. Set on a heat diffuser over low heat and slowly bring the liquid to a boil. Cook until only about ½ cup liquid remains. Remove from the heat and let cool, drain, then rinse and dry.

When cooking in a tagine on a gas or electric stovetop, use a heat diffuser and start at a lower temperature than you ordinarily would with a metal pot, then slowly raise the heat as necessary. Or, to put it another way: avoid thermal shock—sudden changes in temperature—which can cause cracking. Once the heat has permeated the pot, which can take a relatively long time because clay is such a good insulator, the pot will hold the heat evenly for a long time.

When you remove a hot tagine from the stove, use thick pot holders and always place it on a wooden board, folded kitchen towel, or cloth pad. If you place a hot tagine on a cold surface, such as a marble or granite counter, it may crack. By the same token, never place a refrigerated pot in a preheated oven. Instead, bring to room temperature, put it in the oven, and then turn on the heat. Also, never place a hot tagine in cold water, and avoid adding cold food or liquid to a hot clay pot. [Flameware (see below) is an exception to this rule.]

Glazed pots are generally dishwasher-safe, but porous unglazed pots should be washed by hand to prevent absorption of detergent. After washing, if your earthenware tagine is waterlogged, turn it upside down and let it air-dry thoroughly overnight.

Because unglazed earthenware is porous and thus tends to hold tastes and aromas, it's best to dedicate one unglazed earthenware terrine or pot for cooking fish and keep another to use for meat and poultry.

Flameware, the popular name for flameproof ceramic cookware, is newer on the market, but it's extremely practical and doesn't need seasoning. This type of stoneware contains mineral elements that keep the vessels from expanding and contracting with sudden changes in temperature (as conventional stoneware does), thus allowing them to be used over direct heat on all types of stoves: gas, electric, and glass top, or even under the broiler. They are excellent for slowly developing a golden brown crust on fish or poultry and for meat dishes that require caramelization. I use my flameware casseroles for stews, soups, and bean dishes and my flameware skillets for frying eggs and for potato and vegetable gratins.

PRESERVED LEMONS

In Morocco, many types of lemons are put up in salt for use in salads, couscous, fish dishes, and tagines. I'd go so far as to say that preserved lemons are the most important condiment in the Moroccan larder. Fresh lemons are never an adequate substitute. The taste, texture, and aroma of preserved lemons are unique and cannot be duplicated by other means (no matter what some cookbook authors tell you).

The crème de la crème of Moroccan lemons, the fragrant, thin-skinned *doqq*, is similar in aroma and flavor to our thicker-skinned American hybrid, the Meyer lemon. Meyer lemons turn extremely soft during preserving, and they make an excellent flavoring for olives, salads, or brined vegetables or garnish for tagines. California Eureka lemons also work quite well.

PRESERVED LEMONS

The following recipe can be doubled, tripled, or more. Be sure to store your preserved lemons in a glass jar with a tight-fitting lid.

According to the late distinguished food writer Michael Field, the best way to extract the maximum amount of juice from a lemon is to cook it in a microwave or in boiling water for a short time and then allow it to cool before squeezing. Some cooks suggest using commercial lemon juice to top off their preserved lemons. I only use freshly squeezed lemon juice.

⊱ Makes 5 preserved lemons ⊰

5 organic lemons, scrubbed and dried

About ⅓ cup kosher salt

½ cup fresh lemon juice

1. Soften the lemons by rolling them back and forth on a wooden cutting board. Quarter the lemons from their tops to within ¼ inch of their bottoms, sprinkle salt on the exposed flesh, and then reshape the fruit. Pack them into a glass jar, pushing them down and adding more salt between layers. Top off with the lemon juice, but leave some air space before sealing the jar.

2. Allow the lemons to ripen in a warm place for 30 days, turning the jar upside down every few days to distribute the salt and juice. If necessary, open the jar and add more lemon juice to keep the lemons covered.

Variation:

AZIZA BENCHEKOUN'S FIVE-DAY PRESERVED LEMON RECIPE

If you run out of preserved lemons and need some in a hurry, you can use this "quick" method taught to me by a Moroccan diplomat's wife. Lemons preserved this way will not keep more than 1 or 2 days, but are perfectly acceptable in an emergency.

With a sharp knife, make 8 fine 2-inch vertical incisions around the peel of each lemon. Do not cut into the membrane, which protects the pulp. Place the lemons in a stainless steel saucepan with plenty of salt and water to cover and then boil until the peels become very soft, about 5 minutes. Place in a clean jar, cover with the cooled cooking liquid, and leave to pickle for 5 days.

NOTES TO THE COOK

To use: Pluck out a lemon with a wooden fork or spoon and rinse it under cold running water. Remove and discard the pulp, unless it is called for in the recipe—I generally use only the rind, but in a few recipes, I add the pulp to the marinade.

Preserved lemons will keep for up to a year in the refrigerator, and the pickling juice can be used one more time over the course of a year; then it should be discarded. The most important thing to remember is that the lemons must be completely covered with salted lemon juice.

Sometimes you will see a lacy white substance clinging to preserved lemons in their jar. This material is harmless, but it should be rinsed off for aesthetic reasons before the lemons are used. Preserved lemons are always rinsed before use in any case, to rid them of excessive saltiness.

OLIVES

Morocco is blessed in the North with many regions heavily covered with olive trees, mostly the Picholine Marocaine variety. Most of the olives are used to make olive oil, but Moroccan cooking also uses large amounts of whole olives, which are brined or cured and treated in numerous ways. (See Sources.)

In the souks, you will find stalls that sell nothing but olives of every flavor, size, quality, and color, from green to red to black. The color of an olive depends upon when it was picked. As it ripens on the tree, it turns from pale green to green-tan to tan-violet, then to violet-red to deep wine red to reddish black, and finally to coal black. After that, it loses its glistening appearance and begins to shrivel in the sun.

A freshly picked olive is inedible. It must be pickled or cured, and the way this is done determines whether it is tangy, bitter, salty, lemony, or sweet. In the olive market, each seller has his own special seasonings.

Basically there are three types of olives used in Moroccan cooking: green, midway, and black.

GREEN PICHOLINE OLIVES

Unripe green cracked or whole olives (often flavored with preserved lemon, garlic, herbs, and olive oil or simply with the juice of bitter oranges) are added to salads and used in some tagines known as *meslalla*, where they literally "smother" the chicken or lamb or fish (see page 295). Mild and nutty, they are readily available at the olive bar in any better American grocery store.

Though green Picholine olives are delicious on their own, they are even better pitted and tossed with a dressing made of lemon juice, olive oil, parsley, ground cumin, harissa, and a little crushed garlic. Leave to macerate for at least 24 hours before serving.

RIPE OR MIDWAY OLIVES

These are often referred to as *beldi* or country-style olives, and are riper and thus softer than green olives but lighter and not as firm as black ones. Midways can be tan, russet, violet, or deep purple. The most popular are the violet and winy-red ones. When pickled in the juice of bitter oranges, they are especially flavorful. Midways are available online (see Sources).

Most midway American olives are not processed by fermentation and have a mild taste, which works well for many of the tagines in this book. For use in salads, marinate them for a short time in a simple dressing made of lemon juice, olive oil, cumin, paprika, parsley or cilantro, salt, and cayenne to taste.

Midway ripe olives are most often used to garnish a chicken dish or tagine, such as the chicken with lemon and olives on page 306. Some

Moroccan olive merchants gently spice these olives with their own formulae and toss them with pickled carrots, pickled onions, and pickled cucumbers to be sold as salads. Moroccan cooks use them to garnish canned tuna or sardines for a simple summertime meal.

BLACK OLIVES

Sun-dried, salt-cured shriveled black olives are readily available in the United States. You don't have to do much to them, as their flavor has already been concentrated. In Morocco, they're often sold smothered in fiery harissa. But plump, oily black olives are often mixed with garlic, oil, cumin, and thyme to be used in salads, or, best of all to my mind, mixed with some creamy goat cheese, and used to fill appetizer-sized fried pastry triangles.

HANDLING OLIVES

Rinse the olives and taste for saltiness. If they are overly salty, soak them for an hour in water to cover, then drain and rinse well. If they are too bitter, place them in a saucepan, cover with water, and bring to a boil; drain, cover with fresh water, and repeat until the bitterness is gone. If they are too acidic, soak them in several changes of water, until no longer sour.

ARGAN OIL

In the region called the Souss, in the Moroccan southwest, the towns have magical names: Tiznit, Tamanar, Tafraout, Taroudant, Essaouira. Here the local Berbers extract oil from the nuts of the argan tree (*Argania spinosa*), a plant indigenous to the region and famous for its attractiveness to goats, which literally climb up into its branches.

The nuts contain an oil that has a remarkable flavor, akin to that of toasted hazelnuts. Moroccan cooks use the oil to enhance taste and aroma by drizzling it over couscous, corn couscous, corn bread, semolina pancakes, steamed vegetables, warm slices of goat cheese, and fresh cooked fish. Since it is expensive, it is used sparingly, and because it's strongly flavored, a little bit goes a long way.

Please note that there are two kinds of argan oil, one used in cosmetics and the other for adding to food. Be sure to purchase the edible variety (see Sources).

The production of argan oil is artisanal and the technique is passed down from mother to daughter. Both UNESCO and Slow Food protect the argan tree and its oil, but even so, some tainted oils have appeared on the market. For this reason, I suggest you stick to the sources I recommend.

AMLOU

One of the most famous uses of argan oil is in the preparation of *amlou,* a shiny brown dip made with ground toasted almond paste and a light honey. It's delicious on warm *harcha* rounds (see page 116) or semolina pancakes (see pages 125 and 126).

Commercial *amlou* doesn't hold up well, so I suggest you make your own using the traditional method: pounding the nuts in a heavy mortar with a strong pestle, then using the pestle to slowly rub them while adding the argan oil. Finally, you work in the honey. If you know how to make classic mayonnaise, you can make *amlou.*

Yes, it can be made in a food processor, but you will not achieve the proper silken texture and glossy appearance. It will, however, still taste good!

NOTE TO THE COOK

Since *amlou* tends to separate upon long storage, make it in small amounts, and use it within a month.

—— Makes about 1¼ cups ——

8 ounces almonds, blanched, peeled, and toasted in a 300°F oven until golden brown

1 teaspoon coarse sea salt

½ cup argan oil (see Sources)

¼ cup orange blossom honey, preferably clear and thin

Grind the warm almonds with the salt to a smooth paste in a heavy mortar. Slowly work in the argan oil, about 1 tablespoon at a time. When the mixture is smooth and creamy, gradually add the honey, a spoonful at a time. Scrape the glossy *amlou* into an earthenware crock and store it in a cool place, but not in the refrigerator.

SPICES AND SPICE MIXTURES

Wandering among the spice stalls in a great city like Fes, seeing and inhaling the aromas of myriad spices displayed in huge sacks, small boxes, and glass jars, the visitor is struck by the notion that the Moroccans have fallen in love with every spice in the world. In fact, this love of spices is in the tradition of their Arab ancestors, who brought with them, on their great sweep across North Africa from Arabia, a sophisticated knowledge of their use in perfumes and medicines, for the enhancement of food, and as currency for trade.

Since biblical times, spices have been a symbol of luxury in the Middle East, and the spice trade, a way of life. The caravans that crossed the desert and brought these aromatics to people, who treasured them like gold, became one of the economic pillars of the Arabian empire. Later the Moors taught the Spaniards the value of spices, and thus disposed them to finance the spice-seeking voyages of Christopher Columbus. The rest is history!

Here are my notes on the essential spices of Moroccan cooking: frequently used spices; spices that are used less often but are important in particular dishes; and spice mixtures, including the famous and sometimes notorious mixture, *ras el hanout*.

THE TEN MOST FREQUENTLY USED SPICES

There are ten important spices that are used over and over again in Moroccan cooking and that the cook should always have on hand: cinnamon, cumin, saffron, turmeric, ginger, black and/or white pepper, cayenne, sweet paprika, aniseed, and sesame seeds.

CINNAMON: There are two kinds of cinnamon, Ceylon and cassia. Ceylon, light tan and delicate, is the true cinnamon. Cassia cinnamon, available in most supermarkets, has a stronger taste, but I use it in bark form in certain dishes, and so you will need both varieties. Cinnamon is used frequently in Moroccan tagines; for meat, fish, and poultry; in salads; and as a final dusting on a Berber *harira* soup, *bastila*, *kedras*, couscous dishes, and desserts.

CUMIN SEED: Some of the best cumin in the world is produced just west of Marrakech, and I urge you to seek out the Moroccan variety even if you have to go to the trouble of acquiring it by mail order (see Sources). Moroccan cumin seed is so powerful it does not need to be toasted before being ground. Used frequently to add a heady aroma and flavor to fish and chicken dishes, brochettes, and eggs, cumin seed is also an important component of ground-meat dishes (*kefta*) and roasts, salads, and soups. When a recipe calls for ground cumin seed, I simply grind the amount needed with a pinch of coarse salt, using a mortar and pestle, to release its aroma and flavor.

SAFFRON: A very small amount of saffron can totally change the aroma and color of a dish, and happily so, since saffron is the most expensive spice in the world. I am particularly partial to the Moroccan saffron grown in the High Atlas Mountains near the town of Taliouine, and spice importer Mustapha Haddouch (see Sources), who imports from this area, tells me it is the most fragrant variety available. His description: "Strongly perfumed, with an aroma of honey, it has pungent bitter-honey flavor."

Saffron threads should be long and reddish, and they should be brittle before being pulverized, or some of their potency will be lost. To make them brittle, place on a plate set over a pan of boiling water or dry in a warm skillet over very low heat. Once they are brittle, pulverize a pinch or two in a small cup or mortar.

See page 48 for instructions on making saffron water, an economical method of preparing saffron before using it in a recipe.

TURMERIC: Turmeric, which comes from the root of a tropical plant in the ginger family, has a clean, bitter taste. It is sometimes mixed with saffron in tagines and soups for balance and color.

GINGER: Ginger has a sweet, lemony, and peppery flavor. It is used often, along with black pepper, in tagines and in all dishes with a chicken *mqquali* sauce (see page 305). My recipes call only for ground dried ginger.

BLACK AND WHITE PEPPER: A Moroccan cook explained to me that black pepper is always added early in the cooking to allow its coarse taste time to mellow, while the more subtle white pepper is used to finish a dish.

HOT RED PEPPER AND CAYENNE: Hot peppers are used with restraint in Moroccan cooking. A medium-hot paprika called *fefla hamra harra* (which is similar in heat to our New Mexican chile pepper) is used in some fish dishes, in dishes that feature lentils, and in some tagines. I substitute the moderately hot Turkish Marash red pepper flakes, Aleppo pepper, or piment d'Espelette (see Sources).

SWEET PAPRIKA: Though Hungarian paprika is considered the best in the world, sweet Moroccan or Spanish Ñiora paprika, which is readily available in America, is used by Moroccan cooks in salads, vegetable tagines, *kefta,* and virtually any tomato dish except those that use cinnamon and honey, and in the indispensable fish marinade known as charmoula (see page 243). Paprika doesn't keep well, so I suggest you buy it in small amounts and store it in a screw-top jar in a cool, dark place.

ANISEED: There are many types of aniseed, but the best is the green aniseed with a strong, warm, licorice flavor produced in Morocco between Meknes and Fes or in Spain. It's used in breads, cookies, and some fish preparations.

SESAME SEEDS: Sesame seeds are cultivated in Morocco and also in the Far East, as the source of an important oil. Unhulled seeds are used in Moroccan bread and desserts and, when toasted, as a garnish for tagines.

SECONDARY SPICES

Allspice, caraway, cardamom pods, cloves, coriander seeds, cubeb pepper, fenugreek, gum arabic, licorice, mace and nutmeg, and nigella seeds are also used in Moroccan cooking, but much less frequently than the previous group of spices.

ALLSPICE: This reddish-brown berry has a complex flavor that echoes a combination of cloves, nutmeg, and cinnamon. It's used in some old recipes for couscous, in some types of *kefta,* and in a *bastila* made in Fes.

CARAWAY: Caraway seeds appear along with garlic in some hot pepper sauces, as well as in the famous snail soup called *babbouche,* where it joins a dozen or so other aromatics.

CARDAMOM PODS: Cardamom is one of the most expensive spices used in Morocco. Inside each dried, green pod are roughly a dozen seeds, which are aromatic, clean tasting, sweet, peppery, and bitter. Twelve pods will give you 1½ teaspoons seeds. Cardamom is used to flavor coffee and in *ras el hanout*.

CLOVES: Cloves are used in couscous recipes, lentil salads, and desserts.

CORIANDER SEEDS: Coriander is used to season homemade olives (see page 69), in some *harira* soups, in lentil soups, and, with great vigor, as a component of a rub for *mechoui* (see Roasted Whole Lamb, page 343). It also seasons the preserved meat called *khliî* (see page 43) and meat confit (see page 44).

CUBEB PEPPER: This is a personal favorite because of its lovely aroma. I use it in my "stand-in" mixed spice mixture, La Kama (page 37). It also appears in many meat tagines and in some vegetable salads. In northwestern Morocco, it's used to flavor a pastry called *markout*, made with honey, dates, and orange flower water.

FENUGREEK: Fenugreek seeds have no taste unless heated, and then they smell a little like celery and taste a little like burnt sugar or maple syrup. They are soaked before using to remove their raw taste. They are a major ingredient in the chicken dish called *r'fissa* (see page 127)

GUM ARABIC (OR MASTIC): I adore this pellet-shaped, strong-scented spice, especially as a flavoring for sweets such as almond paste, where one or two grains can make a decisive difference, making the paste seem even richer; it also preserves flavor by hindering spoilage. Most popular in Marrakech pastries, it also turns up in an unusual chicken tagine (see page 284) and in a dish of scrambled eggs.

LICORICE: Licorice sticks, the dried rhizomes (underground stems) of the plant, are used in *babbouche*, the famous snail soup, and in a preparation of squid.

MACE AND NUTMEG: Mace, the lacy coat of the nutmeg seed, adds sweetness and a sweet aroma to chicken dishes such as the *r'fissa* (see page 127) or Marrakech *tangia* (see page 409), or guinea hen and spring onions (see page 120). Nutmeg, milder than mace, is used in some desserts and rice dishes, as well as in spice mixtures.

NIGELLA SEEDS: These tiny black seeds have a very sharp, acid taste. They flavor bread and are also used in a chicken tagine with preserved lemons and black olives (see page 298), a specialty of Marrakech, in which they add a savory bitter flavor with mild pepper overtones. Lightly toast the seeds just before using.

SPICE MIXTURES

RAS EL HANOUT, which literally means "top of the shop," seems to fascinate everyone, foreigners and Moroccans alike. It is a very old mixture of many spices, sometimes nineteen, sometimes twenty-six. Moroccans have told me about a *ras el hanout* that contained more than a hundred ingredients. Theoretically almost any addition is permissible.

The aphrodisiacs (Spanish fly and ash berries) that appear in many versions are the reason the mere mention of this mixture will put a gleam in a Moroccan cook's eye. The *attar*, or spice mixer, keeps his recipe to himself. You can purchase excellent blends online (see Sources).

Ras el hanout is used in game dishes, *mrouzia* (Lamb Tagine with Raisins, Almonds, and Honey, page 384), the hashish candy called *majoun* (page 457), and some couscous dishes in areas of Morocco where the winters are particularly harsh. *Ras el hanout*, it is alleged, will "warm the body."

Christine Benlafquih writes of *ras el hanout* on her website (www .moroccanfood.about.com), "Some Moroccans use it almost daily in their cooking." She suggests adding it to spice rubs, beef or lamb tagines, and couscous.

Back in 1972, I bought a packet of *ras el hanout* in the Attarine quarter of Fes, where it was sold in unground form. This enabled me to see exactly

which spices were included. After a long analysis, a spice importer friend in New York came up with the following list of ingredients: allspice; ash berries[1]; belladonna leaves[2]; black peppercorns; cantharides[3]; cardamom pods; wild cardamom pods[4]; cayenne; cassia cinnamon; Ceylon cinnamon; cloves; coriander seed; cubeb pepper; earth almonds[5]; galangal[6]; ginger; gouza al asnab[7]; grains of paradise[8]; lavender[9]; long pepper[10]; mace; monk's pepper[11]; nigella; nutmeg; orrisroot[12]; rosebuds[13]; and turmeric.

Please note that some of the spices listed above are not safe to ingest on their own. If you want to try your hand at making *ras el hanout*, try either of the two recipes on page 36. Neither is a true *ras el hanout*, in that they contain fewer and safer spices, but both will serve you well. Otherwise, purchase *ras el hanout* from one of my suggested mail-order sources (page 502).

Note that these two spice mixture recipes produce small amounts. The reason: once you grind spices, they begin to die. Store the mixtures in small jars in a cool, dark place.

1. A tan elongated spice that looks like a bird's tongue and is alleged to have strong medicinal and aphrodisiacal properties.
2. *Atropa belladonna*, sometimes called "deadly nightshade." The berries are collected and dried in the Rif Mountain area.
3. The very sight of these green metallic beetles, called "Spanish fly," terrifies me.
4. Also known as bitter black cardamom. Similar to green cardamom pods but with a completely different appearance, a sort of brown root with a beard at one end that smells to me like old shoes.
5. These look like small elongated nutmegs and have a perfumed chestnut taste. In Tangier, there is a small Spanish ice cream parlor that sells *horchata*, a very good iced drink made from earth almonds.
6. A highly aromatic spice that tastes like a cross between ginger and cardamom.
7. In Marrakech, mustard seeds are stuck together to form a ball.
8. These reddish-brown grains, also called Malagueta pepper, are about half the size of black peppercorns and are used as a stimulant and an aphrodisiac. Found along the "Pepper Coast" of Africa in Guinea and Sierra Leone, they came to Morocco in caravans from Senegal and Mauritania and were first used by southern Berbers to spice meat and flavor breads.
9. These small purple flowers have a sweet, lemony aroma and must be used with care because they are strongly flavored. Recently I unearthed an old Rif Mountain recipe for couscous in which a few sprigs of dried lavender are infused in a tea, which is then mixed into the couscous after it is steamed twice, then buttered and sugared.
10. These look like elongated and pockmarked black peppercorns and are alleged to have unspecified "magical powers."
11. This pepper, said to come from a "chaste tree," is believed to calm sexual desire, hence the name.
12. When these off-white rhizomes are roasted, they taste a little like coffee, and when they are sucked, they sweeten the breath.
13. These come from dried roses grown in the Valley of Dades. They were not in the Fes *ras el hanout*, but they do appear in most formulae.

In a small village outside Marrakech, I listened as a "wise woman" explained the difference between *ras el hanout* and the spice mixture called *mssâkhen*, which literally means to "warm you up." She lowered her voice to a whisper as she explained that *mssâkhen* not only warms you up in winter, but also, *"inshallah"* (with God's wishes), assists a woman to become pregnant. "You add a little to couscous without vegetables," she told me, "or to *r'fissa* chicken stew (page 127). Or if you just want to warm yourself up from the cold, it is good to add it to a rich lentil and pasta soup." At this point, her whisper became even more intense: "You can give it to a woman who has just given birth to help strengthen her body, but whatever you do, don't let anyone already pregnant eat it!"

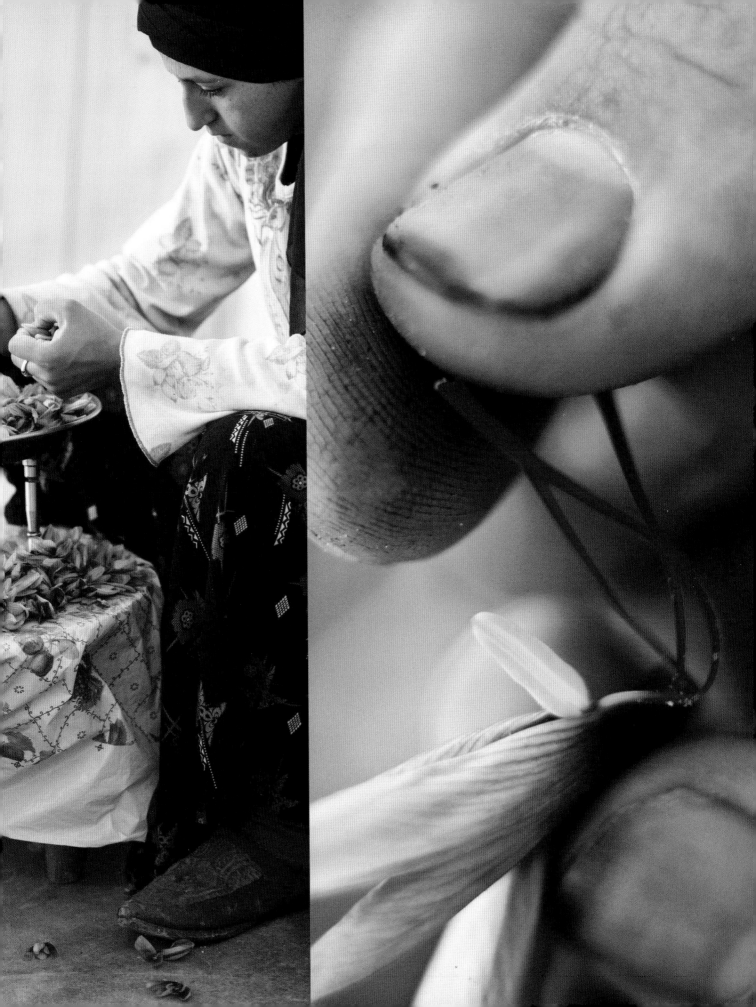

"FAUX" RAS EL HANOUT #1

Added to meat tagines that include honeyed fruits, the following blend will make these sweet-tart Moroccan dishes even tastier. As little as ½ to 1 teaspoon of this mixture added to the other spices called for in a recipe will provide an extra boost.

1 tablespoon each cumin seeds, preferably Moroccan, coriander seeds, black peppercorns, and dried rosebuds

1 teaspoon each ground turmeric, grated nutmeg, ground ginger, and ground turmeric

10 green cardamom seeds

10 cubeb peppercorns

2 cloves

2 mace blades

2 Ceylon cinnamon sticks

A pinch of grated nutmeg

1. Toast the coriander seeds and cardamom seeds in a heavy-bottomed skillet over low heat for 5 minutes, or until aromatic and beginning to crackle and pop.

2. Grind all the spices together in a spice mill. Sift through a fine sieve and store in a closed jar in a cool, dark place.

"FAUX" RAS EL HANOUT #2

This blend delivers a particularly strong flavor bounce to Couscous with Seven Vegetables in the Fes Manner (page 209) and tagines smothered in vegetables. I use it as a substitute for yet another Moroccan spice mixture, called *mssâkhen* (see page 33), in the chicken *r'fissa* on page 127.

2 tablespoons cumin seeds, preferably Moroccan

2 tablespoons coriander seeds

15 cardamom pods

1 tablespoon green aniseed

2 teaspoons black peppercorns

1 teaspoon white peppercorns

One 2-inch Ceylon cinnamon stick or 1½ teaspoons ground Ceylon cinnamon

3 tablespoons ground ginger

¾ teaspoon ground turmeric

½ teaspoon grated nutmeg

1. Toast the cumin seeds (unnecessary if they are Moroccan), coriander seeds, and cardamom pods in a heavy-bottomed skillet over low heat for 5 minutes, or until aromatic and beginning to crackle and pop.

2. Grind the toasted spices, aniseed, and peppercorns in a food processor or spice mill until pulverized. Add the cinnamon stick, if using, and grind again. Force as much of the mixture as you can through a fine sieve; discard the debris. Mix with the remaining ground spices, and store in a closed jar in a cool, dark place.

LA KAMA SPICE MIXTURE

This is used to flavor fish, lamb, and chicken tagines. It's good with winter vegetables such as turnips, rutabagas, butternut squash, and carrots.

1 teaspoon each ground ginger and ground turmeric

1 teaspoon freshly ground white pepper

½ teaspoon ground cinnamon

½ teaspoon cubeb pepper (optional)

A good pinch of grated nutmeg

Mix the ground spices. Sift through a fine sieve and store in a closed jar in a cool, dark place.

HARISSA SAUCE

When I first learned about Moroccan cooking, it was proudly described as "sweet and salty" or "sweet and savory," but never as "sweet and spicy."

Harissa, a spicy paste made from hot chile peppers crushed with garlic and salt and thinned with olive oil, used to be used sparingly, but it is now making huge inroads into the national cuisine. One finds thin or thick harissa sauces accompanying bread, couscous, and kebabs. And in the popular new supermarkets, Tabasco sauce is a steady seller alongside locally produced harissa.

You can purchase imported Moroccan harissa by the jar (see Sources). Or you can substitute Turkish red hot pepper sauce, available at Middle Eastern stores.

Makes about ¾ cup

1 garlic clove	¾ cup water or broth
Pinch of cumin seeds, preferably Moroccan	1 tablespoon harissa paste, or more to taste
Pinch of coarse salt, or to taste	Fresh lemon juice (optional)

Crush the garlic to a paste with the cumin and salt. Mix with the water or broth and harissa in a small saucepan, set over high heat, and bring to a boil, stirring. Pour into a small serving bowl and allow to cool slightly before serving. Correct the seasoning with salt if necessary and, if desired, lemon juice.

HERBS AND AROMATICS

The most important herbs in Moroccan cooking are onions, garlic, cilantro, parsley, bay leaves, and three forms of the famous Moroccan herbs known collectively as *za'atar*—thyme, oregano, and marjoram. Lesser known but important in the Middle Atlas and Rif Mountain regions are purslane, calamint, and mallow.

Herbs for tea making include spearmint, peppermint, wild mint, marjoram, verveine, basil, and absinthe; see Chapter 13 for more information.

ONIONS: In tagine cooking, the most commonly used onions are red onions. Grated and added early on, they break down, enriching and thickening the sauce. Sliced large yellow or white onions are also used in tagines to add heft while retaining their shape. Fat spring onions, three times larger than our scallions, are finely diced and added raw to salads. Sliced onions are also cooked down to jam thickness and used to garnish tagines and couscous.

GARLIC: Garlic is one of the most important ingredients in Moroccan cooking. Surprisingly, it is often used in honeyed dishes, where it helps to balance out the flavors.

CILANTRO: Cilantro, fresh coriander, endows many tagines with its special flavor.

PARSLEY: Moroccans use the flat-leaved Italian variety in huge amounts. Some tagines call for several cupfuls.

BAY LEAVES: Dried bay leaves, imported from Turkey or Greece, are often added to fish soups, preserved olives, and traditional vinegar.

ZA'ATAR: This is a generic word for any one or a combination of herbs in the same family, including Mediterranean oregano, thyme borneal, ordinary thyme, and marjoram. Because the term can be confusing, I rarely use the word *za'atar* in my recipes; instead, I list the actual herb. (Note that the word *za'atar* has a different meaning in the Middle East, where it refers to a spice and herb mixture that includes thyme and sumac.)

PURSLANE: Purslane is used in cooked leafy green salads (see page 81), in soups (see page 176), and with lentils and beans. It is far better steamed than boiled. It can be found at farmers' markets and in many vegetable gardens, where it grows as a weed.

CALAMINT: Known as *manta*, calamint is a strongly aromatic mint used in tea, and the much-acclaimed *harcha* bread of the Hyayna tribe in Taounate province (see page 116). Garden centers specializing in herbs often carry it, or see Sources.

MALLOW: Called *baqqula*, mallow is a leafy green that is steamed and used in salads (see page 81) and soups.

TOMATO MAGIC

I love tomato paste for the way it creates deep, rich, non-acidic flavored sauces. I've often watched Moroccan cooks add some to a pot containing hot olive oil, causing the paste to sizzle and come alive. But with tomato paste, as with many flavorings, less is almost always more.

Because some canned tomato pastes are not dependably good, I've developed a method of making my own homemade tomato paste, a preparation I call "Tomato Magic." I puree the finest sun-dried tomatoes packed in olive oil with the best canned organic tomatoes, and boil the puree down to a thick jam. It can be refrigerated for up to a month or frozen up to a year for future use.

Makes about 1½ cups

One 6- to 8-ounce jar sun-dried tomatoes packed in olive oil

One 28-ounce can organic tomatoes, preferably Muir Glen fire-toasted tomatoes

½ teaspoon salt

Extra virgin olive oil

NOTE TO THE COOK

As you use your tomato magic, make sure to keep the remaining paste covered with olive oil to prevent deterioration.

1. Combine the sun-dried tomatoes, with their packing oil from the jar; the canned tomatoes, with their juices; the salt; and 2 tablespoons water in a food processor or blender and puree until smooth.

2. Scrape the puree into a wide heavy-bottomed saucepan, set over medium-low heat, and cook, stirring often, until reduced to a thick jam, about 30 minutes.

3. Scrape some of the tomato paste into a clean, dry jar for more immediate use. Cover with ¼ inch of olive oil, close the jar, and store in the refrigerator for up to 1 month. For longer storage time, divide the remaining paste into 1- or 2-tablespoon balls and place them side by side on a flat tray. Set in the freezer for 10 to 15 minutes, until firm, then place in a freezer bag and store in the freezer.

HONEY

Honey is an important ingredient in Moroccan cooking, appearing in recipes such as mini pastry triangles stuffed with goat cheese and honey (see page 147); anise-flavored semolina soup (see page 190); numerous pancakes and fritters; skillet breads; couscous dishes; tagines; and, of course, desserts. Moroccans also use honey for medicinal purposes, such as relieving sore throats, headaches, common colds, and sleeplessness.

The best honeys for cooking are the liquid varieties. Honey doesn't go bad. It keeps well in the cupboard. And honey is probably the healthiest way to consume sugar.

Some of the famous honeys of Morocco are the slightly tangy acacia; mildly sweet eucalyptus honey from the Gharb; tart and fruity jujube honey from Bouarfa; strongly aromatic rosemary honey from the region of the Midelt; floral lavender and orange flower blossom honey from the Middle Atlas; and the dark herbal thyme honey produced south of the High Atlas Mountains.

FRAGRANT WATERS

Moroccan cooks use both orange flower water and rose water in cakes, confections, certain tagines, and salads—and also for perfuming themselves after dining.

Arabs invented the process of distillation, and distilling apparati found in modern chemical labs is surprisingly similar to their ancient alembic stills.

Orange flower water is usually made from the flowers of the bergamot orange tree. Rose water is made from rosebuds collected in the Valley of Dades, sold in the souks from enormous baskets. It takes seven pounds of orange blossoms or rosebuds to make a gallon of fragrant water. Although both fragrant waters are used throughout Morocco, there seems to be a preference for rose water in Marrakech and for orange flower water in Fes.

In Morocco, these fragrant waters are often homemade, and they can be very strong.

You can buy small jars of orange flower water and rose water imported from Morocco, France, and the Middle East.

MOROCCAN PRESERVED MEAT

Almost every Mediterranean cuisine employs small quantities of preserved meats as a condiment to enchance the flavor of grain, vegetable, and leafy green dishes, as well as soups and stews. Turkish cooks use *basturma* (thin slices of salted, pressed, and spiced beef), southern French cooks use *ventrèche* (slices of cured pork belly), and Italians use pancetta (dry-cured and spiced pork belly).

The Moroccans have two principal types of preserved meat. The oldest, *gueddide*, is similar to jerky, in that the meat is simply salted and dried. A more elaborate, juicier version, called *khliî*, is spiced meat that has been dried, then simmered in fat and then stored in its own fat. (A simple, more perishable version of *khliî* called *mqila Rabati* has been dubbed by some Moroccan food journalists as the "*khliî* express." I call it Moroccan meat confit.)

GUEDDIDE is produced throughout the Moroccan countryside once a year during the religious festival called the Aid, when lambs are sacrificed and there's plenty of lamb meat around. Choice strips of meat, about ten inches long, are taken from the leg, then rubbed with minced garlic, ground coriander and cumin, and salt, both for flavor and to extract moisture. The strips are placed in the sun for several days to dry out completely, and then the dried pieces are wrapped in cloth and stored in clay jars.

Before cooking, the strips are soaked in water overnight to soften them and remove the salt. Then they may be left whole or diced or shredded for use as a flavoring in couscous, tagines, bean dishes, and soups.

Nowadays city dwellers rely on country relatives for their *gueddide* or buy it in the local souk. *Gueddide* is an acquired taste, and it is not particularly popular with young people today because of the strong salty flavor.

KHLIÎ is made with beef, lamb, or camel. The meat is salted and dried like *gueddide*, then cut up and cooked in fat or suet with water until the water evaporates and only the meat and fat are left. The fat is then used to preserve the meat in jar or jugs, where it can be safely kept for up to a year in the refrigerator.

Fes is famous for *khliî* with camel. On my last visit, I stopped at a butcher shop that specialized in fresh camel meat and camel *khliî*. The butcher assured me that his *khliî* was the real deal and absolutely delicious fried and served with eggs (see page 155).

NOTES TO THE COOK

Save any bits and pieces of meat solids left in the strainer, wrap airtight, freeze, and use to flavor soups, beans, tagines, or even couscous broth.

You can purchase one-pound packets of *khlïi* online (see Sources). It's produced in the United States and tastes like the real thing! It can be safely kept up to a year in the refrigerator. Before using, be sure to crush and shred the amount needed into tiny pieces.

Crush small slices in a mortar or between two small sheets of waxed paper, then shred finely with your fingers. The more you shred, the more flavor is released.

One-quarter cup packed shredded *khlïi* equals 2 ounces. If substituting online *khlïi* for "Express" Meat Confit, be sure to reduce salt in the recipe and use approximately 25 percent less meat.

I've developed an easier method of making *khlïi*, which I highly recommend. If you've ever made French-style duck confit, you'll recognize the method.

This "express" version of Moroccan meat confit will only keep in the refrigerator for a few weeks. I add it to *harira* soups, fry it with eggs, stuff it into bread dough or pastry triangles, use it as a meat substitute in beans and lentil dishes, and add it in semolina or barley couscous dishes made with seven vegetables.

Makes 1½ pounds

1½ pounds flank steak and 1 pound short ribs or 2½ pounds bone-in lamb shoulder

1 head garlic, separated into cloves and peeled

1 teaspoon coarse salt

1 tablespoon coriander seeds

1½ teaspoons cumin seeds, preferably Moroccan

Pinch of cayenne

2 tablespoons white vinegar

About ¾ cup extra virgin olive oil, plus more as needed

7 ounces beef suet

FINISHING SPICES

1½ teaspoons ground coriander

½ teaspoon ground cumin, preferably Moroccan

1 teaspoon La Kama Spice Mixture (page 37)

¼ teaspoon cayenne

Salt and freshly ground black pepper

1. Wash and drain the meat. Place it in a medium enameled cast-iron casserole.

2. Combine the garlic, salt, coriander seeds, cumin seeds, and cayenne in a blender and blend to a paste. Add the vinegar and ⅓ cup of olive oil and blend until smooth. Pour over the meat in the casserole and let stand for 2 hours at room temperature.

3. Meanwhile, add the suet and 1 cup hot water to the unwashed blender and blend until smooth. Pour into a saucepan, add another cup of water and ¼ cup olive oil, and set aside.

4. Warm the contents of the casserole over low heat. Meanwhile, bring the suet mixture to a boil. Pour over the meat. If the meat is not entirely covered, add more hot water. Cover with a round of parchment paper, reduce the heat to low, and cook until the meat is so soft it can be cut with the side of a wooden spoon, about 3 hours.

5. Lift out the meat (set the casserole aside) and remove and discard the bones and gristle. Cut the meat into neat slices, toss with the finishing spices, then pack into a dry 3-cup jar or bowl.

6. Boil down the cooking liquid and fat until almost all the water has evaporated. Strain into a deep bowl and let the fat rise to the top. Spoon the fat over the meat and use a thin skewer to allow the fat to run to the bottom of the jar. Top off with fresh olive oil. Cool completely, then cover and refrigerate.

7. To use, bring the meat to room temperature. Tongs or wooden utensils are best for removing the slices of meat needed for a recipe. Cover the remaining meat with more oil if necessary, and return to the refrigerator.

TEN TIPS FOR PREPARING MOROCCAN FOOD

1. HOW TO MAKE SAFFRON WATER

Nearly all the recipes in this book that use saffron add it in the form of saffron water—crumbled, dried, and crushed saffron threads soaked in warm water. Using saffron this way is economical, and it brings out more of the spice's aroma and flavor than simply adding a few strands to a dish. In fact, I've discovered that if I soak all the ground spices called for in a recipe in a little saffron water before adding them to the dish, their combined flavors are intensified and better distributed.

So, do as many Moroccan cooks do, and prepare a small jar of saffron water. Dry ½ teaspoon crumbled strands in a warm (not hot) skillet. Crush again, then soak in 1 cup hot water and store in a small jar in the refrigerator. This will keep for up to a week.

For longer storage (my favorite method), quadruple the recipe quantities above; pour the saffron water into a plastic ice cube tray and freeze into cubes. Once they are frozen, shake out the cubes and store in a freezer bag. Each cube will be equivalent to 2 tablespoons saffron water or a good pinch of dried saffron threads.

2. HOW TO MAKE QUICK GOLDEN-GLAZED ONIONS AS A BASE FOR TAGINES AND SOUPS

Many recipes in this book start a soup, stock, or tagine by steaming and glazing roughly chopped onions before adding the remaining ingredients. I toss the chopped onions in salt (which will draw out their moisture when they are heated), then set them in the tagine bottom, add a little water and oil, and cover them—this is a good way to slowly heat up your tagine and at the same time soften the onions and develop flavor. After the onions turn soft, I remove the cover, raise the heat a bit, and cook them until golden, creating a tasty base for the other ingredients.

3. WHY AND HOW TO GRATE AN ONION

Moroccan cooks often use grated red onions as a base for a creamy tagine sauce, as a stuffing for vegetables, or as a pastry filling.

Grating is easily accomplished by rubbing the cut side of an onion along the large holes of a box grater. The grated onion is then rinsed to reduce its pungency and drained. This procedure is quick and helps the grated onion dissolve rapidly in a slow-simmered dish. For larger amounts of grated onions, I use the food processor, being careful not to completely mash them.

To prepare grated onions for future use, process 1 large peeled and quartered red onion at a time. Rinse, press dry, and divide into $\frac{1}{2}$-cup balls. Wrap in freezer bags and keep frozen until needed.

4. HOW TO GRATE A TOMATO

The best tomatoes for grating are large Romas (plum tomatoes): they have few seeds and not too much juice, and once one of the ends is cut off, they can be very quickly grated.

Place the cut side against the coarsest holes of a box grater or a flat grater set over a bowl, and rub the tomato in only one direction until you are left with just the tomato skin in your hand (the skin is a good protection against cuts). If using round tomatoes, halve, seed, and grate as directed.

5. HOW TO FINELY CHOP PARSLEY AND CILANTRO

When I lived in Morocco, women didn't have chopping knives and large cutting boards. Their workspace was the size of a milk crate, and chopping was done with a small paring knife. When a cook wanted finely chopped herbs, she ground them to a pulp in a brass mortar, reducing a good handful of fresh leaves to a mere two packed tablespoons. And the flavor of the herbs pulped this way was always more intense than that of herbs cut fine with a knife.

I found that if I used a food processor to grind washed and squeezed dry parsley or cilantro leaves, I obtained a similar texture and flavor. Also, I could freeze the processed ground herbs in small packets for use in soups and tagines (not for fresh salads or garnish).

Parsley and cilantro sprigs will stay fresh for about 10 days in the refrigerator. Stand them up in a bowl of water and cover with a plastic bag.

6. WHY IT ISN'T NECESSARY TO TOAST IMPORTED MOROCCAN CUMIN SEEDS

Moroccan cumin seeds are so strong that toasting them will result in "overkill." It's best to grind them with a pinch of coarse salt just before using. I have watched experienced Moroccan cooks grind cumin seeds, with a pinch of coarse salt, to the consistency of sand using the heel of one hand against the palm of the other. A mortar and pestle does a good job too!

7. WHY YOU CAN PURCHASE COUSCOUS AT THE SUPERMARKET

There's couscous sold out of sacks in health food stores, and there's 100 percent semolina couscous sold in most supermarkets. You can use either type in any of the recipes in this book. Nearly all commercial 100 percent semolina couscous, whether labeled "instant" or not, is virtually the same, since all factory-made couscous is partially precooked.

Artisanal sun-dried couscous is available in limited quantities (see Sources).

8. HOW TO SEAL THE TOP AND BOTTOM OF A COUSCOUS COOKER

Christine Benlafquih, of www.moroccanfood.about.com, gave me this tip: Place a strip of twisted aluminum foil along the rim of the bottom pot. Set the colander or steamer on top and tuck the foil between the pot and steamer. This will create a tight seal so that steam will rise only through the steamer holes. (Remember that the colander or steamer should not make contact with the broth or water below.)

9. WHY MOROCCAN COOKS STEAM PASTA, FRUITS, CHICKEN, LAMB, VEGETABLES, COUSCOUS, AND OTHER GRAINS FOR SOUPS, SALADS, AND MAIN COURSES

A colander set snugly over a tall pot of boiling water is all you need to steam couscous. It is the steam that helps to create the incredible lightness of the grain. But steaming is not only used to cook couscous—it is a very important procedure in Moroccan cooking that preserves shape, color, taste, and vitamins.

Fruits such as quinces, apples, and pears that are first steamed, then caramelized in a pan with butter and sugar or honey will turn silky and soft but hold their shape when added to a tagine or placed on top of a couscous. Cooking pasta, rice, or thin pancakes by steaming them is a revelation. The starch will come out smooth and silky. See Chicken with Caramelized Quinces (page 279), Sweet Steamed Rice (page 450), and Msemmen/R'Fissa (page 127). The same goes for turnips, eggplants, carrots, sweet potatoes, and butternut squash, which are often steamed before being transformed into cooked vegetable salads or glazed and added to tagines or couscous.

Just as steamed starches, fruits, and vegetables keep their original flavors, so do steamed chicken and lamb. Both should be eaten the moment they are ready; if left too long, they will dry out.

10. HOW TO PEEL AND COOK CHICKPEAS

Many Moroccan recipes call for peeled chickpeas, which taste better and are more easily digested than unpeeled chickpeas. Soak overnight in cold water, then drain, spread the chickpeas in a single layer on a kitchen towel, and cover with another towel. Using a rolling pin, firmly (but not heavily) roll it back and forth over the chickpeas about ten times. Almost all the peels will roll off.

Bring a pot of water to a boil, throw in the chickpeas, and boil for 10 minutes. Remove from the heat and let sit for a few minutes. The remaining peels will rise to the surface. Remove them with a skimmer, then continue cooking the chickpeas as directed in the recipe.

The chickpeas can be peeled in advance, drained, and stored in the refrigerator for a few hours. Completely cooked chickpeas can be stored for a week in the cooking liquid. They can also be frozen in their cooking liquid.

chapter three

SALADS

❋

"In one corner, near the archway leading to the *souks*, is the fruit-market, where the red-gold branches of unripe dates for animal fodder are piled up in great stacks, and dozens of donkeys are coming and going, their panniers laden with fruits and vegetables which are being heaped on the ground in gorgeous pyramids: purple eggplants, melons, cucumbers, bright orange pumpkins, mauve and pink and violet onions, rusty crimson pomegranates, and the gold grapes of Sefrou and Salé, all mingled with fresh green sheaves of mint and wormwood."

—edith wharton

❋

SALADS

LATE-SUMMER SALAD
⟨ page 57 ⟩

FRESH TOMATO AND CAPER SALAD
⟨ page 58 ⟩

ORANGE, ROMAINE, AND WALNUT SALAD
⟨ page 61 ⟩

ORANGE, LEAFY GREEN, AND DATE SALAD
⟨ page 62 ⟩

BLOOD ORANGE, LETTUCE,
AND TOASTED ALMOND SALAD
⟨ page 63 ⟩

ORANGE AND GRATED RADISH SALAD
WITH ORANGE FLOWER WATER
⟨ page 64 ⟩

ORANGE AND OLIVE SALAD
⟨ page 67 ⟩

ORANGE SALAD WITH ROSE OR
ORANGE FLOWER WATER
⟨ page 68 ⟩

ORANGE AND GRATED CARROT SALAD
WITH ORANGE FLOWER WATER
⟨ page 68 ⟩

CRUSHED OLIVE SALAD
⟨ page 69 ⟩

GRATED CUCUMBER SALAD WITH
ORANGE FLOWER WATER
⟨ page 73 ⟩

GRATED CUCUMBER SALAD WITH OREGANO
⟨ page 73 ⟩

ROASTED BEET SALAD WITH CINNAMON
⟨ page 74 ⟩

CARROT AND GOLDEN RAISIN SALAD
⟨ page 77 ⟩

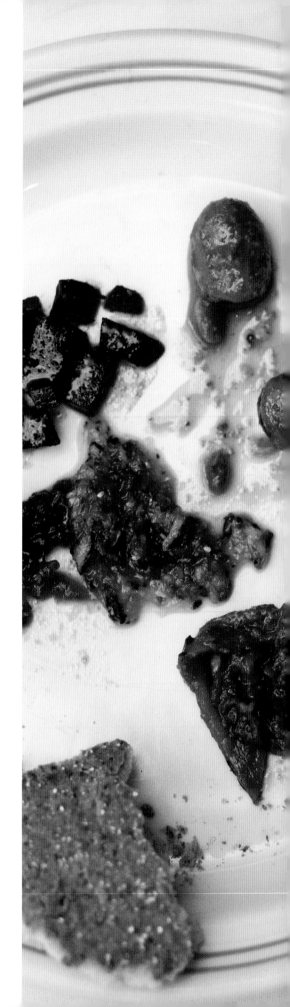

CRUSHED SPICED CARROT SALAD

〜 page 78 〜

SWEET CARROT SALAD

〜 page 78 〜

CARROT SALAD WITH CUMIN, CINNAMON,
AND SWEET PAPRIKA

〜 page 79 〜

FRESH FAVA BEAN SALAD

〜 page 80 〜

COOKED "WILD GREENS" SALAD

〜 page 81 〜

PURSLANE JAM

〜 page 84 〜

OVEN-ROASTED TOMATOES WITH
TOASTED PINE NUTS

〜 page 85 〜

TOMATOES, PRESERVED LEMONS,
AND SWEET RED PEPPERS

〜 page 86 〜

SESAME-STUDDED TOMATO JAM

〜 page 87 〜

GRILLED RED PEPPER SALAD

〜 page 89 〜

MIXED PEPPERS AND TOMATO JAM

〜 page 90 〜

TOMATO AND GREEN PEPPER SALAD

〜 page 91 〜

EGGPLANT ZAALOUK

〜 page 93 〜

LIVER AND OLIVE SALAD

〜 page 94 〜

SPICED BRAIN SALAD WITH
PRESERVED LEMONS (MOKH)

〜 page 95 〜

Moroccan salads are not like ours, mixtures of greens doused with dressings. They're closer to Italian antipasti, served at the beginning of a meal to inspire the appetite and excite the palate: spiced or sweetened, cooked or raw, or pickled or stewed vegetables, as well as cubed and grilled meat or fish.

The glories of these salads are their unexpected contrasts: carrots with cumin and hot paprika, slow-roasted tomatoes with pine nuts, or stewed lamb's brains with preserved lemons. One of my favorites is a salad of garlicky brightly colored wild greens, scented with cumin and slow-cooked down to a savory jam, then topped with slivers of preserved lemon and dotted with olives. Utterly delicious on slices of Moroccan bread!

Serving up four different salads as a starter every day is an amazing feat if you're not well organized. Most of my Moroccan neighbors always had salads on hand that had been made in advance, as well as a repertory of fresh salads that were easy to put together. They are on the table as you sit down. Sometimes they remain there through the meal, sometimes they're whisked away as the tagine or couscous or soup is brought in from the kitchen.

Four salad dishes is typical at a Moroccan home, but at a first-class restaurant such as Al Fassia in Marrakech, you can expect at least a dozen small plates, a symphony of contrasting colors and shapes that might include creamy mashed eggplant cooked with ripe tomatoes and aromatic sweet green peppers; marinated olives and preserved lemon; carrots with raisins; carrots with oranges; grated cucumber; and many more. Moroccan salads like these are like gems that sparkle in the crown of a great national cuisine.

Vegetable salads tend to be seasonal. In the summer, strange-looking green vegetables such as the *feggous* (Armenian cucumber) appear, flavored with *za'atar*, along with salads of tomatoes and green pepper with preserved lemon; grated carrots with orange blossom water; and sometimes, meat dishes such as lamb brains with herbs and spices.

Vegetables were not a traditional part of the cuisine of the southern Berber peoples. For them, there were little more than pumpkin-like gourds, turnips, onions, nuts, and fruit. It is still customary in the south to start a guest off with a plate of dates and a glass of milk, while in the countryside, the first offering is usually some kind of biscuit served with honey and preserved butter. But around Fes and along the coastal areas, vegetables have always been popular. Here are the great agricultural districts of the country, the Sais Plain and the Sebou Valley, the Chaouia area stretching from Rabat to Casablanca, and the gardens of the southern Atlantic coast that culminate in the famous orange groves of Agadir. It is in the heartland, around Fes and Meknes, and along this fruit- and vegetable-laden coast, that one finds the great salads of Morocco.

LATE-SUMMER SALAD

When tomatoes are ripe and local bell peppers are at their sweetest, this raw salad really shines. It also helps to use a really great floral honey, such as lavender, eucalyptus, clover, or acacia, that is delicate and well balanced.

⟶⊷ Serves 4 to 6 as part of a traditional salad course ⊶⟵

3 medium red-ripe tomatoes, peeled, halved, seeded, and cubed

1 large red bell pepper, peeled, cored, and finely diced

1 large green bell pepper, peeled, cored, and finely diced

1 red onion, finely diced

1 tablespoon honey

1 tablespoon fresh lemon juice or mild cider vinegar

¼ cup extra virgin olive oil

Fine sea salt and freshly ground black pepper

1½ tablespoons finely chopped cilantro

1½ tablespoons finely chopped flat-leaf parsley

Mix the tomatoes, peppers, and red onion in a salad bowl. Mix the honey, lemon juice or vinegar, oil, and salt and pepper to taste and toss with the vegetables. Sprinkle the chopped herbs on top. Refrigerate until ready to serve.

FRESH TOMATO AND CAPER SALAD

Although Morocco is one of the leading suppliers of Mediterranean capers, and Moroccan cooks put them into lots of different fish tagines, this is the only Moroccan salad I know in which they're featured. All the vegetables in the salad are cut to the same size as the capers, yet each vegetable retains its distinct texture and flavor.

Make this on the day you intend to serve it and serve it cold but not iced.

Serves 6 as part of a traditional salad course

2 pounds red-ripe tomatoes, peeled, halved, seeded, and cut into small dice (about 3 cups)

1 small red onion, cut into small dice (½ cup)

2 tender celery ribs, cut into small dice (¼ cup)

1 small green bell pepper, peeled, cored, seeded, and diced

¾ preserved lemon (see page 21), pulp removed, rind rinsed and diced

2 tablespoons medium to large capers, rinsed and drained

1¾ teaspoons fine sea salt

½ teaspoon freshly ground white pepper

3 to 4 tablespoons extra virgin olive oil or argan oil (see Sources)

Juice of ½ lemon, or to taste

Combine the tomatoes, onion, celery, bell pepper, lemon rind, and capers in a bowl. Mix the salt, pepper, oil, and lemon juice and pour over the salad. Carefully toss. Refrigerate for about 30 minutes before serving.

ORANGE, ROMAINE, AND WALNUT SALAD

1 head tender romaine lettuce

3 navel or temple oranges

DRESSING

2 tablespoons fresh lemon juice

2 tablespoons sugar

Pinch of salt

½ teaspoon ground Ceylon cinnamon, plus more for dusting

1 tablespoon orange flower water

2 tablespoons reserved orange juice

¾ cup chopped walnuts

1. Wash the romaine lettuce and separate into leaves, discarding the tough outer ones. Drain, wrap in paper towels, and refrigerate until needed.

2. Peel and section the oranges as described on page 62; reserve 2 tablespoons of the juices for the dressing. Cover and keep chilled.

3. To make the dressing: Mix the lemon juice, sugar, salt, cinnamon, orange flower water, and orange juice in a bowl, blending well. Taste; the dressing should be sweet. Add more sugar if necessary.

4. Just before serving, shred the lettuce and arrange in a glass serving dish. Pour the dressing over and toss. Arrange overlapping sections of oranges around the edges, then sprinkle the salad with the chopped walnuts and dust with cinnamon.

ORANGE SALADS

Moroccan oranges are so good that even Floridians and Californians begrudgingly admire them. They make marvelous, clean-tasting salads and superbly refreshing desserts.

ORANGE, LEAFY GREEN, AND DATE SALAD

―――∞ Serves 4 to 6 as part of a traditional salad course ∞―――

3 navel or temple oranges

DRESSING

2 tablespoons fresh lemon juice

2 tablespoons reserved orange juice

Pinch of salt

¼ teaspoon ground Ceylon cinnamon, plus more for dusting

6 Medjoul or Deglat Nour dates, halved and pitted

2 tablespoons orange flower water, or more to taste

5 ounces mixed baby greens, such as Treviso or red radicchio, arugula, and baby spinach, washed and dried

½ cup toasted pine nuts or crushed toasted almonds

1. Peel and segment the oranges; reserve 2 tablespoons of the juices for the dressing.

2. To make the dressing: Combine the lemon juice, orange juice, salt, and cinnamon in a wide bowl. Add the orange sections and toss gently. Cover with a sheet of plastic wrap and chill for 1 to 2 hours.

3. Toss the dates with the orange flower water and set aside.

4. Just before serving, arrange the greens on a wide platter. Tilt the bowl of oranges so the dressing falls over the greens, then gently toss. Arrange the orange sections around the edges of the greens. Scatter the dates and pine nuts over the greens and dust with a little cinnamon.

TO PEEL AND SECTION ORANGES

Roll each orange around on a work surface to soften it. Using a small knife, employ a seesaw motion to peel the orange. Cut away all the white pith from the flesh. Section or cut into slices. Squeeze any juice from the remainder of the orange over the slices or sections to keep them moist, or set the juice aside if it is called for in the recipe.

BLOOD ORANGE, LETTUCE, AND TOASTED ALMOND SALAD

Morocco, Algeria, and Sicily share fame for producing some of the most tender, juicy, and flavorful blood oranges. Look for them imported in the late winter.

Serves 4 to 6 as part of a traditional salad course

4 cups baby romaine lettuce leaves, washed and dried

3 blood oranges, peeled (see page 62) and sliced into rounds

DRESSING

2 tablespoons fresh lemon juice

1 tablespoon extra virgin olive oil

1 tablespoon mild honey, such as lavender, eucalyptus, acacia, or clover

1½ teaspoons orange flower water, or more to taste

Salt and freshly ground black pepper

Ground Ceylon cinnamon

3 tablespoons crushed toasted almonds

1. Arrange the lettuce on a flat serving tray. Arrange the orange slices, overlapping, over the lettuce.

2. To make the dressing: Mix the lemon juice, oil, honey, orange flower water, and salt, pepper, and cinnamon to taste and pour over the oranges. Cover with a sheet of plastic wrap and chill for 1 to 2 hours.

3. Just before serving, scatter the toasted almonds over the oranges.

ORANGE AND GRATED RADISH SALAD WITH ORANGE FLOWER WATER

Please don't dress the grated radishes too far in advance, or they will lose their texture.

⟶ Serves 4 to 6 as part of a traditional salad course ⟵

1 to 2 bunches red radishes (approximately 8 ounces), trimmed

1½ tablespoons sugar

2 navel or temple oranges

DRESSING

2 tablespoons reserved orange juice

2 to 3 teaspoons orange flower water

1½ tablespoons fresh lemon juice, or more to taste

Salt

Pinch of ground Ceylon cinnamon or 3 to 4 spearmint leaves, slivered, for garnish

1. Using the fine shredding disk, shred the radishes in a food processor; sprinkle with the sugar and let sit for 15 minutes (you should have about 1 cup).

2. Drain the excess liquid from the radishes. Wrap tightly in plastic wrap and refrigerate until chilled.

3. Peel and slice the oranges as directed on page 62; reserve 2 tablespoons of the juices for the dressing. Chill the oranges.

4. Just before serving, make the dressing: Mix the orange juice, orange flower water, lemon juice, and salt to taste in a serving bowl. Unwrap the radishes, add to the bowl, and toss. Sharpen the flavor with more lemon juice and correct the salt if necessary. Arrange the orange slices around the edges of the bowl and sprinkle with the cinnamon or mint leaves. Serve at once.

ORANGE AND OLIVE SALAD

Serves 4 to 6 as part of a traditional salad course

3 navel or temple oranges

24 juicy black olives

DRESSING

2 tablespoons extra virgin olive oil

2 tablespoons reserved orange juice

¼ teaspoon ground cumin, preferably Moroccan

¼ teaspoon sweet paprika

Pinch of cayenne, or to taste

1 teaspoon sugar

¼ teaspoon salt, or more to taste

2 tablespoons chopped flat-leaf parsley

1. Peel and section the oranges as directed on page 62; reserve 2 tablespoons of the juices for the dressing. Arrange the oranges in a rimmed serving dish.

2. Rinse and pit the olives, then soak in fresh water for 10 minutes; drain.

3. To make the dressing: Combine the olive oil, orange juice, cumin, paprika, cayenne, sugar, and salt in a bowl. Toss with the olives. Taste and correct the salt if necessary.

4. Scatter the olives and chopped parsley over the oranges and serve at once.

ORANGE SALAD WITH ROSE OR ORANGE FLOWER WATER

Oranges, rose or orange flower water, and cinnamon make an outstanding combination. The orange slices are arranged in a pattern of overlapping circles, and the perfumed water is spooned on top.

Serves 4 to 6 as part of a traditional salad course

6 navel or temple oranges

1½ teaspoons rose water or orange flower water, or more to taste

1 tablespoon sugar, or to taste

1 teaspoon ground Ceylon cinnamon

Confectioners' sugar for dusting

1. Peel and thinly slice the oranges as directed on page 62. Arrange the slices in a pattern of overlapping circles in a rimmed serving dish. Sprinkle with the perfumed water, sugar, and ¼ teaspoon of the cinnamon. Taste for sweetness and adjust as necessary. Cover and refrigerate until chilled.

2. Just before serving, dust the oranges with the remaining ¾ teaspoon cinnamon and confectioners' sugar.

ORANGE AND GRATED CARROT SALAD WITH ORANGE FLOWER WATER

Serves 4 to 6 as part of a traditional salad course

1 navel or temple orange

1 pound carrots, trimmed, peeled, and grated

DRESSING

2 to 3 tablespoons fresh lemon juice

Reserved orange juice

1½ tablespoons sugar

1 teaspoon orange flower water

1 teaspoon ground Ceylon cinnamon

1. Peel the orange as directed on page 62 and cut into dice; reserve the juices for the dressing. Gently mix the oranges and carrots in a serving dish.

2. To make the dressing: Combine the lemon juice, orange juice, sugar, and orange flower water in a small bowl. Pour over the carrots and oranges. Cover and store in the refrigerator until ready to serve; partially drain and dust with the cinnamon just before serving.

CRUSHED OLIVE SALAD

The gentle flavors of preserved lemon peel and bitter orange marmalade give a lovely boost to "midway," or green-ripe olives.

Among the domestic brands available in most large groceries, Lindsay's Select Medium Home-Style cured pitted green-ripe olives and Graber's pitted green-ripe olives work well here. Or you can purchase red olives online (see Sources).

This salad needs a couple of days of mellowing to develop great flavor. If carefully prepared, it will keep for over a week in the refrigerator.

———⊛ Serves 4 to 6 as part of a traditional salad course ⊛———

One 6-ounce can pitted green-ripe olives (about 1½ cups), drained

1 large garlic clove, boiled for 5 minutes, drained, peeled, and crushed

½ teaspoon salt, or more to taste

1 tablespoon chopped cilantro

¼ preserved lemon (see page 21), pulp removed, rind rinsed and dried

1½ teaspoons bitter orange marmalade

1½ tablespoons extra virgin olive oil

1 teaspoon sweet paprika

½ teaspoon cumin seeds, preferably Moroccan

¼ teaspoon ground coriander

¼ teaspoon cayenne

1. Wash the olives. Spread them out on a paper towel, cover with a second sheet, and press down to gently crush them. Place in a bowl and set aside.

2. Combine the garlic, salt, cilantro, lemon rind, and orange marmalade in a small blender or a mortar and grind to a paste. Loosen the paste with the olive oil, then mix with the spices and olives and stir gently. Correct the salt if necessary. Cover and refrigerate for at least 3 days before serving.

GRATED CUCUMBER SALAD WITH ORANGE FLOWER WATER

——— Serves 4 to 6 as part of a traditional salad course ———

2 cucumbers (1 pound), peeled, halved lengthwise, seeded, and grated

2 tablespoons sugar

2 tablespoons strained fresh lemon juice

1 to 1½ tablespoons orange flower water

Pinch of fine sea salt

Pinch of ground Ceylon cinnamon (optional)

1. Wrap the grated cucumber in paper towels or a kitchen towel and squeeze to remove excess moisture. (You should have about 2½ cups.)

2. Combine the sugar, lemon juice, orange flower water, and salt in a serving dish. Add the cucumber and toss. Cover loosely and refrigerate until ready to serve.

3. If desired, sprinkle with the cinnamon just before serving.

GRATED CUCUMBER SALAD WITH OREGANO

——— Serves 4 to 6 as part of a traditional salad course ———

2 cucumbers (1 pound), peeled, halved lengthwise, seeded, and grated

1 tablespoon sugar

2 tablespoons strained fresh lemon juice or cider vinegar

Pinch of fine sea salt

1 scant tablespoon fresh oregano leaves, chopped, or 1 teaspoon dried Mediterranean oregano

A handful of cured black olives, pitted

1. Wrap the grated cucumber in paper towels or a kitchen towel and squeeze to remove excess moisture. (You should have about 2½ cups.)

2. Combine the sugar, lemon juice, and salt in a serving dish. Add the cucumber and toss. Sprinkle the oregano (if using dried, crush it between your fingertips) over the cucumbers. Mix well with two forks, then cover and chill for at least 30 minutes.

3. Decorate the salad with the olives just before serving. Serve chilled.

CUCUMBER SALADS

In late summer, the thinner curved cucumbers called *feggous* arrive at many farmers' markets. They are often sold as "Armenian yard-long cucumbers." They're more flavorful and have fewer seeds than ordinary cucumbers, and their tiny seeds needn't be removed. Their skin is thinner, so they needn't be peeled. In short, they are my idealized version of an ordinary cucumber and the preferred variety for these two cucumber salads. Look for *feggous* that are dark green and marked with pale green puckered longitudinal furrows. When they are ripe, their color fades and they develop a strong muskmelon flavor.

ROASTED BEET SALAD
WITH CINNAMON

In Morocco, community bread ovens are not just used by local families for baking bread. They're also often rented out to vendors who use them to cook products they will sell that day in the street. I remember a young man who'd appear weekly at the community oven in my neighborhood, hauling his father's crop of beets for roasting. The beets, still in their dark red skins and with a bit of the stem still left on each, were shoveled into the oven to bake slowly in the receding heat. Compared to that of quickly baked beets, their flavor was a revelation: intensely sweet, with a hint of caramel.

For this recipe, you could boil the beets, but I strongly recommend subjecting them to a slow roast in your oven. Or you can dry-roast them in a Chinese sand pot or flame-proof bean pot on top of the stove and obtain the same result. Roasted beets will keep in the refrigerator for a week, and they can also be frozen.

Serves 4 to 6 as part of a traditional salad course

1 pound beets (3 to 4)

2 tablespoons coarse salt

1 tablespoon sugar

Juice of 1 lemon, or to taste

1 tablespoon extra virgin olive oil

Large pinch of ground Ceylon cinnamon

1 tablespoon chopped flat-leaf parsley

Salt to taste

1. Rinse and thoroughly dry the beets, being careful not to break their skins. Cut off the tops, leaving about 1½ inches.

2. *To roast the beets in the oven,* tightly wrap the beets, with the salt, in foil or parchment paper and set in a shallow baking dish. Bake at 325°F for 2 hours. To check for tenderness, open one end of the packet and test a beet with the tip of a knife to see if the flesh has softened. *To use an earthenware sand pot or bean pot,* sprinkle the salt on the bottom of the pot. Loosely pile the beets on top of each other, cover with a piece of crumpled parchment paper and the lid, and set over low heat. Cook for 1½ hours, shaking the pot from time to time, without opening. Check for tenderness as directed above, and cook for up to 30 minutes longer if necessary. Transfer the hot clay pot to a wooden surface or folded kitchen towel to prevent cracking. Let the beets cool.

3. Peel the beets, cut into bite-sized pieces, and put in a bowl. Combine the remaining ingredients, pour over the beets, and let marinate for 1 hour before serving. Serve at room temperature.

CARROT AND GOLDEN RAISIN SALAD

This lovely salad is served at Al Fassia Restaurant in Marrakech, where the all-female kitchen staff turns it out in a particularly beautiful way, constructing a dome out of cubes of carrots the size of the raisins, then layering the raisins on the surface in a geometric pattern resembling Moroccan tile work. The visual effect of this presentation is wonderful, the kitchen work involved is labor-intensive, and, of course, the "tile work" is destroyed as soon as diners start to eat. But if you simply mold the ingredients haphazardly in a small bowl, then invert it onto a plate, the appearance of the salad will still be striking, and it will taste exactly the same.

Serves 4 to 6 as part of a traditional salad course

8 ounces large carrots

1 tablespoon sugar

One 1-inch Ceylon cinnamon stick

Pinch of salt

2 tablespoons fresh lemon juice

½ cup golden raisins

1 tablespoon orange flower water

1. Trim and peel the carrots, halve them lengthwise, and cut out and discard the hard core. Cut the carrots into ¼-inch dice, place in a small saucepan, add the sugar, cinnamon stick, salt, lemon juice, and water to cover, cover, and cook until tender. Drain the carrots in a sieve set over a bowl and quickly use the hot liquid to soak the raisins.

2. When the liquid has cooled down, drain the raisins and mix with the carrots and orange flower water. Pack into a 2½- to 3-inch rounded mold and chill overnight.

3. To serve, invert the dome onto a plate.

CRUSHED SPICED CARROT SALAD

Serves 4 to 6 as part of a traditional salad course

12 ounces (4 to 6 medium) carrots, trimmed and peeled

¾ teaspoon cumin seeds, preferably Moroccan

2 garlic cloves, halved

1 teaspoon coarse sea salt, or to taste

½ teaspoon ground Ceylon cinnamon

½ teaspoon sweet paprika

3 tablespoons extra virgin olive oil

Juice of ½ lemon, or more to taste

Freshly ground black pepper

1 tablespoon chopped flat-leaf parsley

1. Steam the whole carrots over boiling water until you can easily crush them with the tines of a fork, 25 to 30 minutes. Drain, place in a deep heavy bowl, and let cool.

2. Crush the cumin seeds, garlic, and salt to a paste in a mortar. Scrape the paste into a skillet, add the cinnamon and paprika, and stir in the olive oil. Turn the heat on for an instant to warm the spices, then pour over the carrots. Use a fork to crush the warm carrots with the spices.

3. Add the lemon juice to taste and correct the seasoning with more salt if necessary and pepper. Mound into a pile on a serving plate and scatter the chopped parsley on top.

STEAMING VEGETABLES

Steaming is one of the most important techniques employed by Moroccan cooks. Many of the vegetables used in Moroccan cooked salads are steamed before being sautéed or marinated. Moroccan cooks use their couscous cooker to steam vegetables such as cauliflower, carrots, and eggplant; all kinds of leafy greens; and even turnips and sweet potatoes.

This method preserves flavor and produces a meltingly soft and creamy texture: it also enables the vegetables to absorb spicing. Stainless steel, ceramic, or even bamboo steamers all work well. But please don't steam in aluminum, which imparts an odd taste to food. And remember: steaming involves intense heat, so when you lift the steamer cover, do so away from your face.

SWEET CARROT SALAD

Serves 4 to 6 as part of a traditional salad course

1 pound (6 to 8 medium) carrots, trimmed and peeled

⅓ cup fresh lemon juice

3 heaping tablespoons sugar

½ teaspoon ground Ceylon cinnamon

¼ cup chopped flat-leaf parsley

Scant ¼ teaspoon ground cumin, preferably Moroccan

¼ teaspoon sweet paprika

Pinch of salt

1. Steam the carrots over boiling water until just tender, 10 to 15 minutes.

2. Dice the carrots and put in a bowl. Mix all the other ingredients, and pour over the carrots. Serve cool.

CARROT SALAD WITH CUMIN, CINNAMON, AND SWEET PAPRIKA

1 pound (6 to 8 medium) carrots, trimmed and peeled

1 teaspoon sweet paprika

½ teaspoon ground cumin, preferably Moroccan

¼ teaspoon cayenne

⅛ teaspoon ground Ceylon cinnamon

Juice of 1 lemon

½ teaspoon sugar

Fine sea salt

Extra virgin olive oil for drizzling

Chopped flat-leaf parsley for garnish

1. Early in the day, or the day before: Steam the carrots over boiling water until just barely tender, 10 to 15 minutes.

2. Dice the carrots and put in a bowl. Mix with the spices, lemon juice, sugar, and a pinch of salt. Cool, then cover and chill until ready to serve.

3. Just before serving, correct the seasoning with salt. Drizzle with olive oil and sprinkle with parsley.

FRESH FAVA BEAN SALAD

Moroccans steam fresh fava beans to preserve both flavor and color. In this recipe, I steam the fava in their pods and then remove both the pods and skins at the same time. This little trick not only preserves the flavor of the favas better but also enables you to perform the arduous task of double-peeling in one fell swoop!

━━━⤜ Serves 4 to 6 as part of a traditional salad course ⤛━━━

1½ pounds young fava beans

2 garlic cloves

Coarse salt

¼ teaspoon cumin seeds, preferably Moroccan

1 teaspoon sweet paprika

2 tablespoons mixed chopped flat-leaf parsley and cilantro

2 tablespoons fresh lemon juice

2 tablespoons extra virgin olive oil

½ preserved lemon (see page 21), pulp removed, rind rinsed and slivered

1. Bring a pot of water to a boil. Set a colander on top, add the fava beans in their pods, cover, and steam until tender, 5 to 8 minutes, depending upon their age.

2. Meanwhile, crush the garlic with ½ teaspoon salt and the cumin to a paste in a mortar. Place in a small saucepan, add the paprika and ½ cup water, and bring to a boil, then simmer for 5 minutes. Remove from the heat.

3. Cool the favas under cold running water. Peel the pods and outer skins from the beans; drop the beans into the saucepan as you work.

4. Add the herbs to the pan, bring to a boil, and cook until the beans are tender. Stir in the lemon juice, olive oil, and lemon rind. Taste for salt, and let cool before serving.

✿

NOTE TO THE COOK

I steam 1 pound of fava beans in their pods at a time. A pound of beans will give you approximately 1 cup double-peeled beans.

COOKED "WILD GREENS" SALAD

Steamed tender greens, crushed to a puree, make a soft creamy salad. Please don't cook them using the usual quick stir-fry method—only steaming will make them tender. Young Swiss chard, purslane, arugula, spinach, and/or beet greens can be substituted for the much-loved wild green mallow (see note).

If your cooked salad isn't sufficiently creamy, beat in enough additional olive oil to achieve a lovely velvety texture.

This salad will keep for several days, if stored covered in the refrigerator.

———⊚ Serves 4 to 6 as part of a traditional salad course ⊛———

1 pound mixed greens, such as spinach, Swiss chard, mallow, purslane, arugula, and/or beet greens (6 cups)

1 cup flat-leaf parsley leaves, roughly chopped

3 garlic cloves, unpeeled

½ cup cilantro leaves, chopped

¼ teaspoon salt, or more to taste

3 tablespoons extra virgin olive oil, plus more as needed

¼ teaspoon sweet paprika

Pinch of cayenne

¼ teaspoon ground cumin, preferably Moroccan, or more to taste

Juice of ½ lemon, or more to taste

½ preserved lemon (see page 21), pulp removed, rind rinsed and slivered

12 Moroccan oil-cured olives, pitted and soaked in several changes of water to remove salt

1. Wash the greens well, drain, stem, and roughly chop.

2. Steam the greens, parsley, and garlic for 10 minutes. Cool.

3. Squeeze out as much moisture as possible from the greens and finely chop. Peel the garlic, place in a mortar with the cilantro and salt, and crush to a paste.

4. Heat the olive oil in a 10-inch skillet. Add the garlic paste and chopped greens and cook over medium-low heat, turning the mixture often to avoid burning, until all the liquid has evaporated, about 10 minutes. Blend in the paprika, cayenne, cumin, and lemon juice. Transfer to a bowl and let cool slightly.

5. Beat enough oil into the greens to create a texture similar to that of whipped potatoes. Cover and refrigerate for at least 1 hour before serving.

6. Correct the seasoning with more salt and/or lemon juice if necessary, and whip once more to lighten the mixture. Shape the mixture into a smooth hemisphere on a plate and decorate with the slivered lemon peel and black olives. Serve cool.

※

MALLOW

Mallow, the green leaf of choice for cooked salads in northern Morocco, grows wild in open fields and in the Rif Mountains. (I've found it growing wild in Sterling Park off Greenwich Street in San Francisco!) Riffians prize it for its richness and unique flavor and make it delicious by adding spices and mixing it with other greens.

When foraging for mallow, pick only the tender leaves that grow on stems no longer than 12 inches. Avoid blemished leaves and leaves that have yellowed. As soon as mallow plants flower, the leaves lose their flavor. Be sure to remove the stems before steaming, as they will turn it gooey.

PURSLANE JAM

Purslane is such a great-tasting "weed," and so rampant in gardens throughout the United States, it's well worth learning how to recognize it. You may also find it at farmers' markets, but if you don't, ask one of the sellers to bring some next time. They are usually happy to do so, as they consider it a nuisance. One farmer on Martha's Vineyard offered me "free lifetime rights" to his purslane if I promised to pick some every week. I accepted!

This salad is one of my favorites. It doesn't always look as good as it tastes, because when crushed to a puree, steamed purslane emerges a homely soft green. But please don't pass it by. This salad will keep for several days, covered, in the refrigerator.

───── ❧ Serves 4 to 6 as part of a traditional salad course ❧ ─────

4 cups stemmed purslane leaves, rinsed and drained	½ teaspoon ground cumin, preferably Moroccan
4 large garlic cloves	Pinch of cayenne
1 teaspoon coarse salt, or to taste	1 tablespoon fresh lemon juice, or to taste
1 cup tightly packed flat-leaf parsley, chopped	1 preserved lemon (see page 21), pulp removed, rind rinsed and slivered
½ cup tightly packed cilantro, chopped	
3 tablespoons extra virgin olive oil	12 green-ripe, midway, or red olives, rinsed, pitted, and drained
¾ teaspoon sweet paprika	

1. Fill the bottom of a deep pot with water and bring to a boil. Insert a colander, add the purslane leaves, and steam, covered, for 12 minutes (or a few minutes longer if the leaves are very thick). Remove from the heat, uncover, and allow to cool.

2. When the purslane is cool enough to handle, squeeze out the excess moisture and set aside.

3. Pound the garlic with the salt to a paste in a mortar. Add the chopped herbs and pound to a paste.

4. Heat 2 tablespoons of the oil in a 10-inch skillet. Add the garlic-herb paste and cook for 1 to 2 minutes, without burning. Add the purslane leaves and sauté slowly until all the moisture has evaporated, turning the greens often to avoid burning, about 5 minutes. Scrape onto a chopping board and finely chop. Blend in the paprika, cumin, and cayenne. Place in a serving dish and allow to cool.

5. Just before serving, blend in the lemon juice and remaining tablespoon of olive oil; adjust the seasoning with salt and/or more lemon juice if needed. Decorate with the slivered lemon peel and olives. Serve at room temperature.

OVEN-ROASTED TOMATOES WITH TOASTED PINE NUTS

A beautiful arrangement of lightly charred slow-roasted tomatoes gently flavored with floral water. This salad is also excellent as an accompaniment to roast chicken or grilled fish.

⊷ Serves 6 as part of a traditional salad course ⊷

6 medium red-ripe tomatoes

Coarse sea salt

1 tablespoon turbinado or other raw sugar

Pinch of ground Ceylon cinnamon

1 tablespoon extra virgin olive oil

2 tablespoons rose water

2 tablespoons pine nuts or sesame seeds, toasted

1. Cut each tomato horizontally in half and squeeze gently to extract the seeds. Lightly salt the tomatoes, turn them upside down on paper towels, and let drain for 30 minutes.

2. Gently squeeze the tomatoes again to rid them of any excess moisture. Arrange cut side up in a single layer in a lightly oiled round shallow 10-inch baking dish. Mix 1 teaspoon salt with the sugar and cinnamon, and sprinkle a pinch over each tomato half. Drizzle with the olive oil.

3. Place the tomatoes in the oven and set the temperature to 250°F. Bake for 3 hours.

4. Raise the oven temperature to 400°F and continue baking for 30 minutes. Turn off the oven and let the tomatoes finish baking in the receding heat, about 30 minutes; they will be wrinkled and slightly charred.

5. Remove the roasted tomatoes from the oven, splash with the rose water, and scatter the toasted nuts on top. Let cool to room temperature before serving.

GRILLING AND PEELING BELL PEPPERS

Ideally one grills bell peppers over glowing embers to add the smoky aroma that makes them so special. If you have a gas stovetop, turn the peppers on all sides until the skins are completely blackened.

If you have an electric or ceramic stovetop, here is an excellent alternative: Core, quarter, and seed the raw peppers, then broil, skin side up, until the skins are blackened.

Once the pepper skins are scorched, wrap in a plastic bag until cool, then wipe away the blackened skin, and, if you blackened them over the stovetop, stem, seed, and quarter lengthwise. Place smooth side up, side by side, on paper towels and cover with more paper towels until ready to use.

TOMATOES, PRESERVED LEMONS, AND SWEET RED PEPPERS

This salad is best when freshly made. It is a great accompaniment to Tangier-Style Fried Chicken (page 322).

⟹ Serves 4 as part of a traditional salad course ⟸

1 pound red-ripe tomatoes, peeled, halved, seeded, and cut into ¾-inch chunks

2 red bell peppers, grilled or broiled (see note), peeled, seeded, and cut into small pieces (¾ cup)

3 tablespoons finely chopped red onion, rinsed, drained, and squeezed dry in a paper towel

3 tablespoons fruity extra virgin olive oil

Juice of ½ lemon, or to taste

½ teaspoon ground cumin, preferably Moroccan

½ teaspoon sea salt

Pinch of sweet paprika

Pinch of cayenne

1 preserved lemon (see page 21), pulp removed, rind rinsed and cut into ⅛-inch dice

1. Combine the tomatoes and peppers in a medium glass serving dish. Add the onion, olive oil, lemon juice, cumin, salt, paprika, and cayenne and toss to mix. Cover and refrigerate until well chilled, about 30 minutes.

2. Just before serving, sprinkle the preserved lemon peel over the chilled salad.

SESAME-STUDDED TOMATO JAM

To make this marvelous jam, tomatoes are first scorched in a hot oven to bring out their natural sweetness, then cooked down in a skillet. Toasted sesame seeds add their inimitable nutty flavor. Chef-owner Fatema Hal of Restaurant Mansouria in Paris says she adds pinches of powdered dried rose petals and nutmeg to flavor her tomato jam.

This jam can be refrigerated for up to 1 week.

Serves 6 to 8 as part of a traditional Moroccan dinner

4 pounds red-ripe Roma (plum) or other tomatoes

2 tablespoons extra virgin olive oil

3 tablespoons honey, preferably orange blossom, clover, acacia, or lavender

½ teaspoon ground Ceylon cinnamon, or more to taste

Salt and freshly ground black pepper

1½ teaspoons orange flower water, or more to taste

2 to 3 teaspoons sesame seeds, toasted

1. Preheat the oven to 450°F.

2. Arrange the tomatoes on a baking sheet and roast, turning occasionally, until charred and soft, about 1 hour. Let cool.

3. Peel, core, halve, and seed the tomatoes, then coarsely chop, to make about 3½ cups. (Do not use a food processor.)

4. Heat the olive oil in a large skillet until shimmering. Add the tomatoes and cook over medium-high heat, stirring frequently, until all the liquid has evaporated and the tomatoes are sizzling and beginning to brown, about 8 minutes.

5. Add the honey, cinnamon, and salt and pepper to taste and cook for a minute to bring out the flavors. Remove from the heat and let cool.

6. Add the orange flower water and correct the seasoning, adding more cinnamon if desired. Spoon into in a flat bowl. Just before serving, garnish with the sesame seeds.

GRILLED RED PEPPER SALAD

Grilled red peppers are wonderful by themselves, but the addition of a small amount of tomato and cumin enhances their flavor.

⟿☙ Serves 4 to 6 as part of a traditional salad course ☙⟾

2 large red bell peppers (1 pound),
  grilled or broiled (see page 86),
  peeled, seeded, and quartered

2 teaspoons coarse sea salt

2 tablespoons extra virgin olive oil

3 tablespoons peeled, seeded,
  and diced fresh or canned
  tomato

1 garlic clove, crushed to a paste
  with ¼ teaspoon salt

Pinch of ground cumin, preferably
  Moroccan

1 teaspoon finely chopped flat-leaf
  parsley

1. Place the pepper quarters on paper towels and cover with more paper towels. Press down gently to remove excess moisture. Flip each quarter over, sprinkle with the sea salt, and roll up like a rug. Let stand for about 1 hour at room temperature.

2. Unroll the peppers and press to remove excess moisture. Warm 1 tablespoon of the olive oil in a medium skillet. Add the peppers and gently sauté for 2 to 3 minutes. Add the tomato, garlic, cumin, and parsley and sauté for an instant. Tilt the pan so you can scoop out the oil and discard it. Toss the peppers and tomatoes with the remaining tablespoon of oil. Serve at room temperature, or refrigerate for up to 3 days.

MIXED PEPPERS AND TOMATO JAM

In this recipe from the Rif Mountains called *taktouka*, peppers and tomatoes are cooked down in their own juices before olive oil is added. This makes a huge difference in lightness and flavor.

This keeps well in the refrigerator for 4 or 5 days and even improves in flavor.

——— ◎ Serves 4 as part of a traditional salad course ◎ ———

2 red bell peppers, grilled or broiled (see page 86), peeled, seeded, and diced

2 green bell peppers, grilled or broiled (see page 86), peeled, seeded, and diced

1 small hot red pepper, stemmed and seeded (optional)

2 pounds red ripe tomatoes, peeled and diced (about 3 cups, including juice and seeds)

2 garlic cloves

1 teaspoon sea salt, or to taste

1 teaspoon cumin seeds, preferably Moroccan

½ teaspoon freshly ground black pepper

2 tablespoons cilantro leaves, coarsely chopped

1 tablespoon sweet paprika

¼ cup extra virgin olive oil

Fresh lemon juice to taste or a pinch of sugar (optional)

1. Set a large skillet over medium-low heat, add the diced peppers, hot red pepper, and tomatoes, and cook until warmed, stirring occasionally.

2. Meanwhile, crush the garlic with the salt, cumin, and pepper to a paste in a mortar. Add the cilantro and crush to a puree.

3. Scrape the puree into the tomato-pepper mixture, add the paprika and olive oil, and continue cooking until thick and most of the moisture has evaporated, about 20 minutes. Remove from the heat, taste, and add more salt and/or, if desired, lemon juice or sugar to taste. Serve at room temperature with bread.

TOMATO AND GREEN PEPPER SALAD

Serves 4 to 6 as part of a traditional salad course

3 green bell peppers, grilled or broiled (see page 86), peeled, seeded, and cut into small pieces

4 large red-ripe tomatoes, peeled, halved, seeded, and chopped

1 garlic clove, crushed

Pinch of sweet paprika

¼ teaspoon ground cumin, preferably Moroccan

2 tablespoons extra virgin olive oil

1 tablespoon fresh lemon juice

½ teaspoon salt

¼ teaspoon freshly ground black pepper

¼ preserved lemon (see page 21), pulp removed, rind rinsed and cut into ⅛-inch dice

1. Mix the peppers and tomatoes in a serving dish, then add all the remaining ingredients except the preserved lemon. Mix well to blend the spices, then toss with the vegetables. Refrigerate until shortly before serving.

2. Just before serving, sprinkle the preserved lemon over the salad. Serve cool.

HOT CHILE RELISH, RABAT-STYLE

Fry 6 hot green chile peppers in vegetable oil. Cool them under a towel, then peel. Toss with a little fresh lemon juice and salt, and serve whole.

SWEET GREEN PEPPER RELISH, FES-STYLE

Mix 6 grilled or broiled (see page 86) peeled and chopped seeded green bell peppers with 2 tablespoons fresh lemon juice, a few tablespoons of olive oil, and sugar to taste.

EGGPLANT ZAALOUK

This recipe is my version of the famous eggplant-tomato salad called *zaalouk*, one of the best of all cooked Moroccan salads. Utterly delicious on slices of warm Berber Skillet Breads (page 110), *zaalouk* will keep for several days in the refrigerator, getting better and better.

In this recipe I use a medium black-skinned eggplant, because this type tastes better than smaller eggplants when grilled.

Begin 1 day in advance, because the salad must be refrigerated overnight before serving.

───── ❧ Serves 6 to 8 ❧ ─────

2 medium black eggplants
 (¾ pound each)

⅓ cup extra virgin olive oil

1 pound red-ripe tomatoes,
 peeled, halved, seeded, and
 chopped, or 2 cups drained
 chopped canned tomatoes

Pinch of sugar (if the tomatoes are
 acidic)

1 tablespoon crushed garlic

¾ teaspoon ground cumin,
 preferably Moroccan

½ teaspoon sweet paprika

¼ teaspoon cayenne

Salt

2 tablespoons finely chopped
 cilantro

Fresh lemon juice (about
 3 tablespoons)

1. Pierce each eggplant in one or two places with a toothpick. If you are cooking over coals, slowly grill the eggplant until blackened, collapsed, and cooked through, 20 to 30 minutes. If you are cooking indoors, preheat the broiler and set the rack on the second highest rung. Halve each eggplant lengthwise, place cut side down on a foil-lined baking sheet, and broil until blackened and tender, about 20 minutes. Dump into a colander set in the sink. Peel while still hot and allow to drain until cool. Squeeze gently to remove any bitter juices.

2. Meanwhile, heat 3 tablespoons of the olive oil in a medium nonstick skillet set over moderate heat. Add the tomatoes, sugar, if using, garlic, cumin, paprika, cayenne, and ½ teaspoon salt, and cook, stirring occasionally, for 20 minutes.

3. Crush the eggplant with a fork and add to the skillet. Stir in the chopped cilantro, and continue cooking, stirring often, until thick and juicy, about 10 to 15 more minutes. Transfer to a bowl and fold in lemon juice and salt to taste. Let cool, then cover and refrigerate overnight.

4. Return the salad to room temperature and toss with the remaining olive oil before serving.

LIVER AND OLIVE SALAD

❊

MEAT SALADS

Though the following two dishes are not built around vegetables, they are nevertheless considered salads, to be served as appetizers.

Moroccans have a great way of pan-frying liver, and also fish: they use semolina pasta flour, rather than all-purpose flour, which they say creates a seal on the food, rather than being absorbed by it.

———— ❧ Serves 4 to 6 as part of a traditional salad course ❧ ————

8 ounces (2 thick slices) calf's liver

2 small garlic cloves

1 teaspoon coarse salt

2 tablespoons coarsely chopped cilantro

2 tablespoons coarsely chopped flat-leaf parsley

½ teaspoon sweet paprika

Pinch of cayenne

⅓ cup fresh lemon juice

3 tablespoons extra virgin olive oil

3 tablespoons pasta flour (semolina)

1 red-ripe tomato, peeled, seeded, and chopped, or ½ cup drained canned diced tomatoes

¼ preserved lemon (see page 21), pulp removed, rind rinsed and diced

8 to 12 green-ripe, midway, or red olives, pitted

Pinch of freshly ground cumin, preferably Moroccan

1. Wash the liver slices and drain on a paper towel. Pound the garlic and salt to a paste in a large mortar. Add half the chopped cilantro and parsley and pound until smooth. Stir in the paprika, cayenne, and half the lemon juice. Slide in the slices of liver and mix to coat evenly. Let stand for 1 hour.

2. Heat the oil in an 8- or 9-inch skillet. Transfer the liver to a flat dish, reserving the marinade in the mortar. Dust the liver with the flour and slide into the hot oil. Fry, turning each piece over once with a spatula, until browned, about 5 minutes. Drain the liver on a cutting board.

3. Add the tomato to the cooking oil and boil until thickened.

4. Meanwhile, cut the liver into ½-inch cubes. Return the liver to the skillet and fry with the tomato for about 30 seconds, tossing the cubes so they brown on all sides. Stir ½ cup water into the marinade, pour into the skillet, and bring to a boil. Stir and cook for 1 minute longer. Add the remaining lemon juice and herbs, the preserved lemon, and the olives, stir once, and remove from the heat.

5. Put the liver in a serving dish and dust with the cumin. Serve at room temperature.

SPICED BRAIN SALAD WITH PRESERVED LEMONS (MOKH)

When I first watched Moroccan cooks prepare brains, I was shocked that they did not follow all the steps I'd been taught when I studied classical French cooking. They didn't soak the brains or parboil them first. Rather, they simply held them under running water, pulled off some of the membranes, and continued from there. Later I came to understand that prolonged soaking and parboiling can remove many of the vitamins and minerals that make brains so nutritionally rich. So I now do as Moroccan cooks do, and I think my brain salad dishes are better for it.

—⊛ Serves 4 to 6 as part of a traditional salad course ⊛—

1 pound lamb brains

¼ cup chopped cilantro

¼ cup chopped flat-leaf parsley

½ teaspoon ground cumin, preferably Moroccan

1 teaspoon sweet paprika

2 to 3 garlic cloves, chopped

¼ cup extra virgin olive oil

⅓ cup fresh lemon juice

1 preserved lemon (see page 21), pulp removed, rind rinsed and diced

Salt

1. Wash the brains under running water, removing the membranes and as much blood as possible. (If this makes you feel squeamish, soak the brains in salted water to cover for 1 to 2 hours, changing the water 3 times; discard the water.) Place the brains in a casserole, along with the herbs, spices, garlic, and oil. Pour 1½ cups water over them and bring to a boil. Reduce the heat, partially cover the pot, and simmer for 30 minutes.

2. Add the lemon juice, then mash the brains into small pieces with the back of a wooden spoon. Simmer for another 30 minutes, stirring often. Ten minutes before the dish is finished, add the diced preserved lemon.

3. Season with salt, and cool to room temperature before serving.

Variation:
BRAIN SALAD WITH TOMATOES

Substitute 1 small tomato, peeled, seeded, and cubed, for the preserved lemon and add a pinch or two of cayenne along with the other spices.

NOTE TO THE COOK

Mokh, presented here in two slightly different versions, makes an excellent appetizer when teamed with a mixed herb salad, a salad of tomatoes and green peppers, and one of grated carrots or radishes. The contrasting textures and flavors make for a great start to a Moroccan feast.

chapter four

BREADS
AND
PASTRIES

❖

"Manage with bread and butter
until God sends the honey."

—*moroccan proverb*

❖

BREADS AND PASTRIES

MARRAKECH TAGINE BREAD
❧ page 101 ☙

BREAD WITH SESAME AND ANISE SEEDS
❧ page 102 ☙

MARRAKECH FLAT BREAD STUFFED
WITH MEAT
❧ page 106 ☙

MOROCCAN COUNTRY BREAD
(MATLOUÂ)
❧ page 108 ☙

BERBER SKILLET BREADS
❧ page 110 ☙

TWO-DAY PRE-FERMENT WITH GARLIC
❧ page 112 ☙

TANGIER STREET BREAD
(KALINTÉ)
❧ page 113 ☙

NO-KNEAD HARCHA
(MIDDLE ATLAS FLAT BREAD)
❧ page 116 ☙

NO-KNEAD HARCHA ROUNDS STUFFED
WITH CHEESE OR MEAT
❧ page 119 ☙

NO-KNEAD HARCHA MADE
WITH CORNMEAL
❧ page 119 ☙

HARCHA WITH GUINEA HEN
AND SPRING ONIONS
❧ page 120 ☙

MSEMMEN PANCAKES
{ page 125 }

M'LAOUI PANCAKES
{ page 126 }

MSEMMEN / R'FISSA
{ page 127 }

TRID
{ page 128 }

WARQA
{ page 130 }

BASTILA OF FES WITH CHICKEN OR QUAIL
{ page 135 }

BASTILA WITH LEMON, TETOUAN-STYLE
{ page 138 }

MEAT BASTILA WITH RED PEPPERS,
RAISINS, AND OLIVES
{ page 140 }

BASTILA WITH SEAFOOD, SPINACH, AND NOODLES
{ page 142 }

STUFFED PASTRIES: BRIWATS AND "CIGARS"
{ page 144 }

GOAT CHEESE AND HONEY FILLING
{ page 147 }

MEAT CONFIT FILLING
{ page 148 }

BRIK WITH TUNA, CAPERS, AND EGGS
{ page 149 }

BREAD

North African bread is sacred and is treated with respect. If you see a piece lying on the ground, you pick it up and kiss it and put it someplace where it will not be stepped on.

Chewy, soft-crusted Moroccan bread is highly absorbent, ideal for dipping into the savory sauces of tagines and for using as a kind of fork for conveying food when eating Moroccan-style, with one's right hand. It is extremely easy to make, and well worth the effort if you are serving Moroccan food. Even today a lot of Moroccans still make bread at home. Or they purchase artisanal bread made locally and baked in the neighborhood wood-burning oven.

When I lived in Tangier, we made bread every day. My housekeeper, Fatima, prepared fresh dough every morning, using a leavening of a piece of dough from the day before, and then, kneeling on the floor over a large unglazed red clay pan, she kneaded it for 30 minutes. She let it rise once and after pressing it down, sent it to the community oven on the head of a local boy wearing a padded cap. It was the pace of the bread bearer that determined the length of the second rise. Timing was everything, because the baked loaves had to be returned to our house in time for lunch. The loaves of each family were identified with a wooden stamp, and the same young boy who carried the bread to the oven brought it back as soon as it was baked.

Fatima used to tell me that she couldn't sleep well unless there was plenty of stone-ground wheat flour in the house.

MARRAKECH TAGINE BREAD

I learned to make this bread in Marrakech, where it's so popular it's sold on the street. The loaves are small and light, with soft golden brown crusts.

Both the shape and taste of this bread make it ideal for grasping chunks of vegetables or meats from a tagine and for soaking up delicious sauces, but it's also great lightly toasted and simply smeared with fresh butter and honey.

—————— ❧ Makes four 5- to 6-inch rounds ❧ ——————

2½ cups pasta flour (semolina), plus a handful for sprinkling

1 cup unbleached all-purpose flour

1½ teaspoons rapid-rise yeast

1½ teaspoons salt

1½ teaspoons sugar

1 tablespoon extra virgin olive oil

2 tablespoons milk or unsalted butter, softened (optional)

1. Combine the semolina, all-purpose flour, yeast, salt, and sugar in a food processor, preferably fitted with the dough blade, and sift by pulsing one or two times. With the machine running, slowly add 1¾ cups lukewarm water and the olive oil and process until the dough is silky-smooth and slightly sticky. Turn out onto a lightly floured work surface and, with lightly floured hands, knead the dough for an instant to achieve the proper consistency—smooth, elastic, and satiny-soft. Cover the dough with a cloth and let rest for 15 minutes.

2. Punch the dough down, turn it around on the floured surface, and divide into 4 equal parts. Flatten each piece into a 5- or 6-inch round. Generously sprinkle a large wooden peel or an upside-down baking sheet with pasta flour and arrange the rounds side by side on it. Cover with a kitchen towel and let rise in a warm place for 45 minutes.

3. Set a baking stone or pizza tiles on the bottom shelf of the oven. Preheat the oven to 400°F.

4. Using the palm of your hand, press on the center of each round to gently deflate it, then prick the top once or twice with a fork. (A well-risen loaf will hold its deflated shape.) For a shiny top, brush each round with milk or softened butter. Immediately slide the breads onto the heated pizza stone and bake for 20 minutes, or until they sound hollow when thumped on the bottom. Transfer to a towel-lined work surface to cool.

SEMOLINA FLOURS

Semolina milled from durum wheat comes in three grades:

The coarsest grade is used for home-made couscous (see page 200). Coarse semolina is available at Middle Eastern grocers or through mail-order (see Sources).

The medium grade is used for all sorts of flat breads such as the Marrakech Tagine Bread opposite, Moroccan Country Bread (*Matlouâ*), page 108, and Northern Moroccan harcha (see page 116), for assorted pasta shapes for soups and main dishes, and for desserts. It is sold as "pasta flour" at most grocers.

Extra-fine semolina flour, also called "patent durum flour," "durum atta," or "durum," is double-milled to the texture of talcum powder. It is used for pancakes, sweet and savory pastries, and *warqa* pastry (see page 130) as well as for Marrakech Flat Bread Stuffed with Meat (see page 106), Berber Skillet Breads (see page 110), and Msemman Pancakes (page 125). It is available at Indian and Pakistani groceries, and online (see Sources).

Semolina should always be bought fresh. If you buy in quantity, store it in heavy earthenware crocks in a cool place or in plastic bags in the freezer.

BREAD WITH SESAME AND ANISE SEEDS

Years ago, Moroccan women would knead their dough for up to 30 minutes to arrive at a silky, smooth mass. They often used a method called "knuckling" to add additional water to dough that was already saturated: the cook simply dips her knuckles into warm water, then uses them to press down on the dough while gradually working in the water. Knuckling is done slowly, adding the water about a tablespoon at a time. When the cook hears squishy sounds, she knows she's doing it right. If the dough gets too wet, she simply switches to an ordinary kneading motion, which tightens the dough, or adds a little low-gluten flour and knuckles in a few more drops of water to loosen the dough again.

Many cooks enjoy doing this sort of kneading. Me? I have to admit that I don't have the patience, but I do like good bread. Enter the food processor! Between pulsing and processing with a little rest in between and adding the liquid gradually, I can produce outstanding bread dough.

This recipe produces an excellent bread for serving with tagines.

Makes 2 round loaves; serves 12

1 packet (2¼ teaspoons) rapid-rise yeast

3 cups bread flour

1 scant cup whole wheat flour, preferably stone-ground

2 teaspoons salt

1 teaspoon sugar

½ cup lukewarm milk (optional)

2 teaspoons sesame seeds

1½ teaspoons green aniseed

Extra virgin olive oil

Coarse cornmeal or pasta flour (semolina) for sprinkling

1. Combine the yeast, two flours, salt, and sugar in a food processor, preferably fitted with the dough blade. Pulse once or twice to sift the mixture. With the machine running, slowly add the milk, if using, and then about 1 cup lukewarm water, and process to form a stiff dough. (Since flours differ in their ability to absorb moisture, a precise amount cannot be given.) Let the dough rest and cool down for 5 minutes.

2. Turn the processor on, add a few more tablespoons of water, and process for 20 seconds. Let the dough rest for 5 minutes, then process until the dough is spongy, soft, and tacky, about 15 seconds. Scrape the dough onto a lightly floured board, cover, and let rest for 5 minutes.

3. Sprinkle the dough with the spices and knead to achieve a smooth, elastic consistency. Divide the dough into 2 balls, cover with a kitchen towel, and let rest for 10 minutes.

4. Lightly oil a wide mixing bowl. Transfer 1 ball of dough to the bowl and form into a cone shape by grasping the dough with one hand and rotating it against the sides of the bowl, held by the other hand. Turn out onto a baking sheet that has been sprinkled with cornmeal. With

the palm of your hand, flatten the cone into a disk about 7 inches in diameter with a slightly raised center. Repeat with the second ball of dough. Cover loosely with a damp towel and let rise for 1 to $1\frac{1}{2}$ hours in a warm place. To see if the dough has fully risen, poke your finger gently into it; it is ready if the dough does not spring back.

5. Dab the tops of the loaves with a light brushing of oil. Let the bread rise a second time.

6. Preheat the oven to 400°F.

7. Using a fork, prick the top of each loaf in 3 or 4 places. Place the loaves on the center shelf of the oven and bake for 12 minutes, then lower the heat to 325°F and bake for about 30 minutes more. When done, the bread will sound hollow when tapped on the bottom. Remove and let cool on a rack, then cut into wedges just before serving.

MARRAKECH FLAT BREAD STUFFED WITH MEAT

Many years ago, I learned a version of this delectable bread that I decided to call "Marrakech pizza"; its actual name is *khboz bchehmar*, which means "bread with little bits of meat." It's made in various ways all over southern Morocco. Some versions include chopped hard-cooked eggs along with the meat, others include almonds or grated carrots, and still others add slices of cheese. Here I use finely diced lean beef or lamb and shredded beef suet. Don't be turned off by the suet—it will run out through holes in the bread during cooking and become a frying medium, producing a delicious cracker-like, thin crust.

———— ✎ Makes 4 breads ✎ ————

STUFFING

4 ounces beef or lamb fillet, finely diced

2 ounces beef suet, well chilled and grated

3 tablespoons roughly chopped flat-leaf parsley

½ cup grated onion, rinsed in a sieve and squeezed dry

½ teaspoon cumin seeds, preferably Moroccan

½ teaspoon coriander seeds

½ teaspoon salt

½ teaspoon harissa or other red pepper paste

1 teaspoon Tomato Magic (page 41) or tomato paste

1½ teaspoons sweet paprika

¼ teaspoon freshly ground black pepper

⅛ teaspoon ground Ceylon cinnamon

DOUGH

1 cup all-purpose flour

1 cup extra-fine semolina flour

1½ teaspoons rapid-rise yeast

½ teaspoon salt

Pasta (semolina) flour, for handling the dough

4 teaspoons unsalted butter, softened

1. To make the stuffing: Mix the meat with the grated suet in a bowl. Combine the parsley, onion, cumin seeds, coriander seeds, and salt in a mortar and pound to a smooth paste. Blend in the harissa, Tomato Magic or tomato paste, paprika, pepper, and cinnamon. Mix with the meat, cover, and set aside in a cool place.

2. To make the dough: Combine the two flours, the yeast, and salt in a food processor, preferably fitted with the dough blade, and pulse once or twice to sift the mixture. With the machine running, slowly add ½ cup warm water and process to form a stiff dough, about 10 seconds. Let the dough rest and cool down for 5 minutes.

3. Turn the processor on, add a few more tablespoons water, and process for 15 seconds. Let the dough rest again, then process until the dough is spongy, soft, and tacky, about 5 seconds.

4. Turn the dough out onto a lightly floured work surface and divide into 4 equal parts. Pat 1 ball of dough down into a disk shape, then stretch and flatten it to make a rectangle approximately 8 by 14 inches. Spread one-quarter of the filling in the center. Lightly sprinkle about 1 teaspoon pasta flour over the dough. Fold the right and then the left side of the dough over the filling. Press down on this package and flatten and stretch it until it is the same size as before. Repeat the sprinkling and the folding, this time the right side over the center and then the left side over. Repeat with the remaining 3 balls of dough. Set aside, covered, in a warm place for 45 minutes.

5. Heat a large cast-iron or nonstick griddle until medium-hot. Prick the breads six or seven times on both sides with a fork. Place on the griddle—they will begin to fry in the fat released from the fillings—and cook for 7 to 10 minutes on each side, until crisp. Dot each bread with a teaspoonful of softened butter before serving.

Variation with Meat Confit:

Substitute ½ cup crushed and shredded Meat Confit (page 44) or ⅓ cup crushed and shredded Moroccankhliî (see Sources) for the meat and 2 ounces of its cooking fat for the suet.

MOROCCAN COUNTRY BREAD (MATLOUÂ)

NOTE TO THE COOK

This dough is sticky to work with, so be generous with the pasta flour as you pat the dough out into rounds.

Matlouâ is another famous leavened Moroccan flat bread. Tender, spongy, and round, it goes perfectly with tagines, whether you eat them Moroccan-style or simply use the bread to mop up sauce from your plate. These rounds are equally wonderful smeared with butter or *smen* (see page 159) and wildflower honey accompanied by a glass of mint tea.

This recipe comes from my favorite boutique hotel in Marrakech, Dar Cigognes, which means "The House of Storks." The kitchen turns out local specialties very well, including numerous tagines, *tangia* (see page 409), and the Jewish dish *dafina*—all fabulous when eaten with torn pieces of this bread.

Traditionally *matlouâ* is slow-baked on a flat clay pan over embers, resulting in a soft, golden-brown exterior and tender, moist interior, edged with a faint smoky aroma. If your stove is equipped with a lava stone grill, you can bake the bread on a clay flowerpot saucer set over the heated lava stones. You can also bake it on a pizza stone set on an aluminum flame diverter over hot coals in your outdoor barbecue, or in an earthenware skillet or shallow casserole on top of the stove. In that case, just before serving, use tongs to hold the bread over an open flame on a gas burner to char the edges ever so slightly. Or char the breads under an electric broiler on each side.

In this version, a long, slow fermentation of the dough enhances the flavor. I shape the bread the day before, wrap it in a linen napkin and Ziploc bag to store in the refrigerator overnight, and then bring it to room temperature before its final rise.

Though this bread is best when freshly baked, it can be baked earlier in the day, wrapped in a cloth, and left in a cool place. Reheat it in a dry earthenware saucer, or wrapped in foil in a medium oven, or simply pop it into a toaster.

Note: An electric mixer is the preferred machine for making this bread; a food processor will not produce a particularly good result.

⌾ Makes 6 breads ⌾

1 cup stone-ground whole wheat flour, plus more for kneading

1 cup pasta flour (semolina), plus more for shaping

1 teaspoon granulated sugar

1 teaspoon salt

1 teaspoon rapid-rise yeast

1 tablespoon extra virgin olive oil

1. Combine the two flours, sugar, salt, and yeast in the bowl of an electric mixer, add the olive oil, and use the paddle on low speed to mix to a gritty consistency. Gradually add up to 1 cup warm water as you knead the dough, still on low speed, for 3 to 4 minutes. Let the dough rest for 5 minutes.

2. Turn the machine to medium-low speed and knead the dough for 5 minutes, or until spongy, soft, and tacky to the touch. Cover the dough and let rest for 10 minutes.

3. Turn the dough out onto a floured work surface, dust lightly with whole wheat flour, and knead until smooth and elastic, about 3 minutes. Gather into a ball, cover with a kitchen towel, and let stand for 30 minutes.

4. Divide the dough into 6 balls. Using your palms, gently flatten each ball into a 4- to 5-inch round. Dust with pasta flour, cover with a kitchen towel, and let stand for 30 minutes.

5. Poke one of the rounds with your finger. If the area remains deeply indented, prick each round with a toothpick 8 or 9 times to release any gas. If the dough springs back, let the rounds rest for another 10 minutes or so.

6. Set a large clay flowerpot saucer over medium heat and heat for 10 minutes (see the headnote for other options). Place half of the rounds of dough on the hot saucer and cook, uncovered, for 8 to 10 minutes, turning each once or twice, until golden brown and nicely charred with black spots on both sides. Stack the cooked breads and cook the remaining rounds. Serve hot or warm.

BERBER SKILLET BREADS

This recipe produces two large flat loaves that look great on the table and go beautifully with vegetable tagines. These loaves are made entirely with extra-fine semolina flour, which makes for very bouncy and light bread. I cook them in a nonstick skillet with a dusting of pasta flour, which allows me to shake each one back and forth as it cooks and develops a lovely thin charred crust. It takes about 10 minutes to cook each round, but if you have two skillets, you can do both at the same time. If not, just keep the first wrapped in a kitchen towel while you cook the second. The rounds can be reheated in a toaster oven or simply swiped across a hot skillet.

If you aren't using a pre-ferment, add another teaspoon of yeast and an additional ½ cup flour to the dough.

Makes two 8-inch round breads

1⅓ cups extra-fine semolina flour	1¼ teaspoons fine salt
¼ cup Two-Day Pre-Ferment with Garlic (page 112)	About ⅓ cup pasta flour (semolina) for handling the dough
¼ teaspoon rapid-rise yeast	

1. Combine the flour, pre-ferment, yeast, and salt in a food processor and pulse once or twice to sift the ingredients. Add ½ cup warm water, then process to knead for 15 seconds. Let the dough rest for 10 minutes.

2. Pulse the processor on and off as you add 1 to 2 more tablespoons water, and process for 10 more seconds. Generously sprinkle a wooden board with pasta flour and turn the dough out onto it. Cover with an upside-down bowl and let stand for 10 minutes.

3. Remove the bowl and divide the dough in half. Place two 12-inch squares of waxed paper side by side and coat each with a little pasta flour. Pick up one half of the dough and turn it around on one of the sheets so it is coated in flour. Repeat with the remaining dough. Flatten each into a disk about 8 inches in diameter, cover with a kitchen towel, and let rise for 1 hour.

4. With the palm of your hand, gently flatten each round, then use a thin-pronged fork to lightly prick the tops. Cover loosely with a kitchen towel and let rest for a few minutes while you heat a nonstick skillet or flat griddle (or two pans or griddles if you have them). Sprinkle the skillet or griddle with a tablespoon of pasta flour, immediately transfer a bread round to the skillet using a large flat spatula, and cook for about 5 minutes. Flip the bread onto a flat metal lid, invert the bread, and quickly slide it back into the pan. Cook for about 2 minutes, shaking the skillet to keep the bread moving. Slide onto a platter and serve at once, or keep warm wrapped in a cloth until ready to serve.

ELIAS CANETTI ON MARRAKECH BREAD

In the evenings, after dark, I went to that part of the Djemaa el Fna where the women sold bread. They squatted on the ground in a long line, their faces so thoroughly veiled that you saw only their eyes. Each had a basket in front of her lined with a cloth, and on the cloth a number of flat, round loaves were laid out for sale. I walked very slowly down the line, looking at the women and their loaves. The smell of the loaves was in my nostrils, and simultaneously I caught the look of their dark eyes. Not one of the women missed me; they all saw me, a foreigner come to buy bread. From time to time each would pick up a loaf of bread in her right hand, toss it a little way into the air, catch it again, tilt it to and fro a few times as if weighing it, give it a couple of audible pats, and then, these caresses completed, put it back on top of the other loaves. In this way the loaves themselves, their freshness and weight and smell, as it were, offered themselves for sale. There was something naked and alluring about those loaves; the busy hands of women who were otherwise shrouded completely except for their eyes communicated it to them.

"Here, this I can give you of myself; take it in your hand, it comes from mine."

There were men going past with bold looks in their eyes, and when one saw something that caught his fancy, he stopped and accepted a loaf in his right hand. He tossed it a little way into the air, caught it again, tilted it to and fro a few times as if his hand had been a pair of scales, gave the loaf a couple of pats, and then, if he found it too light or disliked it for some other reason, put it back on top of the others. But sometimes he kept it, and you sensed the loaf's pride and the way it gave off a special smell.

—Elias Canetti, *The Voices of Marrakesh* (1967)

TWO-DAY PRE-FERMENT WITH GARLIC

❧

NOTE TO THE COOK

My instruction to discard the remaining mixture may strike you as odd. The reason it cannot be saved for later use is that it will continue to blossom unmanageably and become too strong.

North African starters, or pre-ferments, are made with dates, grape skins, or garlic. I love using garlic because the effect is subliminal. The bread does not have a garlic flavor, but it does have something special, a unique "breadiness" that is truly excellent.

⅔ plus ½ cup pasta flour (semolina)

¾ cup all-purpose flour

2 garlic cloves, peeled and rinsed

1. Combine the ⅔ cup pasta flour and the all-purpose flour in a glass, earthenware, or stoneware container. Gradually stir in ¾ cup water to make a wet dough. Stir in the garlic cloves. Cover, wrap the container in a cloth or towel, and let stand in a warm place for 24 hours.

2. Uncover the starter and stir in ¼ cup water and the ½ cup pasta flour. Cover and let stand for another 12 hours. The starter should have a crusty exterior but be blossoming underneath.

3. Remove and set aside ½ cup of the starter; discard the garlic and remaining mixture.

TANGIER STREET BREAD (KALINTÉ)

When I lived in Tangier, I remember how, in the late afternoon, just when school let out, boys (including my son's friend, and now mine, spice importer Mustapha Haddouch) would emerge from the bakeries with large trays of freshly made bread held up on one hand waiter-style, calling out, *"Kalinté, kalinté,"* the Tangier slang word for "heat."

This bread is the Tangier version of a Mediterranean chickpea-flour bread such as the *socca* of Nice and the *farinata* of Genoa. But *kalinté* is actually more like a flan, with a glazed glistening top sprinkled just before eating with ground cumin seeds or a smear of diluted harissa.

You will need a 12- or 14-inch deep-dish pizza pan and at least one pizza stone (two are even better) to simulate a brick bread oven and help develop the glossy topping.

Serves about 18 as a snack

1 large egg

6 tablespoons extra virgin olive oil

2 teaspoons fine sea salt

4½ cups lukewarm water

About 2⅔ cups (¾ pound) stone-ground chickpea flour, sifted

Ground cumin, preferably Moroccan, or Harissa Sauce (page 39) or other hot red pepper sauce for garnish

1. Put the egg and ¼ cup of the oil in a blender or a food processor and whirl until light and foamy. Add the salt and then half the water and blend for an instant. Add half the flour and blend until smooth. Add the remaining flour and just enough water to create a smooth mixture. Press through a very fine strainer into a bowl and stir in the remaining water. Cover and let stand in a cool place for at least half a day. (You can refrigerate the batter for up to 2 days.)

2. About 1½ to 2 hours before serving, set a pizza stone on the middle or upper oven shelf. Preheat the oven to 500°F. Brush the bottom and sides of a 14-inch deep-dish pizza pan with some of the remaining oil.

3. Use a whisk to stir up the chickpea-flour mixture. Pour into the pan and bake for 30 minutes.

4. Brush the top of the bread with the remaining oil and cover partially with a baking sheet or another pizza pan. Turn off the oven and let bake for about 20 minutes more in the declining heat. The top should be golden brown and nicely glazed. Remove from the oven, cut into small rectangles, and sprinkle with cumin or harissa, and serve.

NO-KNEAD HARCHA
(MIDDLE ATLAS FLAT BREAD)

Harcha is a wonderful, true "no-knead," handcrafted flat bread from the Middle Atlas region of Morocco. It is tender and crumbly on the inside and ever so lightly crusty on the exterior.

You can produce *harcha* in small or medium rounds. In the Middle Atlas, I've seen *harcha* the size of truck tires sold on the streets. These enormous rounds are cut up into wedges, smeared with butter and honey, and served with mint tea.

I've long been fascinated by this bread, because its lightness derives from the special way it is handled. All you do is moisten the pasta flour until it becomes a kind of mud pie, then allow it to sit until it turns into dough. That's right! It transforms itself into dough without any kneading. I never cease to be amazed.

After this miraculous 25-minute transformation, you shape the dough, then cook it slowly on top of the stove in a nonstick skillet without fat. The resulting texture may remind you a bit of corn bread, and, in fact, in the region of the Souss in the southern part of Morocco, polenta-type cornmeal is substituted (see the recipe on page 119).

Everyone I talked to about *harcha* in the Middle Atlas told me the finest version was made in the town of Hyayna, about a one-hour drive north of Meknes. When I went there, I learned the secret: they make a tea with a local herb called *manta* and then use the tea to flavor the pasta flour before leaving it to expand. *Manta*, I learned, was the herb *Calamintha nepeta*, which those familiar with Tuscan cooking will know as *nepetella*. It tastes a little like wild mint mixed with marjoram and oregano and is available online (see Sources). If you can't get *nepetella*, you can use any good herbal mint tea or make *harcha* the way it's made in the Rif Mountain area, with buttermilk or yogurt thinned with water. I give both options below, and both types are delicious.

Harcha can be served plain or used for sandwiches, and it can also be stuffed with cheese or meat confit (see page 119). It can also be crumbled and used as a bed for a meltingly tender guinea hen stew (see page 120) or crumbled, steamed, and served with a luscious pairing of spring onions and garlic in milk sauce.

Please note: *Harcha* is fragile, so be sure to use your thinnest, most flexible spatula when flipping.

―❧ Makes 12 to 16 small rounds, two 6-inch rounds, or one 12-inch round ❧―

1⅓ cups pasta flour (semolina) plus another ⅔ cup for shaping and cooking the bread

6 tablespoons unsalted butter, softened

1 tablespoon extra virgin olive oil

1½ teaspoons double-acting baking powder

½ teaspoon fine salt

1½ tablespoons honey or 2 tablespoons sugar

½ cup plus 2 tablespoons warm milk, buttermilk, or strained herbal tea

Melted unsalted butter for garnish

Honey (optional)

1. Spread the 1⅓ cups pasta flour out on a work surface or in a wide wooden bowl. Add the butter and oil and use your fingertips to rub the butter and oil into the flour. When the mass is evenly crumbly, almost as fine as sand, add the baking powder and salt and toss lightly.

2. Combine the honey or sugar with the milk, buttermilk, or strained mint tea. Gradually add this liquid to the mass, using your fingertips to work it in and gathering the mixture into a very wet ball, much like a mud pie. Do not knead! Press down gently with the palm of your hand to flatten the mass into a 12-by-5-by-½-inch rectangle. Let stand, uncovered, for 10 to 15 minutes.

3. To make two 6-inch rounds: Use a pastry scraper to divide the dough in half. Lift each half and sprinkle a little pasta flour underneath, then use your palm to flatten it into a 6-inch round. Sprinkle the tops of each round with a little pasta flour. Lift, flip, and press again. Make sure there are no airholes.

4. Set two nonstick skillets over low heat (or cook the breads one at a time if you have only one skillet). Generously dust the surface of each skillet with pasta flour. Slide each round into a skillet and cook over medium-low heat, shaking the bread in a forward-and-backward motion to keep it from sticking, until the undersides are golden, 7 to 10 minutes. Slide each round onto a flat plate. Invert the first skillet over the round and, holding the skillet and plate tightly, flip the round back into the skillet. Repeat with the second round. Cook both rounds until the second sides are golden brown, 7 to 10 minutes more. Immediately brush the tops with butter and honey, if using, and serve hot.

Variation:

To make one 12-inch round, add a beaten egg to the milk, buttermilk, or tea. Follow the directions above, placing a generously dusted sheet of waxed paper beneath the dough to help move it around as you flatten it out to a 12-inch disk, then dust with more pasta flour. Cover the disk with a flat plate, flip, remove the waxed paper, and slide it into a hot skillet. Cook for 12 minutes on the first side, then flip and continue cooking for about 10 more minutes. Use a knife to cut crisscross lines into the finished bread. Spread with butter and serve honey on the side.

NO-KNEAD HARCHA ROUNDS STUFFED WITH CHEESE OR MEAT

Makes 8 stuffed rounds

¼ cup crumbled or crushed fresh goat cheese, finely shredded

16 small uncooked Harcha rounds

¼ cup "Express" Meat Confit (page 44), seasoned with

extra ground cumin, coriander, and pepper, crushed and finely diced, or 3 tablespoons crushed and finely shredded Moroccan khlii (see Sources)

1. Place a heaping teaspoon or so of the cheese or shredded meat on half the *harcha* rounds. Place another round on top of each and press around the edges to seal. Gently flatten each round to 1¼ inches. If cracks appear, moisten the dough, add a tiny amount of pasta flour, and pinch to seal.

2. Place the rounds in a hot skillet sprinkled with pasta flour, as directed on page 117. Cook 10 minutes over low heat. Press down if rounds start to puff. Turn and cook second side. Serve hot or warm.

NO-KNEAD HARCHA MADE WITH CORNMEAL

Makes 12 small rounds

½ teaspoon salt

2 tablespoons sugar

1 tablespoon green aniseed

2 teaspoons double-acting baking powder

¼ cup fine polenta

⅔ cup pasta flour (semolina), plus ¼ cup for handling the dough

½ cup clarified butter, softened

½ cup milk

¼ cup melted clarified butter, blended with 2 tablespoons honey

1. Grind salt, sugar, and aniseed. Toss with baking powder.

2. Mix the polenta and ⅔ cup pasta flour in a bowl. Add the softened clarified butter and work it into the flour with your fingertips to achieve a sandy texture. Add the seasoned baking powder and toss lightly. Add the milk a spoonful at a time, mixing throughly each time before adding more. The dough will be very wet. Flatten it with your palm into a ½-inch-thick round or rectangle. Let stand for 10 minutes.

3. Cut into 12 small circles. Dust with extra pasta flour and cook as directed on page 117. As soon as the rounds are cooked, brush one side with the butter and honey mixture, and serve.

NOTE TO THE COOK

To make small rounds: Divide the dough into 4 parts. Lift up each part and sprinkle a little pasta flour underneath. Use the palm of your hand to flatten each into a 5-by-6-inch rectangle. Use a 1- to 1¼-inch cookie cutter to cut out small rounds of dough. Lift, flip, and gently press each round again, then slide onto a wide spatula and then into a hot skillet. Cook the rounds as directed on page 117, then brush the tops with butter and honey, if using, and serve hot. To make these small rounds in advance: Cook, but don't butter. Instead, cool and store in a paper bag at room temperature for a few hours. To reheat: Dust a dry skillet with pasta flour, set it over medium heat, add the *harcha* rounds, and quickly reheat on both sides, then brush the tops with butter and honey, if using.

HARCHA WITH GUINEA HEN AND SPRING ONIONS

For this recipe, you make the *harcha*, crumble it while it is still warm, and scatter the bits of bread into a serving dish. Then you moisten the bread with a thick sauce and serve the cut-up guinea hen on top.

This preparation is a specialty of the town of Beni Slimane. My recipe was inspired by a series of answers to posted queries on a Moroccan food website. The dish is quite special and definitely worth the trouble. You can substitute chicken or Rock Cornish game hens, preferably organic and air-chilled, for the guinea hen.

Note that the guinea hen must marinate overnight.

One 2½- to 3-pound guinea hen, giblets and neck set aside

MARINADE

2 teaspoons ground ginger

1½ teaspoons freshly ground black pepper

1 teaspoon ground turmeric

1 teaspoon "Faux" *Ras el Hanout* #2 (page 36)

1 teaspoon crushed dried mint, wild mint, thyme, or marjoram

½ teaspoon crushed mace

2 teaspoons salt

3 tablespoons saffron water (see page 48)

¼ cup extra virgin olive oil

1 tablespoon fenugreek seeds

1 pound spring onions or scallions, trimmed

1 cinnamon stick, bruised

2 teaspoons Tomato Magic (page 41) or 1 teaspoon tomato paste

One 12-inch or two 6-inch rounds No-Knead Harcha (page 116),

made with the addition of 1 teaspoon crushed dried mint, wild mint, thyme, or marjoram, freshly cooked

2 teaspoons Smen, Oudi (pages 159 and 161), or clarified butter

2 tablespoons chopped flat-leaf parsley

1. One day in advance: Wash and dry the bird and giblets. Combine all the marinade ingredients in a bowl. Rub the bird inside and outside with the marinade, place the bird and giblets in a Ziploc bag, and add the remaining marinade. Close up and refrigerate overnight, turning the bag occasionally.

2. Soak the fenugreek seeds in warm water for at least 4 hours; drain.

3. About 1½ hours before serving, bring the bird to room temperature.

4. Halve or quarter the spring onions lengthwise, depending on size. Separate the green leaves from the white bulbs and dice enough of the tender leaves to make 2 cups. Coarsely chop the white bulbs and reserve 3 cups; discard the rest.

5. Place the guinea hen, with the marinade (set the giblets aside), on its side in a medium casserole, set over medium-low heat, and cook until lightly browned. Turn and continue cooking until browned on all sides, about 10 minutes. Add the spring onion whites and tender green leaves and cook for 5 minutes.

6. Make a cheesecloth packet with the drained fenugreek, the cinnamon stick, and neck and giblets and tie up with string. Add 4 cups water, the packet, and the Tomato Magic or tomato paste to the casserole and cook, covered, at a low simmer until the bird is very tender, about 1 hour.

7. Meanwhile, make the *harcha*. While it is still warm, break into small pieces and place in a shallow serving dish.

8. Transfer the guinea hen to a cutting board and allow to rest for 5 minutes, then carve into 6 serving pieces. Discard the backbone and wingtips.

9. Meanwhile, remove and discard the cheesecloth packet and boil down the liquid in the casserole to a thick gravy. Correct the seasoning with salt and pepper and add the *smen, oudi,* or butter and parsley.

10. Spoon some of the sauce over the *harcha*, arrange the guinea hen on top, pour over the rest of the sauce, and serve.

MSEMMEN PANCAKES

These pancakes are made with a well-kneaded dough that is stretched paper thin into a rectangle, then oiled, folded in half, and folded in half again, resulting in a square packet. The packet is then fried on a lightly greased griddle until it browns like a crepe. Properly made it will be so thin you'll be able to see light through it. It is then served with honey and butter.

—∾ Makes about sixteen 5-inch square pancakes ∾—

1½ cups extra-fine semolina flour

1½ cups unsifted all-purpose flour

1½ teaspoons fine sea salt

¼ teaspoon rapid-rise yeast

Vegetable oil for handling the dough

6 tablespoons melted clarified butter

Pasta flour (semolina) for dusting

Butter and liquid honey for serving

1. Combine the two flours, salt, and yeast in a food processor and pulse to sift. With the machine running, add about 1½ cups warm water. Then add more water by the tablespoon if necessary to form a soft ball of dough. Process for 25 seconds more, or until the dough is very elastic, soft, and smooth. Allow the dough to rest for 10 minutes.

2. Turn the dough ball out onto a smooth countertop, Silpat mat, or metal pizza pan. Use oil to grease your hands, the surface, and the dough. With your thumb and forefinger, squeeze and pull off small balls of dough about the size of large prunes; you should have about 16 balls. Coat each ball with oil.

3. Pat 1 ball down into a disk, flattening it with the oiled palms and fingers of both hands and stretching it as you flatten it. If you kneaded the dough well enough, it will practically slide outward. Avoid tearing the dough as it becomes paper-thin; try to keep it evenly thin. Stretch the dough out to a paper-thin 10-by-9-inch rectangle. Lightly brush with butter and dust with pasta flour. Fold the ends of the rectangle over so they meet in the center and brush with butter, then turn 90 degrees and fold again. Pat slightly, again brush with butter, and flatten so you have a 4½-inch square packet; set aside. Repeat with the other balls of dough.

4. Heat a large nonstick griddle or skillet over medium heat. Press each packet out until it is almost double in size. Use a spatula to slide the packet into the skillet. Cook 2 or 3 at a time, turning them over several times, until they are golden brown and the centers are cooked. They should puff a little bit in the center—gently press down the puffing with a spatula. Transfer to a rack to cool. Serve the pancakes reheated in a hot dry skillet with butter and honey.

❋

RGHAIF

Rghaif is to Moroccans what madeleines were to Marcel Proust—a food that opens up all sorts of sweet memories of childhood and home. Many Moroccans living abroad have told me that from time to time they feel an overwhelming longing for *rghaif.*

In 1968, my son Nicholas, then six, visited the mountain village of Joujouka to witness the annual celebration of the Rites of Pan. (The music of Joujouka was recorded by Brian Jones, of the Rolling Stones.) When Nick returned, he was full of stories of a man dressed in animal skins who danced with a fiery branch. But the thing he remembered best was being awakened in the morning by haunting flute music and being fed what he called "an airy pancake." He begged me to make it for him, but it took me quite a while to figure out that the airy pancake he liked so much was actually a type of *rghaif.*

Rghaif means "pancake," and it appears in Moroccan cooking in all sorts of different shapes, sizes, and flour blends, with names such as *msemmen, m'laoui,* and *rezzat el cadi.* All are served with honey and butter for breakfast. Some are coated with confectioners' sugar; others are stuffed with almonds or long-simmered onions flavored with saffron and blended with chopped olives, or spread with a spicy meat confit.

One dish made only in homes, never served in restaurants, is called *r'fissa* (see page 127). It's a little like *trid* (see page 128) in that it employs soft, silky pancake leaves as a bed for a soupy poultry stew; it is often flavored with fenugreek and accompanied by lentils.

M'LAOUI PANCAKES

For these pancakes, the *rghaif* pastry is folded differently but fried the same way as *msemmen* (see page 125). Each piece of dough is squeezed into a ball, then flattened into a long thin strip. One end is flattened very thin, and the pastry is rolled up, much as you might roll up a rug, except that you keep stretching the unrolled part as you roll the pastry. Then you flatten the whole thing into a round pancake. These are excellent hot with butter and honey.

———⊗ Makes about 18 pancakes ⊗———

2¾ cups (1 pound) extra-fine semolina flour	Vegetable oil for handling the dough
1 teaspoon rapid-rise yeast	⅓ cup melted clarified butter
1½ teaspoons salt	¼ cup pasta flour (semolina)
1 teaspoon sugar	½ cup honey

1. Combine the flour, yeast, salt, and sugar in a food processor and pulse to sift. With the machine running, add about 1½ cups warm water, then add more water by the tablespoon if necessary to form a soft ball of dough. Process for 25 seconds more, or until the dough is very elastic, soft, and smooth. Allow the dough to rest for 10 minutes.

2. Turn the dough ball out onto a smooth countertop, Silpat mat, or large metal pizza pan. Lightly oil your hands, the work surface, and the dough. With your thumb and forefinger, squeeze off small balls of dough about the size of large prunes. Coat each ball with butter.

3. Pat 1 ball down into a disk, flattening it with the oiled palms and fingers of both hands and stretching it as you flatten it. Avoid tearing the dough as it becomes paper-thin; try to keep it evenly thin. Stretch the dough out to a 10-by-9-inch rectangle. Lightly brush with butter and dust with pasta flour. Fold the ends of the rectangle over so they meet in the center, brush lightly with butter, and dust with pasta flour. Fold the dough again lengthwise in half. Pat down with buttered fingers and set aside. Repeat with the other balls of dough.

4. Flatten the first strip of dough at one end until very thin, then roll the dough up into a cylinder, stretching the unrolled part at the same time. Flatten the cylinder into a round pancake. Repeat with the remaining strips. Cover with a towel and let rise slightly, about 20 minutes.

5. Lightly brush a nonstick skillet with butter and set over medium heat. One at a time, press each pancake down, then slide into the skillet and fry until it becomes golden brown. Brush a little of the melted butter over the top, turn it, and continue frying for a minute longer. Transfer to paper towels to drain. Serve warm with the honey on the side.

THE CAID'S TURBAN

This form of pancake is the most difficult to execute well, which is why I chose not to include a recipe, but it's such an interesting pastry, I wanted to describe it. The dough is worked into a thin rope about as thick as knitting yarn. While it is being worked and stretched, the completed portion is kept wrapped around the preparer's fingers. When thick as a ball of yarn, it is set aside to rest, then flattened and gently fried in a small amount of oil. After frying, it is pressed down, which loosens the coil of pastry and makes it look like a plate of spaghetti. It is then steamed in a couscousier and served very hot with butter and dark country honey.

These pancakes are also used as the pastry base for dishes served at weddings and religious feasts: country chickens, pigeons, or partridges that have been cooked with the finest saffron and aged *smen*, then topped with toasted crushed almonds.

MSEMMEN / R'FISSA

This popular dish, served on special occasions, is presented like couscous on a large platter. The *msemmen* are torn into pieces while still hot to the touch and set aside until just before serving. Then they are piled into a steamer and reheated. The chicken stew is placed on top and the sauce spooned over. There are many versions of this dish. This one was given to me by Aunt Aicha from the town of Beni Mellal. She said to be sure to add the *ras el hanout*: "It puts the dish up ten notches."

――― ❧ Serves 8 ❧ ―――

¼ cup fenugreek seeds

1½ cups Moroccan or French green lentils

¼ cup extra virgin olive oil

5 large onions, 1 grated, 4 thinly sliced

1½ teaspoons coarse salt

1 teaspoon freshly ground black pepper

¾ tablespoon ground ginger

¾ tablespoon ground turmeric

½ teaspoon "Faux" Ras el Hanout #2 (page 36)

Pinch of ground coriander

One 4-pound chicken, preferably organic and air-chilled

1 teaspoon Homemade Smen (page 159)

4 sprigs each cilantro and parsley, tied together

Msemmen Pancakes (page 125), made without yeast

1. Soak the fenugreek seeds in warm water to cover for at least 4 hours; drain. Soak the lentils for 30 minutes; drain and set aside.

2. Heat the oil in a large pot over medium heat. Add the grated onion, salt, pepper, ginger, turmeric, *ras el hanout*, and coriander. Add the chicken and stir to coat the chicken with spices, then add ⅓ cup water, cover, and let steam for 10 minutes. Add just under 4 quarts water and bring to a boil. Reduce the heat to a simmer, add the drained fenugreek seeds, cover, and cook for 25 minutes.

3. Turn the chicken for even cooking. Add the sliced onions, lentils, *smen,* and herbs and cook for 20 minutes, or until the onions and lentils are tender. Turn off the heat and let sit for 10 to 15 minutes.

4. Meanwhile, tear the *msemmen* into large pieces and steam over boiling water for 10 minutes. Spread the pieces of *msemmen* over the bottom of a large shallow serving platter.

5. Transfer the chicken to a cutting board and cut into serving pieces. Arrange the pieces of chicken evenly over the pastry leaves. Use a slotted spoon to scoop the lentils over the chicken and ladle some of the broth on top. Serve with some of the remaining broth on the side.

❉

NOTES TO THE COOK

You can make *msemmen* a day in advance: flatten each square between two sheets of parchment; roll up and store in a Ziploc bag in the refrigerator. Let return to room temperature before reheating, one by one, in a hot dry skillet.

When making pancakes, for this dish, follow the recipe on page 125, except omit the yeast to avoid unwanted puffy leaves. Tear the *msemmen*, while still hot, into bite-sized pieces, then steam in a couscous cooker to reheat just before serving.

Here is the basic method for washing and seasoning a whole or cut up chicken for R'fissa, Trid, and Bastila (pages 127, 128, and 135).

This process rids the chicken of any bitter flavor that might spoil the sauce; it also helps to bring out its flavor. Wash the chicken well and pull out as much fat as possible. Crush 5 cloves of garlic and make a paste with 2 tablespoons coarse salt. Rub the paste into the flesh of the chicken. Let stand for 30 minutes, then rinse under running water until the chicken no longer smells of garlic. Drain and pat dry.

If the chicken is whole, clip off the wing tips and discard; cross the drumsticks over each other and tie with string.

TRID

NOTES TO THE COOK

Trid, as it is prepared in the city of Fes, is often called the "poor man's *bastila*"—a reference to what is probably the most famous and luxurious dish in Moroccan cuisine (see page 135).

This version has similar spicing to its more famous and far more luxurious cousin. A cooked chicken is nestled in a bed of very thin, white, nearly translucent pastry leaves that may be compared to fine cotton shirting. It is often topped with a drizzling of country honey, in place of the famous sugar and cinnamon topping applied to *bastila*, and in some homes, it is also decorated with toasted almonds.

In this variation from the city of Safi, the leaves are torn up and used as a bed beneath the chicken parts. And in some homes, sugar and cinnamon and a bowl of cold milk are served on the side of the *trid*.

8 cups (2 pounds) all-purpose flour

Salt

¼ cup vegetable oil, plus more as needed

One 4-pound chicken, preferably organic and air-chilled

1 large yellow or red onion, grated

½ teaspoon ground ginger

½ teaspoon freshly ground black pepper

Three 3-inch cinnamon sticks

1 teaspoon black peppercorns

3 tablespoons saffron water (see page 48)

7 tablespoons unsalted butter

10 cilantro sprigs, tied together

1 tablespoon Homemade Smen (page 159)

1 tablespoon dark honey (optional)

1. To prepare the dough: Combine the flour and 1 teaspoon salt in a dry bowl. Add just enough lukewarm water to make a soft dough. Knead for 5 minutes, then add the vegetable oil by the spoonful, kneading well to incorporate each addition before adding more. Then knead the dough in a food processor for 1 minute, or until very elastic and smooth.

2. Separate the dough into 3 equal parts. Coat each one with more oil and cover with a cloth. Let stand for 1 hour.

3. Place the chicken in a 4-quart casserole, along with the onion, 1 teaspoon salt, the spices, saffron water, butter, cilantro, and 6 cups water. Bring to a boil, then reduce the heat to very low, cover, and simmer for 1 hour, or until the chicken is well cooked, turning the chicken from time to time for even cooking.

4. Remove the chicken to a platter. Reduce the sauce to a thick gravy of about 1¾ cups by boiling rapidly, uncovered. Cut the chicken into 8 serving pieces, removing any loose bones. Return to the sauce and keep warm.

5. Meanwhile, place 1 of the balls of dough on a countertop, Silpat mat, or metal pizza pan and flatten it by stretching and rubbing outward with the palms of your hands. Continue to knead and roll the dough until smooth. Repeat with the other 2 balls.

6. Rub the work surface sparingly with oil. Twist the first ball of dough in half and then press and rub the one half between your palms, forming a cylinder. Make a small circle with your thumb and forefinger, push the cylinder partway through, and twist off a small ball the size of a prune. Repeat until you have "popped" 10 "prunes"

through your thumb and forefinger. Repeat with remaining half, and then the other 2 balls.

7. Flatten each piece of dough into a 3-inch disk by tapping with oily fingertips.

8. Set a deep pot of water on the stove and bring to a fast boil. Set a nonstick skillet that sits snugly over the pot on top and secure with kitchen string. Before making the first pastry leaf, use a silicone brush to oil the skillet, then wipe it dry with a paper towel. Oil your fingers and stretch the first pastry disk until you obtain a paper-thin circle approximately 8 inches in diameter. Lightly oil the bottom of the skillet and place the leaf in it to dry; turn after 30 seconds. Meanwhile, stretch and oil the next leaf. Place the second leaf on top of the drying first leaf and wait a second or two, then flip them both over so that the second leaf will start to dry too. Continue in this manner until you have 10 flattened leaves piled together, cooking and drying on the skillet bottom. Fold the pile loosely in half and then loosely in half again, so that the edges have a chance to dry. Remove and keep warm in a wrapped towel while you prepare the next batch. Continue until you've prepared all the leaves.

9. Detach the skillet from the pot of boiling water. Replace it with a snug-fitting colander or steamer. Separate the leaves of pastry, tearing off and discarding any raw edges. Pile into the colander or steamer, cover, and steam for 20 minutes.

10. Meanwhile, preheat the oven to 350°F.

11. Remove the steamed leaves from the colander and cut or tear into small pieces. Place one-third of the steamed leaves, in two layers, in an ovenproof serving dish. Dribble ⅓ cup of the sauce over the leaves. Cover with another third of the leaves, dribble with another ⅓ cup sauce, and top with the final third of the leaves. Nestle the pieces of chicken in the middle. Add the *smen* and honey, if using, to the remaining sauce and dribble it on top.

12. Bake for 10 minutes and serve.

Variation:

CHICKEN WRAPPED WITH TRID AND CABBAGE

For this version, as prepared in the mountains of northern Morocco, use only 1 cinnamon stick and omit the honey. When the chicken is cooked, remove it from the sauce and cover to keep warm. Quarter and core a small green cabbage, add to the casserole, and cook until tender. Return the chicken to the casserole to reheat. Meanwhile, tear the steamed *trid* leaves into small pieces. Line the bottom of a wide, deep serving dish with one-third of the leaves. Spoon a few tablespoons of the sauce on top. Add half of the cabbage, spreading it out evenly, and top with the chicken pieces and some of sauce. Add another layer of torn leaves and then the remaining cabbage and end with a final layer of *trid* leaves. Cover with the remaining sauce and serve.

WARQA

Warqa is the most prestigious pastry in Moroccan cuisine, used to make what is certainly the nation's most impressive dish, *bastila* (see page 135). Though many people compare *warqa* pastry with Greek fillo dough, Hungarian strudel leaves, and Tunisian *brik* pastry, *warqa* is thinner and stronger than all three.

The making of *warqa*, also an essential ingredient in *briwat* and Moroccan *cigars* (see page 144), is always the work of specialists. It's wonderful to watch these talented women as they knead a ball of dough, then tap it multiple times on a metal pan heated over a charcoal brazier, creating a paper-thin pastry leaf dab by dab. It's a time-consuming process, difficult to master, and for this reason, most recipes (including those in my first book) recommend the substituting of commercial fillo dough or *brik* pastry.

But, thanks to the Internet, I recently learned a new and fairly easy way to make this pastry, by using a brush to apply a batter to a skillet heated to a constant temperature. The resulting *warqa* is superb: more tender, crisper, and more flavorful than anything commercial.

To replicate the constant 195° to 200°F heat of a Moroccan copper-and-tin *warqa* pan set over charcoal, I make my *warqa* leaves in a nonstick skillet snugly fitted over a pot of boiling water To keep the skillet stable, I fasten its handle to one of the pot handles with string.

By tradition, *warqa* leaves are cooked on one side only. In pastry dishes such as *bastila*, the cooked (shiny) side of the leaves is always facing out. See the recipe on page 135 for more details.

It takes about 5 minutes to make this batter in a food processor, and, with practice, about 2 minutes to make each leaf. Note that the batter must be made a day ahead.

NOTES TO THE COOK

This recipe works well with very-high-gluten flours such as Guisto's Ultimate Performance Unbleached Bread Flour (13½%) or King Arthur's Sir Lancelot Hi-Gluten Flour (13%); see Sources. If *warqa* is intended for *bastila*, use the ¼ cup all-purpose flour; if intended for *briwat*, use ¼ cup extra-fine semolina flour.

You will need two brushes: a silicone brush to apply oil to the shiny side of each cooked pastry leaf, and a natural bristle pastry brush to apply the batter to the skillet.

To clean the bristle brush, soak it in warm water, then use the prongs of a fork to loosen any solidified batter.

You can freeze the sheets by inserting rounds of waxed paper between each sheet and wrapping in a freezer bag.

Quickly brush the batter evenly over the skillet.

Makes fifteen to twenty-four 10- to 12-inch round leaves, or enough batter for about 3 dozen pastry triangles (see page 144)

8 ounces high-gluten flour (see Note)

¼ cup all-purpose flour or extra-fine semolina flour (see Note)

1 teaspoon salt

1 tablespoon cider vinegar or fresh lemon juice

1 tablespoon extra virgin olive oil

3 tablespoons vegetable oil for brushing the cooked leaves

1. The day before: To prepare the batter, combine the two flours and salt in a food processor and pulse to sift. With the machine running, add 1 cup water and the vinegar. Once the dough forms a smooth ball, add the oil through the tube and process the dough for 30 seconds. With the machine running, slowly pour in ¾ cup more water and process for another 30 to 45 seconds, or until you have a smooth batter. Pour into a container, cover, and refrigerate overnight.

2. The following day: To make the *warqa*, set a deep pot of water on the stove and bring to a fast boil. Set a nonstick skillet that sits snugly over the pot, and secure with kitchen string. Before making the first pastry leaf, use a silicone brush to oil the skillet, then wipe it dry with a paper towel.

3. Use a bristle brush to stir up the batter, then lift up the brush thick with batter and quickly brush the batter evenly over the hot skillet; use a circular motion to create a thin film-like layer. If necessary, stir the batter and apply a thinner second layer to fill in any empty spaces. (Don't worry about lacy edges or tiny cracks in the center.) Cook the leaf for about 2 minutes, or until it turns completely white and the edges begin to curl, but it is still supple. The pastry is cooked only on one side. Use your fingertips to lift the pastry out of the skillet, transfer to a paper towel, shiny cooked side up, and quickly brush all over with oil. Cover with another paper towel and gently press to remove excess oil. Leave the paper towel on the pastry.

Apply a thin second layer to fill in any empty spaces.

4. Stir up the batter and make another pastry leaf as described above, then oil and cover with a paper towel, stacking the leaf on the previous one. Continue making leaves and stacking them, then slide the stack (leaves and paper) into a plastic bag to prevent them from drying out. The package can be kept in the refrigerator for up to 3 days.

Use your fingertips to lift the pastry out of the skillet.

It should be thin enough to detect the outline of your hand through it.

BASTILA OF FES WITH CHICKEN OR QUAIL

Bastila (also written as *pastila*, *bisteeya*, or *bestela*) is so intricate and so grand, so lavish and so rich, that its extravagance always reminds me of the Arabian Nights. The traditional *bastila* of Fes is an enormous flaky pigeon pie never less than twenty inches in diameter. Beneath the perfectly crisped pastry top, which is covered with cinnamon and sugar, are layers of shredded cooked squab, quail, or chicken; two dozen eggs curdled in a lemony spiced onion sauce; and sweetened almonds.

In Fes, this pie is traditionally made with pigeon or squab. I've found that either chicken thighs or quail make highly acceptable substitutes. I've written this recipe so you can make a smaller version of this amazing dish in your home oven, whether you use homemade *warqa* leaves, or commercial fillo.

You can prepare steps 1 through 5 up to one day in advance, and assemble the pie a few hours before baking.

Bastila is best served very hot, so plan accordingly.

Look for semi-boneless quail, which have all but the wing and lower leg bones removed, at specialty butchers.

-----◎ Serves 12 as a first course; makes one 12-inch *bastila* ◎-----

6 bone-in chicken thighs, 6 ounces each, or 6 semi-boned quails, about 6 ounces each

3 tablespoons saffron water (see page 48)

1 teaspoon ground ginger

¾ teaspoon ground black pepper

¼ teaspoon turmeric

¼ teaspoon grated nutmeg

Coarse salt

Two 2-inch soft cinnamon sticks

½ large red onion, grated

½ cup chopped parsley leaves

¼ cup chopped cilantro leaves

½ cup clarified butter

¼ cup vegetable oil

12 ounces whole blanched almonds

⅓ cup confectioners' sugar, plus more for dusting

1½ teaspoons ground Ceylon cinnamon, plus more for dusting

¼ cup fresh lemon juice

9 large eggs

24 Warqa (page 130) or 8 ounces fillo leaves

1 egg yolk, lightly beaten

1. Put the chicken thighs or quail in a wide casserole. Mix the saffron water with the ginger, pepper, turmeric, nutmeg, and 1 teaspoon coarse salt. Toss with the chicken or quail and set aside for 10 minutes.

2. Lightly bruise the cinnamon sticks. Add the cinnamon sticks, grated onion, parsley, cilantro, half the butter, and 1½ cups water to the casserole, and bring to a boil, then lower the heat, cover, and simmer for 30 minutes if using quail, or for 45 minutes if using chicken.

3. Meanwhile, heat the oil in a large skillet and lightly brown the almonds. Drain on paper towels. When the almonds are cool, coarsely grind them in a food processor. Combine them with ⅓ cup confectioners' sugar and 1½ teaspoons ground cinnamon. Set aside.

4. Remove the chicken or quail from the casserole to a work surface; remove and discard the cinnamon sticks. When the chicken or quail is cool enough to handle, remove all the meat from the bones and roughly shred it with your hands. Discard the skin.

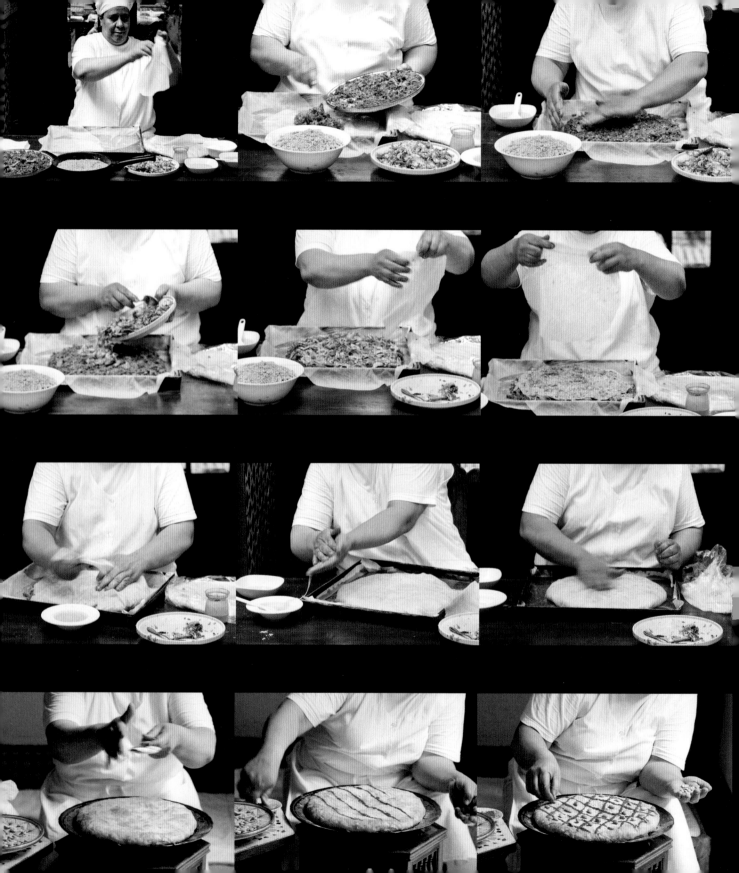

5. Bring the cooking liquid to a boil and reduce, uncovered, to about 1⅓ cups. Add the lemon juice. Beat the eggs until frothy, then slowly pour into the simmering sauce, stirring continuously in one direction, until the eggs cook and set (they should become "curdy"). Taste for salt. Scrape the mixture into a strainer set over a bowl and let drain. At this point, the chicken or quail and egg mixture can be cooled, wrapped separately, and refrigerated overnight. Wrap the almonds and store in a cool place.

6. About 1 hour before serving, preheat the oven to 425°F.

7. Fold 4 *warqa* or fillo leaves in half, place on a baking sheet, and bake for 30 seconds, or until crisp and golden. Or gently fry the folded leaves in a lightly oiled skillet for 30 seconds.

8. Unroll the other *warqa* or fillo leaves and keep them under a damp towel to prevent them from drying out. Warm the remaining clarified butter. Brush some of it over the bottom and sides of a 12-inch deep-dish pizza pan. Cover the bottom of the pan with 1 pastry leaf, shiny side down if using *warqa*. See drawings and captions 1 and 2.

9. Sprinkle the almond-sugar mixture over the pastry. Cover with all but 2 of the remaining pastry leaves; if using fillo, brush every leaf lightly with butter. Fold the overlapping leaves over the top to envelop the pie. Lightly brush the edges with some of the beaten egg yolk and place the remaining 2 leaves, overlapping, on top. Fold the edges under the pie (as if tucking in bed sheets).

10. Brush the *warqa* or fillo with butter and the remaining beaten egg yolk. Bake until golden brown and crisp, about 20 minutes.

11. Shake the pan to loosen the pie and run a spatula around the edges. If necessary, tilt the pan to pour off excess butter (which should be reserved). Invert the pie onto a buttered 14-inch round baking sheet. Brush the pie with any reserved butter and bake for another 10 minutes to crisp the pastry.

12. Remove the pie from the oven. Tilt to pour off any excess butter. Put a large serving platter over the pie and, holding it firmly, invert. (The traditional upper filling is always the almond layer.) Dust the top of the pie with a little confectioners' sugar and then run crisscrossing lines of cinnamon over the top. Serve very hot.

1. Arrange 6 or 7 more leaves, so that each leaf covers a portion of the bottom of the pan and extends over the sides of the pan, until the entire bottom of the pan is covered. If using fillo, lightly brush the extended leaves with butter so they do not dry out. If using *warqa*, arrange 5 or 6 leaves shiny side down around the bottom and sides; do not butter them. Place another pastry leaf in the center of the pan shiny side down.

2. Place some of the chicken or quail around the edges of the pan, then work toward the center so that the pastry is covered with an even layer of the poultry. Cover the chicken or quail with the well-drained egg mixture and then the baked or fried pastry leaves.

BASTILA WITH LEMON, TETOUAN-STYLE

This *bastila*, popular in Tetouan, is much tarter and a lot less sweet than the better-known Fes version, but it's still a splendid and luxurious dish. It will work out best if you do steps 1 through 5 the morning of the day the *bastila* is to be served. Please note that the more thoroughly the eggs are drained, the better the pie will be: crisp on the outside, and moist within.

—— ☞ Serves 12 ☜ ——

4 pounds chicken legs and thighs, bone-in, plus giblets if possible

1 cup grated red onion

3 tablespoons saffron water (see page 48)

¼ teaspoon ground turmeric

½ teaspoon freshly ground black pepper, or to taste

½ teaspoon ground ginger

2 large cinnamon sticks

11 tablespoons unsalted butter

Salt

2 large yellow onions, quartered and thinly sliced lengthwise (about 4 cups)

1½ cups chopped flat-leaf parsley

½ cup fresh lemon juice

8 large eggs, well beaten

24 Warqa (page 130) or 8 ounces fillo leaves

1½ preserved lemons (see page 21), pulp removed, rind rinsed and diced

Ground Ceylon cinnamon for dusting

1. Place the chicken leg and thigh parts in a 4- to 5-quart casserole, along with the giblets, if you have them, the grated onion, half the saffron water, the spices, and 6 tablespoons of the butter. Pour in 1½ cups water, add salt to taste, and bring to a boil. Reduce the heat and simmer for ¾ hour, covered.

2. Remove the chicken, giblets, cinnamon sticks, and any loose bones from the casserole. Reduce the sauce to about 1 cup by boiling it rapidly, uncovered. Add the sliced onions, parsley, a few pinches of pepper, and the remaining saffron water and cook, uncovered, stirring often, until the onions are soft and reduced to a thick mass.

3. Add the lemon juice and eggs and continue cooking until the eggs become "curdy." Transfer this mixture to a colander set over a bowl and drain thoroughly. Reserve the liquid.

4. Remove the chicken from the bones and shred into chunks by hand; discard the bones and skin. Coarsely chop the giblets.

5. Heat the remaining 5 tablespoons butter in a small saucepan. When the foam subsides, pour off the clear liquid into a small bowl, leaving

the milky solids behind. Set this clarified butter aside. The recipe can be prepared up to this point in advance and refrigerated.

6. Preheat the oven to 425°F.

7. Unroll the pastry leaves and place them under a damp towel to prevent them from drying out. Cover the bottom of 12-inch deep-dish pizza pan with half the pastry leaves, overlapping them as illustrated on page 137. Moisten every few layers of pastry with 2 tablespoons of the reserved lemon-egg liquid. Place some of the chicken and the chopped giblets, if using, around the edges of the pan and then work toward the center so that the pastry is covered with an even layer of poultry. Cover with a layer of the onions and eggs. Sprinkle with the preserved lemon peel and about ¼ teaspoon ground cinnamon.

8. Cover the pie with the remaining pastry leaves, brushing some of the remaining lemon-egg liquid on each, using no more than 3 tablespoons. Fold the leaves over the top to envelop the pie. Dribble the clarified butter over the top and down the sides of the pie.

9. Bake as in steps 10 to 12 on page 137 and serve hot, with a light dusting of ground cinnamon.

MEAT BASTILA WITH RED PEPPERS, RAISINS, AND OLIVES

Choumicha is Morocco's own Julia Child, that country's foremost TV cooking personality. After watching her demonstrate a meat and lamb liver *bastila* wrapped in *trid* pastry, I decided to make my own version, using ground beef and grilled red peppers (to simulate the texture of liver) and wrapping the whole in homemade *warqa*, like a classic *bastila*.

I don't usually make up new recipes, but this one turned out really well. As many times as I've served it, it's never failed to delight my friends. Herewith, my personal take on meat *bastila*, with a "tip of the toque" to the fabulous Choumicha.

―――∞ Serves 6 ∞―――

8 ounces ground beef

⅔ cup chopped onion

2 garlic cloves, chopped

1 tablespoon La Kama Spice Mixture (page 37)

3 tablespoons chopped flat-leaf parsley

¼ cup chopped cilantro

Salt

2 ounces rice vermicelli or vermicelli pasta

2 small or 1 large red bell pepper (8 ounces), grilled or broiled (see page 86), peeled, seeded, and roughly diced (¾ cup)

1 large red-ripe tomato, peeled, seeded, roughly chopped, and drained (1 cup)

½ teaspoon harissa paste or Turkish red pepper paste

3 tablespoons golden raisins

10 sliced pitted Picholine or green-ripe olives

1 tablespoon fresh lemon juice, or to taste

Freshly ground black pepper

24 homemade Warqa (page 130) or 8 ounces fillo leaves

1 tablespoon vegetable oil

1 egg yolk, beaten with a teaspoon of water

2 to 3 tablespoons melted clarified butter (use the larger amount if working with fillo)

Lemon slices for garnish

A few cilantro and parsley sprigs for garnish

1. Place the meat, onion, garlic, spices, herbs, and 1 teaspoon salt in a heavy skillet, set over low heat, and cook, covered, until the meat loses its pink color and the onion has thrown off a lot of liquid, about 20 minutes.

2. Meanwhile, cook the rice vermicelli in salted boiling water for 2 minutes and drain. Cut pasta, if using, into 2-inch strands.

3. Add the bell pepper, tomato, hot pepper paste, raisins, and olives to the skillet and cook, uncovered, over medium heat for 5 minutes, or until almost all the moisture has evaporated. Add the vermicelli and

toss to mix. Add the lemon juice and salt and pepper to taste. Makes about 6 cups filling. The filling can be prepared up to 1 day in advance; cool, cover, and refrigerate.

4. Preheat the oven to 400°F. Brush the bottom of a 10- or 12-inch pizza pan with the oil.

5. *If using warqa*, arrange all but 3 of the leaves, shiny side down, overlapping, so that they cover the bottom and overhang the edges of the greased pan. Spread the filling evenly over the pastry leaves, lightly pressing down to create an even layer. Fold the edges of the pastry leaves up over the filling to enclose it. Brush the folded leaves with some of the beaten yolk. Place the remaining leaves, shiny side up, and overlapping, over the top, and tuck in the edges to create a neat pie. Brush the top with 2 tablespoons butter and a light coating of beaten egg yolk. (Reserve the remaining egg yolk.) *If using fillo pastry,* arrange half the fillo leaves, one on top of the other, so that they cover the bottom of the pan and overhang the edges, brushing every other layer with butter. Spread the meat and vermicelli filling evenly over the leaves, lightly pressing down to create an even layer. Fold the edges of the pastry leaves up over the filling to enclose it. Brush the folded leaves with beaten yolk. Cover with the remaining 4 or 5 pastry sheets and tuck the edges under the pie. Brush the top with a light coating of beaten egg yolk. (Reserve the remaining egg yolk.)

6. Bake the pie for 20 minutes, or until golden and crisp.

7. Shake the pan to loosen the pie and run a spatula around the edges. If necessary, tilt the pan to pour off excess fat. Invert the pie onto a greased large baking sheet. Brush the pie with the remaining egg yolk. Return to the oven and bake for another 10 minutes.

8. Remove the pie from the oven. Tilt to pour off any excess fat. Put a serving platter over the pie and, holding it firmly, invert. Decorate the top with a few lemon slices and sprigs of cilantro and parsley. Cut into wedges and serve hot.

REHEATING WARQA-WRAPPED BASTILA

Warqa-wrapped *bastila* can be assembled ahead, partially baked, and frozen, but you must follow this method, which I learned from Chef Mourad Lahlou of Restaurant Aziza in San Francisco, or the pastry will be tough. Please note this method only applies to *bastila* wrapped in *warqa*, not in fillo.

Before freezing, you bake the *bastila* in a steamy hot oven to cook the food through to its center and to "set" the pastry without browning it. Then you can cool it and/or freeze it. When ready to serve, you bake it again in a hot oven.

Here is the procedure: Set a pan of boiling water on the bottom shelf of a preheated 350°F oven. When the oven is steamy, place the assembled *bastila* on the upper shelf and steam-bake for 10 minutes, invert, turn, and continue to bake 10 more minutes. Cool, cover, and keep in a cool place, or cool, wrap, and freeze. For the final baking, place the *bastila* in a preheated 400°F oven and bake for 15 to 20 minutes on each side to crisp the outside and heat the interior.

BASTILA WITH SEAFOOD, SPINACH, AND NOODLES

In the mid-1980s, some years after *Couscous and Other Good Food from Morocco* was published, I started hearing rumors of a fabulous new dish, a seafood *bastila* that was appearing on private Moroccan tables in place of the traditional, very rich squab *bastila*.

I tried for a long time to obtain a good recipe but was never served a version I liked. Then I heard that the world-famous Mamounia Hotel in Marrakech was serving a great version in which spicy noodles replaced the buttery crushed almonds that hold a traditional *bastila* together.

Mohammed Boussaoud, former executive chef at the Mamounia, had by then become chef at the luxurious Jerusalem restaurant Darna ("Your House"), where he was preparing a kosher version of the dish he'd once cooked so famously in Marrakech. An Arab-Moslem Moroccan chef working at an Israeli restaurant! Well, why not? In fact, I was delighted, for it gave me a chance to meet with him on a trip to Israel and learn how to make his original non-kosher (i.e., shellfish) version.

The charmoula-marinated seafood and fish (shrimp, monkfish, and other thick-fleshed fish) are sandwiched between two layers of vermicelli noodles and spinach leaves, which enable them to cook at very low heat to a point of perfect moistness.

I hope you will try this dish. It is extremely tasty and a lot less caloric than classic *bastila*.

——— Serves 6 ———

CHARMOULA

½ cup extra virgin olive oil

3 tomatoes, peeled, halved, seeded, and chopped, lightly fried in 1 tablespoon of the oil until reduced to ½ cup

1 tablespoon crushed garlic

¾ cup torn cilantro leaves

¾ cup torn flat-leaf parsley leaves

1½ teaspoons paprika

Pinch of freshly ground black pepper

½ teaspoon cayenne

1 teaspoon cumin seed, preferably Moroccan

1 teaspoon salt

3 tablespoons fresh lemon juice

½ cup extra virgin olive oil

5 ounces fedelini noodles, broken into 1-inch lengths

1 pound mixed firm fish fillets, such as cod, halibut, and/or monkfish, or other thick-fleshed white fish, thinly sliced

8 ounces large shrimp, shelled and thinly sliced

1 pound spinach, washed and stemmed

8 ounces fillo leaves

1 preserved lemon (optional; see page 21), pulp removed, rind rinsed, quartered, and diced

Olive oil for brushing

3 tablespoons club soda

1. To make the charmoula: Combine all the ingredients in a blender or food processor, and blend until smooth.

2. Cook the fedelini in boiling water for 2 minutes; let drain and immediately put in a bowl with ¼ cup of the charmoula. Let cool until all of the sauce has been absorbed by the pasta. In another bowl, toss the sliced fish and shrimp with the remaining charmoula and refrigerate.

3. Heat a large skillet. Add the spinach by the handful and cook over high heat, turning with tongs, until thoroughly wilted. Transfer the spinach to a colander and let cool. Squeeze the spinach dry and then finely shred it. Divide into thirds.

4. About 1 hour before serving, preheat the oven to 350°F.

5. Unroll the fillo leaves and keep them under a damp towel to prevent them from drying out. Brush a 10- or 12-inch pizza pan with oil. Cover the bottom with two-thirds of the fillo, one leaf on top of the other so they overhang the edges, lightly brushing each layer with oil. Spread half the noodles in an even layer over the pastry. Cover with a layer of the fish and lemon rind, if using, and top with the remaining noodles. Fold the overhanging fillo leaves over to envelop the filling. Cover with the remaining leaves, lightly brushing each layer with oil. Fold the edges under the pie (as if you were tucking in a sheet).

6. Score the top of the pie. Brush with oil, sprinkle with the club soda, and bake until golden brown and crisp, about 20 minutes. Serve hot.

STUFFED PASTRIES:
BRIWATS AND "CIGARS"

Briwats are small pastry envelopes stuffed with such things as goat cheese and honey, rice pudding, almond paste, kefta (cinnamon-flavored ground meat), shrimp and vermicelli, spicy meat confit, and fillings normally used in *bastila* (see page 135), without the almonds, or Bastila with Lemon, Tetouan-Style (page 138). They can be made with homemade *warqa* (see page 130) or commercial fillo.

"Cigars" are tubular in shape and stuffed with the some of the same kinds of fillings. A platter piled high with *briwats* on the buffet table is a handsome sight. You can fry or bake them and serve them as an appetizer or a snack, or as part of a light lunch with a green salad.

See pages 147–148 for some popular Moroccan fillings.

Make 2 long strips of pastry at a time.

PREPARING WARQA FOR BRIWAT AND CIGARS

You can make excellent *briwat* and cigars with commercial fillo pastry, but they'll be even better if you use *warqa*. However, the preparation of your *warqa* will be a little different: Follow the recipe for *warqa* (see page 130), except instead of making single round leaves on the skillet, make 2 long strips at a time that can be rolled up like cigars or folded into triangles like a flag.

Some fillings for *briwats* and cigars require extra layers to stay intact. To do this, you'll need to make the *warqa* strips longer by connecting two of them: Make a paste with flour and water, then use it to paint a 1-inch-wide swath at one end of 1 of the pastry strips. Place a second pastry strip on top of the paste and press to connect, thus forming a longer strip.

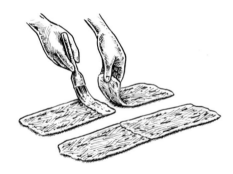

To make the strips longer, patch 2 together with a flour-water paste. Please remember to always place *warqa* strips shiny side down before filling.

PREPARING FILLO FOR BRIWATS AND CIGARS

You will need 6 sheets of fillo to make 2 dozen pastries. Unroll the fillo; work with one sheet at a time. Keep the remaining sheets covered with a damp cloth. Lightly brush the top with butter or oil. Divide each sheet into four 4-by-12-inch strips.

FORMING STUFFED TRIANGLES
WITH WARQA OR FILLO

Place a heaping teaspoon of filling about 1 inch from the top or bottom of each pastry strip. Fold over the strip to enclose the filling, creating a triangle as if you were folding a flag. See illustrations.

Place a spoonful of filling about 1 inch from the top or bottom of each pastry strip. Fold into a triangle like a flag.

FORMING PASTRY CIGARS

Use long *warqa* strips as described earlier, or cut the sheet of fillo into 4 quarters, then fold each quarter in half. Place a heaping spoonful of the stuffing at the bottom of each *warqa* strip or doubled piece of fillo, leaving about a ¼-inch border along the sides, and roll up, tucking in the sides after the first roll, creating a tube resembling an Asian spring roll. Seal with a little flour-and-water paste.

Using a small silicone brush, lightly dap the top of the fillo pastries with oil to keep their tops from drying out.

FRYING AND STORING FILLED PASTRIES

I always double-fry *warqa* or fillo pastries for maximum crispness. If you want to store them overnight or freeze them for later use, do the first frying, cool, and then refrigerate or freeze. Then do the second frying just before serving. The principle is the same as for French fries: cooking them first in oil at a lower temperature sets their exterior skins and partially cooks the interiors, then frying them again at a much higher temperature completes the interior cooking and achieves maximum crispness.

The first frying should be done in oil about 250°F; fry until the pastries are pale golden on each side, about 30 seconds. The second frying is done in 375°F oil; fry until the pastries are very crisp and golden.

BAKING BRIWATS OR CIGARS

If you'd rather bake than fry the filled pastries, use the following method: Preheat the oven to 350°F. Lightly brush one or two baking sheets with olive oil. Place the triangles or cigars side by side on the sheets, without letting them touch each other. Brush the tops with beaten egg yolk and bake for about 10 minutes, or until crisp and golden. Turn each one over and bake for 5 minutes longer. Serve warm.

GOAT CHEESE AND HONEY FILLING

This moist, silken filling is a personal favorite. Fresh creamy goat cheese goes beautifully with a touch of good honey, fresh herbs, and a soft scrambled egg—all wrapped up and fried in a light, crisp pastry triangle.

Makes about 1¼ cups, enough for 24 briwats

2 tablespoons honey, preferably multifloral or lavender

5 tablespoons warm clarified butter

1 teaspoon fresh lemon juice, or more to taste

8 ounces soft fresh goat cheese

¼ teaspoon freshly ground pepper

2 tablespoons snipped chives

1 teaspoon thyme leaves, crumbled

Salt

4 large eggs, lightly beaten

1 recipe Warqa (page 130), or 6 fillo leaves (see directions for folding and frying or baking on pages 144–145)

1. Combine the honey, 2 tablespoons of the butter, and the lemon juice in a medium bowl. Add the goat cheese, pepper, chives, thyme, and a pinch of salt and use a fork to mash until smooth.

2. Slide the eggs into a small buttered nonstick skillet and scramble until soft. Immediately slip them onto the cheese mixture and stir until well combined. Allow to cool before using to fill pastry leaves.

MEAT CONFIT FILLING

Meat confit and its "debris" (which falls to the bottom of the pot when making it), combined with paprika, cumin, cayenne, grated red onion, and chopped parsley and sautéed in some of the confit fat, makes a wonderful filling for *briwats* or "cigars."

———— ☜ Makes enough for 24 pastries ☞ ————

8 ounces "Express" Meat Confit (page 44), plus 1 tablespoon of the fat

Freshly ground pepper

1 teaspoon ground cumin, preferably Moroccan

1 teaspoon hot red paprika

Pinch of ground ginger

1 medium red onion, grated, rinsed, and squeezed dry

1 large garlic clove, crushed

1½ tablespoons Tomato Magic (page 41) or tomato paste

2 large eggs, beaten

1 tablespoon chopped parsley

Salt

1 recipe Warqa (page 130) or 6 fillo sheets (see directions for folding and frying or baking on pages 144–145)

1. Trim the "Express" Meat Confit of excess fat. Crush and shred the meat. Season with black pepper, the cumin, paprika, and ginger, and let stand for 5 minutes.

2. Meanwhile, heat the fat from the confit in a skillet and sauté the onion and garlic for 2 to 3 minutes. Add the Tomato Magic or paste and fry until sizzling. Remove from the heat, add the meat confit and the beaten eggs, and allow the eggs to form soft curds in the receding heat. Fold in the parsley. Season to taste with salt. Cool before using to fill pastry leaves.

BRIK WITH TUNA, CAPERS, AND EGGS

Nowadays most anything might end up inside a Moroccan *brik*, but the most popular stuffing in northern Morocco remains the classic Tunisian combination of quality canned tuna, Moroccan capers, eggs, and cheese.

If you don't feel like making *warqa*, the best pastry for *briks* is Tunisian *brik* leaves, or Chinese spring roll skins. All you do is spread out the leaf, break a raw egg onto one half, add the flavorings, and fold the leaf over diagonally, then "glue" the edges closed with a little frothy egg white.

The *briks* are then deep-fried in hot oil until golden brown and drained on a paper towel. The *briks* should be devoured immediately. To eat one, grasp it by its corners, being careful not to let any egg run down your face.

❈

BRIK

Though most people associate *brik* with Tunisia, where the pastries are extremely popular and sold on the street, they are also prepared in the Moroccan northeast and have lately become popular in all major cities of the country. A *brik* is basically just another kind of stuffed pastry, but it must be served immediately, like a soufflé.

----- ❧ Serves 4 as a snack ❧ -----

1 tablespoon unsalted butter

1 small onion, finely chopped

4 ounces canned tuna, drained and mashed

1 to 2 tablespoons chopped flat-leaf parsley

Salt and freshly ground black pepper

A few capers, rinsed, drained, and mashed

1 to 2 tablespoons freshly grated Parmesan cheese

4 Warqa (page 130) or commercial *brik* pastry (see Sources) leaves or 4 Chinese spring roll skins

4 medium or small eggs

1 egg white, lightly beaten

Vegetable or olive oil for deep-frying

Lemon wedges

1. Melt the butter in a small skillet, and cook the onion over very gentle heat until soft but not browned. Add the tuna, parsley, salt and pepper to taste, capers, and cheese, mix well, and separate into 4 equal parts.

2. Spread out the pastry leaves. Place one-quarter of the filling on one half of each leaf. Break an egg over each portion of filling. Fold each pastry leaf over to form a half circle or triangle and glue the edges shut with the beaten egg white. Then fold each edge over 1/2 inch for a firmer seal, being careful not to break the egg yolk.

3. Pour oil to a depth of 1 inch into a large skillet and heat until hot but not smoking. Slide in the *briks* one at a time and fry, spooning hot oil over the tops until the underside is nicely browned. Turn and continue frying until browned on the second side. Remove and drain on paper towels. Serve at once, with lemon wedges.

chapter five

EGGS, BUTTER, BUTTERMILK, AND CHEESE

❊

"An egg cannot break a stone."

—*berber proverb*

❊

EGGS, BUTTER, BUTTERMILK, AND CHEESE

FRIED EGGS WITH MEAT CONFIT
୧ page 155 ୨

FRIED EGGS WITH MEAT CONFIT
AND TOMATO-ONION PANCAKE
୧ page 156 ୨

HOMEMADE SMEN
୧ page 159 ୨

OUDI
(THYME-SCENTED CLARIFIED BUTTER)
୧ page 161 ୨

MOROCCAN BUTTERMILK
୧ page 164 ୨

MOROCCAN YOGURT (RAIB)
୧ page 164 ୨

QUICK HERB-FLAVORED COUNTRY CHEESE
୧ page 167 ୨

Moroccans have a large repertory of unique egg preparations ranging from the curdled lemony-egg interior of their most famous dish, *bastila*, to hard-cooked eggs sold on the street for dipping into a mixture of salt and ground cumin, then squashed into the hollow of a slice of bread and devoured as a sandwich.

In Fes, a Moroccan cook often will dip hard-cooked eggs into saffron-tinted water and then slice them to decorate the local version of *t'faya* (lamb cooked with a confit of onions with spices and almonds; see page 374). Jewish cooks in Essaouira very slowly simmer eggs all night in their famous meat and bean casserole, *dafina*, a process that turns the whites a soft tan and endows the yolks with a sensuous creamy texture.

A favorite family dish consists of eggs poached in a spicy tomato sauce with *kefta* (meatballs; see page 402), or in a buttery onion sauce with bite-sized pieces of lamb (see page 382). In the pre-Sahara, south of the High Atlas Mountains, flat breads are stuffed and baked with crumbled hard-cooked eggs, spices, almonds, and tiny cubes of lean beef.

And there there's the formidable Berber specialty *djej mefenned* (see page 312), in which a whole braised chicken is turned in sizzling fat while simultaneously being basted with beaten seasoned eggs. In a less complicated version, a chicken cooked in a tagine is thickened with eggs to produce a smooth custard (page 304).

A former ambassador who often dined at the palace of the late King Mohammed V told me about one of the most luxurious of Moroccan egg preparations, presented in silver eggcups. Eggshells, their tops removed, were filled with eggs softly scrambled with powdered gum arabic, saffron, cumin, and salt. The diners imbibed this mixture like shots of whiskey directly from the shells.

Every country has its own version of the omelet. In the coastal town of Larache, I've read, they eat an omelet garnished with local truffles, turmeric, and herbs. South of Marrakech, I was served an elaborate omelet prepared with potatoes, parsley, cumin, paprika, and cubes of bread, garnished with olives and preserved lemons. At the other end of the scale, I've heard that there's an omelet served in the pre-Sahara that's stuffed with bits of locust. Haven't tried it . . . and don't intend to!

FRIED EGGS
WITH MEAT CONFIT

In this recipe, shreds of meat confit, preserved meat seasoned with ground coriander, cumin, and lots of garlic, endow fried eggs with a unique flavor.

⸺ Serves 2 ⸺

Scant ⅓ cup "Express" Meat
  Confit (page 44), or
  2 tablespoons Moroccankhliî
  (see Sources), crushed and
  finely shredded, plus
  1 tablespoon of the fat

2 teaspoons unsalted butter

4 large eggs

Salt (optional)

Freshly ground black pepper

Use your fingers to loosen the shredded preserved meat. Place the fat and the butter in a skillet and set over medium heat. When melted, scatter the shreds evenly over the bottom of the pan. Add the eggs, cover, and cook for 5 minutes, or until the whites are set but the yolks are still runny. Season with a pinch of salt (if using "Express" Meat Confit) and pepper and serve at once.

FRIED EGGS WITH MEAT CONFIT AND TOMATO-ONION PANCAKE

This version yields a full heartwarming breakfast, particularly delicious on cold autumn mornings.

———— ❧ Serves 3 ❧ ————

2 medium onions, halved and thinly sliced (about 3 cups)

1 tablespoon extra virgin olive oil

12 ounces Roma (plum) tomatoes, grated (about 1½ cups)

Scant ½ cup "Express" Meat Confit (page 44), or 2 tablespoons crushed and shredded Moroccankhlii (see Sources), plus 1 tablespoon of the fat

3 large eggs

Salt and freshly ground black pepper

1 tablespoon roughly chopped flat-leaf parsley

1. Toss the onions with the oil in a 9- or 10-inch enameled cast-iron skillet or cazuela. Set over medium heat, cover with lid or a sheet of foil, and cook slowly for 10 minutes. Uncover and cook until the onions are lightly caramelized.

2. Add the tomatoes and meat and its fat and cook, covered, for 15 minutes, or until the mixture is as thick as a normal pancake. (The recipe can be made ahead to this point; reheat the contents of the skillet before proceeding.)

3. Add the eggs, cover, and cook until the whites are firm but the yolks are still runny. Season with salt and pepper and scatter the parsley on top. Serve at once, directly from the skillet.

CLARIFIED BUTTER AND HOMEMADE SMEN

Moroccan country butter, *zebda*, is made by leaving fresh milk in an earthenware jug for two to three days, allowing it to curdle or "turn" naturally. The curdled milk is then poured into an earthenware churn (which, though never washed, is kept clean and used only for butter making) and churned until the butter particles separate out and the remaining liquid turns to buttermilk (*lben*). In southern Morocco, the churning is done in a goatskin bag slung between trees. A woman swings the bag until she hears splashing sounds inside, letting her know that the butter has separated from the milk.

Once a Moroccan cook has fresh country butter in hand, she will use it to make *oudi* (see the accompanying recipe) or the more matured *smen*.

"Exactly what is *smen*?" is a question that comes up frequently in my classes. I tell my students that it's similar to Indian ghee and Middle Eastern *samneh* in that all three substances are created by churning fresh cream into butter and clarifying it, then storing it. But Moroccans take the process a step further, culturing their butter before clarifying it in order to develop an intense aroma and a complex nutty, salty flavor that bears little relation to that of ordinary butter.

Goat's, cow's, and sheep's milk are all used, and methods differ from region to region, resulting in slight differences in taste. Some cooks culture their butter with buttermilk, others with mildly soured cream, and still others with yogurt, to provide the proper bacterial culture and flavor. But however the *smen* is made, it is regarded by Moroccan cooks as a condiment of choice to enrich and add depth of flavor to couscous dishes, soups, casseroles, and numerous tagines. Old-timers often serve it spread on warm semolina bread, accompanied by a glass of mint tea.

Chef Mourad Lahlou, of the Michelin-starred San Francisco restaurant Aziza, told me, "A teaspoon of aged *smen* added to some fresh butter is all I need to perfume two pounds of couscous." Mourad makes his own *smen*, somewhat lighter in flavor than the *smen* made by many families in his hometown of Marrakech, who age their *smen* for a year to increase intensity, then use it in very small amounts to flavor special dishes.

I have even heard tales of Berber families who prepare it, salt it, and bury it in the ground in earthenware jugs at the birth of a daughter, to be brought out many years later on her wedding day. A few spoonfuls will be added to the celebratory couscous, and the rest given to the bride to take to her new home so she can cook wonderful Moroccan food for her husband.

A bit of history: poorly prepared *smen* was the bête noire of early British travel writers, who time and again referred to it as rancid and foul smelling and recounted harrowing tales of how, at the risk of appearing rude, they forced themselves to eat it for breakfast with their Moroccan hosts. Unfortunately, this terrible reputation has persisted to this day, to the extent that at the very mention of the word, Britishers will gag to indicate their revulsion. But the truth is that although good *smen* is strong, it is not at all rancid smelling, and when properly used, it enhances numerous Moroccan dishes.

Because *smen* requires careful preparation and lengthy maturation, I often suggest another more easily made cultured butter such as *oudi* in my recipes. But if you take the time to make *smen*, by all means use it as indicated.

HOMEMADE SMEN

Though *smen* is a quintessentially Moroccan ingredient, *oudi* will make a fine substitute. However, truly dedicated cooks will want to try it, and for them I present this recipe. There are many ways to make *smen* in a Western kitchen. My way, detailed below, combines country methods with modern kitchen devices, yielding a lovely medium-strength condiment that will work well in all my recipes that call for it.

This recipe can be doubled or tripled.

⟶ ❧ Makes about ½ cup ❧ ⟵

3 cups organic heavy cream

2 tablespoons whole-milk yogurt
(goat's, sheep's, or cow's milk)

2 teaspoons coarse sea salt

1. Combine the cream and yogurt in a bowl and let stand overnight at room temperature to culture.

2. Transfer the cultured cream into a food processor and process for 10 to 20 seconds, or until the cream seizes and throws off liquid. Switch to pulsing and continue until the butter separates from the liquid. Pour off all the liquid buttermilk and reserve for some another purpose. (You can freeze it and use it to moisten couscous.)

3. Wash the butter by adding about 3 tablespoons ice-cold water to the processor and pulsing 2 or 3 times. Pour off and discard the liquid. Repeat twice, with ½ cup ice-cold water. The water should run clear. If it doesn't, repeat one more time.

4. Place the butter on a parchment paper–lined work surface. Sprinkle on the salt and knead until well blended. Divide into 6 equal parts. Press each part into a ¼-inch-thick round and arrange side by side on a dry cloth on a large platter. Cover with another cloth and let ripen in a cool, dark place for 2 to 3 days.

5. To clarify the butter, place it in a small heavy saucepan and set over very low heat. Allow the butter to melt slowly, without stirring and without browning. Remove the foam as it appears on the surface. When the butter is golden and clear, remove it from the heat and let stand until cool.

6. Carefully spoon the butter through a double layer of dampened cheesecloth set over a bowl, leaving any white sediment at the bottom of the pan behind. To prevent the *smen* from turning rancid, strain again through clean cheesecloth. The *smen* must be absolutely clear; discard any solids. Pour the butter into a dry sterile container, preferably earthenware. Cover tightly and store in a cool and dark place at room temperature for 1 month before opening. Store in a cool cupboard or the refrigerator after opening.

OUDI
(THYME-SCENTED
CLARIFIED BUTTER)

Allow me to introduce you to *oudi*, an excellent middle-of-the-road alternative to *smen*: clarified butter with a remarkable herbal flavoring, unlike any you'll have tasted before.

I consider it an absolute must in my kitchen for adding an "extra something" that can raise homestyle Moroccan dishes to a higher culinary level. A few tablespoons can be tossed into freshly steamed couscous, dribbled onto dips made with corn or barley, used to sauté eggs, drizzled over a bowl of beans or lentils, whipped into hearty soups, or added to the finest tagines.

Using a little lightly toasted barley grits to clarify butter is an old Mediterranean trick, employed to absorb milk solids and other debris and to endow the butter with a lovely faintly smoky aroma. The addition of dried thyme creates an extra dimension of aroma and taste.

Makes about 1⅓ pounds

¼ cup barley grits

1 teaspoon dried thyme or dried
 Mediterranean oregano

2½ pounds unsalted butter, cut
 into small pieces

1. Lightly toast the grits with the thyme in a medium heavy saucepan over low heat, stirring constantly, until the grits turn a lovely light brown. Add the butter and allow it to melt slowly, without stirring and without browning. Remove the foam as it appears on the surface. When the butter is golden and clear, remove it from the heat and allow to cool.

2. Carefully pour the butter through damp cheesecloth into clean glass or ceramic jars. Discard the milky barley residue. *Oudi* keeps for many months in closed jars in the refrigerator.

MOROCCAN BUTTERMILK

Homemade buttermilk, called *Iben*, is much appreciated by Moroccan Berbers, who use it as a thirst-quencher and often down it with a plate of barley couscous, or a dish of fava beans and well-buttered couscous. American buttermilk is most often made from cow's milk. Moroccans usually make theirs with goat's milk. But any type of buttermilk, whether homemade or commercial, will go well with Moroccan food.

To make a delicious "faux" *Iben*: A day in advance, combine 4 cups water with 1 quart goat's-milk yogurt in a blender and blend well. Keep refrigerated; it will be more delicious on the second day.

MOROCCAN YOGURT (RAIB)

Raib, a thick, luscious, sweet-tasting fermented yogurt with a wonderful herbal aroma, is made by steeping a small sachet of dried wild thistles in simmering milk. The milk then thickens and firms up, attaining the texture of junket. Moroccans don't refrigerate *raib*, but store it in clay pots in a cool part of their kitchens.

Dried wild cardoon thistles are available by mail-order from www.tagines.com.

—— Serves 4 as a snack ——

1 tablespoon dried wild cardoon thistles	2 tablespoons sugar
1 quart milk	2 tablespoons orange flower water, or more to taste

1. Crush the thistle flowers to a coarse powder in a mortar; there should be about 1 teaspoon. Wrap the thistle powder in cheesecloth, and tie securely with kitchen string.

2. Heat the milk to lukewarm in a saucepan. Hold the cheesecloth packet between two wooden spoons, insert into the lukewarm milk, and swirl and press on the bag repeatedly until some brown juices are released, about 1 minute. Discard the packet.

3. Stir the sugar and orange flower water into the warm milk. Cover and set in a warm place for 1 to 1½ hours, until set.

4. To serve, divide the soft yogurt among four custard cups. Serve cool or chilled.

MOROCCAN FRESH CHEESE

The most famous cheese of Morocco is *jben*, made in the Rif Mountain area in the northern part of the country, where there is a cheese-making tradition. *Jben* is a dense goat's-milk ricotta that is served with dates or salads, stuffed into pastry triangles, or spread with honey on freshly made stovetop skillet bread.

AGED GOAT CHEESE (KLILA)

Klila is another Rif Mountain cheese, especially popular in Oujda, Tangier, and Tetouan, where it's used as a condiment. It's made from buttermilk that's been cooked with an acid such as lemon juice, then allowed to curdle and drain to the texture of feta. Then it is crumbled and left to age for at least 6 months, until quite strong and dry.

Riffians use it along with spices such as ginger, coriander, cumin, and cinnamon to perk up winter dishes made with beans and lentils (see Chapter 11). It's also added to butternut squash and tomato soup (page 189) and to chickpea and meat confit soup (page 184).

You can substitute an aged goat Gouda, any American artisanal aged goat cheese such as Shamrock Bouchon or Cypress Grove Midnight Moon, or even a crumbled barrel-aged feta.

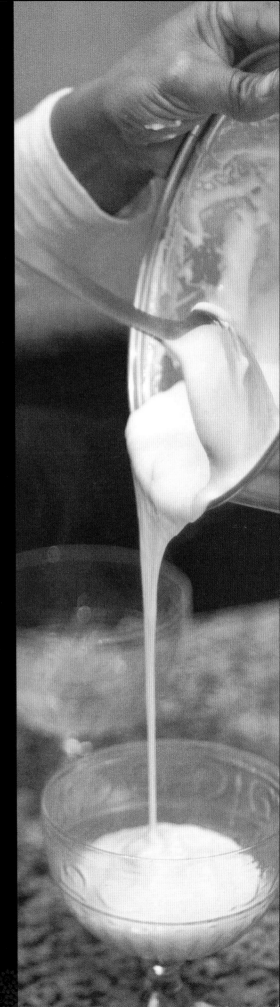

QUICK HERB-FLAVORED COUNTRY CHEESE

There are a number of fine fresh, creamy goat cheeses made in the United States. Look for artisanal goat cheeses such as the creamy goat cheese from Vermont Butter and Cheese Company, or any good local fresh, dense goat cheese.

———⚙ Makes about 1⅓ cups ⚙———

1 cup fresh, dense goat cheese

2 tablespoons heavy cream

Salt and freshly ground black pepper

1 tablespoon minced fresh za'atar herbs—a mix of marjoram, fresh thyme, and/or Mediterranean oregano, plus more for serving

Extra virgin olive oil

1. Whip the cheese with the heavy cream and 1 tablespoon water in a bowl until light and airy. Season with salt and pepper to taste.

2. Scatter half the herbs on the bottom of a flat serving dish. Pile the cheese on top, sprinkle with the remaining herbs, and dribble over the olive oil. Serve with more fresh herbs, and salt and pepper.

chapter six

SOUPS

"Hot water is no playground
for a frog."

—berber saying

SOUPS

BERBER HARIRA WITH LEAFY ZEGZAW
page 173

TANGIER-STYLE HARIRA
page 174

HARIRA WITH LAMB, SUMMER LEAFY GREENS,
AND EGGS
page 176

TROUT WITH PRESERVED LEMONS, RAISINS,
AND PINE NUTS IN BROTH
page 179

CREAMY FAVA BEAN SOUP
page 180

RIFFIAN SPLIT PEA SOUP WITH PAPRIKA OIL
page 182

MEAT CONFIT, CHICKPEA, AND PASTA SOUP
page 184

LAMB, TOMATO, CINNAMON,
AND STEAMED PASTA CHORBA
page 185

BUTTERNUT SQUASH AND TOMATO SOUP
page 189

SEMOLINA SOUP WITH ANISEED
page 190

SOUPS

The most famous soup in Morocco is called *harira*, which, in effect, symbolizes the unification of the Moroccan people during Ramadan, the ninth month of the Muslim calendar. This holy month of fasting is one of the most striking features of the Arab world. During this month, according to Muslim law, between dawn and sunset, not a bit of food nor a drop of water may be consumed. The breaking of the fast, announced at sunset by the report of a cannon, is the moment when all Moroccans, rich and poor alike, sit down to the traditional Ramadan "breakfast at sunset": *harira* soup, dates, figs, and fried honey cakes called *chebbakia* (see page 482).

Every region of the country has its own version of *harira*, which changes as Ramadan rotates through the seasons (it's based on a lunar calendar). The soup is often chunky with meat and beans, or thick with leafy vegetables and herbs, but the underlying texture of the liquid is always silky-smooth. This is the one constant, no matter the regional variation, and, in fact, the word *hareer* in Arabic suggests velvetiness.

Some cooks use a slightly fermented leavening, called *tedouira*, to achieve this desired texture; others simply blend some fine stone-ground flour, such as barley, millet, durum wheat, corn, or sorghum with water, or stir in some beaten eggs. But the final result will always be creamy, the signature texture of the soup.

Most *hariras* are made with an assortment of beans, such as lentils, chickpeas, and fava beans; a few fresh herbs, such as parsley and cilantro; and grated tomatoes or a homemade tomato sauce enriched with sun-dried tomatoes. *Harira* can be vegetarian or loaded with bits of lamb, beef, chicken, or fish. Every city, every region, every family has its favorite *hariras* for each season, and since the soup is served at nightfall for a full lunar month, there are variations upon variations.

Harira is usually made in large amounts to feed a lot of people. I've reduced the quantities in the following recipes while doing my best to maintain authentic flavor.

BERBER HARIRA WITH LEAFY ZEGZAW

I was curious to learn more about Berber *zegzaw*, a leafy green reputed to grow well in the oases of the Sahara that is used as a the base of a sauce for couscous (see page 222). It is also used in this barley-rich vegetarian *harira*. To track down the elusive vegetable, I turned to Jamal Bellahkdar's book on Moroccan plants to find an available equivalent. The solution: a perennial kale (*Brassica oleracea var. ramosa*) that will hold its deep rich flavor and silken texture in this complex soup composed of vegetables, spices, and herbs. Like most *hariras*, this Berber variation is finished off with a thickening agent to develop the proper velvety texture.

Be sure to serve some dates on the side.

NOTE TO THE COOK

Add 1 cup cooked dried fava beans and some of their cooking liquid to the soup. See page 180, steps 1 and 2, for instructions for soaking and cooking dried fava beans.

———— ❧ Serves 8 ❧ ————

1 bunch (about 12 ounces) Red Russian kale or leafy broccoli rabe or broccolini

1 large red onion, grated (about 1¼ cups)

1 medium white turnip, finely grated (¾ cup)

4 Roma (plum) tomatoes, peeled, halved, seeded, and grated (¾ cup)

½ cup minced celery

2 tablespoons chopped flat-leaf parsley

2 tablespoons chopped cilantro

1½ teaspoons ground cumin, preferably Moroccan

Pinch of ground ginger

Coarse salt and freshly ground black pepper

¼ cup extra virgin olive oil, plus extra for drizzling

½ cup barley flour

1. Wash and shake dry the kale; cut away any thick stems. Thinly slice the leaves crosswise, then coarsely chop and place in a large bowl. Add the grated onion, turnip, tomatoes, celery, parsley, cilantro, 1 teaspoon of the cumin, the ginger, 1 teaspoon each salt and pepper, and the ¼ cup oil; mix well. Pack into a straight-sided skillet or cazuela, cover with a round of parchment and a tight-fitting lid, and steam over low heat for 30 minutes.

2. Blend the barley flour, the remaining ½ teaspoon cumin, and 1 cup water to a smooth paste. Stir into the soup and bring to a boil. Reduce the heat to a simmer and cook for 20 minutes. If the soup is too thick, thin with water. Correct the seasoning with salt and pepper, and serve with a swirl of extra virgin olive oil.

TANGIER-STYLE HARIRA

The complex spice mixture known as La Kama makes a particularly good match for this meaty and voluptuous *harira*. The soup is thickened with *tedouira*, a lightly fermented batter made with durum wheat flour, water, and lemon juice.

In this recipe, I opt for bone marrow in place of *smen*, a trick I picked up from a Sephardic cook. She told me that since *harira* is also part of her cuisine, Moroccan Jewish cooks use beef marrow to enrich the soup to avoid mixing meat and dairy.

Be sure to accompany this hot soup with a platter of dates and/or honeyed cakes (see page 482).

— Serves 10 —

¾ cup dried chickpeas

Three 3-inch marrow bones with marrow intact

¼ cup pasta flour (semolina)

Juice of ½ lemon, or to taste

8 ounces boneless shoulder of lamb or beef, trimmed of excess fat and diced

2 tablespoons extra virgin olive oil

¾ cup chopped red onion

Salt and freshly ground black pepper

1½ teaspoons La Kama Spice Mixture (page 37)

2 tablespoons saffron water (see page 48)

3 quarts chicken stock

⅓ cup finely chopped flat-leaf parsley

⅓ cup finely chopped celery leaves

⅓ cup finely chopped cilantro

¾ cup short-grain rice, rinsed, or brown lentils, picked over and rinsed

1½ cups peeled, halved, seeded, and crushed tomatoes

1 teaspoon sugar

1. The day before: Soak the chickpeas overnight in water to cover. Soak the marrow bones in salted water overnight in the refrigerator; drain before using.

2. To make the *tedouira*: Combine the pasta flour, lemon juice, and ½ cup lukewarm water in a medium bowl, partially cover, and set in a warm place to ferment overnight.

3. The following day: Peel the chickpeas (see page 51); put the marrow bones and diced lamb in a deep pot, without any added fat, cover, and steam over medium-low heat until the bones and meat lose their raw color, about 10 minutes. Add the oil and onions and cook, stirring, for 5 minutes. Cover with about 6 cups water and bring to a hard boil, then skim to remove any impurities.

4. Drain the chickpeas and add to the pot, along with salt and pepper to taste, the spices, and saffron water and bring back to a boil. Reduce the heat to a simmer and cook, covered, for 1 hour.

5. Pick out the marrow bones. Extract the marrow and crush to a pulp with the back of a spoon; discard the bones. Combine the chicken stock, marrow, ¼ teaspoon pepper, the parsley, celery leaves, half the cilantro, and the rice or lentils in a second pot, bring to a boil, and cook for 20 minutes.

6. Add the tomatoes, sugar, and the semolina mixture to the rice or lentils and cook, uncovered, for 10 minutes, stirring constantly.

7. Combine the contents of the two pots and adjust the seasoning. Garnish individual portions with a sprinkling of the remaining chopped cilantro.

Variation:

HARIRA WITH POACHED EGGS

Here's a nice way of serving any leftovers from the recipe alone. Simply scrape the leftover soup into a saucepan, thin with water to the right satiny consistency, and bring to a simmer. Meanwhile, preheat the oven to 350°F. Arrange individual ovenproof soup bowls on a baking sheet.

About 10 minutes before serving, divide the soup among the bowls. Break 1 or 2 eggs into each, tilt the bowls, and spoon some of the hot liquid over the eggs. Set the pan with the bowls in the oven and bake for 10 minutes, or until the egg whites are set but the yolks are still runny. Sprinkle with fresh herbs and a light dusting of salt and pepper.

HARIRA WITH LAMB, SUMMER LEAFY GREENS, AND EGGS

Since the Moslem calendar is lunar, the fasting month of Ramadan falls at a different time each year. In summer, *harira* should be nutritious but also light. This version is built around the super-healthy and delicious leafy weed purslane, which provides a refreshingly lively savor. If unavailable, substitute a mild soft-textured green such as young Swiss chard. The soup is thickened at the end with a few beaten eggs flavored with cinnamon.

Serves 8 to 10

2 teaspoons La Kama Spice Mixture (page 37)

¾ teaspoon sweet paprika

2 cloves, crushed

2 tablespoons saffron water (see page 48)

2 bone-in lamb shoulder chops (about 1¼ pounds), trimmed of excess fat and cut into bite-sized cubes, bones reserved

1 large red onion, grated (1½ cups)

1 cinnamon stick

2 large red-ripe tomatoes, halved, seeded, and grated (1 cup)

Salt

2 to 3 flat-leaf parsley sprigs, plus ½ cup chopped parsley

1 cup brown lentils

⅓ cup short- or medium-grain rice, rinsed

¼ cup chopped cilantro, plus extra for garnish

2 cups finely chopped stemmed purslane leaves (about 6 ounces)

2 large eggs

Juice of 1 lemon

Pinch of ground Ceylon cinnamon

1. Early in the day, or about 3 hours before serving: Combine the spice mixture, paprika, cloves, and saffron water in a small bowl. Rub the meat with one-third of the spice mixture and let marinate at room temperature for 1 hour.

2. Put the seasoned lamb and the bones in a 5-quart soup pot, without any added fat, cover, and steam over medium-low heat until the meat loses its color about 10 minutes. Pour in 8 cups water and quickly bring to a boil; skim carefully. Add the onion, cinnamon stick, half the tomatoes, half of the remaining mixed spices, 1 teaspoon salt, and the parsley sprigs, return to a boil, and skim once again, then simmer, covered, for 30 minutes.

3. Meanwhile, pick over the lentils, rinse under hot water, and soak in cold water for 15 minutes.

4. Drain the lentils, add to the pot, and bring back to a boil, skimming. Cover, reduce the heat to low, and cook for 45 minutes. Discard the cinnamon stick and lamb bones.

5. Meanwhile, combine the rice, the remaining spice mixture, and 3 cups water in a saucepan, bring to a boil, and cook for 15 minutes. Add the remaining tomatoes, the chopped parsley, cilantro, purslane, and 1 teaspoon salt and cook for 5 minutes longer, or until the rice is tender.

6. Beat the eggs, 2 tablespoons water, and the lemon juice in a small bowl until foamy, about 2 minutes. Carefully add a ladleful of the meat broth to the eggs, stirring constantly. Slowly pour the egg mixture into the simmering lentils, being very careful not to curdle the eggs. Immediately pour in the rice with its cooking liquid and stir thoroughly over gentle heat, until thickened; do not let boil.

7. Serve hot, with a sprinkling of chopped cilantro and cinnamon.

TROUT WITH PRESERVED LEMONS, RAISINS, AND PINE NUTS IN BROTH

At a restaurant in the Middle Atlas town of Ifrane, known as the "Little Switzerland" of Morocco, I finally tasted the famous regional lake trout. The fish, I learned, was served in numerous ways: fried, in tagines, and, as in this recipe, gently poached in a lovely light broth.

The dish reminded me of a mountain lake trout preparation I learned from the famous French chef Michel Bras. I've based the recipe below on his technique, but the dish is totally Moroccan in character.

—❧ Serves 2 to 4 ❧—

8 ounces lake trout or Arctic char fillets

Coarse salt and freshly ground white pepper

Cayenne

3 tablespoons coarsely chopped cilantro

2 large spring onions or 1 bunch scallions, trimmed, halved lengthwise, and sliced about ⅛ inch thick on a slight diagonal

1 medium carrot, scraped and sliced about ⅛ inch thick on a slight diagonal

1 teaspoon honey, such as orange blossom, jujube, eucalyptus, or thyme

1 preserved lemon (see page 21), pulp removed, rind rinsed and cut into ¼-inch dice

1 tablespoon golden raisins, soaked in water for 10 minutes and drained

1 tablespoon pine nuts

1 to 2 tablespoons extra virgin olive oil

NOTE TO THE COOK

If you can, use small lake or salmon trout to make this soup, catching and then filleting, skinning, and boning the fish yourself. Or you can purchase farmed lake trout fillets at your local fish market. Arctic char can also be substituted.

1. Cut the fillets into small pieces. Season with salt, pepper, and cayenne. Put on a plate, scatter a small amount of the cilantro on top, cover with plastic, and refrigerate.

2. Simmer the spring onions or scallions and carrots in 3 cups water in a 10-inch deep skillet until tender, 10 to 15 minutes.

3. Add the honey, preserved lemon, raisins, pine nuts, and a little salt and pepper to the vegetables and bring to a boil, then simmer for 10 minutes. (The soup can be made in advance up to this point; bring to a simmer before proceeding. Add more water if necessary to keep the mixture submerged by about 1 inch.)

4. Slip in the pieces of fish and cook gently until the fish is silky smooth and tender, about 10 minutes. Adjust the seasoning with salt and pepper, drizzle with the extra virgin olive oil, scatter with the remaining cilantro, and serve.

CREAMY FAVA BEAN SOUP

❈
NOTE TO THE COOK

Local cooks told me not to cover the pot while the beans cook, since they believe that the gassiness of these particular beans leaves with the steam.

The best Bysscera is laced with new olive oil made from green, unripe olives, available in the autumn.

This is the soup version of an earthy dip, *byssara* (page 436), popular in northern Morocco. It's an authentic *plat de pauvre* that's beloved by all strata of society, as reflected in the following vignette in Madame Zette Guinaudeau's book on Moroccan cooking:

> *A gentleman from Fès to a Berber mountaineer: What would you do if you were the sultan?*
> *The mountaineer's reply: I would eat* byssara *every day.*

Dried fava beans are one of the oldest of Mediterranean food staples. When peeled and cooked slowly in an uncovered casserole, they break down to a luscious smooth, delicately flavored soup. In northern Morocco, the women leave the soup to cook all night over dying embers and then serve it up for breakfast.

Byssara is easy to make ahead, and it can be thinned out if necessary by adding water, then reseasoned before serving. The soup is served with a drizzle of heated olive oil reddened with sweet paprika and cayenne.

Some cooks make more of this soup than they need, then allow the leftovers to thicken further and become a dip (see page 436).

In the province of Taounate in the Rif Mountains northeast of Fes, local cooks use a very unusual whisk that has a group of two-inch-long supple wooden spokes at the end of a long stick. The cook plunges the whisk into the soup pot and rolls the wooden stick between her hands to crush the cooked beans until smooth and silky. Without that particular whisk, a sieve or a run though a food mill is adequate. But I was curious about a "look-alike" 10-inch silicone tornado whisk I found at Sur La Table, and I discovered that it actually makes the beans fluffier. Although it's not a necessary tool for making this soup, I always use it when I have dried beans that I want to break down to a creamy state.

Purchase peeled and split fava beans at a local Middle Eastern store or obtain them from a mail-order source such as Kalustyan's in New York City (see Sources).

———— ❧ Serves 4 ❧ ————

8 ounces large skinned dried fava beans

1 dried red chile pepper, split and seeded

¼ cup extra virgin olive oil

5 large garlic cloves

1 teaspoon cumin seeds, preferably Moroccan

Coarse salt

1 teaspoon sweet paprika

Cayenne

1. The night before: Soak the fava beans in 3 to 4 times their volume of cold water; discard any favas that float.

2. The following day: Bring 6 cups water to a boil in a saucepan. Rinse and drain the fava beans. When the water is boiling, add the beans and the chile pepper, reduce to a simmer, and cook, uncovered,

for 1 hour, skimming off any surface debris. Remove and discard the chile pepper.

3. Add 2 tablespoons of the oil and the garlic to the beans and continue cooking down to a nice thick soupy consistency, about 1 more hour. (You should have about 5 cups.) Remove from the heat to cool slightly. Whisk or puree the soup. Return to the pan.

4. Meanwhile, crush or grind the cumin seeds and 1 teaspoon coarse salt to a powder in a mortar. Thin the soup with warm water if necessary and bring to a boil. Stir the cumin salt into the soup. Correct the seasoning with more salt if needed.

5. Divide the soup among four individual bowls. Quickly heat the remaining 2 tablespoons olive oil in a small saucepan until sizzling, then add the paprika and a few pinches of cayenne, and cook until the oil turns red.

6. Dribble the oil over the soup and serve.

RIFFIAN SPLIT PEA SOUP
WITH PAPRIKA OIL

Serves 4

¼ cup extra virgin olive oil

1 cup chopped onion

Salt and freshly ground pepper

1 cup (8 ounces) dried split
  green peas

3 large cloves garlic

2 tablespoons finely chopped
  cilantro

1 teaspoon ground cumin,
  preferably Moroccan

1½ teaspoons sweet paprika

A few drops of lemon juice

½ cup crumbled dried aged goat
  cheese (see Sources)

⅓ cup heavy cream

Cayenne

1. Combine 3 tablespoons of the olive oil, the chopped onion, and salt and
   pepper to taste in a deep saucepan and set over medium heat. Cover
   and cook for 5 minutes, or until the onions are golden and softened.
   Add the split peas, garlic, cilantro, cumin, and 1 teaspoon of the paprika
   and cook, stirring, for a minute. Then add 4 cups water and bring to a
   boil. Cover and cook for 1 hour, stirring occasionally.

2. Remove from the heat to cool slightly. Puree the soup in batches
   in a blender. Add the cheese and cream to the last batch of soup and
   puree until velvety. Return to the saucepan; thin the soup to the desired
   consistency, and correct the seasoning with salt and a few drops of
   lemon juice.

3. Reheat the soup to boiling. Divide the soup into 4 individual
   bowls. In a small bowl, mix the remaining tablespoon olive oil with the
   remaining ½ teaspoon paprika and pinch of cayenne and dribble over
   each portion.

MEAT CONFIT, CHICKPEA, AND PASTA SOUP

——— ❧ Serves 4 to 6 ❧ ———

NOTE TO THE COOK

In Morocco, the pasta of choice for this northeastern soup is the bead-like *berk-oukch*, but I use the larger *mhamsa* (see Sources) or any top-quality small Italian pasta, such as acini di pepe, orzo, or bird's tongue.

The recipe for this luscious rustic soup was inspired by one in a booklet prepared by a Moroccan pasta company.

¾ cup dried chickpeas

¼ cup split dried peeled fava beans

⅓ cup brown lentils, picked over and rinsed

1 medium onion, chopped

Salt

1 cup "Express" Meat Confit (page 44), or ⅔ cup Moroccan *khliî* (see Sources), plus 2 tablespoons of the fat

2 Roma (plum) tomatoes, grated (½ cup)

1 tablespoon chopped flat-leaf parsley

1 teaspoon freshly ground black pepper

½ teaspoon sweet paprika

Pinch of cayenne

¾ teaspoon ground ginger

⅓ teaspoon ground turmeric

½ teaspoon *ras el hanout* (see page 36)

2 tablespoons saffron water (see page 48)

2 tablespoons crumbled dried aged goat cheese (see Sources)

10 ounce *mhamsa* (see Sources) or top-quality Italian pasta such as acini di pepe, orzo, or bird's tongue

1. The night before: Soak the chickpeas in water to cover. Soak the peeled favas separately in plenty of water.

2. The following day: Cook the fava beans in 3 cups water in a small saucepan for 30 minutes, skimming often.

3. Meanwhile, soak the lentils in water to cover for 30 minutes; drain.

4. Drain the chickpeas and peel as directed on page 51.

5. Toss the onion with ½ teaspoon salt and the fat from the meat confit in a soup pot, cover, and cook over medium heat for 10 minutes, or until the onion is golden. Crush and shred the meat confit and add to the pot, along with the tomatoes, parsley, chickpeas, lentils, all the spices, and the saffron water. Add 5 cups water, the fava beans and 1 cup of their cooking liquid, and the crumbled cheese and bring to a boil. Then cover and cook over low heat for 45 minutes.

6. Meanwhile, fill a large pot with water and bring to a boil. Set on a steamer or colander over the boiling water, add the pasta to the steamer, partially cover, and steam for 10 minutes.

7. Add the steamed pasta to the soup and simmer for a few minutes, stirring. Serve hot.

LAMB, TOMATO, CINNAMON, AND STEAMED PASTA CHORBA

Here is a simple, hearty soup from the northeastern part of the country that has a special twist: the pasta is steamed over boiling water rather than cooked in it. The resulting silky texture never ceases to amaze me.

Serves 4

2 tablespoons extra virgin olive oil

4 ounces ground lean lamb or beef

1 small red onion, grated

1½ teaspoons La Kama Spice Mixture (page 37)

Pinch of cayenne

½ teaspoon ground caraway

2 tablespoons Tomato Magic (page 41) or tomato paste

2 Roma (plum) tomatoes, grated

(½ cup)

Salt and freshly ground black pepper

½ cup rice-shaped pasta, such as orzo or bird's tongue

½ cup canned or freshly cooked chickpeas (see page 51), drained

2 tablespoons finely chopped flat-leaf parsley

2 tablespoons finely chopped cilantro

1. Heat the oil in a medium heavy saucepan. Add the meat, onion, and spices and cook, stirring, for 2 to 3 minutes. Add the Tomato Magic or tomato paste and let it sizzle for an instant. Stir in the grated tomatoes, salt and pepper to taste, and 3 cups water and bring to a boil. Cook, covered, over medium heat for 20 minutes.

2. Meanwhile, fill a deep saucepan with water and bring to a boil. Fit a colander snugly on top, cover partially, and steam the pasta until tender, about 10 minutes.

3. Add the chickpeas, herbs, and tender pasta to the soup and serve at once.

BUTTERNUT SQUASH
AND TOMATO SOUP

Here is a family favorite inspired by the winter soups prepared in the Rif Mountains, soups that keep both body and soul warm, as Fatima, our housekeeper, liked to say.

———— ❧ Serves 4 ❧ ————

1 yellow onion, coarsely chopped (1¾ cups)

Coarse salt

1½ tablespoons extra virgin olive oil

2 pounds butternut, kabocha, or calabaza squash, halved, peeled, seeded, and cut into 1½-inch chunks (about 6 cups)

2 tablespoons Tomato Magic (page 41) or tomato paste

1 teaspoon La Kama Spice Mixture (page 37)

½ cup heavy cream or crème fraîche

¼ pound shredded or crumbled aged goat cheese or goat gouda (see Sources)

1 teaspoon or more to taste harissa paste (see Sources)

Salt and freshly ground black pepper

1. Toss the onion with 1 teaspoon coarse salt and the oil in a medium casserole, preferably earthenware or enameled cast iron, cover, and steam over medium-low heat until the onion is soft, about 10 minutes.

2. Add the squash, cover with a sheet of parchment paper and a lid, and steam for 20 minutes.

3. Add the Tomato Magic or paste, spices, and 4 cups hot water and bring to a boil, then cook at a simmer until the squash is tender, about 20 minutes. Remove from the heat.

4. Transfer the soup in batches to a blender, and puree until smooth; add the cream, three-quarters of the cheese, and the harissa to the last batch of soup and puree until velvety.

5. Return the soup to the pot and season with salt and pepper to taste. Ladle the soup into warm bowls and top each portion with a light sprinkling of the remaining cheese.

❉

NOTE TO THE COOK

When reheating, if the soup thickens too much, thin it with hot water and readjust the seasoning.

SEMOLINA SOUP WITH ANISEED

Here's a nourishing, ivory-colored, homey soup made with semolina flour, milk, and butter and flavored with lightly toasted aniseed. The soup is alleged to have medicinal qualities, but I think it's worth making simply because of its flavor. It's particularly good served with a dollop of honey and a drizzle of olive oil. The first time I had this soup, my hostess gave me a sugar cube to suck on as I ate it!

A variation of this soup, called *her-bel*, is traditionally served for breakfast on the feast day commemorating the birth of the prophet. It is made without the aniseed and with peeled cracked wheat instead of the semolina. In the Middle Atlas, the soup is cooked in a clay pot over a brazier through the night, then flavored in the morning with butter, sugar, and orange flower water.

—⟶ Serves 4 to 6 ⟵—

2 cups milk

⅔ cup pasta flour (semolina)

1 tablespoon unsalted butter

1 teaspoon green aniseed

1 pea-sized piece gum arabic

1 teaspoon sugar

1 teaspoon salt

2 tablespoons floral honey, preferably acacia

Argan oil (see Sources), extra virgin olive oil, or melted butter

4 to 6 sugar cubes (optional)

12 Medjoul dates, pitted and sliced

1. Bring the milk to a boil in a large heavy-bottomed saucepan. Reduce the heat and simmer, stirring to keep the milk from sticking, until it reduces by half. Pour into a bowl and set aside.

2. Pour 6 cups water into the saucepan and quickly bring to a boil. Reduce the heat to a simmer, add the flour and butter, and cook, stirring, for 10 minutes, or until thick and smooth. Pour in the reduced milk and continue cooking for 10 more minutes.

3. Meanwhile, lightly toast the aniseed in a dry skillet until aromatic. Combine the aniseed, gum arabic, sugar, and salt in a mortar or an electric spice grinder and grind to a fine powder.

4. Stir the spice mixture into the soup and continue cooking, stirring occasionally, over very low heat until smooth and light beige in color, about 5 minutes.

5. Pour into individual bowls, add the honey and oil or butter, and serve with the sugar cubes, if desired, and sliced dates on the side.

CORNMEAL PORRIDGE

A cornmeal porridge from southern Morocco is strangely called "the hamburger of the Souss." Made from white corn (hominy grits), the porridge is boiled for hours, until transformed into a thick, pale yellow, creamy pudding, then embellished with a good dollop of thyme-flavored butter called *oudi* (see page 161). Moroccans eat it with the first three fingers of their right hands, plucking some porridge from a communal plate, dipping it into more liquid butter, and then conveying it to their mouths.

MARRAKECH SNAIL SOUP

I've always loved the food offered by outdoor vendors in the Djemaa el Fna in Marrakech, the huge, magnificent square set in the center of the city. By day, the place is filled with self-styled "doctors" and "dentists," as well as purveyors of most anything you can think of. At nightfall, after the storytellers, snake charmers, dancers, acrobats, and God knows what else have exited, this vast exterior space is suffused with the aromas of meat (everything from lamb heads to expensive cuts) being cooked over charcoal braziers. There are circles within circles of vendors offering sweets and ginseng tea, tagines, *harira*-style soups, and you-name-it. Yes, you'll see tourists here, but the food by night and entertainment by day are primarily for the Moroccans who throng the square.

For me, nightfall is the best time. The light is wonderful, the aromas intense. And whenever I come here, I am drawn to a line of six or so vendors who offer a wonderful and quite unforgettable snail soup.

The snails piled into the soup are not the large escargots you eat with garlic butter in France, nor does the soup resemble the snail stews I learned to make in Greece. The vendor dishes out some broth into a porcelain cup, then tops it with a heap of snails from a huge pot. You sit at a kind of bar in front of him, using a toothpick to extract the snails from their shells and ferry them to your mouth. Then you get to the really good part: a delicious clear soup hauntingly seasoned with a dozen herbs and spices, including gum arabic, licorice, bitter orange, absinthe, paprika, caraway, green aniseed, wild mint, thyme, bay leaves, and hot peppers. When I bring a cup of this nectar to my lips, inhale the aroma, and then take my first sip, I know I am back in Marrakech, a city I love, perhaps the most fascinating and exotic city I've visited over my many years spent exploring Mediterranean lands.

On my last visit, I wondered if it would be possible to reproduce this soup, to work up a recipe for my American readers. Once I decided to try, I knew my first task would be obtaining the proper wild snails.

My research quickly led me to the work of François Picart, author of *Snails from Your Garden to Your Table*, who, as it happened, also lived, as I do, in Sonoma County. His book includes detailed instructions on how to raise, purge, and clean snails for consumption. (The book is now out of print, but you can find excerpted instructions from it at www.bertc.com/subfive/recipes/gardensnails.htm.) Then, as if by serendipity, I noticed an item in my local newspaper, the *Sonoma Index-Tribune*, by my friend culinary columnist Kathleen Hill, in which she mentioned that a garden snail had mysteriously turned up in one of her stews.

Aha! I thought, perhaps Kathleen can help me obtain snails!

When I told her I needed a good number of garden snails for testing, she immediately agreed to publicize my request in her column. The call went out, and the snails started coming in—from neighbors, town gardeners, and folks as far away as Healdsburg and Napa. Soon I had a snail soup, which appeared over and over in exactly the same words on a variety of French and Moroccan culinary websites.

With snails and recipe in hand, and using my taste-memory as my guide, I set to work. And I invited everyone who'd contributed "livestock" to meet me at our local Tuesday-afternoon farmers' market, held on the great square of Sonoma—admittedly not quite as grand as the Djemaa el Fna, but we do have music, entertainment, and prepared food in addition to excellent local produce. Here, I promised, I'd be dishing out snail soup to my "happy few," just like a Moroccan soup vendor.

The day finally came. I prepared the soup, using all the proper spices. And, in truth, the snails themselves tasted pretty good. But I'm sorry to report that the broth itself was, well, just awful. This happens to food writers more often than you might think. Some recipes just don't work out. Usually, if a dish has great potential, I'm inspired to keep at it, adjusting here and there until I finally get it right. But in this case, I realized I didn't have it in me to send out a new request for snails and then go through the two-week-long purging/cleaning process again. So, alas, I could not dazzle my contributors. Instead, I had to tell them I'd failed and could not dish out soup to them as promised, and suggested instead that we all meet up one day at nightfall in the Djemaa el Fna in Marrakech to devour the real thing.

chapter seven

COUSCOUS

❖

"... A mountain of couscous
surrounded by a sea of sauce."

—*paul bowles*

❖

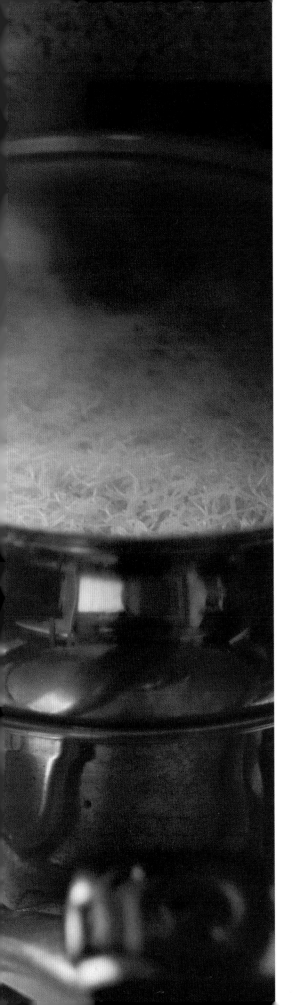

COUSCOUS

FAMILY COUSCOUS
❧ page 204 ❧

COUSCOUS WITH LAMB, PUMPKIN,
CARROTS, CHICKPEAS, AND RAISINS
❧ page 206 ❧

COUSCOUS WITH SEVEN VEGETABLES
IN THE FES MANNER
❧ page 209 ❧

ECLECTIC COUSCOUS
❧ page 212 ❧

BERBER COUSCOUS FOR SPRING
❧ page 214 ❧

BERBER COUSCOUS
❧ page 217 ❧

BARLEY GRITS COUSCOUS WITH
BEEF AND LEAFY GREENS
❧ page 222 ❧

BARLEY GRITS COUSCOUS WITH
FRESH FAVA BEANS
❧ page 224 ❧

FINE-GRAIN COUSCOUS WITH
CHICKEN OR LAMB
❧ page 226 ❧

STEAMED NOODLE COUSCOUS
(CHAARIYA MEFTOUN)
❧ page 230 ❧

STONE-GROUND CORN GRITS COUSCOUS
WITH SHELLFISH, CARAMELIZED ONIONS,
AND GLAZED TURNIPS
❧ page 235 ❧

COUSCOUS

The couscous concept is simple and it is brilliant. Take a container with a perforated bottom, fill it with a grain (in most cases, semolina that has been previously moistened, then dried out a bit), place the perforated container over a pot of boiling liquid, and allow steam to rise up through the perforations, soften the grain, and make it swell.

After a certain amount of time, the steamed grain is dumped into a large shallow tray, tossed with a little cool water until evenly moistened, and then left to dry before repeating the steaming. Depending upon the type of grain, its size, age, and whether it was hand- or machine-made, it may have to be steamed a third time to achieve the desired light, tender fluffiness.

When the grain is properly cooked, it is tossed with butter or, in some parts of Morocco, with *smen*, argan oil, or extra virgin olive oil, then doused with milk, or a sauce, and garnished with vegetables, meat, poultry, or fish.

Couscous is the crowning achievement of Berber cooking. I consider it magical.

The word *couscous* and its various phonetic soundalikes in North African Berber dialects (*seksu*, *keskesu*, *utsu*, and *kouski* in southern Tunisia) are probably a verbal approximation of the hissing sound as steam rises up through the perforations and into the grain. There are other theories, but the one fact that no one denies is that the dish itself is Berber.

Though the word *couscous* is applied to various grains, it really is a description of the process by which these grains are steamed. Although the prevalent grain used is pellet pasta made from semolina flour, couscous can also be made with barley, barley sprouts, millet, green wheat, crushed acorns, corn, and crushed bread crumbs.

Today the dish can be as simple and pure as the Berber version of steamed barley coated in preserved butter and downed with a cup of buttermilk, or as elaborate and spectacular as the couscous preparations allegedly served in palaces: great pyramids of semolina concealing mounds of pigeons, each stuffed in turn with couscous and other mysterious things.

In Morocco, couscous is traditionally served for Friday lunch, when the whole family is home from work and school, or on special occasions such as weddings, births, and circumcisions—or, of course, whenever anyone feels like eating it. It isn't a dish you will find in a Moroccan restaurant catering to Moroccans, but you will inevitably find it featured on the menu of a restaurant catering to tourists.

Couscous is surely, if unofficially, the national dish of Morocco. It's also the central image in a famous Moroccan proverb about the virtues of almsgiving: "A handful of couscous [given in charity] is better than Mecca and all its dust."

When I lived in Morocco, couscous was rarely served at the evening meal. Also—and many people don't realize this—it was not considered a main course. At a Moroccan banquet or *diaffa*, it was served at the end of a string of courses to finally and fully satiate the hunger of the guests. "No guest should go home hungry" is the basis of Arab hospitality. And although this idea is often carried to the point of absurdity, when, after being offered course after course, the possibility of going home hungry is out of the question, still, satiation is symbolized by the appearance of a mound of couscous, highly flavored, laden with vegetables and meats. Such a dish is served as a finale so that the guests will achieve *shabaan* (total satisfaction) and know that their host has held back nothing that could give them pleasure.

Of course, Moroccan restaurants that cater to tourists and European and American chefs who serve couscous are serving it as a main course and there is nothing wrong with them doing so, as long as they prepare it the proper way. That being the case in today's world, all of the couscous recipes in this book can be served as a main course for lunch or dinner or, in the traditional way, as the final dish in a succession at a banquet.

EQUIPMENT FOR STEAMING COUSCOUS

If you love couscous as much as I do, you'll want to acquire a true couscousier. But you can steam couscous perfectly well in a colander (metal or, even better, stoneware) that fits snugly over a tall pot, or in the type of pasta pot that comes with a shallow steam insert. (See Sources for couscousiers, pasta steamers with inserts, stoneware colanders, and Khafel silicone strips to fasten a colander to a tall pot.

Don't worry about the size of your steamer. Since semolina couscous is best steamed uncovered, you can simply shape the grains into a pyramid as they expand and it doesn't matter if the peak of the pyramid is higher than the steamer itself. The steam will still move perfectly well right up through the pile of grain.

The piece of equipment you do need is a substitute for the Moroccan *gsaa*, a large shallow basin of earthenware, wood, or metal in which the couscous is worked and where it dries. I've found that a large pizza pan is ideal. I've also used rimmed baking sheets and large flowerpot saucers.

I now steam my couscous grains over boiling water, rather than over the broth and vegetables. Some cookbook writers will tell you that the steam from the broth will imbue the grain with flavor, but this is doubtful, since anything imparted by the broth is minimal, and in any event, the grain is saturated and flavored when doused with broth just before serving. Also, it is much easier to monitor the preparation of broth and vegetables by cooking them in a separate pot. For one thing, you'll avoid overcooking, and there's also no need to take the steamer off the pot numerous times to check the progress of the vegetables. Finally, when you pour your broth over your grains just before serving, you'll be truly flavoring the grain as opposed perpetuating to the illusion of flavoring it via "aromatic" steam.

SEMOLINA COUSCOUS: INSTANT OR HAND-ROLLED?

You can purchase hand-rolled, sun-dried couscous imported from Morocco in Middle Eastern stores and top-of-the-line groceries and online (see Sources). This couscous is a true artisanal product made with high-quality durum wheat flour and is thus superior in taste and texture. If you like top-of-the-line pasta, you will like hand-rolled, sun-dried couscous.

Or you can use so-called "instant couscous," provided it is 100 percent semolina. My preferred brands are Ferrero, Dari, Rivera, Tria, and Tripiak, which come with instructions for the traditional steaming of the grain. The problem with most other "instant couscous" is that the grain won't properly expand, and the result will be mediocre at best. If you follow the directions on a 1-pound box of ordinary instant couscous, you will get about 6 cups of couscous after 10 minutes of preparation. But if you instead moisten and steam ordinary instant couscous, three times for 10 to 20 minutes each time, you will end up with about 10 cups. And if you use one of my preferred brands of instant couscous and steam it three times, you will get up to 12 cups. As for hand-rolled, sun-dried couscous, 1 pound steamed four times will give you about 18 cups! This isn't magic. Hand-made couscous, unlike "instant couscous," has not been pre-steamed.

Please note: In the "Desserts" chapter, I tell you how to make your own couscous out of semolina flour. It's easy to do and a lot of fun, but really only necessary when making sweet couscous such as the luxurious Handmade Dessert Couscous (page 444). Imported fine-grain couscous can be substituted (see Sources). Homemade couscous is so special, so fine, so light, and so fluffy, it will quickly become apparent that it's well worth your effort.

If you wish to use your own homemade couscous in the following recipes, by all means do so. Simply follow the directions below, and be sure to steam the grain three times.

HANDLING AND STEAMING SEMOLINA COUSCOUS

The directions for steaming and handling semolina couscous, whether hand-rolled or instant, are the same except for the timing and the extra steaming required to cook the hand-rolled variety.

Hand-rolled, sun-dried couscous requires three steamings of 20 minutes each and a final steaming of 10 minutes. The first three steamings can be done early in the day, the final steaming just before serving.

Instant couscous (no matter what the directions on the box say) requires two steamings of 20 minutes each and a final steaming of 10 minutes. As is the case with hand-rolled grains, the first two or three steamings can be done hours in advance.

What follows are the master instructions for handling and steaming 1 pound of hand-rolled or instant semolina couscous. If preparing more than 1 pound, add up to 50 percent more water when moistening the grain and add an extra 5 minutes to each steaming time.

Though this may sound complicated, the principle is very simple: all the gradual moistening, careful raking and aerating, and multiple steamings of the semolina grain is done to maximize its swelling without allowing it to become lumpy or soggy. (If you do get lumps, simply wet your fingers with cold water and rub the lumps apart.)

Slowly dribble the swollen couscous grains into the steamer, allowing the grains to form a soft mound.

STEP 1: Fill a deep pot (or the bottom of a couscousier) with water and bring to a rapid boil. Be sure to leave room between the top of the boiling water and the bottom of the perforated steamer that will sit above it. I also suggest tossing a penny into the pot. When it stops clicking, it will be a signal that it's time to add more water.

STEP 2: *If using hand-rolled, sun-dried couscous,* place the grain in a fine strainer and quickly moisten under running water. Dump into a wide shallow pan, smooth out, and allow the grains to swell for about 5 minutes, then toss with ½ cup water and allow to stand for 5 minutes more. *If using instant couscous,* place the grains in a large pan, cover with 2 cups water, and allow to stand for about 1 minute, then stir and pour off the excess water.

With wet hands, lift up the grains, rubbing them gently and letting them fall back into the pan two or three times. This process should break up any lumps that formed. Next, rake the couscous with your fingers to circulate it and cause the grains to swell. An important thing to remember about couscous is that it increases in volume in the pan, not in the steamer where it cooks.

Liberally rub oil on your fingers and palms, and rake the grains.

STEP 3: Line the inside of the perforated couscousier top or a colander with a sheet of cheesecloth. (Note: The cheesecloth is not there to prevent the couscous from falling through the holes; the grains won't fall if steam is rising. It is there to help you transfer the grains back and forth from the steamer to the wide pan without having to unseal and reseal the steamer and the bottom pot.) Set the container snugly on top of the pot of boiling water and check to see that no steam is escaping out the sides. If steam is escaping, place a long strip of foil or a dampened strip of kitchen cloth or a silicon strip around the pot top and tuck it between the steamer and pot. You want the steam to rise only through the perforated holes.

Steam for 20 minutes. Unless instructed otherwise in the recipe, do not cover the couscous as it steams.

STEP 4: Use the cheesecloth to transfer the couscous back to the large shallow pan. Spread the grains out with a large wire whisk. Gradually sprinkle about 1 cup cold water, or ¹⁄₂ cup cold water and ¹⁄₂ cup milk, plus 1 teaspoon salt and 1 teaspoon oil over the grains. Separate and break up lumps by lifting and stirring the grains gently. This will help to keep each grain separate. Smooth the grains out and allow to dry for about 10 minutes.

STEP 5: Repeat steps 3 and 4 for a second steaming, but do not add more salt or oil. (Repeat a third time for hand-rolled couscous.) When you moisten the grains, this time use only water (if you added milk the first time). If you are preparing the couscous in advance, cover it with a damp kitchen cloth. Covered, it will hold well for several hours.

STEP 6: About 30 minutes before serving, break up any lumps with a whisk, then by working the grains lightly between wet fingers. Bring the water in the bottom pot to a boil. Pile all the couscous at once into the perforated top and steam for 10 minutes. Dump the couscous onto a wide serving dish and toss with butter and *smen*, if using. Then gradually add your broth as instructed in the recipes, up to 1 cup for instant couscous and up to 1¹⁄₂ cups for hand-rolled. (You may not need all the broth listed in the recipe.) Toss the grains, then let stand for 10 minutes before shaping and garnishing the couscous. Serve any remaining broth on the side for those who like their couscous very moist.

FAMILY COUSCOUS

⁕

NOTE TO THE COOK

Freeze any remaining broth for another use.

What makes this recipe unique is its size. Most traditional couscous recipes call for 1½ to 2 pounds of grain, enough to feed 12 to 16 people as part of a Moroccan feast, or 8 to 10 as a main dish. This one, which has all the trimmings of one of the most lavish of all couscous presentations, is pared down to feed 6 as a main course. If you want to make it for a larger number, it doubles easily.

The chicken is slowly poached in a highly seasoned broth, then drained, quartered, brushed with honey, and glazed in a hot oven just before it is placed in the center of the steaming couscous grains. Equally stunning is the caramelized onion-raisin sauce topping, decorated with sautéed almonds and halved hard-cooked eggs.

——— ❧ Serves 6 as a main dish ❧ ———

1 pound (2¾ cups) hand-rolled or 1 box (2¼ cups) instant couscous	1 teaspoon ground Ceylon cinnamon
8 tablespoons (1 stick) unsalted butter	2 tablespoons sugar
Coarse salt and freshly ground black pepper	¾ cup dark raisins, soaked in water for 15 minutes and drained
1½ teaspoons La Kama Spice Mixture (page 37)	½ cup blanched almonds, whole
¼ cup saffron water (see page 48)	Oil for frying
2½ to 3 pounds large yellow onions, halved and thinly sliced	1 tablespoon herbed Smen or Oudi (optional; page 159 or 161)
One 3½-pound chicken, preferably organic and air-chilled, trussed, plus the giblets	3 tablespoons honey, such as lavender, acacia, or orange blossom
1 cinnamon stick	3 hard-cooked eggs, peeled and halved
1 small bouquet flat-leaf parsley sprigs, tied together	

1. Prepare the couscous as directed in steps 1 through 5 on pages 202–203.

2. Meanwhile, prepare the broth and the onion topping: Place 1 tablespoon of the butter, 1½ teaspoons salt, ½ teaspoon pepper, 1 teaspoon of the spice mixture, 2 tablespoons of the saffron water, and one-fifth of the sliced onions in a deep casserole. Swirl the casserole once so the contents gently mix, cover, and cook over medium heat to soften the onions, about 10 minutes. Add the chicken and cook, turning it on all sides to gently firm up the skin, then set it breast side up. Add the giblets, cinnamon stick, parsley sprigs, and 6 cups water and bring to a boil, then cover with a sheet of parchment paper and a tight-fitting lid and simmer over very low heat until the chicken flesh

begins to draw away from the bones, about 1¼ hours. Remove from the heat.

3. Meanwhile, put the remaining onions and just enough water to cover them in a medium saucepan and bring to a boil, then simmer for 2 to 3 minutes. Drain in a large sieve, pressing hard on the onions to remove excess moisture, then return the onions to the saucepan and add 1 tablespoon of the saffron water, ½ teaspoon salt, and 3 tablespoons of the butter. Cover and cook over medium heat for 10 minutes.

4. Stir in the remaining spice mixture, the ground cinnamon, and the sugar and continue to cook for 15 more minutes.

5. Add 1 cup of the chicken broth and the drained raisins to the onions and bring to a boil, then lower the heat and cook, uncovered, until the onions thicken to a syrupy sauce. Remove from the heat, cover, and keep warm.

6. Preheat the oven to 450°F.

7. Carefully transfer the chicken to a rimmed baking sheet and allow to rest and cool slightly. When the chicken is cool enough to handle, carefully divide into serving pieces and place them side by side on the pan.

8. Fry the almonds in oil in a small skillet until golden brown. Set aside.

9. About 30 minutes before serving, rake and steam the couscous for the third time as directed in step 6 on page 203. Spread the couscous out on a serving platter. Toss with the remaining 1 tablespoon saffron water, the remaining 4 tablespoons butter, and the *smen* or *oudi*, if using. Use a whisk to break up any lumps. Gradually add up to 1 cup of the cooking liquid for instant couscous and up to 1¼ cups for hand-rolled. (You may not need all the broth.) Toss the grains, then let stand for 10 minutes.

10. Meanwhile, blend the honey with 1 tablespoon of the hot broth and brush the skin side of the chicken parts with it. Set in the oven to glaze, about 10 minutes.

11. Nestle the glazed chicken parts in the center of the couscous and spoon over the onion and raisin glaze. Scatter the almonds evenly on top and place the hard-cooked egg halves around the edges of the plate. Serve with the remaining broth in a bowl with a ladle for those who want their couscous moist.

COUSCOUS WITH LAMB, PUMPKIN, CARROTS, CHICKPEAS, AND RAISINS

This superb lamb couscous makes a warm and inviting presentation. The grain is spread out on a serving platter, the lamb and onions are placed in a well in the center, and chunks of pumpkin and carrots are arranged attractively over the meat.

The couscous, silky and moist, scattered with chickpeas and raisins, is ultrarefined and rustic at the same time: ultrarefined because its relatively few ingredients suggest a great purity of gastronomic thinking, and rustic because the inclusion of pumpkin in place of Old World gourds is reminiscent of the earliest vegetable couscous preparations of the Berbers.

NOTE TO THE COOK

Some cooks sprinkle a little cinnamon over the vegetables just before serving. Others serve it with a red pepper sauce.

— Serves 8 as a main dish —

½ cup dried chickpeas

4 large yellow onions, quartered and sliced lengthwise

½ tablespoon coarse salt, or more to taste

1½ to 2 teaspoons freshly ground black pepper, or to taste

1 teaspoon ground ginger

½ teaspoon ground turmeric

2 tablespoons saffron water (see page 48)

12 tablespoons (1½ sticks) unsalted butter

1½ pounds lamb neck, cut into 5 pieces

4 cups hand-rolled couscous or 1½ pounds instant couscous

1 pound carrots, scraped, halved lengthwise, and cut into 2½-inch lengths

¼ cup granulated sugar

1⅓ cups (½ pound) dark raisins

1½ pounds pumpkin or winter squash, peeled, seeded, and cut into 2-inch chunks

2 teaspoons Smen or Oudi (page 159 or 161)

Red Pepper Sauce (page 211; optional)

Ground cinnamon, as garnish (optional)

1. One day in advance: Soak the chickpeas in water to cover generously.

2. The following day: Peel the chickpeas as directed on page 51.

3. To prepare the broth: Place the onions in a large casserole and add the salt, pepper, ginger, turmeric, saffron water, and 4 tablespoons of the butter. Swirl the casserole once or twice to gently mix the contents, cover, and cook over medium heat to soften the onions, about 10 minutes. Uncover and cook, stirring, until the onions turn golden. Add the lamb and lightly brown on all sides. Add 8 cups water and bring to a boil, then cover and simmer over medium heat for 2½ hours, adding the chickpeas after 2 hours.

4. Meanwhile, prepare the couscous as directed in steps 1 through 5 on pages 202–203.

5. Add the carrots, sugar, and raisins to the broth and continue cooking for 30 minutes. Remove the lamb and let it cool.

6. Cut the meat into small pieces, discarding the bones, gristle, and fat, and return to the broth. (The dish can be prepared in advance up to this point.)

7. About thirty minutes before serving, rake and steam the couscous for a third time as directed in step 6 on page 203.

8. Meanwhile, reheat the broth to a boil, add the pumpkin, and cook until tender, about 15 minutes. Correct the seasoning.

9. Dump the couscous onto a large serving dish and toss with the remaining 8 tablespoons butter and *smen* or *oudi,* if using. Use a long wire whisk to smooth out any lumps. Moisten the couscous by gradually adding up to $1\frac{1}{3}$ cups of the cooking liquid for instant couscous and up to $1\frac{2}{3}$ cups for hand-rolled. (You may not need all the broth.) Toss the grains again, then let stand for 10 minutes.

10. Spread out the couscous, form a well in the center, and add the meat and onions. Top with the pumpkin and carrots. Spoon the raisins and chickpeas over the couscous. Serve with a bowl of the broth on the side for those who like their couscous very moist.

COUSCOUS WITH SEVEN VEGETABLES IN THE FES MANNER

Fes is one of the great gastronomic centers of Morocco, and many people believe the best food in the country is to be found in Fassi homes. A traditional Fes couscous is made with chickpeas, raisins, and onions. A modern variation includes the legendary Berber seven vegetables (pumpkin, cabbage, zucchini, turnips, sweet potatoes, carrots, and tomatoes), two kinds of meat (chicken and lamb), and both sweet (raisins or stewed quinces) and savory (vegetables). This assemblage is rich and glorious, and if you want, you can add other things: hot pepper (early in the cooking), fava beans (30 minutes before serving), or even potatoes (which should be cooked separately with the pumpkin). However, in Fes, the number seven is considered lucky, so it is probably best to limit the vegetables to that number.

According to Robert Landry, in *Les Soleils de la Cuisine*, it is extremely chic to serve a Moroccan couscous with seven-year-old *smen*, seven vegetables, and seven spices. I have yet to taste seven-year-old *smen* (though two-year-old *smen* is fairly common). As for seven spices, the only recipe I have found is one noted down by the great English travel writer Budgett Meakin in his book *The Moors*, published seventy years ago. He describes a couscous flavored with pepper, ginger, nutmeg, coriander seeds, allspice, turmeric, and saffron. I'm happy using just saffron, turmeric, and cinnamon in this recipe.

———— ❦ Serves 8 as a main dish ❦ ————

- 1 cup dried chickpeas
- 3 cracked lamb shanks, trimmed of excess fat
- 2 sets chicken wings and backs
- 12 tablespoons (1½ sticks) unsalted butter
- 1½ tablespoons coarse salt
- 1 tablespoon freshly ground black pepper
- 2 tablespoons saffron water (see page 48)
- ½ teaspoon ground turmeric
- 4 medium yellow onions, quartered
- 2 cassia cinnamon sticks
- A small bundle of cilantro and parsley sprigs, tied together
- 4 or 5 red-ripe tomatoes, peeled, halved, seeded, and quartered
- 8 ounces carrots, scraped and cut into 1½-inch lengths
- 8 ounces white turnips, peeled and cut into 1½-inch lengths
- 1 pound sweet potatoes, peeled and cut into chunks
- 4 cups hand-rolled couscous or 1½ pounds instant couscous
- 8 ounces pumpkin, peeled, seeded if necessary, and cut into chunks
- A handful of dark raisins, soaked in water for 15 minutes and drained
- 8 ounces zucchini, trimmed and quartered
- 1 small cabbage, cut in half
- 2 tablespoons Smen or Oudi (optional; page 159 or 161)
- Red Pepper Sauce (page 211)

1. One day in advance: Soak the chickpeas in water to cover generously.

2. The following day. Drain the chickpeas and peel as directed on page 51. Cook the chickpeas in water to cover for 20 minutes; drain and set aside.

3. To prepare the broth: Place the meat and chicken in a large casserole, along with half the butter, the salt, pepper, saffron water, turmeric, half the quartered onions, the cinnamon sticks, herbs, and tomatoes. Cover and cook gently over low heat for 10 minutes, giving the pan a swirl from time to time. Add 4 quarts water and bring to a boil, then reduce the heat and simmer, partially covered, for 3 hours. Midway through, remove and discard the chicken wings and backs.

4. Turn off the heat under the casserole and allow the broth to cool down. Remove the surface fat and discard. Cut the meat into chunks, discarding the bones, gristle, and fat, and return to the broth. Bring it to a boil, add the carrots, turnips, sweet potatoes, and chickpeas, and cook for 30 minutes.

5. Meanwhile, prepare the couscous as directed in steps 1 through 5 on pages 202–203. (The dish can be prepared in advance up to this point.)

6. Thirty minutes before serving, cook the pumpkin with the raisins in a separate pan, in the lamb broth–flavored water until the pumpkin is tender.

7. Rake and steam the couscous for the third time.

8. Add the zucchini and cabbage to the lamb broth, bring back to a boil, and cook until tender. Strain the broth into a saucepan and correct the seasoning. Boil down to about 8 cups. Keep the meat and vegetables warm and moist.

9. Dump the couscous onto a serving platter and toss with the remaining butter and the *smen* or *oudi*, if using. Use a fork to smooth out any lumps. Moisten the couscous by gradually adding up to 1⅓ cups of the cooking liquid for instant couscous and up to 1⅔ cups for hand-rolled. (You may not need all the broth.) Toss the grains again, then let stand for 10 minutes.

10. Spread out the couscous and form a large well in the center. With a slotted spoon, transfer the meat and vegetables to the well. Decorate with the drained raisins and pumpkin slices. Serve with the remaining broth and the red pepper sauce on the side.

Variation:

COUSCOUS WITH SEVEN VEGETABLES IN THE MARRAKECH MANNER *(see page 208 for photo)*

This version is similar to the couscous above, but chickpeas and chicken are usually omitted and any number (up to seven, for good luck) of the following vegetables are used: onions, fava beans, tomatoes, sweet potatoes, pumpkin, turnips, carrots, zucchini, sweet and hot peppers, and cabbage.

Variation:

MOUNTAIN-STYLE COUSCOUS WITH MEAT CONFIT AND SEVEN VEGETABLES

This is a hearty dish, appropriate for winter. Replace the chicken and lamb with 1 pound lamb neck and 1 pound crushed and shredded "Express" Meat Confit (page 44). Replace a portion of the butter with 3 to 4 tablespoons of the meat confit drippings, 30 minutes before serving.

Variation:

COUSCOUS WITH LAMB'S HEAD AND SEVEN VEGETABLES

In Fes, this popular couscous, said to make the diner strong and smart, is usually served on Fridays. Substitute 2 lambs' heads (soaked in water, halved, well cleaned, and tied together) for the chicken and lamb. Lamb's tongue is meaty and lamb brains are delicate and sweet. As for the eyes (everything but the pupils), they are considered the best part and are plucked and handed to the guest of honor! *Chacun à son gout!*

RED PEPPER SAUCE

Makes 1 cup

1 cup lamb or chicken broth

1 teaspoon harissa paste or more to taste

1 tablespoon fresh lemon juice

1 to 2 tablespoons olive oil

A few pinches of ground cumin, preferably Moroccan, to taste

Sprinkling of chopped flat-leaf parsley and cilantro

Combine all the ingredients in a small saucepan over high heat. Cook 2 to 3 minutes, mix well, and pour into a small serving bowl.

ECLECTIC COUSCOUS

NOTES TO THE COOK

Fatema Hal, one of Morocco's most famous food writers, has written an entire book on the subject of Moroccan couscous. When we met in Marrakech, she told me, "In the nation of couscous, onion is king."

Though not all great recipes for couscous employ an onion garnish, many do—not surprising, since there is a stunning affinity between couscous and onions, an affinity that shows itself in regional couscous recipes from every part of the country. One of the most famous of these garnishes, credited to the period of the Andaluz, is a rich unctuous blend of caramelized onions, raisins, and chickpeas placed over, under, or in the center of a huge plate of couscous.

In this recipe, I pay homage to this extraordinary onion garnish, as well as to the concept of using whatever vegetables are in season. And to make the dish even more eclectic, I've added a hot red pepper sauce, which anchors both ideas. The result: a vegetable couscous with lamb, raisins, onions, and almonds, sweet, savory, and spicy all at the same time.

½ cup dried chickpeas

12 medium yellow onions

Coarse salt and freshly ground black pepper

2 tablespoons saffron water (see page 48)

¼ teaspoon ground turmeric

2 teaspoons ground Ceylon cinnamon, plus more for dusting

½ pound (2 sticks) unsalted butter

1½ to 2 pounds lamb neck or shoulder, cut into 2-inch chunks

4 cups hand-rolled couscous or 1½ pounds or instant couscous

½ cup dark raisins

½ teaspoon ground ginger

¼ cup sugar

5 carrots, scraped, halved lengthwise, and cut into 2-inch lengths

4 red-ripe tomatoes, peeled, halved, seeded, and chopped

4 to 5 flat-leaf parsley sprigs and 2 to 3 cilantro sprigs, tied together

4 small zucchini, trimmed, halved lengthwise, and cut into 2-inch lengths

3 tablespoons extra virgin olive oil

1 cup blanched whole almonds

Red Pepper Sauce (page 211)

1. One day in advance: Soak the chickpeas in water to cover generously.

2. The following day, drain the chickpeas and peel as directed on page 51. Cook the chickpeas in boiling water for 20 minutes; drain and set aside.

3. To prepare the broth: Quarter and slice 3 of the onions and place in a large casserole. Add 1 tablespoon salt, 1 teaspoon pepper, half the saffron water, half the turmeric, ½ teaspoon of the cinnamon, and 4 tablespoons of the butter. Swirl the casserole once or twice to let the contents mix gently, cover, and cook over medium heat to soften the onions, about 10 minutes. Uncover and cook, stirring, until the onions turn golden. Add the lamb and lightly brown on all sides. Add 3 quarts water and bring to a boil, then cover, reduce the heat, and simmer for 2 hours.

4. Meanwhile, cut the remaining onions into ¼-inch-thick "quarter-moons." Cook in boiling water to cover for a few minutes, and drain.

5. Prepare the couscous as directed in steps 1 through 5 on pages 202–203.

6. Meanwhile, begin the preparation of the glazed topping: After the lamb has been cooking for 1 hour, transfer 2 cups of the simmering

broth to a saucepan. Add the raisins, along with the drained onion quarter-moons, the remaining saffron water, turmeric, and $1\frac{1}{2}$ teaspoons cinnamon, the ground ginger, sugar, 3 tablespoons of the butter, and salt and pepper to taste. Cook, covered, for 1 hour.

7. Remove the lid and continue cooking the onions until the liquid has evaporated and the onions have a glazed appearance, about 30 minutes. Set aside uncovered.

8. While the glazed topping mixture is cooking, add the carrots, tomatoes, chickpeas, herb sprigs and, if necessary, more water to the broth and continue cooking for 30 minutes. (The dish can be prepared in advance up to this point.)

9. Thirty minutes before serving, steam, rake, and butter the couscous as directed in step 6 on page 203, using the remaining 9 tablespoons butter. And the scented butter, if using.

10. Meanwhile, skim the fat off the surface of the lamb broth and heat the broth. Add the zucchini and cook until tender. Strain the broth and reserve the broth and vegetables separately. Let the meat cool down, then cut it into small pieces, discarding the bones, fat, and gristle, and return to the hot broth to keep moist.

11. Reheat the glazed onions and raisins, and correct the seasoning with salt and pepper.

12. Heat the oil in the skillet and fry the almonds until golden brown. Drain and set aside.

13. Correct the seasoning of the broth, and moisten the couscous by gradually adding up to $1\frac{1}{3}$ cups of the broth for instant couscous and up to $1\frac{2}{3}$ cups for hand-rolled. (You may not need all the broth.) Toss the grains, then let stand for 10 minutes.

14. Shape the couscous into a mound. Make a well in the center and fill with some of the lamb and vegetables. Top with the glazed onions and raisins and dust with ground cinnamon. Decorate with the almonds. Serve with the extra lamb and vegetables in an accompanying tureen, the remaining broth in a bowl, and the red pepper sauce in a small bowl on the side.

BERBER COUSCOUS
FOR SPRING

Serves 8 as a main dish

JAMES BEARD AND ME

Back in the late seventies, the great American food writer James Beard came to my home in New York to interview me for an article he was writing about Moroccan couscous. Excited about Mr. Beard's impending visit, I wanted very much to present him with a new and exciting couscous dish I hadn't yet published.

I called an old friend, the wife of Moroccan ambassador Abselam Jaidi, for advice. She told me that on a recent trip back to Morocco, she and Abselam had eaten one of the most delicious couscous dishes of their lives. She had no idea how it was made, but she promised to try and find out. Days passed. No word came from Mrs. Jaidi. Perhaps she'd forgotten or had been unable to unearth the secret.

Since it was late spring, I decided to make a slightly new version of the Berber couscous in my book. Then, the night before Mr. Beard's visit, Mrs. Jaidi called. She had the secret: milk! All I had to do, she said, was toss the couscous with milk instead of water after the first steaming, and the couscous flavor would come alive.

I knew Berbers sometimes added rich, creamy milk to their couscous sauce, but I was worried that moistening the couscous with milk would reduce its fluffiness. So I decided to make my Berber couscous in two batches: the first, the traditional way; the second using the "secret."

I couldn't get over the difference, and neither could Mr. Beard. We agreed that the addition of milk really made the couscous "sing."

4 cups hand-rolled couscous or 1½ pounds instant couscous

6 tablespoons unsalted butter

1½ cups milk

1 large yellow onion, halved and thinly sliced

8 sprigs each flat-leaf parsley and cilantro, tied together

1 cinnamon stick

Coarse salt and freshly ground black pepper

1 tablespoon saffron water (see page 48)

8 to 10 chicken thighs

1½ tablespoon Smen or Oudi (optional; pages 159 or 161)

8 to 10 white pearl onions

1 pound very small white turnips or very fresh radishes, scrubbed and trimmed

¼ cup golden raisins

1½ pounds small zucchini, trimmed and halved lengthwise

2 cups double-peeled fresh fava beans (see page 80)

2 large red-ripe tomatoes, halved, seeded, and grated

1 green or red chile pepper, stemmed and seeded (optional)

1 cup heavy cream

Vegetable oil for sauteeing the chicken

1. Prepare the couscous as directed in steps 1 through 5 on pages 202–203; use 4 tablespoons of the butter in step 3, and substitute the 1½ cups milk for the water in step 4.

2. Meanwhile, prepare the broth: Put 2 tablespoons of the butter, the onion, herbs, cinnamon stick, 1½ teaspoons salt, 1½ teaspoons pepper, and the saffron water in a large casserole. Swirl the casserole once or twice so the contents gently mix, cover, and cook over medium heat to soften the onion, about 5 minutes. Uncover and cook, stirring, until the onion turns golden. Add 6 cups water and bring to a boil, then slide in the chicken thighs, cover, reduce the heat to low, and cook for 45 minutes.

3. Carefully transfer the chicken to a work surface and let cool slightly. Pull out the bones from each thigh and cut away fat and gristle. Season the chicken with salt and pepper, reshape each thigh, and wrap them in foil to keep moist. (The dish can be prepared in advance up to this point. Cool, cover, and set aside the broth.)

4. Thirty minutes before serving, rake, steam, and butter the couscous as described in step 6 on page 203; if using the scented butter, now is the time to add it.

5. Meanwhile, skim the broth and bring to a boil. Add the baby onions, turnips or radishes, and raisins and cook, partially covered, for 20 minutes. Add the zucchini and continue cooking until tender.

214 ❧ THE FOOD OF MOROCCO

Add the favas, tomatoes, chile pepper, if using, and cream, bring to a boil, and continue cooking until all the vegetables are very tender. Remove from the heat and correct the seasoning.

6. Separate the cooking liquid from the vegetables. Sauté the chicken in hot oil in a covered skillet until well browned on all sides. At the same time, wrap up the vegetables to keep them warm.

7. Moisten the couscous by gradually adding up to $1\frac{1}{3}$ cups of the cooking liquid for instant and up to $1\frac{2}{3}$ cups for hand-rolled. (You may not need all the liquid.) Toss the grains again, then let stand for 10 minutes.

8. Spread out the couscous and form a well in the center. Put in the drained chicken, top with the vegetables, and serve with the remaining sauce on the side.

BERBER COUSCOUS

This is the kind of couscous you will find in small villages in the foothills of the Middle Atlas Mountains, and it is extraordinary. It is served in spring, when everything that grows is fresh and young and tender, and it has a miraculous clean taste. Everything in it should be as fresh as possible, except, of course, the *smen*, which, ideally, should be about a year old. But I think a month-old clarified butter made with oregano water (*oudi*, page 161) makes an excellent substitution.

— Serves 8 as a main dish —

- 4 cups hand-rolled couscous or 1½ pounds instant couscous
- 1 small chicken, preferably organic and air-chilled
- 8 tablespoons (1 stick) unsalted butter
- 2 teaspoons coarse salt
- 2 teaspoons freshly ground black pepper
- ¼ teaspoon ground turmeric
- 2 tablespoon saffron water (see page 48)
- 2 large red-ripe tomatoes, halved, seeded, and grated, peel discarded
- 8 sprigs each flat-leaf parsley and cilantro, tied together
- 1 large yellow onion, quartered
- 1 cinnamon stick
- 8 white baby onions, peeled
- 1 pound small, tender white turnips, cut in half
- 1½ pounds small zucchini, trimmed and quartered lengthwise
- 2 cups baby peas, peeled fava beans, or lima beans
- 1 green or red chile pepper (optional)
- 2 to 3 tablespoons Smen or Oudi (page 159 or 161) or 3 tablespoons clarified butter
- 2 cups half-and-half or fresh, creamy milk

1. Prepare the couscous as directed in steps 1 through 5 on pages 202–203.

2. Meanwhile, prepare the broth: Wash the chicken and trim off all excess fat. Melt the butter in a deep casserole over low heat. Add the salt, pepper, turmeric, saffron water, half the grated tomatoes, the herbs, yellow onion, and cinnamon stick. Take the casserole in your hands and give it a good swirl to mix the ingredients. Add the chicken, cover, and cook gently for 15 minutes.

3. Add 4 cups water, cover, and simmer for 30 minutes.

4. Add the white onions and turnips to the simmering broth and cook for 15 minutes, adding more water if necessary. (The dish can be prepared in advance up to this point.)

5. Thirty minutes before serving, rake and steam the couscous for a third time as directed in step 6 on page 203.

6. Meanwhile, add the remaining grated tomato, the zucchini, peas, and optional chile pepper to the broth and bring to a boil, then lower the heat and simmer for 20 minutes.

7. Dump the couscous out onto a large serving dish and mix in the *smen* or clarified butter with your fingertips, working it in gently. Smooth out any lumps with a fork. Make a well in the center and place the chicken in the well. Cover with the vegetables.

8. Meanwhile, add the half-and-half or milk to the broth and bring to a boil. Strain the broth and gradually add about 1½ cups to moisten the couscous. The remaining broth can be served in small cups for additional moistening of individual portions, or as a soup. Serve at once.

Variation:
BERBER COUSCOUS WITH CRACKED BARLEY

If you want to make a couscous unlike any other, try this. It is precisely the same as the Berber couscous in the recipe above, except that instead of semolina, it is made with cracked barley. The flavor is nutty, rustic, and extraordinarily good.

The first time I tasted this couscous, it was served on a wooden tray. The vegetables looked very bright piled over the pearl-colored grains, and there was one vegetable that was uncut, a fourteen-inch-long pale green, long-cooked, bottleneck gourd called a *slaoui*, placed on top.

Below you will find instructions on the steaming and handling of cracked or Scotch barley (available in organic and health food stores). The grain is different in texture from semolina and requires three covered steamings. If you like this dish, you can substitute cracked barley for semolina in any of my couscous recipes, using this recipe as a guide. The most important thing to remember is that water must be added to this kind of grain very slowly, as described in step 4.

Substitute 4 cups cracked barley (1½ pounds) for the couscous in the recipe above.

1. Prepare the broth and vegetables as in steps 2 through 4 on page 217.

2. Meanwhile, wash the cracked barley grains in a large shallow pan by pouring 6 cups water over them, stirring, and then draining off the water. Let stand for 30 minutes.

3. Butter the inside of the upper container of the couscousier. Squeeze the cracked barley to extract excess water and slowly add the barley grains to the top container by rubbing them between your palms as you drop them in. Before sealing the top container with foil

or silicone wrap (see Sources), make sure there is plenty of liquid in the bottom of the pot. Steam the grains for 20 minutes.

4. Dump the barley out into the roasting pan and break up the lumps with the fork. Add 1 tablespoon butter. Slowly add 2 cups water while raking and working the grains to help them swell and separate; it should take about 3 minutes to add the water. Do not let the grains become soggy. Rake and toss them, then smooth them out and let dry for at least 10 minutes.

5. Steam the barley again for 20 minutes.

6. Dump the barley out into a large roasting pan and break up the lumps. Allow to stand at least 5 minutes, then work the grits from time to time to keep them from becoming lumpy. Do not add water.

7. Thirty minutes before serving, add the vegetables as in step 6 of the previous recipe. Cook until tender. Meanwhile, steam the cracked barley for 10 more minutes.

8. To serve, dump the cracked barley into the serving dish. Add the *smen* or clarified butter and work it in lightly. Form a mound and then make a well, in it. With a slotted spoon, transfer the vegetables and chicken to the well. Taste the sauce after adding the half-and-half or milk and readjust the seasoning. Strain the hot, creamy broth over the cracked barley and vegetables to moisten well. Serve at once.

MANY KINDS AND TYPES OF BARLEY USED TO MAKE COUSCOUS

Barley is grown in great quantity in Morocco and is used in many forms to make couscous.

Barley for couscous comes in two sizes: a large grind that is similar to cracked or Scotch barley and a small grind that is sold as barley grits. Both are usually available at well-stocked health food stores. (If your local health food store doesn't stock either, pulse hulled barley to either a fine or a coarse grind in a spice mill or an electric blender, not a food processor). Large or cracked barley is used to make hearty, festive couscous dishes such as the Berber Couscous on page 218. The smaller barley grits are used to make a fava bean couscous (see page 224) and a beef and leafy greens couscous (see page 222).

For me, the most interesting barley couscous is one in which immature barley grains are transformed into the Moroccan version of Middle Eastern *fireek*, or green wheat. The immature barley is steamed, dried, slowly toasted on earthenware plates over embers, and then cracked by hand. The largest pieces are used to make a special couscous called *azenbu*, available only in the Rif Mountains and the Souss, that is regarded by some connoisseurs as one of the most delicious of all couscous presentations. Admired for its purity and utter simplicity, it is the ultimate country dish. The barley is toasted in a pan with oregano, then cracked and sifted. The smaller grains are used in a soup and the larger grains are steamed over boiling water, placed on a platter, buttered, and served with bowls of cold milk or buttermilk in the Berber style.

In the province of Zagora, they roll an unusual couscous fondly called "big couscous accompanied by its little brother." Cracked barley grain rather than coarse semolina is used as a "magnet" for fine semolina flour. The two grains are then rolled together, creating a fascinating two-tone couscous, combining the deep full taste of semolina with the nutty warm flavor of barley. Though I have never tasted the particular sauce that accompanies this couscous, it was described to me as being made with camel head meat garnished with pumpkin, turnips, dried fava beans, and carrots and flavored with dried onion, coriander seeds, dried rosemary, cumin, and bay leaves.

HANDLING AND STEAMING
BARLEY GRITS FOR COUSCOUS

These directions are for both barley grits and commercial barley couscous (Dari brand). You can substitute either for semolina couscous in any of the recipes in this book.

STEP 1: Prepare the couscous steamer as described on page 199.

STEP 2: Meanwhile, dampen the barley grits with one-third of its volume of cool water. Allow to swell for 10 minutes.

STEP 3: When the steam is coming through the perforated holes, immediately rake the barley, pile into the couscous pot lined with cheesecloth, and steam, uncovered, for 10 minutes.

STEP 4: Dump the barley grits out into a large pan and break up the lumps with a fork. Add 1 tablespoon butter or olive oil. Slowly add ¾ cup salted water while raking and working the grains to help them swell and separate; it should take about 3 minutes to add the water. Do not allow the barley grits to become soggy. Smooth them out and let dry for at least 5 minutes.

STEP 5: Pile the barley grits back into the steamer, and steam, uncovered, for 10 more minutes.

STEP 6: Dump the grits back into the pan and again break up the lumps. Allow to stand for 15 minutes, working the grits from time to time to keep them separate and prevent them from becoming lumpy; do not add water. The barley grits can be prepared in advance up to this point. Cover with a cloth and let stand until 30 minutes before serving.

STEP 7: Steam the barley grits for 10 minutes. Dump into the serving dish. Add *smen* or *oudi* or clarified butter and work it in lightly. Form a mound and then a well, and fill the well with meat and vegetables. Strain some of the sauce over the barley grits to moisten. Let stand for 10 minutes, then serve.

BARLEY GRITS COUSCOUS WITH BEEF AND LEAFY GREENS

NOTES TO THE COOK

The green in question, which bears the charming name *zegzaw*, is a type of perennial kale with a soft texture and a slightly astringent flavor. If you can't find this type of kale, you can use broccoli rabe, as I do. Either one steamed keeps its green color even as its strong and unique flavor mellows.

Since you'll be using your steamer to prepare the barley, I suggest steaming your green of choice using a popular method called *étouffée*, or "smothering"—cooking the greens in their own moisture in a tightly covered pot. I fill a straight-sided skillet with the greens, herbs, a pinch of cumin, and some tomatoes, then push all the ingredients down with a weighted plate. The result is a reduction to one-third the original volume as the greens acquire a delicious, soft, piquant, yet wild flavor.

This version of a popular Berber barley couscous comes from an oasis town called Rissani, deep in southern Morocco. It's similar to yet different from one I discovered in Tozeur, an oasis in southwest Tunisia. In the Tunisian version, finely shredded Swiss chard was used to thicken a meat, vegetable, and hot pepper sauce, which was then spread over the steamed grain. In this version, barley is steamed and flavored with a spicy broth enriched with goat's milk and topped with meat, vegetables, and steamed roughly shredded greens.

Serves 6 as part of a Moroccan dinner

½ cup dried chickpeas

1 pound cracked lean beef shanks or short ribs, trimmed of excess fat and cut into 1-inch cubes

1 or 2 bunches young soft leafy Russian kale, or substitute leafy broccoli rabe or broccolini, washed, trimmed, and roughly sliced crosswise

8 ounces small carrots, peeled and halved lengthwise

8 ounces (1) parsnip, peeled and halved lengthwise, or 1 turnip, peeled and halved lengthwise

Coarse salt

3 tablespoons extra virgin olive oil

1 cup diced red onion

1 tablespoon ground ginger

1 teaspoon ground turmeric

½ teaspoon toasted and ground cumin, preferably Moroccan

½ teaspoon freshly ground black pepper, plus more to taste

1 pound tomatoes, halved, peeled, seeded, and cubed

1 pound barley grits or barley couscous (see Sources)

¼ cup chopped cilantro

¼ cup chopped flat-leaf parsley

2 cups milk, preferably goat's milk

2 teaspoons Smen, Oudi (page 159 or 161), or clarified butter

1. The day before: Soak the chickpeas in water to cover generously.

2. The next day: Drain the chickpeas and place in a 5-quart heavy casserole. Add the beef, one-third of the greens, the carrots, and parsnips or turnips, cover, and cook over medium heat without browning, 10 minutes. Add 1 teaspoon salt, 2 tablespoons of the oil, the onion, spices, and half the tomatoes and cook, stirring, for 15 minutes.

3. Add 6 cups water and bring to a boil, then cover and cook over medium-low heat until the meat and chickpeas are tender, 2½ to 3 hours.

4. Meanwhile, steam the barley grits or barley couscous 3 times as directed on page 221.

5. While the barley cooks, brush the remaining tablespoon of olive oil on the bottom of a heavy-bottomed 10-inch straight-sided skillet or cazuela. Spread half the remaining greens in the pan. Spread the herbs on top and cover with the remaining greens. Cover with a paper towel and a heavy plate or a lid that fits inside the pan to weight everything down. Set over low heat and cook for 30 minutes. Uncover, add the remaining tomatoes, and cook uncovered, stirring, until most of the moisture has evaporated, about 10 minutes. Season with salt and pepper. Set aside.

6. Skim the meat and vegetable broth and adjust the seasoning with salt and pepper. Transfer the broth to a saucepan, add the milk, and boil down to reduce by half. Stir in the *smen* or *oudi* or clarified butter, then pick out the meat and remove and discard all the bones and hard fat.

7. Moisten the barley couscous with about 1½ cups of the broth. Use a long whisk to smooth out any lumps. Arrange the meat, vegetables, and greens on top of the couscous. Let stand for 10 minutes, then serve at once, with a bowl of the remaining broth on the side.

BARLEY GRITS COUSCOUS WITH FRESH FAVA BEANS

NOTE TO THE COOK

Some cooks like to sprinkle a little sugar over the barley just before serving.

A long time ago, Mr. Abselam Bennis, president of a gastronomic society in Rabat, gave me this very simple recipe. The dish is very Moroccan, and very elegant, and it should be made only in spring, when fava beans are tender and fresh. The combination of bright fava beans with a bed of off-white barley couscous is most attractive and truly delicious.

Present this dish with glasses of iced buttermilk or goat's-milk yogurt blended with water.

— Serves 4 —

2 pounds fresh fava beans

1 pound barley grits or barley couscous (see Sources)

2 scallions, trimmed and thinly sliced crosswise on the bias

Salt and freshly ground black pepper

1 tablespoon extra virgin olive oil

8 tablespoons (1 stick) unsalted butter

1. Steam the fava beans in their pods until tender, 5 to 8 minutes, depending upon their age. Cool under running water. Peel off both the pod and the outer skin of each bean, dropping the beans into a small wide saucepan as you work.

2. Steam the barley 3 times as directed on page 221.

3. Meanwhile, add the scallions, salt and pepper to taste, and a small quantity of water to the fava beans and cook until tender. Drain and toss with the freshly steamed barley couscous and the extra virgin olive oil and butter.

LARGE-GRAIN COUSCOUS (MHAMSA)

A hand-rolled semolina couscous called *mhamsa*, which is twice the size of the regular packaged grain, is available by mail-order from www.mustaphas.com and www.zingermans.com. *Mhamsa* is extremely popular in the mountainous parts of Morocco, particularly in the Souss area, where it is prepared as a holiday dish with chicken, onions, chickpeas, and raisins. Commercial Israeli couscous can be substituted.

In the Rif Mountains, it's more often served with *khlii* (preserved meat), or with meat confit (see page 44). Sometimes it is steamed, and other times it is cooked like a pasta and served in a soup. See page 184 for a wonderful version from the Rif made with meat confit, aged goat cheese, and spices. Perfect winter food!

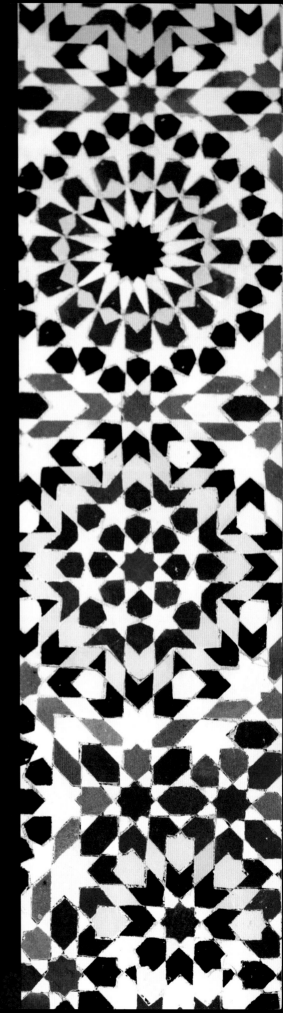

FINE-GRAIN COUSCOUS WITH CHICKEN OR LAMB

Seffa is an extremely fine couscous grain of great delicacy, which is steamed and used for desserts or in place of an ordinary couscous when you want to "upgrade" your couscous dinner. It is available at some Middle Eastern grocers (see Sources).

Seffa is made by moistening 1 pound rough-grained semolina flour and a pinch of salt with 2 tablespoons saffron water. The semolina is rubbed into tiny pellets and pressed through a fine sieve. It is steamed for 20 minutes, loosely covered with a kitchen cloth, then poured into a large shallow pan and "worked" with ½ cup saffron water added very slowly by handfuls. A final sieving through a fine colander or coarse-mesh sieve prepares the grain for a second steaming just before serving. Homemade *seffa*, as opposed to commercial varieties, must be steamed twice.

Serves 10 as part of a Moroccan dinner

1½ pounds chicken thighs, or lean lamb, or chicken giblets, wings, and necks

Salt

½ teaspoon freshly ground black pepper

½ teaspoon ground ginger

¼ teaspoon ground turmeric

2 tablespoons saffron water (see page 48)

¾ cup grated onion

Three 2-inch cinnamon sticks

8 tablespoons (1 stick) unsalted butter

3 cups hot chicken stock

2 pounds store-brought fine-grain couscous or homemade *seffa*

Confectioners' sugar

Ground Ceylon cinnamon

1. Cut the poultry or lamb into 1-inch pieces, discarding the skin, bones, excess fat, and gristle. Place in a heavy-bottomed casserole with salt to taste, the pepper, ginger, turmeric, saffron water, grated onion, cinnamon sticks, and 3 tablespoons of the butter, and cook gently, covered, for 5 minutes. Add the hot chicken stock and bring to a boil, cover, reduce the heat, and simmer for 45 minutes.

2. Meanwhile, steam the *seffa*. If using homemade *seffa*, dampen the grain very lightly with salted water. If using prepared couscous, wash and dry it as directed for handling regular couscous on pages 202–203. Steam the *seffa* for 20 minutes, covered loosely with a kitchen cloth.

3. Dump the *seffa* into a large, shallow pan. Sprinkle with 1 cup water, ¼ cup at a time, and rake the grain for the greatest absorption before adding more water. Add 2 tablespoons of the butter and toss well. Return to the steamer, reseal, and steam again for 20 minutes.

4. If using homemade *seffa*, proceed to the next step. If using prepared couscous, dump it out and work it again, adding more water as necessary, but avoid making the couscous soggy. Dry for 10 minutes,

rake the grains, then return to the steamer and steam again for
20 minutes.

5. Remove the poultry or lamb from the broth and keep warm. Boil
rapidly, uncovered, to reduce the broth to ¾ cup. Discard the cinnamon
sticks.

6. To serve, dump half of the *seffa* onto a large serving dish. Dot with
half of the remaining 3 tablespoons butter, add ¼ cup of the sauce,
and then toss. Spread out evenly and arrange the pieces of poultry
or lamb on top in one layer. Spoon over another ¼ cup broth. Toss
the remaining butter and sauce with the remaining *seffa* and spread
over the poultry or meat. Making sure no meat is visible, form it into
a hemisphere, then sprinkle with a little confectioners' sugar and
decorate with lines of cinnamon. Serve with a bowl of confectioners'
sugar on the side.

STEAMED NOODLE COUSCOUS (CHAARIYA MEFTOUN)

Chaariya are inch-long noodles formed between the thumb and forefinger from pellets of semolina dough. Moroccans steam them two or three times and toss them with cold water between each steaming, so the noodles stay separate and soft. They are used in this recipe and in soups and various other dishes, where they are treated precisely the same as couscous grains.

I substitute broken pieces of vermicelli or capellini. Some food writers will instruct you to boil the noodles. Please don't do it! Boiling will make the *chaariya* too pasta-like. Steaming, on the other hand, keeps them light and silky.

The word *meftoun* in a recipe name means "a surprise" or something hidden. In this dish, the surprise is spicy bits of lamb, pigeon, chicken, or giblets, cooked in a rich sauce with spices and onions, then hidden beneath a layer of the steamed noodles. The whole is garnished with a sprinkling of ground toasted almonds, cinnamon, and confectioners' sugar.

It sounds sweet, but the sugar nicely balances the spicy sauce.

———— ❧ Serves 8 as a main dish ❧ ————

3 meaty lamb shanks (about 3 pounds), each cracked into 3 pieces

3 large red onions (about 2 pounds), halved and sliced ½ inch thick

8 tablespoons (1 stick) unsalted butter

1 tablespoon ground ginger

1½ teaspoons ground turmeric

1½ teaspoons freshly ground black pepper, plus more to taste

½ teaspoon finely ground cubeb pepper (optional)

Two 2-inch cinnamon sticks

12 cilantro sprigs, tied together

Coarse salt

3 tablespoons saffron water (see page 48)

3 teaspoons extra virgin olive oil

1½ pounds vermicelli or capellini

½ cup golden raisins, soaked in water for 15 minutes and drained

⅓ cup confectioners' sugar

1½ teaspoons ground Ceylon cinnamon

¾ cup blanched almonds, toasted and coarsely chopped

1. Place the lamb, onions, 3 tablespoons of the butter, the ginger, turmeric, black pepper, cubeb pepper, if using, cinnamon sticks, cilantro, and 2 teaspoons salt in a large heavy casserole. Heat over low heat, swirling the pan once or twice to let the contents gently mix. Add the saffron water and 2 cups water and bring to a boil, then cover with a sheet of parchment paper and a lid and cook at a slow simmer for 1 hour.

2. Uncover the casserole, lift out the lamb, and set aside. Use a slotted spoon to transfer the onions and cinnamon sticks to an ovenproof skillet. Add ½ cup of the cooking juices and 2 tablespoons of the

butter to the onions and cook slowly until the liquid has evaporated and the onions begin to turn golden, about 1 hour. Remove from the heat; when the onions are cool, pat away congealed fat.

3. Meanwhile, return the lamb to the casserole, cover, and cook for another hour, or until the meat is tender and pulls easily away from the bones.

4. Transfer the lamb to a work surface and cut it into 1-inch chunks, discarding the skin, bones, excess fat, and gristle. Carefully skim the cooking juices in the casserole, discard the cilantro, and season lightly with salt and pepper.

5. Add the lamb and cooking juices to the onions in the skillet. (The dish can be prepared 1 day in advance to this point, covered, and refrigerated. Bring to room temperature before continuing.)

6. About 1 hour before serving, add 1 cup water to the lamb and onions, set the pan in a cold oven, and turn the heat to 350°F. Bake, uncovered, until you are ready to assemble the dish.

7. Meanwhile, prepare for steaming couscous as directed on page 199. Use 1 teaspoon of the olive oil to grease the colander.

8. Break the noodles into 1-inch pieces in a wide shallow bowl. Toss the noodles with the remaining 2 teaspoons olive oil, scrape into the steamer, cover, and steam for 20 minutes.

9. Dump the noodles into a large pan. Gradually sprinkle with $1/2$ cup heavily salted cool water, then use a pair of tongs to aerate the noodles. Return them to the steamer, add the drained raisins, cover, and steam for 20 minutes more.

10. Lift up the colander, scrape the noodles and raisins into the simmering water, and cook for 2 minutes, or until tender. Immediately drain the noodles in the colander and shake to remove all moisture. Toss the noodles with the remaining 3 tablespoons butter and 1 to 2 pinches of salt.

11. Spread out about one-quarter of the noodles in a large serving bowl. Remove the lamb, sauce, and onions from the oven, season with salt and pepper, and spread on top of the noodles. Cover with the remaining noodles, creating a dome. Make a well in the center and place about 3 tablespoons confectioners' sugar inside the well. Combine the remaining confectioners' sugar, the cinnamon, and almonds in a small bowl and use to decorate the noodles. Serve at once.

HANDLING AND STEAMING STONE-GROUND CORN GRITS FOR COUSCOUS

Corn couscous is popular in the southern Souss region, where, in summer, it is often served with shellfish and baby turnips, and in the mountains, where it is a winter staple with meat confit (see page 44) and vegetables.

Coarse stone-ground corn grits are available in most groceries or by mail-order (see Sources). The steps for handling and cooking them are a bit different from those for semolina couscous, but not at all difficult. The steaming takes much longer and the steamer must be covered with a tight-fitting lid. You end up with a very light airy mound of grain that will remind you of the taste of polenta.

Corn couscous doesn't expand as much as semolina couscous. After three steamings, a 1½-pound bag of grits will yield about 12 cups of a sublime corn-flavored couscous in a stunning shade of yellow.

Vegetable oil for greasing the container

1½ pounds coarse corn grits, preferably stone-ground

3 tablespoons argan oil (see Sources), butter, or extra virgin olive oil

Salt and freshly ground black or white pepper

STEP 1: Up to 3 hours before serving, bring plenty of water to a boil in the bottom of a deep pot or couscousier. Lightly grease the inside of the steamer insert with vegetable oil and place on top of the pot. See the directions on page 50 for sealing the two parts.

STEP 2: Moisten the grains with ½ cup water and rub and toss until well absorbed, then add another ½ cup water and allow to stand for about 10 minutes. Gradually add another ½ cup water and spread out the grains to stand for 5 more minutes. Sprinkle with argan oil and rub the grains between your palms for an even coating. Pile the corn into the steamer, cover, and steam for 45 minutes.

STEP 3: Dump the steamed grits into a large pan. Using a long wire whisk, toss and break up any lumps while you moisten the grits with 1 cup lukewarm water. Allow to stand for 5 minutes, toss with another 1 cup water, sprinkle with salt and pepper, and allow to rest for 10 more minutes. Moisten a third time with 1 cup water, then return the grits to the steamer, cover, and steam for 45 additional minutes.

STEP 4: Return the grits to the large pan. Repeat step 3, tossing and breaking up any lumps as above. Toss with a little argan oil, butter, or olive oil. At this point, you can cover the couscous with a damp kitchen cloth. Covered, it will hold well for a few hours.

STEP 5: About 30 minutes before serving, bring the water in the pot back to a boil. Pile the corn grits back into the steamer, cover, and steam for 20 minutes. The grits should be perfectly tender. Dump the corn grits into a wide serving dish and toss with the remaining argan oil, butter, or olive oil. Add the broth and garnish as directed in the recipe.

STONE-GROUND CORN GRITS COUSCOUS WITH SHELLFISH, CARAMELIZED ONIONS, AND GLAZED TURNIPS

This shellfish couscous, a specialty of the southern coastal city of Essaouira, consists of a mound of golden corn couscous in the center of a huge platter surrounded with distinct piles of garnishes, including luscious, raisin-rich caramelized onions, tender and sweet-fleshed charmoula-soaked shrimps, fast-cooked opened mussels still in their shells, and baby glazed turnips tangled up with their leafy greens.

—— ✤ Serves 8 as a main course ✤ ——

✤

NOTE TO THE COOK

The squid stock, shrimp, caramelized onions, and red pepper sauce should all be prepared 1 day in advance.

SQUID STOCK

1 large yellow onion, roughly chopped (2 cups)

Coarse sea salt

2 tablespoons extra virgin olive oil

1 pound cleaned baby squid (fresh or thawed frozen), cut into bite-sized pieces, rinsed, and drained

2 garlic cloves, peeled and crushed

1 teaspoon ground ginger

1 teaspoon sweet paprika

½ teaspoon freshly ground black pepper

2 pinches cayenne

3 tablespoons saffron water (see page 48) or 2 pinches saffron threads

1 tablespoon Tomato Magic (page 41) or tomato paste

2 cups canned or fresh tomatoes, peeled, seeded, and diced

6 or 7 sprigs each flat-leaf parsley and cilantro, tied together

½ preserved lemon (see page 21), pulp removed and rinsed

SHRIMP WITH CHARMOULA SAUCE

3 garlic cloves, crushed to a paste

2 teaspoons ground cumin seed

2 teaspoons sweet paprika

¼ teaspoon cayenne

2 tablespoons chopped flat-leaf parsley

¼ cup chopped cilantro

2 tablespoons extra virgin olive oil

Salt and freshly ground black pepper

32 to 36 (about 2 pounds) jumbo peeled shrimp

CARAMELIZED ONIONS

2 tablespoons extra virgin olive oil

1 pound large white onions, peeled, halved, and thinly sliced

Coarse sea salt

2 tablespoons saffron water (see page 48)

¼ teaspoon ground ginger

Pinch of freshly ground black
pepper

1 cup golden raisins

1 cup squid stock (see above)

RED PEPPER SAUCE

1 cup squid stock

1 teaspoon harissa or Turkish hot
red pepper paste

1 tablespoon fresh lemon juice

1 to 2 tablespoons extra virgin
olive oil

Ground cumin, preferably
Moroccan

Sea salt

Freshly chopped flat-leaf parsley
and cilantro for garnish

COUSCOUS, TURNIPS, AND MUSSELS

1½ pounds stone-ground corn grits

5 bunches (about 24) baby white
turnips with leafy turnip greens

Salt and freshly ground black
pepper

3 tablespoons olive oil

2 tablespoons sugar

2 pounds fresh mussels, scrubbed
and debearded

Argan oil or extra virgin olive oil
for the corn grits (optional)

3 tablespoons butter

2 tablespoons chopped cilantro

Red pepper sauce

1. The day before, make the squid stock: Combine the onion,
2 teaspoons salt, and the olive oil in a deep saucepan, cover, and
cook slowly for 10 minutes. Uncover and cook until the onions are
lightly caramelized and the oil is sizzling, about 10 minutes.

2. Add the squid to the saucepan, and cook until the water it gives
off evaporates. Continue cooking until the pieces begin to turn golden,
about 10 minutes. Stir in the garlic, spices, saffron water, Tomato Magic
or tomato paste, diced tomatoes, herbs, preserved lemon, and 6 cups
water and bring to a boil. Reduce the heat to medium-low, cover, and
simmer for 1 hour. Turn off the heat and let the pot stand, partially
covered, for 1 hour.

3. Strain the stock and return the squid to the stock; discard the
debris. Cool, cover, and refrigerate.

4. To marinate the shrimp: Mix the garlic, spices, herbs, oil, and ½ cup
water. Add salt and pepper to taste. Rub onto the shrimp and allow to
marinate in the refrigerator overnight.

5. To prepare the onions: Heat the olive oil in a large skillet. Add the
onions, ½ teaspoon salt, the saffron water, ginger, pepper, and raisins,

cover, and cook over medium heat for 10 minutes. Add the stock, cover, and cook for 30 minutes more, or until the onions are tender and juicy. Cool, cover, and refrigerate overnight.

6. To prepare the red pepper sauce: Combine the stock, harissa, lemon juice, oil, cumin, and salt to taste and soak overnight.

7. The following day: About 2½ hours before serving, prepare the corn grits as directed in steps 1 through 4 for handling stone-ground corn grits (see page 232).

8. About 45 minutes before serving, bring the water in the deep pot back to a boil. Meanwhile, peel and trim the turnips, reserving the greens. Wash and stem the leaves. Set the steamer in place, add the turnips and leaves, cover, and steam for 15 minutes. Remove to paper towels to drain.

9. Return the grits to the steamer, season with salt and pepper, cover, and steam for 15 to 20 minutes.

10. Meanwhile, heat 2 tablespoons of the olive oil with the sugar in a large skillet. Add the turnips and greens and sauté until glazed. Remove to a side dish.

11. Scrape the marinated shrimp into the skillet, add the remaining tablespoon of oil, raise the heat, and sauté until firm and curled, 2 to 4 minutes. Remove to a side dish.

12. Scrape the caramelized onion and raisins mixture into the skillet and heat until sizzling. Correct the seasoning and move to a side dish.

13. Raise the heat, add the mussels, cover the skillet, and cook until the mussels open; discard those that do not open. Remove to a side dish. Add the remaining squid stock to the skillet and bring to a boil. Remove the pieces of squid and add them to the shrimp. Keep the stock at a low simmer.

14. Heat the red pepper sauce in a small saucepan and garnish with herbs.

15. Dump the grits onto a large serving dish. Add 1 to 2 tablespoons argan oil, if using, and the butter. Use a whisk to break up lumps, then add about 2 cups of the simmering stock and toss well. Shape the corn grits into a mound in the center of the dish. Surround with piles of the mussels, shrimp, squid, turnips and leaves, and caramelized onion mixture. Scatter the cilantro on top, and serve with the remaining warm squid stock and the warm red pepper sauce.

chapter eight

FISH

✤

"The fish in the trap begin to think."

—*berber proverb*

✤

FISH

CHARMOULA
❧ page 243 ❧

BROILED FISH WITH CHARMOULA GLAZE
❧ page 244 ❧

FISH TAGINE WITH TOMATOES, OLIVES,
AND PRESERVED LEMON
❧ page 246 ❧

TAGRA OF FRESH SARDINES WITH
PEPPER OIL CHARMOULA
❧ page 248 ❧

FRIED SARDINES, TANGIER-STYLE
❧ page 251 ❧

FISH TAGINE WITH CREAMY ONION CHARMOULA
❧ page 254 ❧

TAGINE OF BABY CALAMARI WITH
RED PEPPER AND TOMATO
❧ page 257 ❧

SAUTÉED SHRIMP CASA PEPE (PIL PIL)
❧ page 259 ❧

TAGINE WITH FRESH MUSSELS, OLIVES, PEPPERS,
AND ARGAN OIL
❧ page 260 ❧

STEAMED CALAMARI WITH PRESERVED LEMON
AND ARGAN OIL
❧ page 262 ❧

FISH SMOTHERED WITH ONION JAM
❧ page 264 ❧

FISH BAKED WITH ALMOND PASTE
❧ page 265 ❧

GRILLED FISH STUFFED WITH SEAFOOD
❧ page 266 ❧

FISH

Morocco is blessed with an abundance of fish. It is not only surrounded on two sides by the Mediterranean and the Atlantic, each a magnificent fishing ground, but also laced by rivers filled with trout and carp.

Rivers from the Middle Atlas filled with trout and carp flow toward the Atlantic. (Shad has almost disappeared!) The town of Oualidia, situated on a lagoon off the Atlantic coast, just two hours west of Marrakech, has impressed many with the quality, flavor, and texture of its farmed oysters. And all along the Atlantic coast, cities such as El Jadida, Essaouira, and Safi have joined Rabat and Casablanca as places to enjoy spider crabs, shrimp, sea urchins, lobsters, and an incredibly vast array of fresh fish served grilled or in couscous, soups, tagines, and gratins. In Tangier, situated on the northwest corner of Africa, touching both the Atlantic and the Mediterranean, I've often heard locals, speaking of the bounty of available fish and shellfish, recite the proverb "If a man is with God, he can put his arm into the water and by each of its hairs pull up a fish." To which I could have added, "Yes, and if you are speaking of the fish market in Tangier, each of the fish hanging from your hairs will be different."

In that wet, noisy place, I used to find shad and trout from the Middle Atlas, and skate, whiting, red mullet, porgy, Saint Pierres, sardines, eels, anchovies, sea breams, turbots, sole, changuete, crabs, lobsters, angelfish, shrimp, mussels, mackerel, bass, carp, squid, swordfish, tuna, loup, weevers, gurnards, and a variety of clams called *amandes de mer* from the two coasts. And there were many other varieties I couldn't name. One time when living in Tangier, I decided to cook a different fish in a different way each day, alternating between sweet flavorings (cinnamon, ginger, and nutmeg blended with caramelized onions, toasted nuts, or dried fruits) and the savory marinade charmoula, a blend of cumin, sweet and hot paprika, garlic, herbs, lemon juice, and olive oil. I actually continued for three weeks before my family balked and put an end to this admittedly self-indulgent project.

CHARMOULA

The charmoula marinade is quite miraculous. If made without the addition of olive oil, it can be brushed on the insides of an oily fish to great effect. It will also keep oily fish such as sardines fresh a day longer than usual. In the case of shad, the eight hundred or so tiny bones will dissolve after an overnight soak in charmoula. The fish can then be fried the following day in simmering olive oil.

So much charmoula is used along the coast that many home cooks make two or three cups at a time, then store the marinade in the refrigerator for 2 to 3 days, a maturation that makes it taste even better.

A whole fish to be baked gets an overnight charmoula rub. Thick fish steaks receive a charmoula brushing and then are left to marinate for an hour or two before being dusted with semolina and quick-fried. Additional charmoula is served with the fish as a sauce.

Fragile fish fillets such as sole or flounder are simply brushed with charmoula, floured, fried, and served with the sauce. They are not marinated, as this would cause the fish to break down during cooking.

There is no one best recipe for charmoula. In Marrakech, a cook might add some ginger to the spice mix. In Agadir, creamed onions are often added (see page 254); in Tetouan, a little hot red pepper oil; and in Tangier, our housekeeper always added a little thyme.

Makes enough marinade for
3 pounds fish or sauce to serve 4 to 6

2 teaspoons cumin seeds, preferably Moroccan	¼ teaspoon freshly ground white or black pepper
3 garlic cloves	Pinch of cayenne
1 teaspoon coarse sea salt	Juice of 1 lemon (or the rinsed pulp from a preserved lemon; see page 21)
¼ cup finely chopped cilantro	
3 tablespoons finely chopped flat-leaf parsley	2 tablespoons extra virgin olive oil, or more to taste
2 teaspoons sweet paprika, or more to taste	

Combine the cumin, garlic, salt, herbs, and spices in a blender or a mortar and blend or pound until pasty. Add the lemon juice or preserved lemon pulp and olive oil and mix to combine.

NOTE TO THE COOK

To store the sauce for up to a week, scrape the mixture into a small saucepan, add 3 to 4 tablespoons water, and heat slowly, stirring, just until hot and aromatic, about 30 seconds; do not boil. Let cool, then store in a jar in the refrigerator. Bring to room temperature before using.

BROILED FISH WITH CHARMOULA GLAZE

You can cook the fish steaks either whole or cubed for skewering. In either case, save some of the charmoula for a dipping sauce.

⌐◈ Serves 4 ◈⌐

Four 1-inch-thick wild halibut
steaks (or substitute cod fillets)

Charmoula (page 243)

1. Place the fish steaks or skewered cubes on a large flat plate or tray. Brush half of the charmoula over the fish, turning to coat. Cover and refrigerate for up to 2 hours.

2. Set the oven rack about 5 inches from the heat source and preheat the broiler. Cook the steaks or skewered cubes for 3 to 4 minutes on each side. Serve at once, with the remaining charmoula as a sauce.

FISH TAGINES

There is no doubt in my mind that fish cooked in earthenware tastes better than fish cooked in ovenproof glass or enameled cast-iron. (As for tin-lined copperware and aluminum, they will definitely degrade the flavor.) I am very partial to cooking fish in the traditional clay pots of Morocco. Usually wide or oval, these are unglazed and used exclusively for cooking or baking fish, and because they are so attractive, they can be also used as serving dishes.

When Moroccan cooks make fish tagines on the stovetop or in the oven, they almost always first arrange pieces of bamboo (or carrots or celery sticks) in a crisscross pattern in the bottom of the earthenware cooking vessel. This base prevents the fish from sticking to the bottom and ensures that there is always sauce beneath to give flavor and keep the fish moist.

FISH TAGINE WITH TOMATOES, OLIVES, AND PRESERVED LEMON

In this fish tagine, the rich tastes of tomatoes, green peppers, and hot peppers are off-set by the tart, briny flavor of a single preserved lemon. Traditionally tagines such as this would contain an entire fish, with head intact, but I found it easier to make the tagines for this book with the fish cut into thick fillets.

This recipe has been adapted for a 3- or 4-quart, 4-inch-deep ceramic baking dish that can be brought to the table.

—— Serves 4 ——

CHARMOULA

- 2 teaspoons cumin seeds, preferably Moroccan
- 1 teaspoon coarse salt
- 3 garlic cloves
- 1 tablespoon sweet paprika
- 1½ teaspoons crushed red pepper flakes
- 2 tablespoons coarsely chopped flat-leaf parsley

- 2 tablespoons chopped fresh cilantro
- 1 preserved lemon (see page 21), rinsed, pulp and peel separated, reserved for the fish
- 3 tablespoons fruity extra virgin olive oil

- 1 pound thick white fish steaks, such as halibut, cod, or monkfish
- 1 large carrot, peeled and very thinly sliced
- 2 celery ribs, stringed and very thinly sliced
- 1 pound red-ripe tomatoes, peeled and sliced into thin rounds

- 1 small green bell pepper, cored, seeded, and sliced into very thin rounds
- 24 green-ripe, midway, or red olives, rinsed and pitted
- 2 bay leaves
- Cilantro sprigs for garnish

1. To make the charmoula: Combine the cumin, salt, and garlic in a mortar or blender, and pound or blend to a paste. Add the paprika, red pepper, parsley, cilantro, preserved lemon pulp, and olive oil and puree to a smooth sauce.

2. Rinse the fish and pat dry with paper towels. If using monkfish, cut away any gray membrane and cut the fish into 4 even chunks. Rub half of the charmoula all over the fish and let stand for 1 hour at room temperature, or for up to 24 hours in the refrigerator. Add ¼ cup water to the remaining charmoula, cover, and refrigerate.

3. About $1\frac{1}{2}$ hours before serving, preheat the oven to 300°F.

4. Spread 2 tablespoons of the reserved charmoula over the bottom of a 3- or 4-quart shallow baking dish. Scatter the carrot and celery on top. Add half of the tomatoes and bell pepper and sprinkle with a little charmoula. Lay the fish over the vegetables and cover with the remaining tomatoes and peppers. Spread the remaining charmoula on top. Scatter the diced preserved lemon peel, olives, and bay leaves around the fish.

5. Cover the dish tightly with a sheet of foil and bake for 1 hour.

6. Pour off the liquid from the dish into a small nonreactive saucepan, bring it to a boil over medium-high heat, and boil until it is reduced to $\frac{1}{2}$ cup. Meanwhile, raise the oven temperature to 425°F. Pour the reduced cooking liquid over the fish. Baste the fish with the pan juices and bake, uncovered, in the top third of the oven for 10 minutes, or until a nice crust has formed over the vegetables.

7. Transfer the baking dish to a wooden surface or folded kitchen towel to avoid cracking. Garnish with the cilantro sprigs and serve hot or warm.

NOTE TO THE COOK

To avoid overcooking the fish steaks, be sure to nestle them between layers of vegetables. The vegetables act as insulation, allow the proper evaporation of moisture during cooking, and also help coax all the ingredients to the desired state of tenderness.

TAGRA OF FRESH SARDINES WITH PEPPER OIL CHARMOULA

Many of the fish dishes from northern Morocco are prepared in a locally made clay vessel called a *tagra* and cooked in a baker's oven. This oval, flat-bottomed, porous, unglazed earthenware pan, made by potters near the Oued Laou River, which empties into the Mediterranean, encourages slow evaporation of moisture during cooking while giving a delectable earthy flavor to fish dishes. A cazuela or deep tagine can be substituted.

In the North, the preparation of the charmoula is a little different from elsewhere in Morocco. Instead of powdered paprika added directly to the marinade, the paprika is added in the refined form of paprika oil, made by boiling paprika in water and oil, then pouring off the liquid and leaving the sediment behind. The vibrant oil is not only used to flavor the *tagra*, but is also swirled over the entire dish just as it's served.

❧ Serves 6 ❧

2 pounds large fresh sardines (about 12)

Sea salt and freshly ground black pepper

⅓ cup plus 2 tablespoons extra virgin olive oil

1 tablespoon sweet paprika

Pinch of cayenne

2 teaspoons cumin seeds, preferably Moroccan

3 large garlic cloves

2½ tablespoons chopped cilantro

2½ tablespoons chopped flat-leaf parsley

1 pound red or Yukon Gold potatoes, peeled and thinly sliced

12 ounces carrots, peeled and thinly sliced

1 pound Roma (plum) tomatoes, thinly sliced

1 large red bell pepper, cored, seeded, and sliced into thin strips

1 large lemon, thinly sliced

1. Cut the heads off the sardines. Slit the bellies lengthwise and remove the backbones and innards; do not separate the fillets. Rinse well under cold running water and pat dry. Season lightly with salt and pepper.

2. Heat ⅓ cup of the olive oil in a small skillet. Add the paprika, cayenne, and ¼ cup water, bring to a boil, and boil for 2 to 3 minutes. Remove from the heat and let cool slightly.

3. Meanwhile, pound the cumin seeds, 1 teaspoon salt, the garlic, cilantro, and parsley in a mortar until pasty. Scoop the cooled oil and some of the water into a bowl; discard the sediment. Add half the paprika oil to the cumin seed mixture, and smear over the flesh of the sardines. Fold the sides of the sardines together, so they resume their original shape. Arrange on a plate, cover, and refrigerate for 1 hour. (Reserve the remaining pepper oil for serving.)

※

NOTE TO THE COOK

The website www.tagines.com sells traditional Moroccan *tagras*. If you buy one, be sure to season it before using. Rub it with grated onion, oil, and salt, then set it in a 300°F oven to heat up. When it is hot, raise the oven temperature to 450°F and bake until the seasonings turn black. Turn the heat off and let the pan cool slowly in the oven. When cool, wash well and let dry. Use your *tagra* for fish cookery in the oven or over charcoal or lava stones set on low. A *tagra* must be bone-dry when packed with food and set over heat.

To cook the sardines in the tagra over heated coals or lava stones, cover with a sheet of foil and cook for 40 minutes, or until the potato slices are tender. Remove from the heat and place on a wooden surface or folded kitchen towel to prevent cracking. Uncover and let stand for about 30 minutes before serving.

4. About 1½ hours before serving, layer one-third of the potatoes, carrots, tomatoes, and bell pepper in a dry *tagra*. Arrange half the sardines skin side down over the vegetables. Repeat, ending with a layer of potato slices. Spread the lemon slices on top. Pour over the reserved paprika oil, and gently press down so the liquid rises to cover the potatoes.

5. Place the *tagra* in the oven, turn the heat to 350°F, and bake for 1 hour. Remove from the oven and put on a wooden surface to let settle for 30 minutes before serving.

FRIED SARDINES, TANGIER-STYLE

This dish is known in Tangier as "husband and wife" because of the positioning of the sardines. The fish heads are left on, and pairs of fish are arranged so that the heads are facing away from one another, like an old alienated married couple!

Serve hot or cold, brushed lightly with oil and lemon juice.

————— Serve 2 —————

4 fresh or frozen small sardines (about 12 ounces)

1 tablespoon roughly chopped cilantro

1 tablespoon roughly chopped parsley

1¼ teaspoons cumin seeds, preferably Moroccan

2 garlic cloves

1 teaspoon coarse sea salt

1 teaspoon sweet paprika

¼ teaspoon hot paprika or cayenne

1 tablespoon fresh lemon juice

Oil for deep-frying

Flour for dusting

Olive oil

1 lemon, halved

1. Wash the sardines under cool running water. Slit the bellies lengthwise and remove the backbones and innards. Use scissors to snip away any bones near the head. Rinse and pat dry.

2. Crush the herbs to a paste in a heavy mortar or finely chop in a small blender. Add the cumin seeds, garlic, and salt and crush or blend to a thick cream. Blend in the sweet paprika, hot paprika or cayenne, and lemon juice. Smear the mixture over the flesh of all the sardines, then fold back together so that each sardine resumes its original shape. Arrange on a plate, cover, and refrigerate for 1 hour.

3. Heat the oil to 375°F in a straight-sided skillet. Dust the sardines with flour, then fry them until golden brown and crisp on both sides. Drain on paper towels. Brush with a little olive oil and lemon juice, and position "husband and wife" pairs, heads facing away from each other. Serve at once, or allow to cool, cover, and refrigerate to serve cold.

FISH TAGINE WITH CREAMY ONION CHARMOULA

This recipe, from the Atlantic coast city of Agadir, is very good with a firm-textured white fish, such as sea bass, cod, or monkfish.

———— ✆ Serves 4 ✆ ————

ONION CHARMOULA

1½ teaspoons cumin seeds, preferably Moroccan

3 garlic cloves

2 teaspoons coarse sea salt

2 teaspoons sweet paprika

½ teaspoon ground black pepper

Pinch of cayenne

Pinch of turmeric

Pinch of saffron threads

⅓ packed cup mixed cilantro and flat-leaf parsley leaves

⅓ cup extra virgin olive oil

1 medium red onion (7 ounces), roughly chopped

1 pound 1-inch-thick firm-textured white fish steaks

One 2-inch Ceylon cinnamon stick, gently bruised

5 small red-ripe tomatoes (8 ounces), cored and cut into ¼-inch-thick slices

Coarse sea salt

2 medium Yukon Gold potatoes, peeled and cut into 1-inch dice

1 pound narrow zucchini, trimmed and cut into 1-inch chunks

1 red bell pepper, peeled, cored, seeded, and diced

Juice of 1 lemon

GARNISH

½ preserved lemon (see page 21), pulp removed, rind rinsed and diced

12 green-ripe, midway, or red olives, pitted

2 tablespoons chopped cilantro

1. To make the charmoula: Toast the cumin seeds (not necessary if they are Moroccan) by tossing them in a hot dry skillet over medium heat for about 1 minute.

2. Blend the cumin seeds, garlic, and salt to a paste in a large mortar. Moisten the paprika, black pepper, cayenne, turmeric, and saffron with 2 tablespoons water. Add the spices, herbs, and oil to the garlic mixture and blend until smooth. Add the onion and ¾ cup water and blend to a smooth, velvety puree. (Makes about 3 cups.)

3. Wash the fish under cold running water. Trim off any skin, cut into small dice, and reserve. Pat the fish dry and cut into 1-inch chunks. Place the fish and cinnamon stick in a bowl, add ½ cup of the charmoula, and toss. Cover and refrigerate for 1 to 2 hours.

4. Meanwhile, arrange the tomato slices side by side on sheets of paper towels lightly dusted with coarse salt. Dust the tomatoes with salt, cover with more paper towels, and press down to help absorb excess moisture. Leave the tomatoes to dry out until ready to use.

5. Arrange the diced fish skin, if you have it, the potatoes, zucchini, and red bell pepper in an 11- to 12-inch tagine set on a heat diffuser over medium-low heat. Pour over the remaining charmoula and slowly bring to a boil. Cover and cook until the vegetables are tender and the sauce is thick, about 45 minutes. Remove and discard the cinnamon stick. (The tagine can be prepared 1 to 2 hours in advance up to this point; let stand at room temperature.)

6. About 30 minutes before serving, preheat the oven to 400°F.

7. Gently reheat the tagine on the heat diffuser over low heat. Remove the fish from the refrigerator and toss with the lemon juice. Spread the fish chunks and dried tomatoes on top of the cooked vegetables. Transfer to the oven and bake, uncovered, for 10 minutes. Transfer the hot tagine to a wooden surface or a folded towel to prevent cracking.

8. To serve, decorate the tagine with cubes of preserved lemon, olives, and chopped cilantro.

TAGINE OF BABY CALAMARI WITH RED PEPPER AND TOMATO

———— Serves 4 ————

CHARMOULA

¾ teaspoon cumin seeds, preferably Moroccan

3 garlic cloves

Sea salt

1 tablespoon saffron water (see page 48)

1 teaspoon ground ginger

½ teaspoon paprika

½ teaspoon ground turmeric

½ teaspoon cayenne

1 tablespoon extra virgin olive oil

1 pound baby calamari (12 pieces), cleaned and cut into bite-sized pieces, washed, pressed dry in paper towels to remove excess moisture, and placed in a bowl and refrigerated until ready to use

2 tablespoons extra virgin olive oil

1 cup finely chopped onion

1 cup peeled, cored, and diced red bell pepper

1 pound red-ripe tomatoes, peeled, diced, and drained

2 teaspoons sugar

Salt

2 tablespoons fresh lemon juice

2 tablespoons chopped cilantro

Cayenne

NOTE TO THE COOK

Calamari can take either two minutes or an hour and two minutes to cook to perfection. For this dish, I prefer the slow method. (In the recipe on page 262, I cook the calamari quickly.) Excellent with freshly boiled white rice.

1. To make the charmoula: Toast the cumin seeds (not necessary if they are Moroccan) by tossing them in a hot dry skillet over medium heat for about 1 minute. Pound the cumin seeds, garlic, and 1 teaspoon salt to a paste in a mortar. Dilute with the saffron water, then add the spices and olive oil. Toss with the calamari, cover, and refrigerate.

2. About 1¼ hours before serving, set a 10-inch flameware tagine, Spanish cazuela, or heavy-bottomed straight-sided skillet over medium-low heat. Warm the olive oil, then add the onion and cook until soft, about 5 minutes. Add the chopped red pepper, cover, and cook for 5 minutes. Add the seasoned calamari, raise the heat to medium-high, and cook, stirring, until most of the moisture evaporates.

3. Add the tomatoes, sugar, salt, half the lemon juice, and half the cilantro and bring to a boil. Lay a sheet of crumpled wet parchment directly over the contents of the pan, cover with a lid, reduce the heat to a simmer, and cook for 1 hour, or until the squid are tender (no longer chewy). Transfer the hot tagine to a wooden surface or a folded towel to prevent cracking.

4. Correct the seasoning as necessary with the remaining lemon juice, salt, and/or cayenne to taste. Scatter the remaining cilantro on top and serve with rice.

SAUTÉED SHRIMP CASA PEPE (PIL PIL)

Casa Pepe was a fun, modest café-restaurant in the small Atlantic town of Asilah, a half-hour drive west from Tangier. In season, the specialty there was delicious angulas, tiny eels cooked in peppery olive oil. We used to go and eat them every Saturday during the season.

Off-season, Pepe served an Andalusian-influenced shrimp dish, pil pil, that soon became very popular along the coast. Whole peeled shrimp are quickly cooked in a tomato sauce infused with red pepper, cumin, cilantro, and parsley. Pepe used the Moroccan *fefla hamra harra*, a mildly hot red pepper. I use the robust Basque piment d'Espelette as a substitute.

Pil pil is great with rice or slices of soft Moroccan bread.

— Serves 4 to 6 as a first course —

1 pound peeled medium-large shrimp (24 to 36), deveined

½ teaspoon cumin seeds, preferably Moroccan

4 garlic cloves

½ teaspoon coarse sea salt

¾ teaspoon piment d'Espelette or other mildly hot red pepper (see Sources)

1 tablespoon saffron water (see page 48)

2 cups peeled, seeded, and chopped fresh or canned tomatoes

⅓ cup extra virgin olive oil

2 tablespoons chopped flat-leaf parsley

1½ tablespoons chopped cilantro

1. Rinse the shrimp and wipe dry with paper towels. Leave the shrimp at room temperature so they are not ice-cold when they hit the skillet.

2. Crush the cumin seeds, garlic, and coarse salt to a paste in a mortar. Add the piment d'Espelette and saffron water and stir until smooth.

3. Put the tomatoes, garlic-spice mixture, and olive oil in a large skillet, set over high heat, and fry for several minutes to develop the flavor. Add the shrimp and cook, stirring, until they are firm and curled, about 4 minutes. Sprinkle with the herbs, stir once, and serve immediately.

TAGINE WITH FRESH MUSSELS, OLIVES, PEPPERS, AND ARGAN OIL

In southern Morocco, along the road from Agadir to Tifnit, you'll see vendors standing beside large canvas bags. Most likely they are filled with mussels gathered by the local fishermen, opened by their wives and then dried on the rocks. The sellers will tell you these mussels keep well for years and that all you need do is hydrate them and cook them with olives, hot peppers, turnips, tomatoes, and argan oil for a superb tagine. Dried mussels are definitely an acquired taste and, frankly, their odor isn't one you'd want to have permeate your kitchen.

Here is my fresh-mussel adaptation of that tagine, quite wonderful and very easy to make.

Serves 2 to 3

2 pounds fresh mussels, scrubbed and debearded

½ teaspoon cumin seeds, preferably Moroccan

1 large garlic clove

½ teaspoon coarse sea salt

2 tablespoons finely chopped flat-leaf parsley

2 tablespoons finely chopped cilantro

½ teaspoon sweet paprika

2 teaspoons Tomato Magic (page 41) or tomato paste

12 Picholine olives, pitted, rinsed, and drained

1 green Anaheim pepper, cored, seeded, and cut into julienne

1 teaspoon cider vinegar

1 tablespoon fresh lemon juice, or more to taste

2 tablespoons argan oil (see Sources)

1. Steam the mussels in a covered pan over high heat, shaking the pan occasionally, until they open, about 3 minutes; discard any mussels that do not open. Remove the mussels from their shells and set aside. Strain the liquor and reserve.

2. Crush the cumin, garlic, and salt to a paste using a mortar and pestle. Add the herbs, paprika, and ⅓ cup of the reserved mussel liquor and blend until smooth, then pour into an 11- to 12-inch tagine or cazuela set over a heat diffuser. Add the Tomato Magic or tomato paste, olives, pepper strips, vinegar, and the remaining mussel liquor and cook, stirring occasionally, over medium heat for 10 minutes, long enough for the flavors to blend and the pepper strips to soften.

3. Add the mussels, lemon juice, and argan oil and simmer for 5 minutes. Remove from the heat, cover, and let stand on a wooden surface or a folded towel to prevent cracking, for about 20 minutes to allow the mussels to absorb the flavors.

4. Just before serving, reheat gently.

STEAMED CALAMARI WITH PRESERVED LEMON AND ARGAN OIL

In Essaouira, one of Morocco's most important fishing ports, there's a row of tourist restaurants right on the dock that feature freshly caught fish. Among the many dishes offered is grilled calamari served either with a harissa-aioli spread on slices of toasted brioche or swimming in a spicy tomato sauce. At one lovely place, I ate this wonderful calamari salad made with preserved lemon and cumin and a splash of argan oil.

—— Serves 4 ——

12 ounces cleaned baby calamari tubes (12 pieces), rinsed, drained, split lengthwise, and cut into ¾-inch squares

¼ teaspoon cumin seeds, preferably Moroccan

1 clove garlic

Salt and freshly ground black pepper

Pinch of cayenne

2 tablespoons fresh lemon juice

2 tablespoons argan oil (see Sources) or extra virgin olive oil

¼ preserved lemon (see page 21), pulp removed, rind rinsed and finely diced

1½ tablespoons rinsed capers

2 tablespoons minced scallion

½ cup peeled, halved, seeded, and diced tomato

½ cup grilled or broiled (see page 86) peeled, seeded, and finely diced red bell pepper

1½ tablespoons chopped cilantro

1½ tablespoons chopped flat-leaf parsley

1. Bring a large pot of water to a boil. Set a colander or steamer snugly on top, add the calamari, cover, and steam for 2 to 3 minutes, or until the squares are just tender.

2. Meanwhile, toast the cumin seeds (not necessary if they are Moroccan) by tossing them in a hot dry skillet over medium heat for about 1 minute.

3. Crush the cumin seeds and garlic with ½ teaspoon salt, ¼ teaspoon black pepper, and the cayenne in a mortar. Stir in the lemon juice and then the oil. Scrape into a medium bowl.

4. Add the calamari to the oil mixture and toss to combine. Add the preserved lemon, capers, scallion, tomato, red bell pepper, and half the chopped herbs and mix well. Cover and refrigerate for 1 to 2 hours before serving.

5. Add the remaining herbs, toss, and serve.

REGIONAL FISH SPECIALTIES

There are many regional fish dishes that taste better on Moroccan soil, which you may want to try if you visit any of the following cities.

RABAT: Red mullet prepared whole in a tagine. The fish is stewed on a bed of finely minced onions seasoned with saffron, sugar, and cinnamon and surrounded by a layer of golden raisins. The fish turns crusty and golden, the raisins caramelize, and the result is delicious.

SAFI: You will always find a certain finesse in Safi cookery. For example, the *smen* here is washed with herbs and spices, not just *za'atar*; the charmoula for fish is more aromatic than elsewhere, no doubt on account of the addition of pure saffron. Other Safi specialties, besides those recorded in this book, are fish with lemon and olives, fish with butter, cumin, and onions; fish with tomatoes and fennel stalks; and fish stuffed with chopped fresh tomatoes, rice, and plenty of herbs.

FES: This is, of course, an inland city, where fish dishes tend to be built around the Sebou River shad. Due to overfishing and damming to provide water for irrigation, shad is no longer available. River trout makes a good replacement: baked with stuffed fruit; with wild artichokes; with fava beans; and with hot or sweet green peppers.

TETOUAN: The fish specialties here have mostly to do with stuffing, though the tagine of anchovies in garlic sauce is not to be missed, and the Tetouanese are renowned for their skill in the making of fish omelets. Among the great stuffings for fish are tomatoes, rice, onions, olives, and preserved lemons; onion and eggs flavored with lemon and cinnamon; a thick, rich jam made of sweet green peppers and tomatoes cooked down with spices; and other "Andalusian-type" mixtures.

ESSAOUIRA: Here you will find squid stuffed with rice, tomatoes, and charmoula, as well as such Jewish specialties as fish balls poached in tomato sauce, or stuffed inside pastry leaves and fried, and whole fish baked after being coated with cumin paste. There is also a scrumptious sardine tagine made with charmoula and wild greens from the nearby hills.

FISH SMOTHERED WITH ONION JAM

This is my take on a dish I learned in Safi. The original is prepared with conger eel, which I find impossible to source here. So, I've substituted monkfish, with excellent results. Being thicker, it takes a little longer to cook, but as a result, it has more time to absorb the flavors of the honey, raisins, and sweet spices in the onion jam.

    The onions are cooked down to a jam, then a little lemon juice is added to bring the flavors into balance. The fish fillets are arranged in a baking dish with the onion jam and baked until they are opaque and juicy. All in all, a perfect example of good Moroccan home cooking.

———— ✑ Serves 4 ✑ ————

Four 1¼-inch monkfish fillets or other thick white-fleshed fish fillets, about 1½ pounds

Coarse sea salt

¼ cup extra virgin olive oil

2 pounds red onions, halved and thickly sliced lengthwise

2 tablespoons saffron water (see page 48)

Fine sea salt and freshly ground white pepper

1¾ teaspoons ground Ceylon cinnamon

¼ teaspoon grated nutmeg

Pinch of ground ginger

3 tablespoons floral honey

⅓ cup golden raisins

Juice of ½ lemon, optional

A handful of flat-leaf parsley sprigs

1 lemon, quartered

1. Sprinkle the fish on both sides with sea salt. Cover and refrigerate for at least 1 hour.

2. Meanwhile, heat 3 tablespoons of the olive oil in a wide straight-sided skillet over medium-low heat. Add the onions, saffron water, ½ teaspoon salt, ½ teaspoon ground white pepper, and the cinnamon, nutmeg, and ginger, cover, and cook over very low heat until the onions are golden, about 30 minutes.

3. Add the honey and raisins to the onions and continue cooking until the onions have a glazed appearance, about 15 minutes. Correct the seasoning with salt, pepper, and a few drops of lemon juice. Set the onion jam aside, uncovered.

4. Preheat the oven to 400°F.

5. Brush the bottom of an 9-inch baking dish with the remaining tablespoon of oil. Scatter the sprigs of parsley over the bottom. Sprinkle with 3 tablespoons water and place the fish fillets side by side on top. Spread the onion jam over the fish and bake for 10 minutes. Turn off the heat, prop the oven door ajar (about 2 inches), and leave the dish inside for 20 more minutes. Serve with the lemon wedges.

FISH BAKED WITH ALMOND PASTE

This dish, which comes from the fishing city of Safi, was served often at a former Moroccan United Nations ambassador's residence, where it never failed to create a sensation. Here is my adaptation.

———— ❧ Serves 4 ❧ ————

1 red snapper, sea bass, or
  striped bass (3 pounds),
  cleaned and scaled, head and
  tail left intact

Sea salt

¼ cup extra virgin olive oil

1½ cups (½ pound) blanched
  whole almonds

4 to 5 tablespoons unsalted
  butter, softened

1 tablespoon orange flower water

1 teaspoon ground Ceylon
  cinnamon

1 cup confectioners' sugar

1 cup grated onion

1 tablespoon saffron water
  (see page 48)

¼ teaspoon freshly ground black
  pepper

1. Rinse the fish under cold running water. Rub inside and out with 2 teaspoons salt. Let stand for 10 minutes, then rinse again and pat dry with paper towels.

2. Heat the oil in a medium skillet. Fry the almonds, stirring constantly until just golden. Drain on paper towels.

3. Pulverize the almonds in a blender. Add 2 tablespoons of the softened butter, the orange flower water, cinnamon, confectioners' sugar, and 3 tablespoons water (or more if needed) and blend to make a smooth paste. Set aside.

4. Preheat the oven to 375°F.

5. Stuff the cavity of the fish with half the almond paste. Use 1 tablespoon of the butter to grease an ovenproof serving dish, then add the grated onion, ¼ cup water, and the saffron water and mix well. Sprinkle with salt and the pepper. Place the fish on the onion bed. Use a spatula to spread the remaining almond paste over the fish, forming a ripple design.

6. Melt the remaining 1 to 2 tablespoons butter and dribble over the fish. Bake for 45 minutes, or until the fish is completely cooked and the almond paste is crusty yet soft, just beginning to fall into the onion sauce. Serve hot.

GRILLED FISH STUFFED WITH SEAFOOD

On a recent trip to Tangier, I found an eating place unlike any other. Called, simply, Mohammed Belhaj (the name of its owner-chef), it bills itself as Morocco's "first health food restaurant."

The food is excellent and as interesting as its impassioned owner. Mohammed is quite the character, smiling and flapping his arms while talking a blue streak about the healthful properties of his food. As one regular customer confided, "If you don't enjoy his theater, he really doesn't want you in the place."

I was especially impressed by a delicious dish of spiced grilled fish stuffed with shrimp and cubes of swordfish. Though an original creation of an accomplished chef, it's fairly easy to make and brims with traditional Moroccan flavorings.

I recommend you serve this splendid dish with a simple rice pilaf.

Serves 4

2 small striped bass or sea bass (about 1½ pounds each), scaled and cleaned

Coarse sea salt

1 tablespoon extra virgin olive oil

2 teaspoons fresh lemon juice

¼ teaspoon freshly ground white pepper

STUFFING

½ teaspoon cumin seeds, preferably Moroccan

2 tablespoons olive oil

1 tablespoon fresh lemon juice

¼ teaspoon cayenne

½ teaspoon sweet paprika

⅓ cup finely chopped cilantro

⅓ cup finely chopped flat-leaf parsley

2 tablespoons finely diced celery

4 ounces swordfish or ahi tuna, cut into ¾-inch cubes

4 ounces shrimp (about 12), shelled, deveined, and cut in half

TOPPING

¼ teaspoon salt

¼ teaspoon freshly ground white pepper

¾ teaspoon ground cumin, preferably Moroccan

¼ teaspoon ground ginger

Pinch of ground turmeric

2 to 3 tablespoons fresh lemon juice

1. Rinse the fish, then rub each one inside and out with 1 tablespoon salt. Let stand for 20 minutes. Rinse again and pat dry with paper towels.

2. Preheat a grill or the broiler.

3. Mix the olive oil, lemon juice, ½ teaspoon salt, and white pepper in

a small bowl. Brush the fish inside and out with this mixture. Score the fish crosswise, being careful not to cut through to the bone.

4. To prepare the stuffing: Toast the cumin seeds (not necessary if they are Moroccan) by tossing them in a hot dry skillet over medium heat for about 1 minute. Transfer to a medium bowl.

5. Add all the remaining ingredients to the cumin and mix well. Fill the cavity of each fish with half the stuffing and brush the outside with any remaining liquid mixed with 1 tablespoon olive oil. Place in an oiled double-hinged fish rack to keep the stuffing from falling out when the fish is turned. (If you lack this kind of rack, wind kitchen string around the body of each fish to hold stuffing in place.) Grill or broil until the skin is crisp and the flesh is firm, about 8 minutes per side.

6. To make the topping: Combine the salt, white pepper, cumin, ginger, and turmeric in a small bowl. Sprinkle the fish with the spices and drizzle the lemon juice on top. Serve with a cruet of olive oil.

chapter nine

POULTRY

"When the chicken's feathers are of
gold, it isn't smart to make broth
out of the hen."

—*berber saying*

POULTRY

CHICKEN TAGINE WITH PRUNES AND ALMONDS IN
THE STYLE OF THE RIF MOUNTAINS
❧ page 276 ❧

CHICKEN WITH CARAMELIZED QUINCES
AND TOASTED WALNUTS
❧ page 279 ❧

CHICKEN COOKED "BETWEEN TWO FIRES"
❧ page 281 ❧

CHICKEN WITH DRIED APRICOTS AND PINE NUTS
❧ page 282 ❧

CHICKEN STEAMED OVER A BED OF ONIONS
❧ page 284 ❧

CRISPY CHICKEN FES-STYLE, WITH SPICES,
HONEYED ONIONS, AND SAUTÉED ALMONDS
❧ page 286 ❧

CHICKEN SMOTHERED WITH TOMATO JAM
❧ page 289 ❧

CHICKEN WITH EGGPLANT-TOMATO JAM
❧ page 290 ❧

CHICKEN SMOTHERED WITH OLIVES
❧ page 295 ❧

CHICKEN WITH PRESERVED LEMON AND
OLIVES (M'CHERMEL)
❧ page 296 ❧

CHICKEN WITH PRESERVED LEMON,
SOFT BLACK OLIVES, AND NIGELLA SEEDS
❧ page 298 ❧

CHICKEN WITH FENNEL, PRESERVED LEMON, AND OLIVES
❧ page 302 ❧

CHICKEN WITH EGGS, PRESERVED LEMON, AND OLIVES
❧ page 304 ❧

CRISPY CHICKEN WITH PRESERVED LEMON
AND OLIVES MQQUALI
❧ page 305 ❧

ROAST CHICKEN ON A FAUX SPIT WITH LEMON AND OLIVES
⁊ page 306 ⁊

CASSEROLE-ROASTED CHICKEN WITH
PRESERVED LEMON AND OLIVES
⁊ page 308 ⁊

CHICKEN WITH LEMON AND EGGS
⁊ page 310 ⁊

RAKIA'S BRILLIANT CHICKEN COATED WITH EGGS
⁊ page 312 ⁊

CHICKEN MECHOUI
⁊ page 315 ⁊

STEAMED CHICKEN
⁊ page 316 ⁊

DOUBLE-COOKED RED CHICKEN, MARRAKECH-STYLE
⁊ page 317 ⁊

BRAISED AND FRIED GAME HENS
WITH SAUTÉED ALMONDS
⁊ page 320 ⁊

TANGIER-STYLE FRIED CHICKEN
⁊ page 322 ⁊

CHICKEN KEDRA WITH CHICKPEAS AND TURNIPS
⁊ page 323 ⁊

CHICKEN KEDRA WITH ALMONDS AND CHICKPEAS
⁊ page 324 ⁊

CHICKEN KEDRA WITH ALMONDS AND RICE
⁊ page 326 ⁊

CHICKEN SIMMERED IN SMEN
⁊ page 327 ⁊

CHICKEN STUFFED WITH EGGS, ONIONS, AND PARSLEY
⁊ page 328 ⁊

CHICKEN STUFFED WITH RICE, ALMONDS, AND RAISINS
⁊ page 331 ⁊

POULTRY

There are so many chicken and other poultry dishes in Moroccan cuisine, I could write an entire book about the subject and still not include them all. The recipes offered here are a personal selection including my favorite sweet fruit and vegetable chicken tagines and my favorite chicken with lemon and olives dishes, as well as various roasted, steamed, and fried poultry dishes; stuffed chicken dishes; and last but not least, the chicken stews called *kedra*.

SWEET FRUIT AND VEGETABLE CHICKEN TAGINES

A few years ago, an old friend took me to lunch at the home of Saad Hajouji, grandson of El Glaoui, the legendary pasha of Marrakech. The food was lavish: triangular pastries filled with *bastila* stuffing, pigeon smothered in raisins, and huge amounts of "peeled" chickpeas and "peeled" green grapes in a sauce seasoned with onions, nutmeg, saffron, ginger, black pepper, cubed lamb's liver, and a touch of vanilla.

This was Moroccan palace cookery at its finest, labor-intensive, reproducible only with a staff of old women cooks called "dadas."

I knew I couldn't reproduce the work of these experienced Moroccan women cooks, but the intricate spicing of their dishes, the control of sweetness, inspired me to start this chapter with sweet chicken tagines.

TAGINES

The very word *tagine* has reached folkloric status. People are charmed by both the promise of a complexly flavored dish and by the visually seductive image of the cooking pot of the same name, with its round, low-rimmed earthenware bottom and high conical top.

This two-part vessel was devised to condense steam back into moisture, enhancing the slow-cooked stewing effect while maximizing cooking efficiency. At a certain moment in tagine cookery, moisture has either evaporated or been reabsorbed by the poultry or vegetables, or both, and both top and bottom, now well heated, become, in effect, a portable oven in which the food continues to bake gently, preserving nutrition, color, and flavor.

If you're worried that the very small amount of evaporation will cause your food to burn, try this trick until you feel comfortable with tagine cooking: crumple a piece of parchment paper and place it directly over the contents of the tagine before covering and cooking. The moisture will quickly recycle. Midway during cooking, you can remove and discard the paper, then continue cooking so that the "portable oven" aspects of tagine cookery can come into play.

Tagine pots are versatile, and I strongly recommend that you acquire one. But you can still prepare those recipes that call for a tagine by substituting the parchment paper and a cazuela with a dome-like lid or even a heavy-bottomed shallow casserole.

NOTES ON CHICKEN TAGINES

The quality of chicken is especially important when cooking Moroccan food, and especially in a tagine. This said, commercial chicken is labeled in so many different ways, choosing the right one can be confusing.

I am particularly partial to chickens labeled "air-chilled" or "air-dried," to brands such as Bell & Evans, Smart Chickens, and Maverick Ranch Chickens, and also to those labeled "100 percent certified organic and free-range." (The problem with so-called "all natural" chickens is that the USDA allows up to 15 percent saltwater processing and all kinds of feed. Always check the label to ensure there's been no saltwater processing, which both dilutes flavor and adds weight to the bird.) Kosher chicken is also a good choice, but remember to reduce salt, as it has already been subjected to a mild salt brine.

You may wonder why most of my tagine recipes call for the chicken thighs rather than breasts. This is because the breasts on most commercial chicken raised in the United States will cook too quickly, without allowing sufficient time to build up the complex flavor you should expect from a successful chicken tagine.

If you prefer to substitute all bone-in chicken breasts in the tagine recipes, use air-chilled chicken breasts, place a peeled medium potato or onion in the center of the tagine, and position the chicken breasts, narrow end up and slightly overlapping, around it. Cover and cook as directed in the recipe for the first 30 minutes, then remove and discard the potato or onion and finish cooking the chicken as directed. For a mix of thighs and breasts, stack or tilt the breasts over the legs and thighs for the first 30 minutes.

Also, please note that not all tagines are cooked in tagine pots. Although certain dishes such as *kedras* (see pages 323–326) are called "tagines," meaning stews, the pot has to be much deeper than a tagine pot to arrive at a successful result.

Regarding cooking times: A covered tagine needs at least 15 minutes to come to a simmer; then most of my recipes call for cooking over the lowest heat to maintain a slow simmer. Here is the approximate timing for an air-chilled organic chicken cooked until the flesh just begins to fall away from the bone in a tagine or slow-cooked in a deep casserole: a quartered chicken, about 1 hour; a 3-pound whole chicken, about $1\frac{1}{4}$ hours; a $3\frac{1}{2}$-pound whole chicken, about $1\frac{1}{2}$ hours; and a 4-pound whole chicken, about $1\frac{3}{4}$ to 2 hours.

Please remember to transfer a hot tagine to a wooden surface or a folded towel to prevent cracking.

CHICKEN TAGINE WITH PRUNES AND ALMONDS IN THE STYLE OF THE RIF MOUNTAINS

I heard about this dish from many members of the Tangier "literary set," who told me the Moroccan writer Mohammed Mrabet had cooked it for them. Despite all the descriptions, I couldn't figure out the recipe. Finally Paul Bowles, who had discovered and translated Mrabet, recalled the measurements for me from memory.

In the Rif Mountains, Mrabet's home, the people are individualistic and do things their own way—as in this recipe, where they rub cumin into the flesh of the chickens, a procedure unknown in other parts of the country.

Serves 4

One 3¼-pound chicken, preferably organic and air-chilled

Coarse salt and freshly ground black pepper

2 teaspoons ground cumin, preferably Moroccan, or more to taste

12 ounces moist prunes, pitted

2 to 3 teaspoons ground Ceylon cinnamon

2 large yellow onions, halved and sliced lengthwise

1 teaspoon ground turmeric

1 teaspoon ground ginger

1 cup blanched whole almonds

Vegetable oil for frying

1. Rinse the chicken and pat dry; trim away excess fat. Cut off the wings and legs, leaving the breast in one piece. Rub all the pieces with salt, pepper, and the cumin. Let stand for 1 hour.

2. Meanwhile, cover the prunes with cold water in a small saucepan and add the cinnamon. Bring to a boil, reduce the heat, and simmer for 10 minutes. Set aside.

3. Place the onions in a wide, shallow casserole, with the turmeric, ginger, salt and pepper to taste, and ¼ cup water, cover, and steam for 15 minutes.

4. Meanwhile, brown the almonds in 4 or 5 tablespoons oil in a large skillet; remove with a slotted spoon and drain on paper towels. Brown the chicken evenly on all sides in the same oil, then transfer to the steamed onions. Cover with a sheet of parchment paper and cook over the lowest possible heat for about 1¼ hours.

5. Discard the parchment paper. Add the cooked prunes to the casserole and bring to a boil. Remove from the heat. Arrange the chicken breast in the center of a serving dish, place the legs and wings around, and cover all with the prunes and sauce. Sprinkle with the almonds and serve at once.

CHICKEN WITH CARAMELIZED QUINCES AND TOASTED WALNUTS

In this tagine, the quinces are steamed over boiling water, then slipped into a skillet to caramelize with honey and butter. This initial steaming not only provides a moist silky texture but also intensifies the flavor of the quinces far more than if they were simmered in water.

As is often the case in Moroccan cooking, the grated red onion will quickly turn into liquid. This tagine is a perfect example of a recipe neatly balanced between sweet and savory.

⁓ Serves 4 ⁓

4 large chicken thighs (about 2 pounds), preferably organic and air-chilled

½ preserved lemon (see page 21), pulp removed, rind rinsed and chopped

1 teaspoon La Kama Spice Mixture (page 37)

½ teaspoon ground turmeric

½ teaspoon crushed mace

½ teaspoon freshly ground black pepper

1 tablespoon saffron water (see page 48)

2 tablespoons extra virgin olive oil

1 red onion, grated (about 1 cup)

Coarse salt

1 teaspoon Smen (optional; page 159)

12 sprigs each flat-leaf parsley and cilantro, tied together

3 large quinces

1 lemon, halved

1 cup chicken stock, heated

½ teaspoon ground Ceylon cinnamon

2 tablespoons unsalted butter

2 tablespoons floral honey, such as lavender, acacia, or orange blossom, thinned with 2 tablespoons water

½ cup toasted and chopped walnuts

1. Trim the chicken thighs of excess fat; wash and pat dry. Slide your fingers under the skin to loosen it from the flesh.

2. Combine the preserved lemon, spices, and saffron water and rub all over the chicken thighs and under the skin. Let stand for at least 15 minutes.

3. Set an 11- to 12-inch tagine on a heat diffuser over medium-low heat. Add the oil, onion, and 1 teaspoon salt and cook, stirring occasionally, for 5 minutes. Slip in the seasoned chicken, the *smen*, if using, and the herb bouquet. (The grated red onion will provide enough moisture.) Cover and cook, without disturbing, over the lowest possible heat until the flesh just begins to fall away from the bone, about 1 hour.

4. Meanwhile, halve and core the quinces (do not peel), dropping them into water to cover with the juice of the lemon. Fill the bottom of a couscous pot or pasta pot with water, set a snug-fitting vegetable steamer or colander on top, and bring to a boil. Add the quince halves, cover, and steam until completely tender, about 1 hour. Transfer to a rack to drain.

5. Remove the chicken to a side dish, cover, and keep warm. Add the hot chicken stock and cinnamon to the tagine (which should now be able to accept medium heat), and boil the liquid down to a thick sauce. Correct the seasoning, and remove from the heat.

6. Melt the butter in a 10-inch nonstick skillet over medium heat. Add the honey and bring to a boil, stirring. Carefully cut each quince half in half, add to the skillet, and cook, uncovered, over medium heat, turning occasionally until glazed on all sides, about 5 minutes. Arrange the quince quarters attractively around the edges of the tagine.

7. Add the chicken to the same skillet and brown on the skin side in the remaining syrupy juices. Place skin side up in the center of the tagine, coat with the sauce, and set over low heat to reheat.

8. Transfer the hot tagine to a wooden surface or folded kitchen towel on a serving tray to prevent cracking. Let the tagine stand with its top on for 5 minutes, then remove the cover, scatter the walnuts on top, and serve at once.

CHICKEN COOKED "BETWEEN TWO FIRES"

In this super-moist recipe from the city of Fes, a quartered chicken bakes extra slowly in a zesty sauce of grated tomatoes and onions. The thick, intensely flavored sauce is then sprinkled with cinnamon and raw sugar, and the whole is broiled for a final few minutes until lightly charred on top.

∽ Serves 4 ∾

One 3½- to 4-pound
  chicken, preferably organic
  and air-chilled,
  quartered

2 pounds red-ripe tomatoes,
  halved, seeded, grated, and
  drained (2 cups)

1 medium red onion, grated,
  rinsed, and squeezed dry

1 teaspoon La Kama Spice Mixture
  (page 37)

2 tablespoons saffron water
  (see page 48)

Salt

2 tablespoons extra virgin olive oil

One 3-inch Ceylon cinnamon stick

½ teaspoon ground Ceylon
  cinnamon

3 tablespoons turbinado or other
  raw sugar

1. Preheat the oven to 275°F.

2. Rinse the chicken quarters and pat dry; trim away excess fat. Place the chicken quarters skin side up and side by side in a tagine or cazuela. Add the tomatoes, onion, spices, saffron water, 1 teaspoon salt, and the oil to the tagine and mix well with the chicken. Gently crush the cinnamon stick to release its aroma and add to the tagine. Set the tagine on the middle oven rack and bake, uncovered, without disturbing, for 1½ hours.

3. Transfer the tagine to a wooden surface or folded kitchen towel on a tray to prevent cracking. Turn on the broiler. Move the chicken quarters toward the center of the tagine to create a loose "mound." Spread the tomato sauce over the chicken. Tilt the tagine to collect all excess liquid and carefully spoon it into a small skillet.

4. Add the ground cinnamon and sugar to the cooking liquid and bring to a boil. Reduce to a thick sauce, and drizzle over the chicken.

5. Set the tagine on a rack about 9 inches from the heat source and quickly broil until the tomato coating is lightly charred. Transfer the hot tagine to the wooden surface or folded kitchen towel to prevent cracking. Let the tagine stand with its top on for 5 minutes. Remove the cover, discard the cinnamon stick, and serve at once.

NOTES TO THE COOK

Keep in mind that the tagine should be able to support the heat of your broiler. If you have doubts, switch to an oven-proof serving dish in step 5.

In the days before home ovens, Moroccan cooks placed a shallow earthenware plate over the filled tagine, then piled on glowing olive wood embers. This "between two fires" method sealed in the moisture, turned the top crusty and brown, and infused the dish with a subtle smoky fragrance.

Serve with Moroccan Country Bread (page 108).

CHICKEN WITH DRIED APRICOTS AND PINE NUTS

NOTE TO THE COOK

If you are cooking in a flameware or another tagine that can support high heat, you do not need to transfer the chicken to another ovenproof serving dish.

California sun-dried apricots are a perfect choice for this delicious tagine. Simmered in sweetened orange juice, they maintain their silky texture and end up tasting very similar to the Moroccan variety. Here the chicken, stewed with gentle spices, is finished off under the broiler for a faint charring effect. The result: a fascinating juxtaposition of tastes.

Serves 4

- 4 large chicken thighs (about 2 pounds), preferably organic and air-chilled
- 1 small garlic clove
- Coarse salt
- 2 tablespoons saffron water (see page 48)
- 1 tablespoon La Kama Spice Mixture (page 37)
- 1 teaspoon Smen (optional; page 159)
- 3 tablespoons sugar
- 2 tablespoons extra virgin olive oil
- 1 medium red onion, halved and thinly sliced
- 7 to 10 sprigs each cilantro and flat-leaf parsley, tied together
- 20 dried apricots (about 5½ ounces), preferably moist and chewy, rinsed and drained
- ⅓ cup orange juice
- 2 tablespoons unsalted butter
- One 2-inch cinnamon stick
- Freshly ground white pepper
- 2 tablespoons pine nuts or sesame seeds

1. Trim the chicken thighs of excess fat; wash and pat dry. Slide your fingers under the skin to loosen it from the flesh.

2. Crush the garlic with ½ teaspoon coarse salt in a mortar. Stir in the saffron water, spices, *smen*, if using, and 1½ teaspoons of the sugar. Coat the chicken with the spice mixture on all sides and under the skin. Allow to stand for 30 minutes.

3. Meanwhile, put the oil, onion, a pinch of salt, and ¼ cup water in a medium tagine, preferably flameware, set on a heat diffuser over medium-low heat, and cook, covered, until the onion is soft and golden, about 20 minutes.

4. Add the chicken and marinade to the tagine and lightly color each piece on both sides. Add the herbs and ¼ cup hot water, reduce the heat to a bare simmer, and cook, covered, for 45 minutes, turning the chicken thighs once for even cooking.

5. Meanwhile, place the apricots, orange juice, the remaining 2½ tablespoons sugar, the butter, and cinnamon stick in a saucepan and bring to a boil, then reduce the heat and simmer, uncovered, until the liquid is reduced and syrupy, about 30 minutes. Remove from the heat; discard the cinnamon stick when ready to use.

6. Uncover the tagine and skim off excess fat from the cooking liquid. Add the apricots and their syrupy juices and continue to cook until the chicken legs and thighs are cooked through and the flesh is nearly falling off the bone. Correct the seasoning of the sauce with salt and a good pinch of white pepper.

7. Spoon the sauce over and around the chicken and cook for 10 more minutes. Discard the herbs.

8. Meanwhile, place an oven rack about 7 to 9 inches from the broiler and turn on the broiler.

9. Arrange the chicken thighs attractively on an ovenproof serving dish, spoon over the combined sauce, and top with the apricots. Broil just until well glazed. Sprinkle with the pine nuts or sesame seeds and serve at once.

CHICKEN STEAMED OVER A BED OF ONIONS

Here a whole chicken steams slowly over a bed of baby onions for 2 to 3 hours, and the texture of the poultry just keeps getting better! The recipe is based on the style of cooking I remember from the years I lived in Morocco. We made tagines with whole country chickens, cooking them for hours without ever opening the tagine top. The resulting chickens were delicious, scented by the steam-infused spices, and always emerged incredibly tender.

For this recipe to work, you should use an air-chilled chicken, and you really should cook it in a tagine with a tall top. But if you don't have one, all is not lost! Simply quarter the chicken and use any tagine. If you don't have a tagine, you can use a cazuela or a shallow casserole: simply arrange the chicken over the onion as described, add ⅓ cup water, cover the chicken with parchment paper and a lid, and simmer for 2 hours without disturbing.

―――― ◎ Serves 4 to 6 ◎ ――――

One 4-pound chicken, preferably organic and air-chilled

Coarse sea salt and freshly ground black pepper

1 large onion, halved and sliced

1½ tablespoons extra virgin olive oil

3 tablespoons unsalted butter, softened

2 tablespoons saffron water (see page 48)

½ teaspoon ground ginger

½ teaspoon ground turmeric

2 pounds small white onions

Two 2-inch cinnamon sticks

1½ teaspoons cumin seeds, preferably Moroccan, wrapped in a cheesecloth bag

2 grains gum arabic, pulverized with a pinch of salt to a powder

2 tablespoons floral honey, such as orange blossom, acacia, or lavender

½ teaspoon freshly ground white pepper

1. About 4 hours before serving: Trim the chicken of excess fat, rinse, and pat dry. Slide your fingers under the skin to loosen it from the flesh. Season the cavity with salt and pepper. Tie the legs together. Tuck the wings under the chicken and tie them in place.

2. Toss the sliced onion with 1 teaspoon salt and the olive oil in an 11- to 12-inch tagine, set on a heat diffuser over low heat, and cook, covered, until soft and golden, about 20 minutes.

3. Meanwhile, use a fork to blend half the butter with the saffron water, ginger, turmeric, and salt and pepper to taste. Rub half of the mixture under and over the skin of the chicken.

4. Add the remaining butter mixture to the tagine, along with ¼ cup water. Place the baby white onions over the softened onions, add the

cinnamon sticks and cumin, and place the chicken breast side up on top. Cover and cook, without disturbing, over the lowest possible heat for 2½ hours.

5. Preheat the oven to 350°F.

6. Remove the chicken to a side dish. Tilt the tagine and spoon as much of the cooking juices as possible into a small saucepan. Let the fat rise to the top and remove it. Stir the gum arabic and honey into the cooking juices and boil down to a thick sauce. Correct the seasoning with salt and pepper.

7. The tagine should now be hot enough that you can raise the heat to medium. Add the remaining butter and cook the small onions until glazed.

8. Carve the chicken. Return the parts to the tagine, placing them among the glazed onions, and pour the sauce on top. Set the tagine, uncovered, in the oven to reheat and brown the chicken, 10 to 15 minutes.

9. Transfer the hot tagine to a wooden surface or folded kitchen towel on a serving tray to prevent cracking. Let the tagine stand with its top on for 5 minutes. Remove the cover and serve at once.

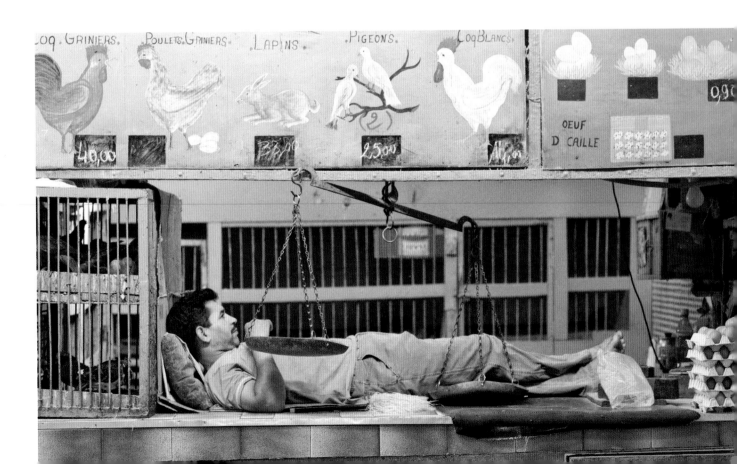

CRISPY CHICKEN FES-STYLE, WITH SPICES, HONEYED ONIONS, AND SAUTÉED ALMONDS

In this recipe, the effect of the marinated spices intensifies as steam drives them into the flesh of the chicken. You can prepare the chicken and its onion-based sauce ahead of time, then reheat the sauce and brown the chicken just before serving. In Fes, the chicken is fried in hot oil and butter until its skin turns golden and crisp, then topped with some buttered and browned almonds.

For this recipe, I suggest you use a large earthenware or flameware tagine or a wide cazuela with a tight-fitting lid.

—◈ Serves 4 ◈—

One 3½-pound chicken, preferably organic and air-chilled, backbone, neck, and wing tips removed and reserved for some other purpose, liver reserved

MARINADE

½ red onion, grated (about ¼ cup)

2 tablespoons chopped flat-leaf parsley

2 tablespoons chopped cilantro

3 garlic cloves, chopped

1 teaspoon coarse salt

1 tablespoon La Kama Spice Mixture (page 37)

1 tablespoon extra virgin olive oil

2 tablespoons saffron water (see page 48)

3 tablespoons extra virgin olive oil

1 pound red onions, halved and thinly sliced

1 to 2 tablespoons floral honey, such as orange blossom, acacia, or lavender

Salt and freshly ground black pepper

⅔ cup blanched whole almonds

2 tablespoons clarified butter

1. The day before: Rinse the chicken and pat dry; trim away excess fat. Slide your fingers under the skin to loosen it from the flesh.

2. To prepare the marinade: Combine the grated onion, herbs, garlic, salt, spices, and olive oil. Rub the mixture under and over the skin of the chicken. Place in a bowl and refrigerate, covered, for at least 4 hours and up to 24 hours.

3. The next day: Bring the chicken to room temperature.

4. Remove the chicken, and add the saffron water and ¼ cup water to the marinade in the bowl. Spread 1 tablespoon of the olive oil and the sliced onions over the bottom of an 11- to 12-inch tagine set over a

heat diffuser and place the chicken breast side up on top. Pour over the marinade. Cover with a piece of parchment paper and cook, without disturbing, over low heat for about 1 hour and 15 minutes. The chicken should be very tender, with the flesh just about to fall off the bone. Carefully transfer it to a side dish, cover with foil, and let it rest and firm up.

5. Dice the reserved chicken liver and add to the onion sauce. Raise the heat to medium and cook, stirring occasionally, for about 10 minutes. Add the honey and correct the seasoning with salt and pepper.

6. Meanwhile, fry the almonds in 1 tablespoon of the oil and 1 tablespoon of the butter until golden brown. (The recipe can be prepared to this point up to 2 hours ahead.)

7. Gently reheat the onion sauce in the tagine.

8. Meanwhile, heat the remaining 1 tablespoon oil and butter in a large skillet over high heat, or set an oven rack about 8 inches from the heat source and turn on the broiler. Divide the chicken into 4 to 8 portions; discard any loose bones. Add the chicken, in batches if necessary, to the skillet, to brown and crisp on all sides. (Use a spatter screen to protect yourself from the hot fat.) Or baste the chicken with the oil and butter and broil on both sides. As the chicken pieces brown, transfer them to the tagine.

9. Transfer the hot tagine to a wooden surface or folded kitchen towel on a serving tray to prevent cracking. Let the tagine stand with its top on for 5 minutes. Remove the cover, scatter the browned almonds on top, and serve at once.

CHICKEN SMOTHERED WITH TOMATO JAM

——— ❧ Serves 6 ❧ ———

6 large fat chicken thighs (about 3 pounds), preferably organic and air-chilled

2 large garlic cloves

Coarse salt

½ teaspoon freshly ground black pepper

¼ teaspoon ground ginger

2 tablespoons extra virgin olive oil

2 tablespoons saffron water (see page 48)

⅓ cup grated red onion

2 tablespoons finely chopped cilantro

1 teaspoon ground Ceylon cinnamon

2½ pounds red-ripe tomatoes, peeled, halved, seeded, and chopped

1 tablespoon Tomato Magic (page 41) or tomato paste

2 tablespoons thyme or floral honey

2 tablespoons sesame seeds, toasted

1. The day before: Rinse the chicken thighs and pat dry; trim away excess fat. Slide your fingers under the skin to loosen it from the flesh. Crush the garlic and 2 teaspoons salt to a paste in a mortar. Mix with the pepper, ginger, olive oil, and saffron water, and rub under and over the skin of the chicken. Let stand, covered, in the refrigerator overnight.

2. The next day: Place the chicken, with its marinade, in an 11- to 12-inch tagine set on a heat diffuser. Add the grated onion, cilantro, ¾ teaspoon of the ground cinnamon, and ½ cup water and mix thoroughly with the chicken pieces. Cook, covered, over low heat, stirring once, for 20 minutes. Then begin to slowly raise the heat to medium and cook, uncovered, for 20 minutes.

3. Add the tomatoes and the Tomato Magic or tomato paste to the tagine and continue to cook over medium heat, uncovered, turning the chicken pieces often in the sauce, until very tender, about 20 more minutes. Take the chicken out and wrap in foil to keep warm and moist. Allow the tomatoes to cook down until all the moisture evaporates, stirring occasionally to avoid scorching, about 1 hour. The tomatoes will begin to fry and the sauce will thicken considerably.

4. Add the honey and the remaining ¼ teaspoon cinnamon to the tomatoes and cook for several minutes to bring out their flavors. Reheat the chicken parts in the sauce, rolling them around to coat evenly.

5. Remove the cover, scatter the sesame seeds on top, and serve hot or warm.

NOTES TO THE COOK

Recently I asked my daughter, Leila, to test this recipe, since she remembered it from her girlhood in Tangier. She was thrilled with the results, telling me that two of her friends liked it so much "they actually licked the bottom of the tagine pot."

For best results, make this dish, as Leila did, in summer, when tomatoes are at their peak.

Please remember to transfer a hot tagine to a wooden surface or a folded kitchen towel on a serving tray to prevent cracking.

CHICKEN WITH EGGPLANT-TOMATO JAM

Here chicken parts simmer in a sauce of garlic, ginger, saffron, and black pepper until they are so tender they're falling off the bone. The chicken parts are then piled in the center of the tagine and topped with a thick, intensely flavored "jam" made from fried eggplant that has been crushed with spices and garlic, refried with tomatoes, and enriched with some of the sauce from the chicken. The remaining sauce is poured around the chicken, and the tagine is reheated to blend the flavors.

You can prepare the recipe through step 4 up to 3 days in advance.

—— ✑ Serves 4 to 6 ✑ ——

2 pounds eggplant (about 2 large)

Coarse salt

Olive oil for shallow-frying, plus 2 tablespoons

3 medium garlic cloves, crushed

¼ cup chopped flat-leaf parsley

¼ cup chopped cilantro

1 teaspoon sweet paprika

¼ teaspoon ground cumin, preferably Moroccan

Pinches of cayenne to taste

2 large tomatoes, peeled, halved, seeded, and chopped (2 cups)

2 to 3 tablespoons fresh lemon juice

1 tablespoon cider vinegar or other mild vinegar

4 large chicken thighs, preferably organic and air-chilled

2 large chicken breasts on the bone, preferably organic and air-chilled

1¼ teaspoons ground ginger

2 tablespoons saffron water (see page 48)

¼ teaspoon freshly ground black pepper

1 medium red onion, grated (½ cup)

Cilantro sprigs and thin lemon slices for garnish

1. Trim off the ends from each eggplant. With a channel knife, remove 3 or 4 thin vertical strips from each, leaving the eggplants striped. Cut each eggplant crosswise in half, and then cut each half lengthwise into 3 or 4 thick strips. Sprinkle with salt and allow to drain in a nonaluminum colander for at least 1 hour.

2. Rinse and drain the eggplant strips; pat dry with paper towels. Heat ¼ inch of oil in a large nonstick skillet over medium heat. Fry the eggplant strips in batches until golden brown on both sides, about 4 minutes. Drain the strips on paper towels and place them on a cutting board. Strain the oil and reserve.

3. With a potato masher, mash the eggplant strips with 1 of the garlic cloves, 2 tablespoons each of the parsley and cilantro, the paprika, cumin, and cayenne.

4. Put 3 tablespoons of the reserved oil in a heavy skillet and reheat. Add the tomatoes and 1 teaspoon salt and cook over medium-high heat, stirring frequently, until most of the moisture evaporates, about 5 minutes. Add the mashed eggplant and cook over low heat, stirring frequently, until most of the moisture evaporates and the mixture is very thick, about 20 minutes. Remove the skillet from the heat and stir in 2 tablespoons of the lemon juice and the vinegar. (The recipe can be made in advance to this point; cool, cover, and refrigerate.)

5. About 2 hours before serving, rinse the chicken and pat dry; trim away excess fat. Pound the remaining 2 garlic cloves and 1 teaspoon salt to a paste in a mortar. Blend in the ginger, saffron water, and black pepper. Gradually whisk in the 2 tablespoons olive oil and 2 to 3 tablespoons hot water, as if you were making mayonnaise.

6. Toss the chicken parts with the garlic-spice mixture, coating each piece, in a large tagine or cazuela. Cover and cook over low heat for 15 minutes. Add the onion, the remaining parsley and cilantro, and 1 cup hot water and slowly bring the mixture almost to a boil. Lift the chicken breasts and "park" them on top of the chicken legs and thighs; reduce the heat to low, cover, and cook, without disturbing, for 30 minutes.

7. Slide the chicken breasts back into the cooking juices and turn to coat both sides. Cover and continue cooking until the flesh just begins to fall off the bone, about 20 minutes.

8. Remove the chicken parts to a side dish and cover to keep moist. Skim off most of the fat, raise the heat to medium, and continue cooking the pan juices, uncovered, until they are reduced to $1\frac{1}{2}$ cups.

9. Preheat the oven to 350°F.

10. Remove half the cooking juices to a bowl. Mix the eggplant-tomato puree with the remaining cooking juices and adjust the seasoning, adding additional salt, cayenne or black pepper, and/or lemon juice to taste. Return the chicken parts to the tagine and coat with the remaining pan juices. Pile the eggplant-tomato mixture on top, forming a pyramid. Cover the dish loosely with parchment paper or foil and set in the oven to reheat, about 15 minutes.

11. Transfer the hot tagine to a wooden surface or folded kitchen towel on a serving tray to prevent cracking. Let the tagine stand with its top on for 5 minutes. Remove the cover, garnish the puree with sprigs of cilantro and lemon slices, and serve at once.

CHICKEN WITH LEMON AND OLIVES

Chicken with lemon and olives is one of the great combinations in Moroccan cookery, the dish that most often seduces foreigners and turns them into devotees of Moroccan tagines. But there are many ways to make this dish, and some of these recipes do not require an earthenware tagine. For this reason, I think of chicken with lemon and olives as a theme with numerous variations. I present some of my favorites here, but there are many more.

That being said, there is no substitute for preserved lemons in Moroccan food. I cannot emphasize this enough. To not use preserved lemons when they're called for in a recipe is to completely miss the point and also to miss an entire dimension of culinary experience. Preserved lemons are easy to make (see page 21), and if carefully put up, they will keep for more than a year.

Regarding olives, unless otherwise specified, the ideal olive for most of these tagines is often referred to as "red," though they're actually closer in color to violet or red-brown. I call them "midway olives," as they are halfway between green and black. When Moroccans pick them at this stage, they soak them in bitter orange juice, which keeps them soft and gives them a lovely bitter citrus flavor. See page 22 for how to marinate green ripe olives to simulate the country olives that are the traditional accompaniment to preserved lemons. Red olives imported from Morocco are available online (see Sources).

You can also use domestic green ripe olives produced by Lindsay or Graber. They have a similar texture but are better if placed in a marinade for a few days before using (see page 22).

Kalamata and Gaeta olives can be substituted if soaked in several changes of water to remove their vinegar marinade.

CHICKEN SMOTHERED WITH OLIVES

In this subtle, nutty-flavored dish, olives are boiled to release some of their oil into the sauce, but it's really the fresh lemon juice (as opposed to the more typical preserved lemons) that gives the dish its special twist.

——— ❧ Serves 6 to 8 ❧ ———

4 pounds chicken legs and thighs, preferably organic and air-chilled

2 large red onions

3 tablespoons extra virgin olive oil

1 tablespoon finely chopped garlic

1 teaspoon ground ginger

1 teaspoon freshly ground black pepper

½ teaspoon ground cumin, preferably Moroccan

½ teaspoon sweet paprika

2 tablespoons saffron water (see page 48)

½ cup chopped flat-leaf parsley

½ cup chopped cilantro

2 pounds Picholine or green-ripe olives, pitted, soaked in water for 10 minutes, rinsed, and drained

⅓ cup fresh lemon juice or to taste

Salt

1. Wash and dry the chicken; trim away excess fat.

2. Cut up 1½ of the onions and pulse in a food processor until coarsely grated. Place the grated onion in a strainer and press to remove excess moisture. Measure out ¾ cup (freeze the rest for some other purpose). Thinly slice the remaining half onion.

3. Blend the oil, garlic, ginger, pepper, cumin, paprika, and saffron water to a paste in a 4-quart casserole. Stir in the grated onion and herbs. Then continue stirring while slowly adding 3 cups water (as if you were making mayonnaise). Add the chicken and bring to a boil, then reduce the heat to low and simmer, covered, for 30 minutes.

4. Preheat the oven to 450°F.

5. With a slotted spoon, remove the chicken parts from the casserole and place skin side up on a baking sheet. Bake on the upper shelf of the oven for 15 minutes, or until the meat is falling off the bone and the skin is crisp and nicely browned.

6. Meanwhile, add the reserved half onion and the olives to the casserole and bring to a boil. Reduce to a simmer and cook until the contents are thick and creamy, about 15 minutes. Add lemon juice to taste. Season with salt if necessary.

7. Remove the chicken to a rimmed serving platter, cover completely with the olives and sauce, and serve at once.

CHICKEN WITH PRESERVED LEMON AND OLIVES (M'CHERMEL)

I first ate this dish in a home in Meknes, sometimes called "The City of Olives." *Djej m'chermel* is a classic Moroccan chicken preparation, served in a sublime, intricately spiced, creamy, lemony sauce with a scattering of olives. It is best to use a large wide casserole to cook this dish. If desired, transfer the contents to an attractive serving dish or a large tagine in step 7.

⟶ ❧ Serves 8 ❧ ⟵

2 chickens, preferably organic and air-chilled, quartered, with their livers

2 garlic cloves, thinly sliced

Salt

1 teaspoon ground ginger

1 teaspoon sweet paprika

¼ teaspoon ground cumin, preferably Moroccan

¼ teaspoon freshly ground black pepper

¼ cup extra virgin olive oil

3 large red onions, grated, rinsed, and squeezed dry (about 2½ cups)

¼ teaspoon ground turmeric

2 tablespoons saffron water (see page 48)

¼ cup chopped cilantro

¼ cup chopped flat-leaf parsley

1½ cups green-ripe, midway, or red olives

2 preserved lemons (see page 21), rinsed, pulp removed if desired, and quartered

2 to 3 lemons, halved

1. The day before: Rinse the chickens and pat dry; trim away excess fat. Slide your fingers under the skin to loosen it from the flesh.

2. Mix the garlic with 1 teaspoon salt, the ginger, paprika, cumin, black pepper, and oil and rub the mixture under and over the chicken skin. Mix the excess with the livers. Cover and refrigerate overnight.

3. The next day: Place the chickens, livers, and marinade in a large wide casserole. Add ½ cup of the grated onion, the turmeric, saffron water, herbs, and ½ cup water and slowly heat almost to a boil. Cover and cook at a simmer for 30 minutes, turning the chickens often in the sauce.

4. Remove the chicken livers from the casserole and finely mash them. Return to the casserole along with the remaining onions. (This will give a good deal of heftiness to the sauce.) Add water if necessary and continue cooking, partially covered, for 20 minutes, or until the chicken is very tender and the flesh is just beginning to fall easily from the bone.

5. Meanwhile, rinse and pit the olives. If they seem a little bitter, cover with cold water, bring to a boil, and drain. Set aside.

6. Add the olives and preserved lemon quarters to the sauce.

7. Transfer the chicken to a serving dish or large tagine and spoon the olives and lemons around them. Cover and keep warm. Reduce the sauce to $1\frac{1}{2}$ cups by boiling rapidly, uncovered. Add the juice of 2 lemons to the sauce. Then add salt to taste and more lemon juice, if desired.

8. Pour the sauce over the chicken and serve at once.

CHICKEN WITH PRESERVED LEMON, SOFT BLACK OLIVES, AND NIGELLA SEEDS

An absolutely delightful dish from Marrakech, inspired by a recipe in *L'Authentique Cuisine Marocaine* by Jörg Zipprick and Ben Marrakchi.

———— ❧ Serves 4 ❧ ————

One 3-pound chicken, preferably organic and air-chilled, quartered, backbone and wings removed

1 small garlic clove

2 teaspoons nigella seeds, briefly toasted before using

2 teaspoons coarse salt

¼ cup extra virgin olive oil

1 large onion, halved and thinly sliced

2 tablespoons saffron water (see page 48)

1 teaspoon ground ginger

½ teaspoon freshly ground black pepper

8 ounces Yukon gold potatoes, peeled and cut into 1-inch dice

2 small tomatoes, peeled, halved, seeded, and diced

2 tablespoons finely chopped cilantro

Juice of 1 lemon, or to taste

12 Kalamata or Gaeta olives, pitted, soaked in water to remove excess salt and vinegar, and drained

1 preserved lemon (see page 21), pulp removed, rind rinsed and quartered

1. Rinse the chicken quarters and pat dry; trim away excess fat. Slide your fingers under the skin to loosen it from the flesh.

2. Crush the garlic, half the nigella seeds, and the salt to a paste in a mortar. Loosen with 1 tablespoon of the olive oil. Rub this mixture under and over the skin of the chicken.

3. Heat the remaining 3 tablespoons olive oil in a 12-inch heavy-bottomed skillet over medium-high heat. Add the chicken pieces and fry, turning occasionally, until golden brown on all sides, about 5 minutes. Reduce the heat to medium-low, shove the chicken to one side, tilt the skillet to the other side, and use a spoon to remove almost all the fat.

4. Spread out the chicken pieces, flesh side down, add the onion, cover, and steam for 5 minutes. Add 1 scant cup hot water, the saffron water, ginger, and pepper and bring to a boil. Cover, reduce the heat to low, and cook for 20 minutes. Remove the chicken breasts to a side dish. Cover to keep moist.

5. Add the potatoes, tomatoes, the remaining nigella seeds, and half the cilantro to the sauce in the pan. Cover and cook over medium-low heat for 15 minutes, or until the potatoes and chicken legs are fully cooked.

6. Return the chicken breasts to the skillet and reheat. Correct the seasoning with lemon juice, and baste the chicken with the sauce. Decorate the dish with the olives, the preserved lemon wedges, and the remaining cilantro.

CHICKEN WITH FENNEL, PRESERVED LEMON, AND OLIVES

Mustapha Haddouch, based in Seattle, now imports all the good spices, lemons, and olives needed for true traditional Moroccan cooking.

While I was working on this book, Mustapha suggested I try this recipe, which he described as "bright on the palate" and one of his favorite comfort foods. It's now one of mine too!

⟿ Serves 4 ⟾

4 large chicken legs and thighs (about 2 pounds), preferably organic and air-chilled

2 tablespoon coarse salt

3 tablespoons extra virgin olive oil

8 ounces onions, sliced

1 teaspoon crushed garlic

1 large or 2 small preserved lemons (see page 21), pulp removed, rind rinsed, drained, and quartered

2 tablespoons saffron water (see page 48)

1 teaspoon ground ginger

1 teaspoon green aniseed, preferably Moroccan

Sea salt

2 pounds small fennel bulbs, trimmed and cut into thin, lengthwise slices, plus a few fronds reserved for garnish

18 green-ripe, midway, or red olives

1 tablespoon chopped flat-leaf parsley, for garnish

1. Trim the chicken legs and thighs of excess fat. Soak in 1 quart water and the salt for up to 2 hours. Drain and pat dry.

2. Heat the oil in a large ovenproof skillet. Add the chicken skin side down and fry, without turning, until golden. Transfer the chicken to a side dish. Add the onion and garlic to the pan and cook over medium heat until tender.

3. Add the preserved lemon, ⅓ cup water, the saffron water, ginger, and aniseed and stir once. Return the chicken to the pan, and bring to a boil, then cover, lower the heat, and cook for 25 minutes.

4. Preheat the oven to 325°F.

5. Turn each piece of chicken over and bring the cooking juices to a boil. Add the fennel and olives, cover, and place in the oven to cook for 25 to 30 minutes.

6. If the chicken is not brown enough, turn on the broiler and brown for a few minutes. Taste the sauce and correct the seasoning. Serve hot, sprinkled with the parsley and fennel fronds.

CHICKEN WITH EGGS, PRESERVED LEMON, AND OLIVES

———— Serves 4 ————

This tagine, popular in northern Morocco, is not unlike an Italian frittata, or a Tunisian "tagine," or even a French quiche! Slow-simmered, well-spiced young chickens or cornish hens are cooked and boned. Then, arranged in a shallow baking/serving dish, they are smothered with beaten eggs, studded with olives and diced preserved lemons, and finally baked in the oven.

Please remember to transfer a hot tagine or cazuela to a wooden surface or folded kitchen towel on a serving tray to prevent cracking.

2 young broiler-fryers, poussins, or Cornish game hens (about 1½ pounds each)

1 cup chopped flat-leaf parsley

3 garlic cloves, chopped

¾ cup grated red onion

Salt

1 teaspoon freshly ground black pepper

½ rounded teaspoon ground ginger

2 tablespoons saffron water (see page 48)

4 tablespoons unsalted butter, melted

3 large or 6 small cinnamon sticks

10 large eggs

2 preserved lemons (see page 21), rinsed, pulp removed if desired, and diced

8 green-ripe, midway, or red olives, pitted and chopped

½ cup fresh lemon juice

1. Wash and dry the chickens. Cut each into 3 parts: cut off the legs and thighs, but leave the breasts whole.

2. Mix ⅔ cup of the chopped parsley, the garlic, grated onion, salt to taste, pepper, ginger, saffron water, half the butter, and the cinnamon sticks in a wide 11- or 12-inch tagine or cazuela set on a heat diffuser. Add the poultry and toss to coat on all sides. Add ¼ cup water, cover with a sheet of parchment and the lid, and cook, without disturbing, over medium-low heat, until the poultry is very tender and the flesh is almost falling off the bone, about 1 hour.

3. Preheat the oven to 350°F.

4. Transfer the poultry to a side dish, remove and discard all bones, cover the chicken with foil, and keep warm. Remove any loose bones and the cinnamon sticks from the liquid in the tagine, and cook down to a rich, thick sauce. Slide in the poultry and coat each piece with a spoonful of sauce.

5. Beat the eggs to a froth with the remaining ⅓ cup parsley. Stir the preserved lemon and chopped olives into the eggs, and pour the egg mixture over the poultry. Cover the dish with aluminum foil and bake on the middle shelf of the oven for 20 minutes.

6. Raise the heat to the highest setting. Remove the foil and drizzle the eggs with the remaining melted butter. Transfer the dish to the upper oven shelf and bake for 10 minutes more, or until the eggs are completely set and the poultry has slightly charred. Sprinkle with the lemon juice and serve.

CRISPY CHICKEN WITH PRESERVED LEMON AND OLIVES MQQUALI

—— Serves 4 ——

1 chicken, preferably organic and air-chilled, quartered

2 garlic cloves

1 teaspoon ground ginger

Salt

¼ teaspoon freshly ground black pepper

1 preserved lemon (see page 21), rind rinsed and quartered

¼ cup extra virgin olive oil

2 chicken livers

2 tablespoons saffron water (see page 48)

¼ teaspoon ground turmeric

½ cup grated onion, drained

6 cilantro sprigs, tied together

½ cup green-ripe, midway, or red olives, pitted

1. One day in advance: Wash and dry the chicken; trim off excess fat. Slide your fingers under the skin to loosen it from the flesh.

2. Combine the garlic cloves, the ginger, a little salt, the pepper, the pulp of the preserved lemon (reserve the rind for step 7), and the oil in a blender and blend until smooth. Rub over and under the skin of the chicken, and mix the excess with the livers. Cover with plastic wrap and refrigerate overnight.

3. The next day: Place the chicken pieces, livers, and marinade in a tagine set on a heat diffuser over medium-low heat. Add the saffron water, turmeric, onion, cilantro sprigs, and ¼ cup water. Cover with a sheet of parchment and the tagine top and cook at a low simmer until the chicken flesh is just beginning to fall easily from the bone, about 1 hour.

4. Preheat the oven to 450°F.

5. Remove and discard the parchment paper and cilantro. Carefully transfer the chicken, skin side up, to a baking sheet and place on the upper shelf of the oven for 15 minutes, or until the skin is crisp and brown.

6. Meanwhile, remove the livers, mash them, and return to the sauce. If the sauce is thin, pour it into a saucepan and boil down to ¾ cup, then return to the tagine.

7. Add the quartered preserved lemon peel and olives to the sauce in the tagine. Return the chicken to the tagine and spoon over the sauce. Cover and cook over low heat for 10 more minutes. Let the tagine stand with its top on for 5 minutes. Remove the cover and serve at once.

ROAST CHICKEN ON A FAUX SPIT WITH LEMON AND OLIVES

In this recipe, I marinate the chicken in a yellow sauce called *daghmira*: a blend of chopped parsley, cilantro, ginger, pepper, saffron, lots of garlic, and, very often, the pulp of a preserved lemon.

I prefer to roast the chicken in an upright position so it will self-baste as the fat flows downward. There are a number of excellent devices for doing this, including various ceramic and metal cones. You can also use a beer can roasting device or a wire roaster in a shallow roasting pan.

— Serves 4 —

One 3½-pound chicken, preferably organic and air-chilled

1 preserved lemon (see page 21), rinsed

4 large garlic cloves

Coarse salt

1 teaspoon ground ginger

½ teaspoon freshly ground white pepper

½ teaspoon ground turmeric

3 tablespoons saffron water (see page 48)

2 tablespoons chopped flat-leaf parsley

2 tablespoons chopped cilantro

2 tablespoons extra virgin olive oil

2 tablespoons Smen, Oudi (page 159 or 161), or clarified butter

1 cup chicken stock

2 medium onions, grated, rinsed, and squeezed dry

12 green-ripe, midway, or red olives, pitted

1. About 4 hours before serving, rinse the chicken inside and out and pat dry with paper towels. Slide your fingers under the skin to loosen it from the flesh.

2. Remove the pulp from the preserved lemon, chopping and saving the peel for the sauce. Add the lemon pulp, garlic, 1 teaspoon salt, the ginger, pepper, turmeric, saffron water, herbs, oil, and *smen* or butter to the jar of a blender and grind to a paste. Insert some of the paste under the skin of the chicken and massage into the flesh. Put some of the paste into the cavity and rub the remainder all over the skin. Put the chicken in a bowl, cover, and refrigerate for 1 to 2 hours.

3. About 2 hours before you plan to serve the chicken, remove it from the refrigerator. Position a rack on the lowest shelf and preheat the oven to 400°F.

4. Set a standing ceramic or metal cone, beer can, or wire roaster in a shallow baking dish. Add about 1 cup water to the dish. Stand the chicken up on the cone (or can or wire roaster); set the bowl of marinade aside. Roast until an instant-read thermometer set deep into the inner thigh reaches 165°F, about 45 minutes to 1 hour.

5. Meanwhile, add the chicken stock to the bowl in which you marinated the chicken, then scrape all the liquid and marinade into a 9-inch skillet. Add the onions and cook, stirring, until the onions turn golden brown. Add the olives and reserved lemon peel and bring to a boil, then reduce the heat and simmer for 10 minutes. Remove from the heat and set aside.

6. Transfer the chicken to a carving board and let rest for 5 to 10 minutes before carving.

7. Meanwhile, skim the fat from the juices in the baking dish, add the juices to the skillet, and boil down to a thick, unctuous sauce.

8. Carve the chicken and serve with the sauce.

CASSEROLE-ROASTED CHICKEN WITH PRESERVED LEMON AND OLIVES

Here's a slightly different take on the preceding recipe, using a sophisticated blend of spices created for Mustapha Haddouch in Morocco, which he calls "Mélange #2 Spices" (see Sources). It does impart a deep, haunting, vivid flavor to chicken. It's not easy to substitute, but the combination of ¾ teaspoon La Kama Spice Mixture (page 37) and ½ teaspoon each of ground coriander, ground cumin, and sweet paprika works well.

⟶ Serves 4 ⟵

One 3- to 4-pound chicken, preferably organic and air-chilled

Sea salt and freshly ground black pepper

½ cup finely chopped flat-leaf parsley

½ cup finely chopped cilantro

2 teaspoons "Mélange #2 Spices" (see headnote on La Kama Spice Mixture, page 37)

3 tablespoons extra virgin olive oil

1 medium red onion, finely chopped (1 cup)

1 preserved lemon (see page 21), pulp removed, rind rinsed and chopped

10 to 12 green-ripe, midway, or red olives, pitted

1. Rinse and dry the chicken; trim away the excess fat. Slide your fingers under the skin to loosen it from the flesh. Season the chicken inside and out with salt and pepper.

2. Combine the herbs, spice mixture, 2 tablespoons of the oil, and 2 tablespoons water in a food processor and process to a paste. Rub some of the mixture inside the chicken and under the skin and use the rest to heavily coat the skin on all sides. Let stand for 20 minutes.

3. Preheat the oven to 350°F.

4. Add the remaining tablespoon of the olive oil, the chopped onion, and a good pinch of salt to an enameled cast-iron casserole just large enough to hold the chicken, set over medium heat, cover, and let the onion steam for about 10 minutes. Add the chopped preserved lemon and cook, uncovered, until it begins to caramelize.

5. Tie the legs of the chicken together with kitchen string. Place the chicken on its side in the casserole and cook until browned, about 5 minutes. Carefully turn the chicken onto its other side and cook until browned, about 5 minutes longer. Turn the chicken breast side up, cover, place in the oven, and bake for 1¼ hours.

6. Transfer the chicken to a shallow baking pan, placing it on its side (set the casserole aside). Turn on the broiler and deeply brown the chicken, 3 to 5 minutes. Turn the chicken onto the other side and brown for another 3 to 5 minutes. Transfer to a carving board and let rest for 10 minutes.

7. Meanwhile, skim off any fat from the casserole. Add the olives and ¼ cup water, bring to a boil, and cook, stirring, until reduced to a thick sauce. Correct the seasoning.

8. Carve the chicken and serve with the sauce poured on top.

CHICKEN WITH
LEMON AND EGGS

Back in the 1970s, when I was living in Tangier and working on my first Moroccan cookbook, I was invited to Rabat to learn what was described to me as "a great dish that will be demonstrated for you by a virtuoso cook." The demonstrator turned out to be a short, squat, very dark-skinned Berber woman named Rakia, a specialist at making *djej mefenned*, one of the most difficult to execute dishes in Moroccan cuisine.

Rakia turned out to be quite the character. She cracked jokes as she worked and sang and belly danced around the kitchen, the whole while puffing on strong Koutoubia-brand cigarettes. When she dropped something on the floor, which she did several times, she bent straight down from the waist like a jackknife blade to pick it up.

For all her amusing traits, her technique was truly dazzling, as she twirled a whole chicken in sizzling fat while simultaneously basting it with seasoned beaten eggs. This procedure resulted in an herbed, silken cloak that bonded to the bird just before it was brought to the table.

"Yes, it's very hard to do," Rakia assured me with one of her laughs, implying that I would probably never be able to master the technique. "Of course there is an easier way, the one the cooks down near Agadir follow. But it's not the same at all!" she added with another cackle.

I offer both recipes so you can try them, in the process discovering how diverse and rich these dishes are. First the easier Agadir version: in this preparation, chicken parts are submerged in lemon-flavored eggs, which then surround the chicken like a rich custard.

—◦❀ Serves 4 ❀◦—

4 large chicken legs and thighs, preferably organic and air-chilled, separated into drumsticks and thighs

3 large garlic cloves

Coarse salt

1 teaspoon ground ginger

Freshly ground black pepper

Pinch of ground Ceylon cinnamon

4 tablespoons unsalted butter, softened

1 tablespoon Smen or Oudi (page 159 or 161)

2 tablespoons saffron water (see page 48)

1 large onion, grated, rinsed, and squeezed dry

½ preserved lemon (see page 21), pulp removed, rind rinsed and diced

3 tablespoons chopped flat-leaf parsley

1 tablespoon chopped cilantro

5 large eggs

Juice of 1 lemon

1. About 2 hours before serving, rinse the chicken and pat dry; trim away excess fat.

2. Pound the garlic and 1 teaspoon salt to a paste in a mortar. Mix in the ginger, $\frac{1}{2}$ teaspoon pepper, the cinnamon, 2 tablespoons of the butter, and the *smen* (or thyme-scented butter). Mix the saffron water with $\frac{1}{3}$ cup hot water and gradually stir it into the spice mixture, as if making a mayonnaise. Add half the grated onion and pour into an 11- to 12-inch tagine. Place the chicken pieces skin side up on top and allow to stand at room temperature for about 15 minutes.

3. Cover the tagine, set on a heat diffuser over medium-low heat, and cook, without disturbing, until the chicken is tender, about 1 hour. Transfer the chicken pieces to a broiling pan, skin side up, and pat dry. Pour the contents of the tagine into a bowl and let stand for a few minutes.

4. Preheat the broiler. Skim off the fat that has risen to the top of the cooking liquid and reserve $\frac{1}{4}$ cup; discard the remaining fat. Return the tagine to medium-low heat and add the rest of the grated onion and half of the reserved fat. Cook, stirring occasionally, until the onion is lightly caramelized, about 10 minutes. Scrape into the sauce in the bowl and mix to combine. Add the diced preserved lemon and herbs. Set the sauce aside. (Do not wash the tagine.)

5. Brush the remaining reserved fat over the chicken legs and thighs, set them under the broiler about 6 inches from the heat, and cook for about 5 minutes to crisp the skin. Set aside in a warm place while you finish the sauce.

6. Melt the remaining 2 tablespoons butter in the tagine over medium-low heat. Whisk the eggs in a bowl until well blended. Season with a pinch each of salt and pepper. When the butter is foaming, add the eggs and cook, stirring gently and continually scraping the bottom. As the eggs begin to thicken, gradually add the lemon juice, 1 tablespoon at a time, stirring slowly to a creamy consistency. Immediately turn off the heat and fold in the sauce. Season with additional salt and pepper to taste.

7. Nestle the broiled chicken, skin side up, in the custardy sauce, cover, and let stand for a few minutes. Transfer the hot tagine to a wooden surface or folded kitchen towel to prevent cracking. Serve warm.

RAKIA'S BRILLIANT CHICKEN COATED WITH EGGS

This is the famous *djej mefenned*, one of the most difficult of all Moroccan chicken dishes to execute well; see Rakia's story on page 310. If the technique of twirling the whole chicken in sizzling butter while basting it with seasoned eggs seems too difficult, you can do it the Tetuanese way: quarter the chicken, coat the pieces separately, and fry them as you might fry chicken in America.

———— Serves 8 ————

Two 3-pound chickens, preferably organic and air-chilled

¼ cup saffron water (see page 48)

1 teaspoon mashed garlic

¼ teaspoon ground turmeric

2 teaspoons paprika

¼ teaspoon ground cumin, preferably Moroccan

Salt

3 chicken livers

¼ cup grated onion

12 tablespoons (1½ sticks) unsalted butter

1 tablespoon finely chopped cilantro

EGG COATING

8 large eggs

½ cup finely chopped flat-leaf parsley

Heaping ½ teaspoon sweet paprika

¼ teaspoon ground cumin, preferably Moroccan

⅛ teaspoon salt

¼ cup fresh lemon juice

1. Rinse and dry the chickens; remove the excess fat.

2. Mix the saffron water with the garlic, spices, and 1 teaspoon salt and rub into the chickens. Lay the chickens on their sides in a wide casserole. Add the livers, onion, and half the butter. Pour in 1 cup water and slowly bring to a boil. Add the cilantro and simmer, covered, over medium-low heat for about 1 hour, turning the chickens from time to time until they are very tender. Midway through, remove and mash the livers, then return them to the sauce.

3. Remove the chickens from the casserole. Boil the sauce until reduced to ¾ cup. Keep the sauce warm. Heat the remaining butter in a large skillet. Brown one chicken at a time, turning occasionally, until crusty all over. Strain the fat left in the pan and reserve. Tie the chickens' legs together with kitchen string.

4. Beat the eggs with the parsley, paprika, cumin, and salt to a good froth. Transfer to a large shallow pan. Roll the first crusty chicken in the eggs until well coated.

5. Clean the skillet and return the reserved fat to the pan, along with the butter. Heat the fat and butter, then add the egg-coated chicken. As the egg coating browns, start spooning additional beaten eggs from the pan over the chicken. The eggs will slip over the chicken into the hot butter and begin to congeal. Immediately lift the congealing eggs with a spoon and press them lightly against the chicken. As you continue to do this, more and more of the egg mixture will adhere. (Regulate the heat as you work: it takes about 4 minutes to do each bird.) Continue to patch pieces of egg onto empty spaces and slowly turn the bird so the egg crust browns in the butter. (At the same time you can apply more egg coating to the other side of the bird.) Carefully remove the first chicken to an ovenproof serving platter and keep warm in a low oven, then repeat with the next chicken. Sprinkle the chickens with the lemon juice.

6. Reheat the sauce, pour over the chickens, and serve at once.

CHICKEN MECHOUI

In one of the palaces of the royal family in Marrakech, there is a courtyard devoted to the spit-roasting of chickens. At least a dozen spits are slanted diagonally over piles of burning-hot coals, each attended by two men—one to crank the spit, the other to paint the roasting chickens with spiced butter.

———◎ Serves 4 ◎———

Two 2-pound broiler-fryers, whole, split, or quartered

3 scallions, white part only, chopped

1 garlic clove (optional)

2 tablespoons roughly chopped cilantro

2 tablespoons roughly chopped flat-leaf parsley

1 teaspoon salt

1½ teaspoons sweet paprika

Pinch of cayenne

1½ teaspoons ground cumin, preferably Moroccan

4 tablespoons unsalted butter, softened

1. Rinse the chicken and pat dry; trim away excess fat. Slide your fingers under the skin to loosen it from the flesh.

2. Pound the scallions with the garlic, herbs, salt, and spices in a mortar. Blend in the butter to make a paste. Rub the paste under and over the chicken skin (and into the cavities if left whole). Arrange in a roasting pan and let marinate for at least 1 hour.

3. Heat an outdoor grill or preheat the broiler.

4. Arrange the pieces of chicken skin side up over the coals or skin side down on a broiler pan under the broiler. After 5 minutes, turn and baste with any extra paste or the juices in the broiler pan. Continue turning and basting every 5 minutes until the chickens are done; timing will depend on the heat of the coals.

STEAMED CHICKEN

This dish is quite beautiful because of its simplicity. The chicken is rubbed with saffron, butter, and salt, then steamed until its flesh is very tender and has acquired a delicate flavor.

In Tangier, small white onions are placed inside the chicken, along with a few sprigs of parsley. In Tetouan, the chicken is often stuffed with wild greens or rice, tomatoes, olives, and preserved lemons and spiced with cayenne. Some northern Moroccan cooks gently brown the chicken in butter after removing it from the steamer, but I think this method interferes with the delicacy.

Please note: A steamed chicken must be served at once if you want to eat it hot. It does not reheat well, but it is excellent served cold, accompanied, in the Tetouan style, by sliced raw onions and chopped parsley.

⸙ Serves 4 ⸙

One 3-pound chicken, preferably organic and air-chilled

2 good pinches pulverized saffron threads

1 teaspoon salt

4 tablespoons unsalted butter, softened

Ground cumin, preferably Moroccan

Coarse salt for serving

Cayenne (optional)

1. Rinse the chicken and pat dry; remove the excess fat.

2. Pound the saffron with the salt in a mortar. Blend with the softened butter. Rub into the skin of the chicken. Rub salt into the interior of the chicken.

3. Fill the bottom of a couscousier or steamer with water and bring to a boil. Seal on the perforated top or colander as directed in step 2 in the couscous master instructions on page 199. Place the chicken in the steamer top, breast side up, and cover with a double layer of cheesecloth. Cover tightly and steam for 1 hour without lifting the cover.

4. Serve at once, as is, with accompanying bowls of ground cumin and coarse salt, or, if desired, mix some cumin and salt with a sprinkling of cayenne pepper.

DOUBLE-COOKED RED CHICKEN, MARRAKECH-STYLE

The generous use of Moroccan mild paprika in this classic recipe explains the name, *mhammer*, meaning "reddish." The double-cooking method adds complexity and depth of flavor. Garnish with slices of preserved lemon (see page 21) if desired.

===== Serves 6 to 8 =====

5 garlic cloves

1 tablespoon coarsely chopped cilantro

1¼ teaspoons coarse salt

2 tablespoons saffron water (see page 48)

2 tablespoons unsalted butter, melted

Two 3-pound chickens, preferably organic and air-chilled, backbones removed and reserved (see Notes)

1½ tablespoons sweet paprika

1 teaspoon ground cumin, preferably Moroccan

¼ teaspoon freshly ground black pepper

Pinch of ground ginger

Cayenne

1 small onion, grated

1. Mash or pulse the garlic, cilantro, and 1 teaspoon of the salt to a coarse paste in a mortar or mini food processor. Transfer the paste to a bowl and stir in the saffron water and melted butter.

2. Rub the garlic paste all over the chickens. Cover loosely with plastic wrap and let marinate at room temperature for 1 hour.

3. Cut up the chicken backbones and put in a large enameled cast-iron casserole. Add the chickens, breast side up. Combine 1 tablespoon of the paprika, half the cumin, the pepper, ginger, and a pinch of cayenne in a bowl. Sprinkle the spice mixture over the chickens. Cook over medium-low heat until steam begins to rise, about 5 minutes.

4. Mix the onion with 1½ cups water and pour around the chickens. Bring to a boil over high heat, then reduce the heat to low, cover, and simmer until the juices run clear when the thighs are pierced near the bone with a knife, about 1 hour. Transfer the chickens to a cutting board and remove the strings; keep the chickens intact. Discard the backbones. Skim off the fat from the sauce, reserving 3 tablespoons fat. Boil the sauce until it is reduced to 1 cup, about 15 minutes. Transfer to a small saucepan and keep warm.

5. Preheat the broiler. Stir the remaining spices into the reserved chicken fat. Add the remaining ½ teaspoon salt. Put the chickens in a roasting pan, breast side up, and rub with the spiced fat. Broil 8 to 10 inches from the heat for 10 minutes, or until browned. Carve the chickens and pass the warm sauce at the table.

NOTES TO THE COOK

Ask your butcher to remove the backbones from the chickens. Or use kitchen shears or a large sharp knife to cut down both sides of the backbones to remove them.

Rinse the chickens and pat dry; trim away any excess fat. Re-form the chickens and tie them with kitchen string.

BRAISED AND FRIED GAME HENS WITH SAUTÉED ALMONDS

In this recipe, the hens remain moist and silky because of the extra-slow cooking. Then, just before serving, their skins are crisped in sizzling butter and oil. As with the previous recipe, this type of dish is called *mhammer*, which means "reddish," the result of a generous quantity of paprika in the spicing.

The livers are cooked along with the hens in a mildly seasoned sauce, then mashed to a paste and returned to the sauce, where they act as a subtle thickener. Serve the hens surrounded with wedges of Moroccan bread, and finish the meal with fresh fruit and cups of mint tea.

꙳ Serves 6 ꙳

Three 1-pound Cornish game hens, livers and necks reserved

2 tablespoons saffron water (see page 48)

Coarse salt

3 tablespoons unsalted butter, melted

1½ teaspoons paprika, preferably medium-sweet, plus more to taste

1¼ teaspoons ground ginger

¼ teaspoon ground cumin, preferably Moroccan, plus more to taste

2 large garlic cloves

10 cilantro sprigs, tied together

¾ cup grated red onion

½ cup vegetable oil

¼ cup clarified butter

1 cup blanched whole almonds, lightly browned in vegetable oil

1. Rinse the hens and pat dry; remove the excess fat. Mix the saffron water with salt and the melted butter in a small bowl. Rub the mixture all over the skin of the hens. Set aside at room temperature for 1 hour.

2. Place each hen on its side in a large flameproof casserole and add the livers and necks. Sprinkle with the paprika, ginger, cumin, and 1 teaspoon salt. Heat gently. Cover, take the pot in your hands, and give it a good swirl.

3. Meanwhile, crush the garlic and ½ teaspoon salt to a paste in a mortar. Add to the casserole along with the cilantro, onion, and enough water to just cover the hens. Cover and bring just to a boil. Reduce the heat to low and cook until the hens are very tender, about 1 hour. Remove the casserole from the heat and let the hens cool for 5 minutes in the liquid.

4. Carefully remove the hens, without allowing them to break apart, and set on a platter to cool and drain. Transfer the livers to a work surface or a wide bowl. With a slotted spoon, remove and discard the necks and cilantro. Skim off and discard the fat that rises to the surface.

5. Crush the livers with a fork. Gradually work 3 tablespoons of the cooking liquid into the livers to form a smooth puree.

6. Bring the remaining cooking liquid in the casserole to a boil over high heat and boil until reduced to 1½ cups. Stir or whisk in the liver and simmer until the sauce is thickened. Adjust the seasoning with salt. Add pinches of cumin and paprika to perk up the flavor. (The recipe can be prepared to this point up to 3 hours in advance. Set the hens and sauce aside in a cool place.)

7. About 20 minutes before serving, heat the oil and clarified butter in a large skillet over high heat. Add the hens, in batches if necessary, and brown on all sides. (Use a splatter screen to protect yourself from the hot fat.) As the hens brown, transfer them to a deep round serving platter, and hold them in a 200°F oven. (The hens can instead be halved and browned under the broiler, but the skin will not be as crusty.)

8. Gently reheat the sauce, stirring occasionally. Serve the hens surrounded with the sauce and topped with the browned almonds.

TANGIER-STYLE
FRIED CHICKEN

⟿ Serves 4 ⟾

8 small chicken legs and thighs
  (2 pounds), each separated into
  2 pieces and boned

3 tablespoons extra virgin olive oil

3 tablespoons fresh lemon juice

3 garlic cloves, thinly sliced

1½ tablespoons chopped flat-leaf
  parsley

Pinch of ground ginger

Pinch of ground Ceylon cinnamon

Coarse sea salt and freshly ground
  black pepper

About 4 cups vegetable oil, for
  deep-frying

3 large eggs

1½ tablespoons milk

1½ cups fine dry bread crumbs

1 cup bite-sized pieces butter
  lettuce, such as Boston

3 lemons, cut into wedges

8 to 12 soft black olives,
  for garnish

NOTES TO THE COOK

This is a take on a popular Spanish-Moroccan dish, *criadillas*, made with lamb sweetbreads. Here chicken is marinated in olive oil, garlic, and lemon juice, then cooked in a highly unorthodox manner: dipped first in bread crumbs, and second in beaten eggs, and deep-fried. As soon as the poultry hits the hot oil, a thin, lacy web of egg seals it, keeping the chicken juicy and tender, and almost grease-free. Accompany this very easy dish with a salad of red peppers and preserved lemons (see page 86). The flavors mingle perfectly, making for a very fine light supper.

I usually prepare this recipe in an electric frying pan, but you can also do it in a deep skillet on the stovetop.

1. Pound each boned chicken piece until ¼ inch thick. Trim away any fat and gristle. Mix the oil, lemon juice, garlic, parsley, ginger, cinnamon, and salt and pepper to taste in a bowl. Add the chicken and let it marinate for 1 hour at room temperature, tossing occasionally, or in the refrigerator for up to 4 hours.

2. Heat at least 3 inches of oil to 360°F in an electric frying pan or deep skillet.

3. Meanwhile, beat the eggs and milk in a small bowl until well combined. Drain the chicken pieces, but do not pat them dry; discard the marinade. Dip the moist chicken pieces in the bread crumbs and arrange them side by side on a large tray.

4. Dip 3 or 4 pieces of breaded chicken at a time (enough to fit in the pan without crowding) into the beaten eggs and add them one at a time to the hot oil. Fry until the pieces float to the surface and turn golden brown, about 2 minutes. (Cooking time may vary, depending on the thickness of the chicken.) Turn the chicken and fry until the second side is golden, about 2 minutes longer. Remove with a slotted spoon and drain on paper towels. Repeat with the remaining chicken pieces.

5. Cover a large platter with the pieces of lettuce. Arrange the chicken on top and sprinkle with coarse salt. Decorate with the lemon wedges and olives.

CHICKEN KEDRA WITH CHICKPEAS AND TURNIPS

For this *kedra,* try to use turnips that are young and freshly picked and still retain their stalks and leaves. If you don't have a vegetable garden, you'll probably find them at your local farmers' market in season. It's the stalks that make this dish.

——— ◈ Serves 4 ◈ ———

½ cup dried chickpeas

2 pounds young white turnips

1 (3- to 3½-pound) chicken, preferably organic and air-chilled, quartered

2 onions, quartered and sliced lengthwise

Salt

1 teaspoon freshly ground pepper

½ teaspoon ground turmeric

¼ teaspoon ground ginger

2 tablespoons saffron water (see page 48)

2 tablespoons Homemade Smen (page 159)

6 cups chicken stock or water

Juice of ½ to 1 lemon

Chopped flat-leaf parsley

1. One day in advance: Soak the chickpeas in water to cover generously.

2. The following day: Drain the chickpeas and peel as directed on page 51.

3. Trim the turnips, reserving the greens. Finely chop enough of the leaves and the stems to make 1 cup each.

4. Rinse and drain the chicken; trim away excess fat. Place in a medium to large casserole with the onions, 1 teaspoon salt, the spices, saffron water, and *smen.* Pour in the chicken stock or water and bring just to a boil. Add the chickpeas, turnips, turnip leaves, and turnip stalks, cover, reduce the heat to low, and cook for 45 minutes.

5. Lift out the chicken and, using a slotted spoon, remove the turnips, stalks, and greens to a bowl; keep warm. Return the chicken to the pot and cook for 15 more minutes, or until its flesh is just coming off the bone. Remove the chicken and the chickpeas from the casserole.

6. Bring the cooking juices back to a boil and reduce to a thick gravy. Add the juice of ½ lemon, then correct the seasoning. Return the chicken and the chickpeas, and the turnips, stalks, and greens to the sauce and reheat. Serve with a sprinkling of parsley.

❈

TRADITIONAL CHICKEN KEDRAS

A *kedra* is a particular type of stew, cooked in a deep casserole rather than in a tagine. It's made with the strong Moroccan butter called *smen* and a good deal of onion, reduced to butter softness, spiced with pepper and saffron, and usually cut at the end with a dash of lemon juice. The reason you don't use a tagine is that a *kedra* is a brothy style of stew and thus requires a deeper pot.

Kedras are delicious and rich, and if they have a failing, it is their somewhat unattractive, pale yellow appearance. To make them look more appetizing, some Moroccan cooks brown the chickens in a hot oven or in a skillet in the skimmed-off fat while finishing the sauce, but this is not done in classic *kedra* cooking.

In Fes, *kedras* are always made pure—that is, without ginger, paprika, or cumin added. But in Rabat, Marrakech, and Tangier, this strict constructionist view is usually ignored. Use any or all of the above-mentioned spices if you wish, but if you are entertaining Fassis, do so with the knowledge that they will smile behind your back.

CHICKEN KEDRA WITH ALMONDS AND CHICKPEAS

Variation:

CHICKEN KEDRA WITH
ALMONDS

. . . .

This is a simple variation on this
recipe. Omit the chickpeas and
double the amount of almonds.

Here is one of the most famous chicken *kedras*, called *djej kedra touimiya*. It is made with whole blanched almonds and chickpeas. You might think that crisp almonds would go well with chicken, but, in fact, the almonds should be soft. If they are old, it can sometimes take more than 2 hours to transform them to this state.

—— Serves 4 to 5 ——

½ cup dried chickpeas

1 cup blanched whole almonds

One 3- to 3½-pound chicken, preferably organic and air-chilled, quartered

2 tablespoons saffron water (see page 48)

Salt

1 teaspoon freshly ground white pepper

½ teaspoon ground ginger

1 large Ceylon cinnamon stick

¼ teaspoon ground turmeric

2 tablespoons Smen or Oudi (page 159 or 161)

2 large yellow onions, 1 grated, the other quartered lengthwise and thinly sliced

4 cups chicken stock or water, plus more if necessary

¼ cup chopped flat-leaf parsley

Juice of 1 lemon, or to taste

1. One day in advance: Soak the chickpeas in water to cover generously.

2. The next day: Drain the chickpeas and peel as directed on page 51; set aside.

3. Cover the almonds with cold water in a saucepan and simmer, covered, for at least 2 hours, or until soft. (The cooking time depends upon the freshness of the almonds.)

4. Rinse and dry the chicken; remove the excess fat. Combine half the saffron water, salt, the spices, cinnamon stick, *smen*, grated onion, and chicken in a medium casserole. Cook over low heat for 2 to 3 minutes. Add the stock or water. Bring to a boil, add the peeled chickpeas and a little more water, if necessary, reduce the heat, and simmer for 30 minutes, covered.

5. Add the remaining sliced onions and the chopped parsley and continue cooking for 30 minutes more, or until the chicken is very tender (the flesh almost falling off the bone).

6. Transfer the chicken to a warm serving plate. Boiling rapidly, uncovered, reduce the sauce in the casserole to a thick gravy.

7. Drain the almonds and add to the sauce, along with the remaining saffron water, and cook together for 1 to 2 minutes. Correct the seasoning, add lemon juice to cut the richness of the sauce, and spoon over the chicken. Serve hot.

CHICKEN KEDRA WITH ALMONDS AND RICE

In this recipe, you sew the rice into a cheesecloth bag, then poach it in the sauce, an ingenious technique in that the rice captures the flavor of the sauce yet stays moist—and does not stick to the bottom of the pan.

———— Serves 4 or 5 ————

1 cup blanched whole almonds

1 cup long-grain rice

One 3- to 3½-pound chicken, preferably organic and air-chilled, quartered

¼ cup saffron water (see page 48)

1 teaspoon freshly ground white pepper

½ teaspoon ground ginger

¼ teaspoon ground turmeric

2 tablespoons Smen or Oudi (page 159 or 161)

2 large yellow onions, 1 grated, the other quartered lengthwise and thinly sliced

Salt

4 cups chicken stock or water, plus more if necessary

¼ cup chopped flat-leaf parsley

Juice of ½ lemon, or more to taste

1. Cover the almonds with cold water in a saucepan and simmer, covered, for at least 2 hours, or until soft. (The cooking time depends on the freshness of the almonds.)

2. Meanwhile, fold a piece of cheesecloth in half and sew up two of the sides. Make the bag large enough so the rice has room to expand (a capacity of 3 cups). Spoon in the rice and sew up the remaining side.

3. Rinse and pat dry the chicken; remove the excess fat. Place the chicken in a medium casserole and add half the saffron water, the spices, *smen*, grated onion, and ½ teaspoon salt. Cook over low heat for 2 to 3 minutes. Finely chop half the onions and add to the casserole, along with the 4 cups stock or water, and bring to a boil, then reduce the heat and simmer the chicken for 30 minutes.

4. Add the remaining sliced onion, the parsley, the bag of rice, and more stock or water if necessary. (Be sure there is enough liquid in the casserole to accommodate the rice.) Simmer for 20 to 25 minutes, then remove the bag of rice and keep warm. Continue to cook until the chicken is very tender, falling off the bones. Remove the chicken and keep warm.

5. Drain the almonds and add to the sauce. Add the remaining saffron water and a little more water if necessary and cook together for 5 minutes.

6. Meanwhile, open the bag of rice and form a pyramid of rice in the center of a serving dish. Arrange the pieces of chicken around the rice. Add the lemon juice to the sauce, and pour over the chicken. Serve hot.

CHICKEN SIMMERED IN SMEN

This is an updated version of a very old dish from Fes, using a blender to facilitate the making of the sauce.

⊸ Serves 4 ⊶

One 3-pound chicken, preferably organic and air-chilled, quartered

2 chicken livers

¾ cup grated red onion

2 tablespoons saffron water (see page 48)

¼ teaspoon ground turmeric

½ teaspoon freshly ground white pepper

1 teaspoon salt, or to taste

¼ cup roughly chopped flat-leaf parsley

2 to 3 tablespoons Smen or Oudi (page 159 or 161)

2 tablespoons unsalted butter, preferably clarified

½ preserved lemon (see page 21), pulp removed, rind rinsed and diced

2 tablespoons fresh lemon juice

1. Rinse and dry the chicken; remove the excess fat. Place the chicken in a casserole with the livers and onion. Sprinkle with the saffron water, spices, and salt and toss to coat evenly.

2. Puree the parsley in a blender with ¼ cup water. Add half the "parsley water" and all the *smen* to the casserole. Pour in 1 cup water and bring to a boil. Reduce the heat and simmer, covered, for 1 hour, or until the chicken is very tender, adding more water if necessary. Remove the chicken to a colander to drain. Keep warm while the sauce simmers for few more minutes.

3. Heat the butter in a large skillet and gently brown the drained chicken quarters. Transfer to a flameproof serving dish, cover, and keep warm.

4. Meanwhile, add the remaining parsley water to the sauce in the casserole and boil rapidly, uncovered, to reduce to 1½ cups. Dump the sauce, livers, and odd bits of skin and bits into a blender jar. Whirl until the sauce is smooth. Pour over the chicken.

5. Sprinkle the diced lemon peel over the chicken and simmer for 5 minutes. Taste for seasoning and add salt if necessary. Sprinkle with the lemon juice and serve at once.

CHICKEN STUFFED WITH EGGS, ONIONS, AND PARSLEY

This recipe is freely adapted from *Moorish Recipes*, collected and compiled by John, Fourth Marquis of Bute, K.T. Though Lord Bute, whose book is both charming and instructive, claims that his recipes from the Mennebi Palace in Tangier "follow more closely the Marrakesh taste," this particular recipe is decidedly Tetouanese, with a strong Andalusian influence, indicated by its egg crust.

———— ❧ Serves 4 ❧ ————

One 3- to 3½-pound chicken, preferably organic and air-chilled, neck and giblets reserved

Coarse salt and freshly ground black pepper

5 large eggs

2 tablespoons unsalted butter

¾ cup minced onion

¼ cup chopped flat-leaf parsley

2 tablespoons saffron water (see page 48)

1½ teaspoons ground turmeric

½ teaspoon ground ginger

3 tablespoons extra virgin olive oil

2 cups chicken stock or water, plus more if needed

2 cinnamon sticks

1. Rinse the chicken. Remove the excess fat and rub with coarse salt, then rinse and pat dry. Sew up the neck opening securely. Rub the inside of the large cavity with salt and pepper.

2. Fry the eggs in the butter until almost set, then break the yolks and begin stirring to create large fluffy but firm scrambled eggs. Remove from the heat; mix with the onion, parsley, saffron water, turmeric, salt to taste, ½ teaspoon black pepper, and the ginger. Allow to cool for 10 minutes.

3. Stuff the chicken with a little more than half of this mixture. Sew up the rump opening and tie the feet together. Reserve the remaining egg mixture.

4. Place the chicken breast side up in a heavy-bottomed casserole, with the neck, giblets, oil, and chicken stock. Bring to a boil. Add the cinnamon sticks, reduce the heat, and simmer, partially covered, for 1 hour, basting the chicken often and adding more stock or water if necessary. Remove the chicken when it is very tender and place in an ovenproof serving dish.

5. Preheat the oven to 500°F.

6. Boil the sauce to reduce it to a thick gravy, about ¾ cup. Discard the cinnamon sticks.

7. Spoon the remaining egg mixture over the chicken and surround with the gravy. Place in the oven long enough to brown nicely, then serve at once.

CHICKEN STUFFED WITH RICE, ALMONDS, AND RAISINS

I can't resist introducing this recipe with the same story I included years ago in *Couscous and Other Good Food from Morocco*. Rereading it put a smile on my face as I recalled this culinary adventure, my trepidation and "triumph" as I went after recipes the way a prospector goes after gold.

Winter nights are cold in Marrakech. I shivered as I moved through the narrow passageways of the medina, searching out El Bahia Restaurant in the maze. Moorish restaurants are often located in old palaces with windows starting on the second floor—a type of architecture that reflects the Moroccan desire to shroud life in mystery and to hide secrets from prying eyes. My visit to a restaurant kitchen would be an unprecedented invasion into a world of jealousy and intrigue, a fact I did not fully understand as I pounded on the wooden door.

An unveiled young girl wearing floppy pantaloons led me through the empty dining room, across an open courtyard, and into a white-tiled shed. This large, stark place was the kitchen. Four women, ranging in age from twenty-six to sixty, were waiting there, talking and laughing.

When I came in, they stopped and looked me up and down with a small measure of scorn. They had been informed of my request. They knew that a foreign lady was coming, and, in fact, my list of requested dishes was posted on the wall.

Three of them gave me shy smiles, but one, who was huge, fat, and black, expressed her derision with an outraged sniff. It was she, a Chleuh Berber from the Anti-Atlas Mountains of southwestern Morocco, who had the recipes, whispered the owner's wife, she who had once worked in the kitchens of El Glaoui, the pasha of Marrakech. There was no doubt that she was the "Queen Bee" of the group. I gaped as she fluttered her elbows and batted her eyes and ran a monologue in her native Berber dialect, which neither the owner nor his wife could understand.

Whatever she said seemed to embarrass the youngest of the cooks; she stole off to the far corner and quietly began to knead dough. The pastry cook, a short, fair Berber woman with enormous breasts, set to work frying almonds. She was helpful and answered all my questions, giving long descriptions of desserts she could make for me if I wished. From time to time, she threw indecipherable cracks in the Chleuh language at the Queen Bee, who sat in the corner plunging a chicken, up and down like a yo-yo, into boiling water. I felt that I had at least one friend in that kitchen, but I was hoping for a shift in alliances. I knew—I could feel—that the Queen Bee was the best cook, and I wanted her to like me so she would reveal at least some of her culinary secrets.

At this precise moment, one of the almonds popped out of the pan onto the floor. Suddenly all kitchen work came to a stop and everyone stared. I looked first at the pastry cook, but she turned hastily and avoided my eyes. Then the young one turned back to her dough. But the Queen Bee leered at me, and at that moment I knew what I had to do.

I bent down, retrieved the almond, sniffed it, and tossed it back into the pan. When I glanced again at the Queen Bee, she gave me a mischievous smile. I had moved too quickly for her—she'd intended to return the almond herself, to show contempt for my American "hygiene." But I'd beaten her to the punch, and in some strange way, this

One of my early experiences with Moroccan hospitality took place at an orange grove outside Rabat. After we had consumed one-tenth of a delicious *bastila* that was twenty-five inches in diameter, a servant brought out two young turkeys that had been braised in a huge vat. The stuffing was heavenly—rice, spices, raisins, and crushed almonds—and the turkeys were coated in thick thyme-flavored country honey. Then came a forequarter of lamb, heavily spiced with paprika and cumin, followed by a vegetable couscous, and, last, two enormous platters of fresh fruits. After all, we were six at the table!

won her over. In her enthusiasm, she revealed some of her recipes, including a version of the following one for chicken stuffed with rice and raisins. Then she suddenly stopped, as if realizing these secrets were her wealth. They say in Morocco, "What the tongue refuses, the eyes and hands can say." She smiled and squeezed my hand, and I knew the lesson was over.

———— ✺ Serves 4 to 6 ✺ ————

One 4- to 4½-pound chicken, preferably organic and air-chilled, neck, liver, heart, and kidneys reserved

1 small Ceylon cinnamon stick

¾ cup long-grain rice

8 tablespoons (1 stick) unsalted butter

½ teaspoon *ras el hanout* (see page 36)

Coarse salt and freshly ground black pepper

⅔ cup whole blanched almonds

¾ cup golden raisins, soaked in warm water for 10 minutes and drained

1 large red onion, halved and sliced

1 tablespoon chopped garlic

½ teaspoon ground ginger

3 tablespoons saffron water (see page 48)

1 tablespoon floral honey, such as orange blossom, acacia, or lavender

1. About 3½ hours before serving, bring the chicken to room temperature. Rinse the giblets and neck, wrap in cheesecloth with the cinnamon stick, and set aside.

2. Cook the rice in boiling water for 10 minutes; drain in a sieve, cool down under running water, and drain again. Transfer to a bowl and add 2 tablespoons of the butter, ¼ teaspoon of the *ras el hanout*, ½ teaspoon salt, and ¼ teaspoon pepper and toss to mix.

3. Toast the almonds in a dry skillet, and then crush them in a mortar or a food processor until crumbly. You should have about ¾ cup.

4. Add the almonds and raisins to the rice. You should have about 3 cups stuffing.

5. Melt 2 tablespoons of the butter in a deep heavy-bottomed 4-quart casserole. Add the onion, garlic, ginger, half the saffron water, and 1 teaspoon salt, cover the casserole, and cook over medium heat until the onion turns soft and golden, about 10 minutes.

6. Meanwhile, rinse the chicken well under running water. Rub the chicken with coarse salt, then remove and discard as much fat as possible. Try not to tear the skin. Rinse off the salt and pat dry with

paper towels. Place the rice mixture in the cavity of the bird and close the opening at neck and rump, sewing securely using a poultry needle and heavy thread. Tuck the wings under the chicken and tie the legs together. Rub the chicken with 2 tablespoons of the butter and the remaining saffron water.

7. Place the chicken breast side up over the onion and add water to cover the chicken halfway, about 2 cups. Tuck in the cheesecloth bag of giblets, neck, and cinnamon stick and bring to a simmer. Cover and cook over medium-low heat for 2 hours, basting the chicken every 30 minutes, or until the chicken is very tender and the flesh is almost falling off the bone.

8. Carefully remove the chicken to a lightly buttered ovenproof serving dish, arranging the chicken so it sits attractively in the dish. Cover and keep warm. Discard the giblets and neck packet from the casserole.

9. Preheat the oven to 400°F.

10. Quickly boil down the cooking liquid to about 1 cup. Add the honey and the remaining 2 tablespoons butter and boil down to a thick sauce.

11. Carefully cut away the string on the chicken and discard. Spoon the sauce over the chicken and place in the oven to brown, about 10 minutes, then serve.

Variation:
CHICKEN STUFFED WITH COUSCOUS, ALMONDS, AND RAISINS

Substitute 2 cups cooked couscous for the rice.

chapter ten

MEATS

"No land without stones,
no meat without bones."

—berber saying

MEATS

ROAST FOREQUARTER OF LAMB
{ page 344 }

MARINATED AND ROASTED GOAT MECHOUI
{ page 345 }

BREAST OF LAMB STUFFED WITH
COUSCOUS AND DATES
{ page 346 }

SLOW-COOKED LAMB SHOULDER WITH
BROWNED ALMONDS
{ page 350 }

MEAT TAGINE WITH CARROTS AND CELERY
{ page 354 }

BERBER MEAT TAGINE WITH SEVEN VEGETABLES
{ page 356 }

BEEF TAGINE WITH
ROASTED CAULIFLOWER
{ page 358 }

LAMB TAGINE WITH CARDOONS,
LEMON, AND OLIVES
{ page 360 }

LAMB TAGINE WITH RUTABAGA
AND SESAME SEEDS
{ page 362 }

LAMB TAGINE WITH BABY SPINACH,
LEMON, AND OLIVES
{ page 364 }

LAMB TAGINE WITH GLOBE ZUCCHINI
AND FRESH THYME
{ page 367 }

LAMB TAGINE WITH TOMATOES
AND EGGPLANT
{ page 368 }

LAMB TAGINE WITH QUINCES AND OKRA
❨ page 370 ❩

LAMB TAGINE WITH RAISINS AND ALMONDS,
TIZNIT-STYLE
❨ page 372 ❩

MEAT TAGINE WITH PRUNES AND APPLES
❨ page 373 ❩

LAMB WITH ONIONS, ALMONDS,
AND HARD-COOKED EGGS
❨ page 374 ❩

LAMB TAGINE WITH HONEYED SQUASH AND
TOASTED PINE NUTS
❨ page 376 ❩

LAMB KEDRA WITH CHICKEAS, BUTTERNUT SQUASH,
AND RAS EL HANOUT
❨ page 378 ❩

LAMB TAGINE WITH LAYERED ONIONS
❨ page 380 ❩

LAMB TAGINE WITH PRUNES AND ALMONDS
❨ page 382 ❩

LAMB TAGINE WITH RAISINS, ALMONDS,
AND HONEY
❨ page 384 ❩

LAMB TAGINE WTIH PEARS OR GREEN APPLES
❨ page 385 ❩

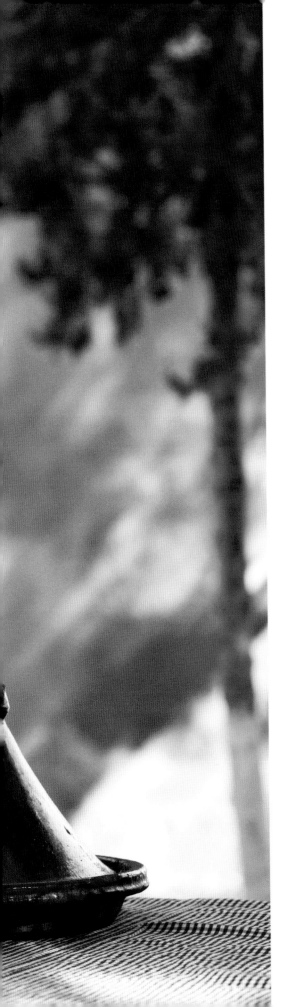

LAMB TAGINE WITH MEDJOUL DATES
❧ page 387 ❧

LAMB TAGINE WITH QUINCES
❧ page 388 ❧

STEAMED LAMB SHOULDER WITH BABY ONIONS
❧ page 390 ❧

SKEWERED AND GRILLED LAMB
❧ page 393 ❧

SEARED LAMB KEBABS COOKED IN BUTTER
❧ page 394 ❧

GRILLED LIVER, BERBER-STYLE
❧ page 397 ❧

GRILLED MERGUEZ SAUSAGES
WITH HARISSA
❧ page 397 ❧

KEFTA BROCHETTES
❧ page 399 ❧

KEFTA TAGINE WITH HERBS,
SPICES, AND LEMON
❧ page 401 ❧

KEFTA TAGINE WITH TOMATOES AND EGGS
❧ page 402 ❧

TANGIA
❧ page 409 ❧

Most of the dishes in this chapter utilize relatively inexpensive tougher cuts of meat: neck, shoulder, shanks, and ribs, cuts that take to the "magic" of the tagine. And it is magical! The tagine (I'm speaking here of the cooking vessel) is an ingenious device invented by Berbers in which to cook meat. For it isn't just the cut of meat but the environment in which it is cooked that creates these wonderful Moroccan meat dishes which are braised, steamed, and baked in the same vessel, and which somehow confusingly are also called tagines.

These shallow earthenware vessels with high cone-shaped tops allow you to braise your meat and vegetables in a steamy environment with moisture recycling from the cool cone tip back into the stew, where it gets reabsorbed. Then, as the dish begins to dry out, the tagine vessel becomes an oven, finishing off the dish with a deep rich sauce at the bottom, vegetables with a firm exterior yet buttery within, and meltingly tender meat falling off the bone. Yes, I call this process magical.

Some of the following recipes require a little extra browning, and these are run under the broiler at the last minute. In the traditional Moroccan process for achieving browning just before serving, the conical top was set aside, a flat clay dish was put on top of the tagine, and hot coals were piled on top, creating a charred topping that added flavor and beauty to the dish. This method is called "cooking between two fires" and is still followed in the countryside.

Most of the recipes in this chapter call for lamb, the traditional "first meat" in Moroccan cuisine and a favorite. But you may, if you like, substitute beef, veal, or even goat with excellent results. If you don't like lamb, try these recipes with veal knuckle, veal breasts, and veal shanks; goat shoulder; or beef ribs or shanks. The cooking time will be a little different, but you will know the dish is done when the meat is falling off the bone or, if there is no bone, when you press a spoon against a cube of meat and it breaks apart. This degree of softness is important, because traditionally these dishes were eaten with the first three fingers of the right hand.

MEAT TAGINES

As previously stated, Moroccan tagines are ingenious devices for cooking. As the food inside slowly cooks, steam rises, cools, and then falls back, keeping the food moist. The unglazed interior of the cone-shaped top absorbs some of the excess moisture, ensuring a steady, slow reduction of liquid below. Finally, the tagine turns into a "portable oven," allowing the meat to brown while the fruits or vegetables maintain their shape until you take your first bite, at which time their meltingly tender interiors are revealed.

If you're worried that the very small amount of liquid will cause your food to burn, try this trick until you feel comfortable with tagine cooking: crumple a square of parchment paper and place it directly over the contents of the tagine before covering and cooking. The moisture will quickly recycle. Midway during cooking, you can remove and discard the paper, then allow cooking to continue so the "portable oven" aspects of tagine cookery can come into play.

The major characteristic of a Moroccan tagine is a highly seasoned sauce, gently reduced to a silken texture through long, slow cooking. Fruits or vegetables are added in abundance, intended not merely to garnish but to become the dominant component, pushing the taste of the meat into the background flavor of the sauce. This is true Berber cooking at its best.

ROASTED WHOLE LAMB (MECHOUI)

The Berbers claim to be the first to have figured out the best way to barbecue lamb: roasting the animal on a spit over a pit of burning charcoal embers, basting it all the while with herbal butter to create a wonderful crisp exterior and juicy, butter-tender meat beneath. *Mechoui* is so tender, in fact, that you can eat it with your fingers, the way Moroccans prefer, even though it is burning-hot.

Mechoui, like couscous, *bastila*, and chicken with preserved lemons and olives, is one of the most famous of all Moroccan dishes, beloved by tourists and Moroccans alike. I've had great *mechoui* not only at festivals in the Middle Atlas, but throughout Morocco. Some of the best have been in the Souss, where the lambs munch on wild herbs and acquire a strong flavor much like the famous *pre-salé* lambs of Brittany. But in the Saharan town of Tineghir, on the famous Route of the Kasbahs near the beautiful Todra Gorge, I ate a *mechoui* prepared in a totally different style, called Saharan.

The *caid*, or mayor, hired the "master butcher" of the town to make the dish. Before slaughtering the lamb, he prepared charcoal embers inside a huge earthen furnace built against a wall. This furnace was terrifically hot. After the lamb was killed, cleaned, and prepared for roasting, he skewered it onto a thick piece of green wood, then inserted it vertically into the furnace. No spices of any sort were rubbed into the flesh. His assistant pulled undigested grass out of the lamb's stomach, mixed this with mud, and then used the mixture to seal an iron cover on top of the furnace. Three hours later, the *mechoui* was completely done, and meltingly tender. It was served with ground cumin and coarse salt.

ROAST FOREQUARTER OF LAMB

I am not going to suggest you spit-roast or bury a whole lamb in an adobe oven; I understand that for most readers that is out of the question. Instead I recommend that you make *mechoui* with a ten-pound lamb forequarter (the neck, shoulder, one of the front legs, and the ribs close to the shoulder blade). Though it may taste a little better if you can dig a pit, fill it with charcoal, and set up a roasting spit in your backyard, I guarantee that with my adaptation, you will obtain an excellent *mechoui* out of the oven of your home, be it country house or city apartment.

The same problems confront the Moroccan city dweller. She knows that the best place to eat *mechoui* is in the countryside, because if she wants to cook it in the city, where most people do not have a full-sized stove, she will have to send out her meat to a community oven where the workers most likely will not have time to properly baste the lamb. The best Berber *mechoui*, you see, is swabbed every ten or so minutes with butter and spices.

Most Americans, however, have large stoves into which a forequarter will fit and are thus in a better position to cook *mechoui* than the average housewife in Rabat or Casablanca. And buying a whole forequarter in America is not difficult. Some butchers will order one, or you can order one yourself from a top-of-the line lamb farm, such as Jamison Ranch in Pennsylvania (see Sources).

— Serves 10 to 12 —

1 lamb forequarter (10 to 12 pounds), trimmed of excess fat

2 tablespoons extra virgin olive oil

3 tablespoons unsalted butter, softened

2 tablespoons ground coriander

1 tablespoon ground cumin seeds, preferably Moroccan

1½ teaspoons sweet paprika

6 garlic cloves, chopped and crushed to a paste with 1 tablespoon salt

Coarse sea salt and ground cumin, preferably Moroccan, for serving

1. Make deep incisions under the foreleg and bone and along the breastplate of the lamb. Blend the remaining ingredients except the sea salt and cumin into a paste and rub into the meat. Let stand for 30 minutes.

2. Preheat the oven to 475°F.

3. Place the lamb fatty side up in a large roasting pan. Place on the middle shelf of the oven and roast for 15 minutes. Reduce the heat to 300°F and continue to roast for about 5 hours, or until the meat can easily be removed from the bones with your fingers. Baste the lamb thoroughly every 15 minutes with the pan juices. The lamb should be golden brown and crisp on the outside, the flesh moist and tender and almost falling off the bone.

4. Serve hot, along with bowls of salt and cumin for those who like additional seasoning.

MARINATED AND ROASTED GOAT MECHOUI

I recently saw a photo on the Internet of a young Moroccan holding a small skinned goat by one leg, lowering it vertically into a cone-shaped mud oven. The picture, taken in the High Atlas, reminded me of the Saharan-style *mechoui* described on page 343. The goat, like the lamb, was subjected to direct heat in a clay environment. Thinking about it, I realized I could simulate this method using my large Romertopf baker (see note) and my home oven. And when I tested the method with a marinated goat shoulder, I got wonderful results: a golden brown exterior with juicy, tender meat inside.

Serves 6

1 goat forequarter (3½ to 4 pounds), cracked at the "elbow"

4 garlic cloves, chopped and crushed to a paste with 1 tablespoon coarse salt

2 teaspoons ground coriander

1½ teaspoons ground cumin seeds, preferably Moroccan

1 teaspoon sweet paprika

2 tablespoons wildflower honey

Juice of 1 lemon

2 tablespoons extra virgin olive oil

2 tablespoons unsalted butter, softened

Coarse sea salt and ground cumin, preferably Moroccan, for serving

1. One day in advance: Wash and dry the goat forequarter. Tie the thin shank close to the larger piece to make a neat package. Lightly score the meat on the skin side. Blend the garlic, spices, honey, lemon juice, oil, and butter and rub all over the meat. Slip into a plastic bag and refrigerate overnight to marinate.

2. The following day: Soak a Romertopf baker in water for 20 minutes; drain.

3. Line the bottom of the pot with a sheet of parchment paper. Place the marinated goat skin side up on top, add ½ cup water, cover, and place in a cold oven. Turn the heat to 325°F and bake for 4 hours without opening the baker.

4. Use oven mitts to remove the Romertopf to a wooden board or a folded kitchen towel to prevent cracking the earthenware. Carefully lift off the hot cover and place on another towel. Lift out the meat onto a serving platter; discard the fat. Serve at once, with small dishes of salt and cumin.

NOTES TO THE COOK

A Romertopf clay baker is a two-part cooking container made of unglazed earthenware that acts as a miniature oven. These porous vessels work differently from any other pot you're likely to use, and for this reason alone, I consider them indispensable for this recipe and for a few others in this book. I especially like them for roasting chickens and for the stuffed breast of lamb on page 346, as well as for tenderizing tough cuts of meats efficiently in moist heat. I also use them for bread baking.

Prior to each use, the domed cover and the bottom of the Romertopf are soaked in water until thoroughly saturated. As a result, when the pot is heated in the oven, the clay first releases steam, which keeps the food moist. Then, when all the moisture has evaporated, it acts as a dry roaster.

To prepare the recipe without a Romertopf baker, place the goat forequarter skin side up in a shallow roasting pan, cover tightly with foil, and set in a 250°F oven to roast for 4 hours. Raise the oven heat to 400°F, remove the foil, and roast until the goat is well browned, about 30 minutes longer.

BREAST OF LAMB STUFFED WITH COUSCOUS AND DATES

NOTES TO THE COOK

Most breast of lamb recipes call for a boned breast, but I find that the juiciest and tastiest recipes are cooked bone-in.

To prepare this dish without a Romer-topf baker, place the stuffed breast of lamb skin side up in a shallow roasting pan. Tightly cover with foil and roast in a 250°F oven for 3 hours. Raise the heat to 450°F and roast uncovered until the lamb is well browned, about 1 hour longer.

This fantastic dish is a breeze to serve: You carve the lamb before you bring it to the table, first lifting the meaty top off the bones and placing it on your serving platter, then scraping out the couscous and spooning it over the meat, and finally scattering the almond-stuffed dates on top.

This dish is best prepared using a large Romertopf baker, which will simulate the two-step steaming-roasting process achieved in a wood-fired oven. However, if you don't have one, see the Notes to the Cook for an alternative method.

This is one of the few recipes in this book in which I suggest following the directions on a box of instant couscous. It works here, since the couscous is packed into the cavity of the lamb breast and thus will lose the light airy texture one wants in a normal couscous preparation.

Serves 4

One 3-pound bone-in breast of lamb

Salt and freshly ground black pepper

1 cup instant couscous

¾ cup toasted blanched almonds

8 ounces pitted Medjoul dates

⅓ cup golden raisins, soaked in warm water for 10 minutes and drained

1 teaspoon La Kama Spice Mixture (page 37)

2 tablespoons saffron water (see page 48)

6 tablespoons unsalted butter, melted

1 tablespoon orange flower water

¼ cup sugar

1 teaspoon ground Ceylon cinnamon

Salt

½ teaspoon freshly ground black pepper

½ teaspoon sweet paprika

Pinch of cayenne

¼ teaspoon grated nutmeg

1 tablespoon honey

1. About 4 hours before serving, remove the lamb from the refrigerator. Trim away as much fat as possible, as well as the thick outer skin, or fell. Create a pocket for stuffing by sliding a thin-bladed knife along the top of the rib bones to separate the meat from the bones. Sprinkle the breast inside and out with salt and pepper. Let stand at room temperature while you prepare the stuffing.

2. Cook the couscous according to the package directions.

3. Insert a toasted almond into 8 dates and set aside. Chop the remaining almonds and dates and combine in a bowl with the drained raisins.

4. Soak the Romertopf baker in water to cover for 15 minutes.

5. Meanwhile, mix the spice mixture with 1 tablespoon of the saffron water, 5 tablespoons of the butter, the orange flower water, sugar, cinnamon, 1 teaspoon salt, and the pepper in a bowl.

6. Toss the couscous with the spice butter and the dried fruit mixture, and stuff the lamb breast cavity with this filling. You will probably need to shake the lamb to get it all in. Tie or sew the pocket shut with kitchen string. Fold the thinner part of the breast underneath and shape into a flat oblong roast. Combine the remaining 1 tablespoon each butter and saffron water, the paprika, cayenne, nutmeg, and honey, and spread this coating over the exposed meat on top.

7. Drain the Romertopf, shaking off any excess moisture. Lay a rectangular sheet of foil on the bottom of the baker. Place the stuffed breast of lamb on top of the foil, cover with the lid, and place in a cold oven. Turn the oven temperature to 400°F and bake for 2 hours without disturbing.

8. Turn off the oven. Arrange the stuffed dates side by side on a flat ovenproof plate and set on top of the baker. Leave the unopened baker in the hot oven for 30 minutes longer.

9. Remove the dates from the oven. Transfer the hot baker to a wooden surface or a folded kitchen towel to prevent cracking. Carefully open and place the Romertopf cover on a kitchen towel. Transfer the meat to a carving board and let rest for 10 minutes (pour out and discard the fat that has accumulated in the pot).

10. Cut away all the string from the lamb breast and pull out any protruding bones. Carve into 1-inch-thick slices. Arrange the slices on a heated serving dish, scatter the stuffed dates and the couscous on top, and serve at once.

SLOW-COOKED LAMB SHOULDER WITH BROWNED ALMONDS

BRAISING A LAMB
FOREQUARTER IS NOT FOR
EVERYONE!

When I was staying with the late Madame Khadija Jaidi outside Rabat, we needed to cook a 10-pound forequarter of lamb for a large party. It's nearly impossible to find a pot large enough to do this in an American home, but in Morocco, where in a traditional household, a large number of relatives and servants must be fed, there will often be several pots sufficient to hold such an enormous piece of meat. When I helped make this dish in the Jaidi house, we cooked it outside on a charcoal brazier. Otherwise it would have been very difficult to turn the meat over. Even so, it took three of us to brown it in an enormous pot—two to turn the meat and one to steady the foot-high brazier.

In Marrakech, the restaurant Al Fassia specializes in refined women's cooking. On a recent visit, head chef and owner Halima Chab sat with me as members of her all-female staff brought out various dishes for us to try. One in particular, lamb shoulder garnished with browned almonds, struck me on account of its special flavor and texture. I'd learned a similar recipe from my cooking teacher, Madame Jaidi, and published it in my earlier book, but the presentation and the flavoring of the Al Fassia version were so different, I knew I had to learn to make it.

It's a special-order dish at Al Fassia, requiring advance notice, Halima told me, since it requires very slow cooking. She was quite specific about the meat, that it have a lot of bone, and no fat. (See Note for the cut I used to simulate Halima's recipe.) In fact, the dish was presented at table with the bones in, then the server tapped the meat with the side of a spoon, and it fell open quite miraculously, like a flower.

To make this dish easier, prepare through step 4 a day in advance.

Serves 6 to 8

1 head garlic, cloves separated and peeled

1 teaspoon cumin seeds, preferably Moroccan

Coarse salt

2 pinches saffron threads, crumbled

1½ tablespoons sweet paprika

1 teaspoon ground ginger

¼ teaspoon ground turmeric

Pinch of cayenne

7 tablespoons unsalted butter, softened

One 4½- to 5-pound bone-in lamb shoulder roast with some of the rack, cut into 2 pieces and trimmed of fat

2 tablespoons extra virgin olive oil

1 large red onion, finely diced

2 cinnamon sticks and a bunch of cilantro, tied together

1 cup blanched whole almonds

Vegetable oil for frying

1 pound couscous, steamed and buttered (see pages 200–203)

1. One day in advance: Mash 3 of the garlic cloves, the cumin seeds, and 1 teaspoon salt to a paste in a mortar. Add the saffron, paprika, ginger, turmeric, cayenne, and 2 tablespoons of the butter and blend to make a thick cream. Rub the cream into the pieces of lamb and let stand for at least 15 minutes. The flesh should have a reddish sheen.

2. Place both pieces of lamb in a large casserole. Add the oil, the remaining garlic, the onion, cinnamon-cilantro bundle, and enough water to come about halfway up the sides of the meat. Bring to a boil. Place a crumpled sheet of wet parchment paper directly over the contents of the casserole, cover with a lid, reduce the heat to very low, and cook, turning and basting the meat every half hour, for

about 3 hours. The meat should be very tender and almost falling off the bone.

3. Carefully transfer the meat to a foil-lined workspace. Remove the skin and discard any visible fat, but do not remove the bones. When cool, wrap in foil and refrigerate overnight.

4. Meanwhile, discard the cinnamon-cilantro bundle. Strain the sauce through a fine-mesh strainer, pressing on the solids with the back of a wooden spoon. Let cool, then cover and refrigerate overnight.

5. The next day: About 30 minutes before serving, fry the almonds in vegetable oil until golden brown. Drain and set aside.

6. Preheat the oven to 250°F.

7. Skim the fat from the refrigerated sauce, then reheat the sauce in a saucepan to simmering. Heat half the remaining butter in a straight-sided skillet over medium heat. Place one of the lamb pieces in the hot butter and brown on all sides. As the meat begins to produce a deep brown residue on the bottom of the skillet, add a few tablespoons of the simmering sauce and scrape up the flavorful bits clinging to the bottom and spoon some over the meat. Repeat this process 5 or 6 times, or until the meat is beautifully glazed. Transfer the meat to an ovenproof platter and put in the oven to keep warm. Repeat with the remaining butter and lamb.

8. When both pieces of lamb are in the oven, add the remaining sauce to the skillet and boil down until thick enough to coat a spoon. Taste for seasoning.

9. When ready to serve, remove the lamb from the oven and pull out the bones and discard. Arrange the lamb over a bed of the freshly steamed couscous. Dribble some of the sauce over the meat, scatter the fried almonds on top, and serve at once, with the remaining sauce in a small bowl.

✵
NOTE TO THE COOK

Ask your butcher for the "square-shaped cut," bone-in, which should contain some of the blade, arm, and ribs. Ask him or her to halve it, then trim off all of the external fat.

MEAT TAGINE WITH CARROTS AND CELERY

This splendid, utterly meltingly tender, and fresh-looking tagine is best made with long firm celery ribs and sweet fresh carrots. Ideally, the carrots should all be the same size in length and width from top to tip. The carrots and celery ribs are piled vertically against the central mound of meat, creating a cone of food that mirrors the conical shape of the tagine top.

For this recipe, I use a 10-inch-wide tagine bottom to support the inner mound of meat, against which I vertically arrange the vegetables. Be sure to use the outer celery ribs and cut them to the same size, and save the tender center with leaves for the top garnish.

For information on choosing, preparing, seasoning, and cooking in a tagine, see pages 18–19.

⁓ Serves 6 ⁓

2 pounds boneless lamb shoulder, cut into 12 pieces

2 garlic cloves

Salt

1 tablespoon La Kama Spice Mixture (page 37)

2 tablespoons saffron water (see page 48)

3 tablespoons extra virgin olive oil

1 tablespoon chopped cilantro

¼ cup grated red onion

12 medium carrots (1 pound), preferably that are approximately the same size

1 large bunch celery

Juice of ½ lemon, or more to taste

½ cup green-ripe, midway, or red olives, rinsed and pitted

1 preserved lemon (see page 21), pulp removed, rind rinsed and cut into 4 wedges

1. About 3 hours before serving, trim the lamb of all excess fat.

2. Crush the garlic to a paste with the salt in a mortar. Mix with the spices, saffron water, 2 tablespoons of the oil, the cilantro, and grated red onion, and toss with the meat. Transfer to a 10-inch tagine. Add ⅓ cup water, cover, and set the tagine on a heat diffuser over medium-low heat. Cover and cook for 30 minutes.

3. Meanwhile, peel the carrots and trim so they are more or less the same length and thickness from top to tip. Separate the celery ribs and wash them. Peel and trim 8 to 12 outer ribs to match the length of the carrots. Bend the tender leafy inner ribs into half and tie with kitchen string into a bundle.

4. Shift the meat to the center of the tagine pot to form a mound. Lightly coat the carrots and celery with the remaining tablespoon of oil. Arrange the carrots and outer celery ribs around the mound, creating a cone. Place the celery bundle on top. Cover the tagine and cook over low heat for $2\frac{1}{2}$ hours.

5. Remove the tagine from the stove to a wooden surface, gently tilt it, and scoop away excess fat from the cooking liquid. Add 1 to 2 tablespoons lemon juice to the juices, gently swirl to combine, and return to the stove. Scatter the olives and lemon wedges around the vegetables, cover, and cook for 5 more minutes. Serve hot.

BERBER MEAT TAGINE WITH SEVEN VEGETABLES

In the Moroccan south, a finishing touch to this dish is to remove the fat by tilting the tagine and skimming it off, then replace it with a few tablespoons of argan oil for a special nutty flavor.

NOTES TO THE COOK

When I watched a cook from the south make this multivegetable tagine, I noticed that before adding the meat, she started out by slowly heating up an empty tagine over charcoal.

To simulate this process using a gas or electric stovetop, add some sliced onion, salt, a little oil, and a few tablespoons water to your tagine bottom, and then warm it over a low flame, protected by a heat diffuser, for about 15 minutes.

In this rare departure from the traditional making of a tagine, I brown the meat separately, add it to the softened onions, and then use the meat drippings to flavor the vegetables. During the actual cooking, the vegetables will steam, providing the moisture you need to create the unctuous textures of a well-made tagine.

For information on choosing, preparing, seasoning, and cooking in a tagine, see pages 18–19.

Before cooking.

Two to three hours later.

--- ❧ Serves 6 ❧ ---

2 pounds boneless lamb shoulder, cut into 6 to 8 chunks

3 tablespoons extra virgin olive oil

1 medium yellow onion, halved and thinly sliced

Coarse salt

Salt and freshly ground black pepper

1 tablespoon La Kama Spice Mixture (page 37)

2 pinches cayenne

2 tablespoons saffron water (see page 48)

6 carrots, preferably 3 to 4 inches long, blunt, trimmed, and peeled

6 zucchini, preferably 3 to 4 inches long, trimmed

1 small sweet potato, peeled and cut into 6 wedges

6 small white turnips, peeled

1 small bundle flat-leaf parsley and cilantro sprigs, tied together

1 medium red-ripe tomato, peeled, cored, seeded, and thinly sliced

¼ small green cabbage

1. About 4 hours before serving, trim the meat of all excess fat and allow to come to room temperature.

2. Put half the oil, the onions, 3 tablespoons water, and a pinch of coarse salt in a large tagine, and set on a heat diffuser over medium-low heat. Cover, and let the tagine heat up for 15 minutes. Uncover, raise the heat to medium, and allow the excess moisture to boil away. Reduce the heat to low.

3. Meanwhile, heat the remaining oil in a skillet over medium heat. Brown the meat, in batches, on all sides. Transfer the meat to the tagine, fat-side down. Sprinkle with salt and pepper, cover, and cook over low heat while preparing the vegetables.

4. Tilt the skillet and pour off almost all the fat. Add the spice mixture, cayenne, saffron water, and 2 cups water to the skillet, raise the heat to high, and bring to a boil, scraping up the entire meat residue. Boil until reduced by half. Season with salt and pepper. Add the carrots, zucchini, sweet potato, and turnips and toss with the juices in the skillet.

5. Shift the meat and onions to the center of the tagine to form a mound. Position the vegetables so they overlap, lean on, and surround the mound of meat and onions. Place the herbs, tomato, and cabbage on top. Cover the tagine and cook over medium-low heat for 2½ hours.

6. When the meat and vegetables have simmered 2½ hours and the meat is tender, transfer the tagine to a wooden surface or folded towel on a tray to prevent cracking. Let stand, covered, for 10 minutes. Discard the herb bundle.

7. Carefully tilt the tagine and transfer the liquid with a spoon to the skillet. Boil down the liquid in the skillet to a thick sauce and season with salt and pepper. Uncover the tagine, pour the liquid around the vegetables, and serve at once.

BEEF TAGINE WITH ROASTED CAULIFLOWER

Beef tagines can be very good indeed. After hours of slow simmering, the meat comes out buttery and soft, and the sauce acquires excellent flavor. The spicing in this dish follows the Marrakech style, while the particular preliminary browning of the meat is Tetuanese.

―――― ∽ Serves 4 to 6 ∾ ――――

ROBUST MEAT TAGINES

These highly aromatic tagines, flavored with paprika and cumin, are sturdy dishes, nourishing and thick, especially good in winter—satisfying to weary travelers and men who have done hard physical work, or to folk who have just come off the ski slopes an hour outside Marrakech. Though they are not among the most elegant of dishes, these hearty stews are truly toothsome.

Coarse salt

½ teaspoon freshly ground black pepper

¼ teaspoon ground turmeric

5 tablespoons extra virgin olive oil

3 pounds beef short ribs or 2 pounds bone-in beef shoulder, trimmed of excess fat and cut into 1- to 1¼-inch chunks

1 teaspoon sweet paprika

½ teaspoon ground ginger

½ teaspoon ground cumin, preferably Moroccan

1 medium white or red onion, grated

2 tablespoons finely chopped cilantro

2 tablespoons finely chopped flat-leaf parsley

One 2-pound cauliflower

Pinch of red pepper flakes or cayenne, or to taste

12 ounces Roma (plum) tomatoes, peeled, halved, seeded, and chopped

Juice of ½ lemon

1. Heat a tagine, preferably flameware, set on a heat diffuser over medium-low heat until warm. Mix 1 teaspoon salt, the pepper, and turmeric with 1½ tablespoons of the olive oil and add to the warm pan.

2. Add the beef and sauté gently until golden on all sides. Place a crumpled piece of parchment directly over the meat, cover tightly, and cook for 15 minutes, without lifting the cover. (The meat will cook in its own juices, drawn out by the salt over low heat; do not add water.)

3. Add the paprika, ginger, cumin, grated onion, half of the herbs, and ½ cup water. Cover again with the parchment paper and the lid, and simmer gently for 3 hours, until the meat is very tender and has fallen off the bones.

4. Meanwhile, preheat the oven to 400°F.

5. Cut the cauliflower in half, then cut each half lengthwise into ½-inch-thick slices. Lightly brush a jelly-roll pan with 3 tablespoons of the olive oil. Mix the remaining ½ tablespoon oil with ½ teaspoon salt and a pinch of red pepper flakes and gently toss with the cauliflower. Spread the cauliflower out in one layer on the pan and roast for

15 minutes. Use a spatula to turn the slices over and roast for another 15 minutes, or until lightly caramelized. Remove from the oven, cover loosely with paper towels or a kitchen towel, and set aside.

6. Remove the meat from the tagine and remove and discard the bones. Return the meat to the tagine and lightly brown in the fatty juices. Tilt the pan and spoon off and discard the excess fat. If necessary, add a few tablespoons water to make a smooth sauce.

7. Scatter the cauliflower, tomatoes, and the remaining chopped herbs over the beef. Bring to a boil to reheat. Correct the seasoning with salt, black pepper, red pepper flakes, and the lemon juice, and serve at once.

NOTE TO THE COOK

For information on choosing, preparing, seasoning, and cooking in a tagine, see pages 18–19.

Please remember to always transfer a hot tagine to a wooden surface or a folded towel on a tray to prevent cracking.

LAMB TAGINE WITH CARDOONS, LEMON, AND OLIVES

Cardoons are domesticated thistles found in the fall through early spring. You can often find them at Italian grocery stores. They have a taste similar to that of artichokes and an appearance similar to that of celery. They make marvelous eating and should definitely be searched out—or grow them if you have a vegetable garden.

Serves 6

2 pounds boneless lamb shoulder arm chops, trimmed of excess fat

2 garlic cloves

Salt

¾ teaspoon ground ginger

¼ teaspoon ground turmeric

2 tablespoons saffron water (see page 48)

½ cup grated red onion

¼ cup extra virgin olive oil

⅓ cup chopped flat-leaf parsley

3 bundles cardoons (about 15 to 18 tender stalks)

Juice of 2 lemons

1½ preserved lemons (see page 21), pulp removed, rind rinsed and divided into 6 wedges

12 green-ripe, midway, or red olives, rinsed and pitted

1. About 5 hours before serving, rinse the lamb, cut into 6 pieces, and place in an 11- to 12-inch tagine. Crush the garlic to a paste with 1 teaspoon salt. Add the ginger, turmeric, saffron water, grated onion, and oil and use to coat the lamb on all sides. Let marinate for 2 hours.

2. Set the tagine on a heat diffuser, turn the heat to medium-low, and slowly cook the meat until it turns golden brown, about 15 minutes. Add ¾ cup hot water and the parsley, raise the heat to medium, and bring to a boil. Reduce the heat to medium-low, cover, and simmer for 2 hours, turning the lamb often in the sauce.

3. Meanwhile, separate the cardoon stalks and cut away the tough bottom parts and leaves. Wash the inner stalks well. With a paring knife or vegetable peeler, remove the strings. Cut the stalks into 3-inch lengths and keep in acidulated water (with vinegar or lemon juice) to prevent discoloring.

4. After the lamb has cooked for 2 hours, push the meat to one side, slide in the rinsed and drained cardoons, and add enough hot water to cover them. (For the first 15 to 20 minutes of cooking, the cardoons must be covered by liquid.) Place the lamb chops side by side on top of the cardoons and cook for another 40 minutes.

5. Add ¼ cup of the lemon juice to the sauce. Then continue adding the lemon juice by the tablespoon, tasting before adding more each time. Simmer gently, uncovered, to allow the sauce to reduce and the

flavors to blend. If necessary, tilt the tagine, spoon the liquid into a saucepan, and boil rapidly, to reduce the sauce if there's a lot of liquid but the meat is done, to a napping consistency.

6. Rearrange the lamb and cardoons in the tagine so the meat is completely covered with the cardoons. Decorate with the preserved lemons and olives. Taste the sauce for seasoning and add more lemon juice if desired. Serve at once.

LAMB TAGINE WITH RUTABAGA AND SESAME SEEDS

✿

NOTE TO THE COOK

For information on choosing, preparing, and cooking in a tagine, see pages 18–19.

This dish comes from my old housekeeper, Fatima, who made lots of family-style Riffian dishes for us when we lived in Tangier. The tagine can be prepared early in the day, then completely degreased and all the bones removed before reheating. The turnips and rutabaga are steamed, sautéed gently in butter and sugar until just shiny and caramelized, and then spread on top of the meat to look like a flaming nebula in a dark sky. The sesame seeds look like stars.

---❧ Serves 4 ❧---

2½ pounds bone-in lamb shoulder, cut into 4 equal pieces

1 tablespoon ground ginger

1½ teaspoons ground cumin, preferably Moroccan

1½ teaspoons freshly ground white pepper, or to taste

1 teaspoon ground turmeric

Salt

2 tablespoons saffron water (see page 48)

1 tablespoon extra virgin olive oil

1 medium red onion, halved and grated

2 tablespoons chopped flat-leaf parsley

2 tablespoons chopped cilantro

1 pound rutabagas, peeled, halved, and cut into wedges

4 small white turnips, trimmed and halved

2 tablespoons unsalted butter

1½ tablespoons sugar

Pinch of ground Ceylon cinnamon

1 tablespoon sesame seeds, toasted

1. Trim the lamb of excess fat, rinse, and pat dry.

2. Combine the ginger, cumin, white pepper, turmeric, ½ teaspoon salt, and the saffron water in a wide bowl and stir to produce a smooth paste. Stir in the oil. Add the meat, turning to coat on all sides. Let marinate for 1 hour at room temperature, or up to 24 hours in the refrigerator.

3. Heat an 11- to 12-inch tagine set on heat diffuser over medium-low heat. Add the marinated lamb, grated onion, and chopped herbs and gently fry for 5 to 10 minutes. Add 1 cup hot water, cover, and cook for 2½ to 3 hours, until the meat is fork-tender.

4. Meanwhile, set a colander snugly over a pot of boiling water. Add the rutabagas and turnips, cover, and steam until tender, about 15 minutes. Remove from the heat.

5. Melt the butter in a large skillet. Add the steamed vegetables, sprinkle with the sugar and cinnamon, and sauté until lightly glazed.

6. Remove the tagine from the stove to a wooden surface. Discard any loose bones and hard fat attached to the meat. Tilt the tagine and carefully degrease the cooking liquid. Correct the seasoning with salt and pepper. Arrange the turnips in the center of the tagine and surround with the rutabagas. Return the tagine to the stove, scatter the sesame seeds on top, and reheat, then serve.

Variation:

Use only turnips and substitute nigella seeds for the sesame seeds.

LAMB TAGINE WITH BABY SPINACH, LEMON, AND OLIVES

Here is a tagine for spring: soft and delicately spiced lamb cubes under a thick blanket of freshly steamed baby spinach with flecks of olive and strips of preserved lemon.

──── Serves 4 ────

1½ pounds bone-in lamb shoulder, cut into 1½-inch chunks

3 tablespoons extra virgin olive oil

½ cup grated red onion

½ teaspoon ground ginger

½ teaspoon freshly ground white pepper

½ teaspoon ground turmeric

¼ teaspoon ground Ceylon cinnamon

A good pinch of grated nutmeg

¼ teaspoon ground cumin seed ground with ½ teaspoon coarse salt

12 sprigs each cilantro and flat-leaf parsley, tied together

1 pound baby spinach, washed and drained

Salt

12 Picholine olives, pitted, slivered, and rinsed well

1 preserved lemon (see page 21), pulp removed, rind rinsed and cut into strips

1. Trim the excess fat from the lamb.

2. Set an 11- to 12-inch tagine on a heat diffuser over medium-low heat. Add 2 tablespoons of the oil and the onion and slowly heat for about 15 minutes.

3. Add the meat and gently brown on all sides. Add the spices, the herb bundle, and ½ cup water, cover, and cook over low heat for 2½ to 3 hours, turning the meat midway through.

4. Remove the meat from the tagine; remove and discard all the bones. Discard the herb bundle. Tilt the tagine and spoon off the fat, then add a few tablespoons of water and bring to a boil, scraping up any bits and pieces stuck to the bottom of the tagine. Return the meat to the tagine, turn the pieces of meat in the sauce, cover, and keep warm over low heat while you prepare the spinach.

5. Half-fill a medium saucepan with water and bring to a boil. Fit with a steamer insert and brush it lightly with oil, then add half the spinach, cover, and steam until the greens wilt, about 2 minutes. Remove to a side dish. Repeat with the remaining spinach.

6. Toss the spinach with the remaining olive oil and a tiny pinch of salt. Spread the spinach over the meat and scatter the olives and lemon strips on top. Transfer the tagine to a wooden surface or a folded towel on a tray to prevent cracking. Serve at once, with Moroccan bread.

LAMB TAGINE WITH GLOBE ZUCCHINI AND FRESH THYME

——— ✥ Serves 4 to 6 ✥ ———

2 pounds bone-in lamb shoulder, cut into 8 chunks

2 tablespoons saffron water (see page 48)

1 teaspoon ground ginger

½ teaspoon ground turmeric

½ teaspoon freshly ground black pepper, plus more to taste

2 garlic cloves, crushed to a paste with 1 teaspoon salt

2 tablespoons extra virgin olive oil

1 medium red onion, grated (½ cup)

12 sprigs each cilantro and flat-leaf parsley, tied together

4 globe or round zucchini (1½ pounds)

Coarse salt

1 red-ripe tomato, halved, seeded, and grated (½ cup)

Pinch of sugar

1 tablespoon chopped thyme mixed with marjoram and/or oregano, plus a few sprigs of thyme for garnish

NOTES TO THE COOK

For information on choosing, preparing, seasoning, and cooking in a tagine, see pages 18–19.

For this recipe, Moroccan cooks usually use *za'atar*, a wild herb of the thyme-oregano family, but I opt for fresh thyme, oregano, or marjoram, or a mix of all three, to make this tagine fresh and savory.

Please remember to always transfer a hot tagine to a wooden surface or a folded towel on a tray to prevent cracking.

1. Trim and discard the excess fat from the lamb. Place the meat in an 11- to 12-inch tagine set on a heat diffuser. Mix the saffron water with the ginger, turmeric, pepper, garlic, oil, and onion and toss with the lamb to coat each piece. Gently brown on all sides over medium-low heat. Slip the herb bundle into the center of the tagine, cover, and cook over low heat until the meat is almost falling off the bone, 2½ to 3 hours, turning the meat midway through.

2. Meanwhile, halve the zucchini, toss with coarse salt, and let stand for about 1 hour. Rinse and press on each half to remove excess moisture.

3. Remove the meat from the tagine. Pull off all the bones and discard. Cut the meat into 1-inch chunks, season with salt and pepper, put in a bowl, cover with foil to keep moist, and set aside. Discard the herb bundle.

4. Skim all the fat from the cooking juices, then add the tomato and sugar and bring to a boil, scraping up any bits and pieces stuck to the bottom of the tagine. Add the zucchini cut side down, and gently sauté until nicely glazed, 20 minutes.

5. Sprinkle the vegetables with two-thirds of the thyme-oregano mixture, and return the meat to the tagine. "Park" a zucchini half, round side up, on each chunk of meat, cover the tagine, and cook for 20 more minutes. Serve with a sprinkling of the remaining chopped herbs and the thyme sprigs scattered on top.

LAMB TAGINE WITH TOMATOES AND EGGPLANT

NOTE TO THE COOK

For information on choosing, preparing, seasoning, and cooking in a tagine, see pages 18–19.

Here's a tagine with a true Mediterranean spirit. As my old friend chef Lucien Vanel of Toulouse once told me, "Lamb, tomatoes, eggplant, and garlic is a combination before which we must bow down!"

—— Serves 4 to 6 ——

2 large black-skinned eggplant (about 1 pound each)

Coarse salt

Extra virgin olive oil

1½ to 2 pounds boneless lamb shoulder, trimmed of excess fat and cut into 1½-inch chunks

½ teaspoon ground turmeric

3 large garlic cloves, crushed

¾ teaspoon ground ginger

½ teaspoon freshly ground black pepper, or to taste

2 tablespoons saffron water (see page 48)

1 medium red onion, grated (about ⅔ cup)

10 tablespoons finely chopped flat-leaf parsley

6 tablespoons finely chopped cilantro, plus a sprinkling for garnish

1 teaspoon sweet paprika

½ teaspoon ground cumin, preferably Moroccan

Pinch of cayenne

2 medium red-ripe tomatoes, peeled, halved, seeded, and diced (1 cup)

Pinch of sugar

Juice of 1 lemon, or to taste

1. Trim off the top and bottom of each eggplant. With a channel knife, remove 3 or 4 thin vertical strips from each eggplant, leaving the eggplants striped. Cut each eggplant crosswise in half, then cut each half lengthwise into 3 or 4 thick strips. Sprinkle the eggplant strips with salt and allow to drain in a nonreactive colander for at least 1 hour. Rinse and drain the eggplant strips; pat dry with paper towels.

2. Meanwhile, heat 2 tablespoons olive oil in an 11- or 12-inch tagine set on a heat diffuser, over medium-low heat. Add the meat, ½ teaspoon salt, and the turmeric and cook, covered, for 15 minutes. Uncover, raise the heat to medium, and boil off the liquid in the pan, stirring often, then gently brown the meat on all sides.

3. Pound the garlic and 1 teaspoon salt to a paste in a mortar. Divide in half and reserve one half. Blend the ginger, black pepper, and saffron water with the remaining garlic in a bowl, then gradually stir in 2 tablespoons olive oil and ½ cup hot water.

4. Pour the spice mixture over the lamb; add the onion and half the parsley and cilantro, and bring to a boil. Reduce the heat to medium-low, cover, and simmer for 2½ hours, or until the meat is very tender.

5. While the meat is cooking, rinse the eggplant slices well, press out excess moisture, and pat dry with paper towels. Heat $^1/_4$ inch of oil in a heavy skillet over high heat. Fry the eggplant slices in batches, turning once, until golden brown on both sides, about 4 minutes. Drain on paper towels and place on a cutting board.

6. With a potato masher, crush the eggplant with the reserved garlic paste, 2 tablespoons of the remaining parsley, the remaining cilantro, the paprika, cumin, and cayenne.

7. Return 3 tablespoons of the reserved oil to the skillet and reheat. Add the diced tomatoes, 1 teaspoon salt, and the sugar and cook over medium-high heat, stirring frequently, until most of the moisture evaporates, about 5 minutes. Add the mashed eggplant and cook over very low heat, stirring frequently, until most of the moisture evaporates and the mixture is very thick, about 20 minutes. Remove from the heat and stir in the lemon juice.

8. Skim most of the fat from the lamb cooking juices. Add $^1/_2$ cup hot water to the tagine and bring to a boil, stirring. Adjust the seasoning, adding additional salt, pepper, and/or lemon juice to taste. Mix half the pan juices with the eggplant puree and again adjust the seasoning to taste. Pile the eggplant on top of the lamb, forming a pyramid. Surround with the remaining sauce. Reheat just before serving. Scatter the remaining 3 tablespoons chopped parsley and the cilantro on top of the lamb and serve.

LAMB TAGINE WITH QUINCES AND OKRA

—— ∽ Serves 4 to 5 ∾ ——

It was through the Internet that I met Jill Elyse Grossvogel, a fellow New Yorker, who imports spices, argan oil, and ceramics from Morocco. A Cornell University PhD, she is currently serving as a member of the Casablanca-Chicago Sister Cities Program and is devoted to promoting self-sufficiency among impoverished women living in remote Berber villages.

She kindly shared with me this recipe, collected on one of her trips to the Moroccan Sahara. It comes from the town of Erfoud.

For information on choosing, preparing, seasoning, and cooking in a tagine, see pages 18–19.

2½ pounds bone-in lamb shoulder, cut into 8 to 10 chunks	Salt and freshly ground black pepper
5 tablespoons clarified butter	Pinch of hot paprika
1 cinnamon stick	2 teaspoons extra virgin olive oil
1 teaspoon ground ginger	Juice of ½ lemon
2 tablespoons saffron water (see page 48)	2 pounds fragrant, lemon-yellow quinces
1 red onion, finely chopped	2 tablespoons honey
1 pound fresh young okra	Ground Ceylon cinnamon

1. About 4 hours before serving, bring the lamb to room temperature. Mix 3 tablespoons of the butter, the cinnamon stick, ginger, saffron water, chopped onion, and 2 tablespoons water in a tagine set on a heat diffuser over low heat. Arrange the lamb, bone-side or fat-side down, on top. Cover with a wrinkled sheet of parchment paper and a lid and cook for 3 hours without disturbing.

2. Carefully pare the cone tops of the okra pods and trim the tips if they are black, but do not cut into the pods. If properly trimmed, none of the interior gooey substance will be released. Wash and dry immediately. Mix 1 teaspoon salt with a pinch of pepper, the paprika, olive oil, and a few drops of the lemon juice. Toss with the okra, and let stand for at least 2 hours in a warm place.

3. Meanwhile, prepare the quinces: Wash and rub each with a wet cloth to remove dirt and fuzz. Halve each quince and remove the core, but do not peel. As you work, brush each half with a drop of lemon juice to prevent darkening. Drop the quinces into a skillet, cover with salted water and a lid, and cook over medium heat for about 20 minutes, or until almost tender. Carefully pour off all but a few tablespoons of the poaching liquid and add the remaining 2 tablespoons butter, the honey, and pinch of cinnamon. Turn the quinces cut-side down and cook until tender and glazed brown, about 20 minutes. Remove the skillet from the heat, turn each piece over, and set aside.

4. Transfer the meat to a side dish and cut away any loose bones and hard fat. Add 1 cup hot water to the tagine and bring to a boil over medium heat. Skim off any fat, then add the okra and poach for 8 to 10 minutes. Return the meat to the tagine and reheat. Transfer the tagine to a wooden surface or a cloth-lined tray to avoid cracking. Arrange the quinces over the lamb and okra and serve.

LAMB TAGINE WITH RAISINS AND ALMONDS, TIZNIT-STYLE

Tiznit is a strange flat city in the southern Souss, famous for its silverwork and its red-brown crenellated walls. Because it was one of the main stopping places for caravans that crossed the Sahara, its food shows strong Senegalese and Guinean influences (as does the architecture of its most famous mosque).

Moroccans lovingly refer to this dish as "the tagine that leaves nothing out." At the end, it is sprinkled with a thin film of ground black pepper, perhaps a Senegalese touch?

— Serves 5 or 6 —

3 pounds lamb shoulder, cut into 1½-inch chunks

2 tablespoons extra virgin olive oil

1½ cups chopped yellow or white onions

3 garlic cloves, finely chopped

Salt and freshly ground black pepper

1 teaspoon ground turmeric

¼ teaspoon ground ginger

¼ teaspoon cayenne

6 ounces red-ripe tomatoes, peeled, halved, seeded, and chopped, or 1 cup canned Italian tomatoes, drained

1 tablespoon chopped mixed flat-leaf parsley and cilantro

1 cup dark raisins, soaked in warm water for 15 minutes and drained

Vegetable oil for frying

½ cup blanched whole almonds

1. Remove the excess fat from the lamb. Place in an 11- to 12-inch tagine set on a heat diffuser and add the olive oil, chopped onion, garlic, salt to taste, 1 teaspoon pepper, the turmeric, ginger, and cayenne and toss to coat evenly. Add the tomatoes and 1 cup water and slowly bring to a boil, then cover, reduce the heat, and simmer for 2½ hours, turning the meat often in the sauce.

2. Add the herbs and drained raisins and continue cooking, uncovered, another 30 minutes, or until the meat is tender and the sauce has reduced to a thick gravy.

3. Preheat the oven to 325°F. Transfer the tagine to the oven as it is heating up and bake, uncovered, until the meat is glazed.

4. Meanwhile, heat enough vegetable oil to cover the bottom of a medium skillet. Fry the almonds until golden brown. Drain on paper towels.

5. Sprinkle the almonds over the lamb just before serving. Black pepper is traditionally sprinkled over everything at the table, but I don't recommend it.

MEAT TAGINE WITH PRUNES AND APPLES

Here's one of the most unusual and luscious Moroccan combinations for the tagine pot.

──────🐜 Serves 6 🐜──────

- 3 to 3½ pounds bone-in lamb shoulder or beef short ribs, cut into 1½-inch chunks
- 3 tablespoons unsalted butter
- 2 tablespoons extra virgin olive oil
- 2 tablespoons saffron water (see page 48)
- Salt
- ½ teaspoon freshly ground black pepper
- 1 scant teaspoon ground ginger
- About ½ teaspoon ground Ceylon cinnamon
- 3 tablespoons grated onion, plus 1 cup thinly sliced onion
- 4 to 5 cilantro sprigs, tied together
- 1 pound pitted prunes
- ¼ cup honey or sugar
- 4 medium tart apples
- 1 tablespoon sesame seeds (preferably unhulled), toasted

Variation:

LAMB TAGINE WITH APRICOTS AND HONEY

Substitute 2 pounds fresh apricots, pitted and cored, for the apples and prunes. Don't cook the apricots, just heat them in the sauce at the last minute.

1. Trim the meat of excess fat. Melt 2 tablespoons of the butter in a tagine set on heat diffuser over medium-low heat, then mix with the oil, saffron water, salt to taste, the pepper, ginger, $^1/_4$ teaspoon of the cinnamon, the grated onion, and cilantro in a bowl. Dip each chunk of meat into the mixture to allow the aromas of the spices to be released. Add hot water to almost cover the meat, raise the heat to medium, and bring to a boil, then lower the heat, cover, and simmer gently for 2 hours if using lamb, $2^1/_2$ hours if using beef.

2. Meanwhile, soak the prunes in 2 cups water.

3. Add the sliced onion to the tagine and cook for 30 minutes longer, or until the meat is very tender. Discard any loose bones and hard fat attached to the meat.

4. Drain the prunes and add to the meat. Stir in $^1/_4$ teaspoon of the cinnamon and 3 tablespoons of the honey or sugar. Simmer, uncovered, until the prunes swell and the sauce has reduced to 1 cup, about 30 minutes.

5. Meanwhile, quarter and core the apples; do not peel. Heat the remaining tablespoon of honey, a pinch of cinnamon, and the remaining tablespoon of butter in a large skillet. Add the apples, cut side down, and sauté until soft and glazed, 2 to 3 minutes longer.

6. To serve, arrange the lamb and prunes on a serving platter, pour the sauce over, and decorate with the apples. Sprinkle with the sesame seeds and serve at once.

LAMB WITH ONIONS, ALMONDS, AND HARD-COOKED EGGS

This dish, called *t'faya,* is served throughout Morocco at weddings, circumcisions, and other important occasions. It's usually presented atop a deep dish of steamed couscous, but it is also very good served as a tagine accompanied by Moroccan bread.

The sweet and succulent dish was developed during the period of the Andaluz, the great historical era of Arab rule in Spain. In Fes, chickpeas are added and the onions are lightly browned. In this particular version, from the Atlantic coast, the onions are first steamed to make them buttery soft, then very slowly simmered until reduced to a deep caramel confit. The 1½ cups deeply caramelized onions is made from 10 cups thickly sliced raw onions.

Serves 6

2 tablespoons extra virgin olive oil

4 tablespoons unsalted butter

3 tablespoons saffron water (see page 48)

1 teaspoon ground ginger

1 teaspoon ground Ceylon cinnamon

½ teaspoon ground turmeric

½ teaspoon *ras el hanout* (optional; see page 36)

½ teaspoon sugar

1 medium red onion, grated

3 pounds bone-in lamb shoulder, trimmed of excess fat and cut into 6 pieces

Salt and freshly ground black pepper

12 sprigs each cilantro and spearmint, tied together

Two 2-inch Ceylon cinnamon sticks, gently bruised

3 pounds large yellow onions

2 tablespoons honey

1 teaspoon orange flower water

6 hard-cooked eggs, peeled and quartered

¾ cup blanched whole almonds, toasted

1. Set an 11- to 12-inch tagine or cazuela on a heat diffuser over medium-low heat and add the oil, 1 tablespoon of the butter, the saffron water, ginger, ground cinnamon, turmeric, *ras el hanout,* if using, and the sugar. Add the grated onion and cook until it begins to dissolve, about 10 minutes.

2. Raise the heat to medium, add the lamb, and lightly brown on all sides. Add ½ cup warm water and bring to a boil, stirring. Add 1½ teaspoons salt, 1 teaspoon pepper, the herbs, and 1 of the cinnamon sticks, cover tightly, and simmer over low heat for 2½ hours.

3. Meanwhile, peel, halve, and thickly slice the large onions. Pile into a wide heavy-bottomed skillet, add ½ cup water and a pinch of salt, cover, and steam over medium-low heat for 15 minutes. Add the remaining 3 tablespoons butter, stir, and cook over medium heat until all the

moisture evaporates and the onions begin to shrink in volume and develop a golden color. Add another ½ cup water to deglaze and cook, stirring, to remove any bits and pieces stuck to the bottom of the pan. Stir in the honey and the remaining cinnamon stick and cook for 20 to 30 minutes, or until the onions turn a deep golden brown.

4. When the meat has cooked for 2½ hours, lift off the cover, tilt the tagine, spoon off about ¼ cup of the sauce, with some of the fat, and add to the onions. Continue cooking the onions, stirring occasionally, until the sauce is very well reduced. Correct the seasoning with salt and pepper and set aside.

5. Skim the fat from the remaining meat juices, then add a cup of water to the tagine and slowly bring to a boil. Cover and continue cooking until the meat is soft and the bones can be easily removed, about 30 minutes longer.

6. Skim off the fat from the lamb in the tagine, and add the orange flower water and salt and pepper to taste. Pile the caramelized onions on the meat. Decorate with the eggs and toasted almonds. Serve at once.

LAMB TAGINE WITH HONEYED SQUASH AND TOASTED PINE NUTS

✳

NOTE TO THE COOK

For information on choosing, preparing, seasoning, and cooking in a tagine, see pages 18–19. If your tagine is not capable of taking high heat, transfer the lamb to a shallow baking/serving dish in step 5.

This tantalizing recipe utilizes two kitchen *trucs* employed by Moroccan home cooks. The first trick concerns the handling of the butternut squash. The vegetable is grated and the pulp macerated in salt until it "weeps," giving up a lot of its liquid. A small portion of the juice is later used to aid caramelization of the vegetable as it is cooked down to the consistency of jam, which develops a lovely aroma and, most important, concentrates the flavor.

A second *truc* concerns treating onions in two ways to achieve different effects: the grated onions added early in the cooking dissolve into the sauce and sliced onions added later provide heft.

— ❧ Serves 4 ❧ —

2½ to 3 pounds butternut squash

Coarse salt

2 pounds thick bone-in lamb shoulder arm chops

1 large onion, grated, plus 2 medium onions, sliced

1 teaspoon saffron water (see page 48)

Salt and freshly ground black pepper

2 teaspoons La Kama Spice Mixture (page 37)

2 teaspoons Smen, Oudi (pages 159 or 161), or clarified butter

Pinch of ground Ceylon cinnamon

Pinch of ground ginger

1 tablespoon floral honey, such as lavender, acacia, or orange flower

3 tablespoons unsalted butter

2 tablespoons pine nuts, toasted

1. Peel and halve the squash and scrape out the seeds and membrane. Using the shredding disk of a food processor or the large holes on a box grater, shred the squash. Sprinkle lightly with coarse salt and let drain in a colander for about 1 hour.

2. Trim any excess fat from the lamb. Cut the chops into 1½-inch chunks, with the bones.

3. Place the lamb, grated onion, saffron water, 1 teaspoon salt, 1½ teaspoons of the spice mixture, ¼ cup water, and the *smen* in an 11- to 12-inch tagine set on a heat diffuser over low heat, stir to mix well, cover, and cook for 1½ hours.

4. Stir in the sliced onions and continue to cook, covered, for 1½ hours longer. Pick out the pieces of lamb and let stand until cool enough to handle.

5. Cut out and discard the bones. Skim the fat off the cooking liquid in the tagine. Season the meat with salt and pepper and return to the tagine.

6. Meanwhile, rinse the grated squash under cold running water, then squeeze in your hands over a bowl to catch the juices. Measure out and reserve 2 tablespoons of the juices; discard the remainder. Place the grated squash in a 10-inch nonstick skillet, add the cinnamon, ginger, honey, the remaining $\frac{1}{2}$ teaspoon spice mixture, 2 tablespoons of the butter, and the reserved 2 tablespoons squash liquid and cook slowly until the squash is thickened to a jam-like consistency and the color of a golden caramel, about 45 minutes. Remove from the heat.

7. Preheat the oven to 300°F.

8. Ladle half the sauce from the tagine over the squash and stir to combine. Spread the squash evenly over the lamb. Dot with the remaining 1 tablespoon butter and place the uncovered tagine in the top third of the oven. Raise the heat to 425°F and bake until the squash is lightly glazed, about 30 minutes.

9. Transfer the tagine to a wooden surface or a folded kitchen towel on a serving tray to prevent cracking. Serve hot or warm, with the toasted pine nuts scattered on top.

LAMB KEDRA WITH CHICKPEAS, BUTTERNUT SQUASH, AND RAS EL HANOUT

NOTE TO THE COOK

For information on choosing, preparing, seasoning, and cooking in a tagine, see pages 18–19.

To intensify the sweetness of this meat stew, a Moroccan cook will add the spice mixture known as *ras el hanout*. You won't need much; even a small amount will provide an enticing aroma and wonderfully intense flavor.

This dish is made in a Dutch oven called a *kedra*, thus the name of the dish (you could use the bottom of a couscousier). Actually, you don't use it for serving here; in this recipe, you pile the meat and vegetables into an ovenproof serving dish, boil down the broth, pour it over the stew, and finish it in a hot oven.

— Serves 6 —

1 cup dried chickpeas

2 lamb shanks, sawed crosswise into 1-inch pieces (ask your butcher to do this for you)

1 small red onion, grated (about ⅓ cup)

2 tablespoons saffron water (see page 48)

About 1 teaspoon ground ginger

½ teaspoon "Faux" *Ras el Hanout* #1 (page 36), or more to taste

3 Ceylon cinnamon sticks

4 tablespoons unsalted butter

Coarse salt and freshly ground black pepper

5 large yellow onions (3½ to 4 pounds), quartered and sliced lengthwise

1 pound carrots, peeled and cut into 2-inch lengths

1½ cups dark, meaty, large raisins, preferably Muscat

2 pounds butternut squash, peeled, halved, seeded, and cut into 6 slices about 3 by 2 by ½ inch

¼ cup floral honey, such as orange blossom, lavender, acacia, or rosemary

1 tablespoon Smen or Oudi (page 159 or 161)

Ground Ceylon cinnamon

1. The day before: Soak the chickpeas in water to cover.

2. The next day: Drain the chickpeas and peel as described on page 51. Set aside.

3. Trim the lamb of excess fat and bring to room temperature. Place the lamb in a large casserole, add the grated onion, saffron water, 1 teaspoon ginger, the *ras el hanout*, cinnamon sticks, 2 tablespoons of the butter, 1 teaspoon salt, and ¼ teaspoon pepper, and cook over low heat until the grated onions begin to dissolve, about 10 minutes.

4. Raise the heat to medium and lightly brown the meat on all sides. Add ½ cup water and bring to a boil, stirring. Cover tightly and simmer over low heat for 1½ hours.

5. Add the peeled chickpeas and enough water to cover to the pot. Put the cover back on and continue cooking for another 1 hour; add the sliced onions to the casserole midway through.

6. Remove the lamb to a 10-inch shallow ovenproof serving dish and let cool. Leave the broth in the casserole.

7. Remove and discard the lamb bones. Season the meat with salt, pepper, and a sprinkling of ground ginger, return to the serving dish, and set aside.

8. Skim the fat off the broth in the casserole. Add the carrots and raisins and simmer for 15 minutes. Add the squash and simmer until tender. With a slotted spoon, remove the squash slices and set them aside. Use the slotted spoon to transfer the onions, carrots, raisins, and chickpeas to the serving dish, completely smothering the pieces of lamb; discard the cinnamon sticks. Arrange the squash attractively over the vegetables and meat.

9. Preheat the oven to 425°F.

10. Add the honey and *smen* to the broth and bring to a boil. Cook, uncovered, until reduced to 1½ cups, about 20 minutes. Adjust the seasoning with salt, pepper, and *ras el hanout* to balance sweet and savory.

11. Pour the sauce over the lamb and squash and dot with the remaining 2 tablespoons butter. Bake uncovered in the top third of the oven until the squash is slightly glazed, about 20 minutes. Serve the stew hot or warm, with a light dusting of ground cinnamon.

LAMB TAGINE WITH LAYERED ONIONS

This is the Fes version of a famous layered onion tagine called *qamamma*. I love the way the onions are cooked down to a melting unctuous sauce then combined with tomatoes or raisins and/or honey.

With my recipe you do most of the work 1 or 2 days in advance. Then on the day you serve it, you assemble and bake the dish, then switch the oven to broil, dribble over some olive oil, and cook until the onions turn crusty and lightly charred.

──── ✥ Serves 6 ✥ ────

3 pounds thick lamb shoulder arm chops, bone-in, cut into 9 or 10 pieces

Coarse salt

1 tablespoon La Kama Spice Mixture (page 37)

2 tablespoons saffron water (see page 48)

1 tablespoon liquid honey, preferably a floral honey such as orange blossom, lavender, or acacia

1 medium red onion, coarsely grated (½ cup), plus 3 pounds large yellow onions, cut into ¼-inch-thick slices

2 tablespoons extra virgin olive oil

2 tablespoons Smen, Oudi (pages 157 or 159), or clarified butter

One 2-inch cinnamon stick

Freshly ground black pepper

¾ cup golden raisins, soaked in warm water for 15 minutes and drained

2 tablespoons turbinado or other raw sugar

1 teaspoon ground Ceylon cinnamon

1 recipe Marrakech Tagine Bread (page 101) or 3 pita or Indian naan breads

1 tablespoon chopped parsley for garnish

1. One or 2 days ahead, trim the lamb of excess fat. Place the meat in a medium flameproof casserole, and add 1 teaspoon salt, the spice mixture, saffron water, honey, grated onion, and 1 tablespoon of the oil. Stir over low heat until the aroma of the spices is released, about 5 minutes; do not brown the meat. Add 2 cups water, bring to a boil, and reduce the heat to low, cover, and cook for 2½ hours, or until the meat is almost falling off the bone.

2. Separate the cooking juices and the meat. When the meat is cool enough to handle, pull out and discard the bones and trim off any fat or gristle. Cut the meat into 1-inch chunks and transfer to a storage bowl. Degrease the cooking juices. Return the cooking juices to the casserole and boil down to a glaze. Add ½ teaspoon salt, 1 tablespoon of the *smen* or butter, the sliced onions, and cinnamon stick, cover, and cook, stirring occasionally, until the onions are soft and golden, about 45 minutes. Use a slotted spoon to transfer the onions to a storage dish. Discard the cinnamon stick. Boil down the liquid in the casserole to

about ¾ cup. Season with salt and pepper and remove from the heat. Up to this point the recipe can be prepared up to 2 days in advance. Cool, cover, and refrigerate the meat and onions.

3. About an hour before serving, set an oven rack on the middle shelf of the oven. Preheat the oven to 350°F.

4. Grease an ovenproof tagine or shallow baking serving dish with remaining butter. Spread the meat on the bottom and cover with the cooked onions and raisins. Scatter the sugar and ground cinnamon on top. Place in the oven and bake, uncovered, for 40 minutes. Switch the oven heat to broil, dribble over the remaining tablespoon oil, and cook until crusty and lightly charred, about 5 minutes.

5. Reheat the bread in the oven for a few minutes. Split in half, then tear each half into 2 or 3 pieces. Spread about one third over a large serving platter. Spoon about half of the contents of the tagine on top. Repeat with another third of the bread and the remaining contents of the tagine. Top with the last pieces of the bread and a sprinkling of parsley and serve at once.

Variation:
LAMB TAGINE WITH LAYERED TOMATOES AND ONIONS

In step 4, spread 6 tomatoes, preferably Roma, peeled, halved, seeded, and thinly sliced, over the onion slices. Cover and bake for 30 minutes. Uncover, sprinkle lightly with salt, scatter the sugar and cinnamon on top, and bake for another 30 minutes. Then broil and continue as described in the master recipe.

LAMB TAGINE WITH PRUNES AND ALMONDS

This luscious pairing of dried fruit and almonds calls for the North African spice mixture La Kama—a balanced aromatic blend of cinnamon, ginger, turmeric, pepper, and nutmeg. Here the lamb is simmered in a small amount of butter-rich juices and then the meat is cooled to firm up, the fat is removed, and the lamb is sautéed to produce a great glaze and firm exterior texture.

⟶ ⊚ Serves 4 to 6 ⊚ ⟵

3 pounds bone-in lamb shoulder, cut into 2-inch chunks

1 tablespoon extra virgin olive oil

2 tablespoons unsalted butter

3 garlic cloves, crushed to a paste with 1 teaspoon salt

1 tablespoon La Kama Spice Mixture (page 37)

2 tablespoons saffron water (see page 48)

Salt and freshly ground black pepper

1 pound (18 to 20) unpitted large prunes

1 teaspoon ground Ceylon cinnamon

1 tablespoon orange flower water

3 tablespoons sugar or 2 tablespoons floral honey, such as orange blossom, lavender, or acacia

1 cup blanched whole almonds, toasted

1 tablespoon sesame seeds, toasted (optional)

1. Trim the lamb of excess fat. Combine the oil and 1 tablespoon of the butter, the garlic, spices, saffron water, ¹/₂ teaspoon salt, and a pinch of pepper in an 11- to 12-inch tagine set on a heat diffuser over medium-low heat and warm for a few minutes. Gradually mix in the chunks of meat so all surfaces are glazed with the spices. Add 1 cup warm water and bring to a boil, then lower the heat, cover, and simmer gently for 2¹/₂ hours.

2. Meanwhile, soak the prunes in water to cover for 1 hour.

3. After the lamb has cooked for 1 hour, transfer ¹/₄ cup of the meat juices to a medium stainless steel skillet, add the drained prunes, the cinnamon, orange flower water, and sugar or honey, and cook slowly until the prunes are lightly caramelized, about 20 minutes.

4. Tilt the skillet so that the juices run to one side. Using a slotted spoon, carefully lift out the prunes to a large side dish, leaving the syrupy juices behind. Add the remaining tablespoon of butter and another ¹/₄ cup of the meat cooking juices, and set aside until the meat is tender.

5. Once the meat is tender, transfer the tagine to a wooden surface or a folded kitchen towel on a tray to prevent cracking.

6. Reheat the syrupy prune juices in the skillet to sizzling. Working in batches, brown the chunks of drained lamb until glazed on all sides, then add to the prunes.

7. Skim away the fat from the meat juices in the tagine. Add the lamb and prunes to the tagine and cook over low heat for 30 minutes, or until the lamb is so tender the meat is falling off the bone.

8. Remove the bones from the meat and return to the tagine. Decorate with the almonds and sesame seeds, if using, and serve at once.

LAMB TAGINE WITH RAISINS, ALMONDS, AND HONEY

NOTE TO THE COOK

You may reduce the amount of butter, but if you are planning to keep the dish a long time, you will need the full amount.

This is the famous *mrouzia*, a special and extremely sweet condiment of preserved lamb and fruits made after the celebration of the Aid el Kebir, the Feast of the Slaughter of the Lamb.

On these occasions, a family suddenly finds itself in possession of a great deal of meat. In rural areas where refrigeration is a luxury, and home freezing virtually unknown, the traditional solution is to preserve the meat in the form of *mrouzia*. If properly done, the meat condiment will keep for as long as a month. And even though today city dwellers have freezers, they continue to make and eat *mrouzia* out of respect for tradition.

Mrouzia is famous in both Arab and Berber communities throughout North Africa. Because it is so incredibly rich, it can only be consumed in small quantities and is never presented as a full course. Think of it as Moroccan chutney.

— Serves 8 —

3 pounds lamb neck, cut into about 10 pieces, each with some bone

1½ teaspoons salt

1½ teaspoons *ras el hanout* (see page 36)

¼ teaspoon ground ginger

½ teaspoon freshly ground black pepper

Pinch of pulverized saffron threads

1¾ cups blanched whole almonds

2 garlic cloves, cut up

3 small Ceylon cinnamon sticks

8 tablespoons (1 stick) unsalted butter (see Note)

1 pound dark raisins

¾ cup dark, heavy honey, such as Greek thyme

1 tablespoon ground Ceylon cinnamon

1. Place the lamb in a large casserole. Mix the salt, *ras el hanout*, ginger, pepper, and saffron with 1 cup water and rub into the pieces of meat. Add the almonds, garlic, cinnamon sticks, butter, and 2 cups water and bring to a boil, then lower the heat and simmer for 2½ hours. Add more water as necessary to avoid burning the meat.

2. Add the raisins, honey, and ground cinnamon and continue cooking for 30 minutes.

3. Uncover the casserole and reduce the sauce over high heat, turning the meat and fruit often to avoid scorching, until there is only a thick honey glaze coating the meat left in the pan. Serve warm or hot.

LAMB TAGINE WITH PEARS OR GREEN APPLES

A lovely quintessentially Moroccan pairing of meat and fruit.

—⌒ Serves 4 to 6 ⌒—

3 pounds bone-in lamb shoulder, cut into 10 chunks

Coarse salt

1 scant teaspoon ground ginger

1 scant teaspoon freshly ground black pepper

1 to 2 pinches cayenne

2 tablespoons saffron water (see page 46)

¼ cup grated onion, drained, plus 1¼ cups chopped onions

3 tablespoons unsalted butter

2 tablespoons chopped mixed flat-leaf parsley and cilantro

4 to 6 firm pears or green apples

1 cinnamon stick

Ground Ceylon cinnamon

Sugar

1. Trim the excess fat from the chunks of lamb. Mix ½ teaspoon salt, the spices, saffron water, grated onion, 1 tablespoon of the butter, and the herbs with the lamb in a wide tagine set over a heat diffuser, and toss over low heat to release the aromas of the spices, about 10 minutes; do not brown the meat. Pour in ¼ cup hot water and bring to a boil, then lower the heat and simmer, covered, for 1½ hours, adding water if necessary and turning the meat occasionally in the sauce.

2. Add the chopped onions and continue simmering over gentle heat for another hour, or until the meat is very tender and the sauce is thick.

3. Meanwhile, wash, quarter, and core the pears or apples, but do not peel. As you work, keep them in acidulated water. Sauté the drained fruit in the remaining 2 tablespoons butter in a skillet with a sprinkling of cinnamon and sugar until lightly caramelized.

4. Remove the meat to a workspace and cut away all the loose bones and hard fat. Return the meat to the tagine. Arrange the fruit among the pieces of meat, and continue cooking for another 20 minutes to blend the flavors. Correct the seasoning with salt and pepper, and serve hot.

LAMB TAGINE WITH
MEDJOUL DATES

This recipe comes from the Souss, where argan oil is produced and is often used to flavor all sorts of dishes, including this tagine. You don't need to use it, but if you've been to that part of Morocco and have eaten this tagine there, you'll miss it if you don't!

Use Medjoul dates, pitted or unpitted as you wish, for this unusual tagine.

——— ❧ Serves 6 ❧ ———

3½ pounds bone-in lamb shoulder, cut into 1½-inch chunks

2 garlic cloves, chopped

Salt

2 tablespoons saffron water (see page 48)

1 teaspoon freshly ground black pepper

¾ to 1 teaspoon ground ginger

Pinch of cayenne

2 to 3 tablespoons unsalted melted butter, argan oil (see Sources), or extra virgin olive oil

1 medium white onion, finely minced

2 tablespoons finely chopped cilantro

8 ounces Medjoul dates, pitted if desired

Ground Ceylon cinnamon

1. Trim the excess fat from the meat. Crush the garlic with 1 teaspoon salt to a paste in a mortar. Loosen with the saffron water, then stir in the spices and butter or oil.

2. Place the meat and spice mixture in an 11- to 12-inch tagine set on a heat diffuser over low heat and toss and cook to release the aroma of the spices. Stir in half the onion, the cilantro, and 1 cup hot water, raise the heat to medium, and bring to a boil. Cover the tagine, reduce the heat, and simmer for 2 hours.

3. Add the remaining onions and simmer, uncovered, for 1 more hour, or until the meat is very tender and the sauce has reduced to a thick gravy.

4. Meanwhile, place a rack on the upper shelf of the oven and preheat the oven to 400°F.

5. If your tagine is not capable of taking high heat, transfer the contents of the pot to a shallow baking dish. Place the dates around or among the chunks of meat. Sprinkle each date or cluster of dates with pinches of ground cinnamon. Bake for about 15 minutes, uncovered, until the dates become a little crusty. Serve at once.

LAMB TAGINE
WITH QUINCES

In the medina of Marrakech, there's a lovely and quite famous restaurant called Le Tobsil, which serves wonderful traditional Moroccan food. I told the owner, Christina Rios, how much I enjoyed her version of lamb with quinces, and she suggested that its success might be due to the addition of tomatoes, which, she said, enhanced the flavor of both the quinces and the lamb. Excellent with Moroccan bread.

—∾ Serves 4 ∾—

2½ pounds bone-in lamb shoulder, trimmed of excess fat and cut into 12 chunks

3 tablespoons extra virgin olive oil or clarified butter

1 cup grated red onion

1 scant teaspoon ground ginger, or to taste

½ teaspoon freshly ground black pepper, or to taste

½ teaspoon *ras el hanout* (see page 36)

½ teaspoon ground turmeric

3 tablespoons saffron water (see page 48)

1 teaspoon sea salt, or to taste

1 red-ripe tomato, halved, seeded, and grated (½ cup)

2 tablespoons finely chopped flat-leaf parsley and/or cilantro

1 Ceylon cinnamon stick

4 medium quinces (about 2 pounds)

1 teaspoon sugar, plus extra for dusting

3 tablespoons sesame seeds, toasted

1. Mix the lamb with the oil or butter and one-quarter of the grated onion in an 11- or 12-inch tagine set on a heat diffuser and toss together over low heat for 10 minutes to warm the pan. Add the spices, saffron water, and salt and cook over medium-low heat for 5 minutes to release the aromas. Add the tomato, herbs, and cinnamon stick and cook, gently stirring, for 5 minutes.

2. Add the remaining onion, cover with parchment paper and a lid, and continue to cook over medium-low heat for 2 hours.

3. Meanwhile, halve and core the quinces; do not peel. Make a few cross marks on the skin and flesh side of each quince. As you work, place the pieces in a saucepan of cold water to prevent them from discoloring. Set the saucepan over medium-high heat, add the sugar, and bring to a boil, then reduce the heat and poach the quinces for 15 minutes.

4. Use a slotted spoon to transfer the quinces to the tagine, slipping the halves below the chunks of the lamb. Continue cooking, covered, for 45 more minutes.

5. Preheat the oven to 375°F.

6. Transfer the tagine to a wooden surface or a folded towel on a
   tray to prevent cracking. Let stand so that the fat rises to the surface,
   then carefully tilt the tagine and skim off the fat. Pull out and discard
   the lamb bones and return the lamb to the tagine. Taste the sauce and
   correct the seasoning (the taste of ginger and pepper should just peek
   through). Rearrange the quinces so they are sitting on top of the chunks
   of lamb. Lightly dust the contents of the tagine with sugar, set on
   the upper shelf of the oven, and allow the quinces to glaze, about
   15 minutes.

7. Sprinkle with the toasted sesame seeds. Transfer the tagine to a cloth-
   lined serving tray to avoid cracking. Serve at once.

STEAMED LAMB SHOULDER
WITH BABY ONIONS

This wonderful recipe is not well known, probably because it's something of an "ugly duckling." But it is really good and should not be missed.

Moroccan cooks love to steam vegetables, fruits, couscous, pasta, and meat. It transforms these ingredients into silky, succulent food. In this recipe, the addition of onions yields a haunting flavor and an indescribably wonderful aroma.

I've tested this dish two different ways. Choose one or the other—it depends on your type of steamer. If you have a couscousier or a deep colander, you can prepare this dish with a bone-in shoulder of lamb. If you have a shallow insert steamer, such as the type that comes with a pasta pot, you will need to have your butcher bone the shoulder out. In either case, the steaming time will be the same, about 2 hours.

⟶ Serves 6 ⟵

One 5½-pound young spring lamb shoulder roast with part of the rib section, or one 3-pound boned lamb shoulder (blade end)

6 tablespoons unsalted butter, softened

1½ teaspoons coarse salt, plus extra for serving

½ teaspoon freshly ground black pepper

2 tablespoons saffron water (see page 48)

1 bunch flat-leaf parsley

5 to 6 whole baby onions or 1 large onion, halved and cut into 6 parts

Ground cumin, preferably Moroccan, for serving

1. Trim the lamb of excess fat; the thin fell can be left on. Blend 4 tablespoons of the butter, the salt, pepper, and saffron water and rub it into the lamb flesh. Press down on the boned shoulder, if using, so it will easily fit into the steamer (be sure there is room for the onions as well).

2. Bring plenty of water to a boil in the bottom of a couscousier or steamer. (To borrow a trick from Diana Kennedy, author of *The Cuisines of Mexico*, toss in a penny—when the penny stops clicking, you'll need to add more water.) Set the container snugly on top of the pot of boiling water and check to see that no steam is escaping out the sides. If steam is escaping, place a long strip of foil or a dampened strip of kitchen cloth across the length of the circumference of the pot top, and tuck it between the steamer and the pot. You want steam to rise only through the perforated holes.

3. Make a bed of parsley in the steamer top and rest the shoulder of lamb on it. Surround with the onions. Cover with a sheet of parchment paper or aluminum foil, tucking the edges down under the meat. Place the lid on top, seal with a strip of aluminum foil, and weight down with a heavy saucepan, to prevent steam buildup from

dislodging the lid. Steam for 1¾ hours, without lifting the lid. When you do lift it to test the meat, stand back to avoid a blast of steam. If the lamb is not falling off the bone, continue steaming for 15 minutes longer.

4. Preheat the broiler. As soon as the lamb is removed, brush it with the remaining 2 tablespoons butter and brown it under the broiler until sizzling. Slice and serve at once, with bowls of ground cumin seed and coarse salt to be used as a dip.

SKEWERED AND GRILLED LAMB

One of the most famous dishes of the Middle East and the Arab world is skewered lamb or beef, known variously as shish kebab, *shaslick,* brochettes, and *quodban* in Morocco. In some parts of the country, these are eaten with a good sprinkling of hot spices, followed by a glass of mint tea. On the road between Meknes and Rabat, there is a small town, called Khemisett, that specializes in serving spicy *quodban* to travelers. Here vendors of the many competing stalls grill the meat on skewers, then place the meat inside pieces of barley bread encrusted with salt crystals, and serve it with soothing glasses of highly sweetened mint tea.

——— 🍃 Serves 4 🍃 ———

1¼ pounds boneless leg of lamb, trimmed of fat and cut into ¾-inch cubes

1 cup beef suet cut into 16 chunks

1 onion, grated

¼ cup finely chopped flat-leaf parsley

Salt

½ teaspoon freshly ground black pepper

Moroccan County Bread (page 108)

Harissa Sauce (optional; page 39)

Cayenne (optional)

Ground cumin seeds, preferably Moroccan (optional)

1. Place the lamb in a shallow dish with the chunks of suet. Add the onion, parsley, salt to taste, and pepper, toss well, and let marinate for 2 hours.

2. Heat a grill.

3. Thread the meat alternately with the suet chunks onto 4 long skewers, pressing the pieces together. (There should be 6 pieces of meat and 4 pieces of suet on each skewer.) Grill the meat a few inches from the heat until well browned. Turn and grill the other side. (Moroccans usually grill meat until well done.)

4. To serve, each guest slides the pieces of meat off the skewer and into a wedge of Moroccan Country Bread, then spreads some harissa sauce, if using, on top or sprinkles on some cayenne, cumin, and salt.

NOTE TO THE COOK

For a spicier kebab, add a scant teaspoon each paprika and cumin. Also, 1½ pounds beef fillet can be substituted for the lamb.

SEARED LAMB KEBABS COOKED IN BUTTER

NOTES TO THE COOK

Moroccans grill the kebabs over charcoal before simmering the meat in butter and spices, but you can broil them on aluminum foil under the broiler, so long as they sear fast.

Though not obligatory, I like the traditional way of serving this dish with eggs poached in the sauce during the final minutes of cooking. If you think you might have difficulty extracting the eggs neatly from a central serving dish, you can finish this off in 4 or 6 individual au gratin dishes. Divide the meat and sauce among them, drop 1 egg into each dish, cover with foil, and bake for 10 minutes in a preheated 375°F oven.

In Marrakech, where this dish, *tagine maghdor,* is most frequently served, it's affectionately known as the "ABC of Moroccan cooking." A stands for the grilled kebabs, the aspect of Moroccan cooking usually first observed by a tourist in the Djemaa el Fna. B is for the tagine, the cooking vessel in which the seared kebabs are next cooked. And C is for the sauce, which, the tourist finally learns, is really the point of the dish. So, the thinking goes, if you eat *tagine maghdor,* you'll eat a dish that will tell you what Moroccan cooking is all about.

—— Serves 4 to 6 ——

1½ pounds boneless leg of lamb, trimmed of fat and cut into 1-inch pieces

1 cup grated onion

Salt and freshly ground black pepper

3 garlic cloves, crushed

4 tablespoons unsalted butter

¼ cup mixed chopped flat-leaf parsley and cilantro

1 teaspoon ground cumin, preferably Moroccan

1 rounded teaspoon sweet paprika

Pinch of cayenne

1 cinnamon stick

Juice of 1 lemon

4 to 6 large eggs

Moroccan Country Bread (page 108)

1. Toss the lamb with half the grated onion, salt and pepper to taste, and the crushed garlic. Allow to "ripen" for at least 1 hour.

2. Preheat the broiler to the highest setting. Arrange the lamb on an aluminum-foil-lined baking sheet and, when the broiler is very hot, sear quickly on both sides. (Or thread onto skewers and sear over charcoal.) The lamb will not be fully cooked.

3. Melt the butter in a tagine or cazuela set over a heat diffuser. Add the meat, the remaining onion, the herbs, spices, and cinnamon stick, and cook briefly, then add enough water to almost cover the meat. Bring to a boil, reduce the heat, and simmer, partially covered, for 45 minutes, stirring from time to time and adding water if necessary to maintain about 1 cup sauce.

4. Add the lemon juice and correct the seasoning with salt and pepper. Break in the eggs carefully, cover the tagine, and cook until the eggs are set.

5. Serve at once, with plenty of pita bread or Moroccan Country Bread for mopping up.

GRILLED LIVER, BERBER-STYLE

In Tangier, harissa (see page 39) thinned with water and a drop of olive oil is often served with this dish.

⟶ Serves 4 to 6 ⟵

1 pound lamb's liver, in one piece

4 ounces beef suet

Salt

½ teaspoon ground cumin, preferably Moroccan

1½ teaspoons paprika

Pinches of cayenne, to taste

Moroccan Country Bread (page 108)

1. Heat a grill.

2. Firm up the liver by lightly searing it on both sides on a hot griddle or in a well-seasoned cast-iron skillet. Cut into smallish chunks. Cut the suet into smaller chunks.

3. Mix the liver and suet with salt to taste and the spices. Thread on skewers, beginning and ending with pieces of liver. Grill quickly on both sides, and serve very hot, with Moroccan Country Bread.

GRILLED MERGUEZ SAUSAGES WITH HARISSA

⟶ Serve 4 ⟵

Four 4- to 6-ounce lamb merguez sausages (see Sources)

Harissa Sauce (page 39)

Moroccan Country Bread (page 108)

1. Heat a grill to medium-high heat.

2. Grill the sausages, turning frequently, until crusted and cooked through, 10 to 15 minutes. Serve with harissa sauce and Moroccan Country Bread.

KEFTA

Kefta is the savory spiced ground meat (lamb or beef) of Morocco, served in meatball form or used as stuffing. In traditional Moroccan homes, I've seen it chopped by hand with a heavy steel knife, then kneaded with the spices into a smooth paste.

In Tangier, my butcher usually added some ground lamb's-tail fat to enhance the texture. Here in the States, I use lean beef or lamb, then blend in a small amount of crème fraîche or grated beef suet to create the right "mouthfeel." Some Moroccan cooks add a beaten egg.

Moroccans have dozens of recipes that use *kefta*, including a wonderful summer tagine in which *kefta* balls are poached lightly in a flavorful tomato sauce, then topped with poached eggs (see page 402). In winter, *kefta* balls are smothered and simmered in an herb sauce. And all year round, you'll find them placed over a bed of simmered slices of potatoes and garnished with green olives, or over spring onions and garnished with golden raisins. *Kefta* is also great-tasting when simply skewered and grilled, accompanied by a grouping of traditional salads. And it is stuffed into vegetables, as well as the triangular fried pastries called *briwats* (see page 144).

KEFTA BROCHETTES

This is the easiest and most classic way to serve grilled ground meat on skewers.

Serves 2 to 4

KEFTA

1 pound ground lean lamb
or beef

3 tablespoons crème fraîche or
grated beef suet

1 garlic clove

2 tablespoons roughly chopped
cilantro

2 tablespoons roughly chopped
flat-leaf parsley

12 spearmint leaves

1 tablespoon sweet paprika

½ teaspoon ground cumin,
preferably Moroccan

½ teaspoon ground Ceylon
cinnamon

½ teaspoon ground ginger

¾ teaspoon salt

Pinch of cayenne

Harissa Sauce (page 39) for
serving

4 skewers (if using bamboo
skewers, soak for 1 hour)

1. To make the *kefta*: Combine all the ingredients in a food processor and blend until pasty. Let stand at room temperature for at least 1 hour.

2. Heat a grill.

3. With wet hands, divide the meat mixture into 8 portions and shape into sausage shapes, packing them onto the skewers, 2 sausages on each. Grill rapidly, 2 to 3 inches from the broiler flame or over charcoal, turning once, until done to taste (Moroccans prefer them well cooked). Serve hot, with some warm harissa sauce.

KEFTA TAGINE WITH HERBS, SPICES, AND LEMON

In some Moroccan homes where fiery dishes are appreciated, a whole dried red pepper is added to the sauce.

———————— ✎ Serves 4 or 5 ✎ ————————

KEFTA

1 pound lean ground lamb or beef

3 tablespoons crème fraîche or grated beef suet

2 teaspoons sweet paprika

1 teaspoon ground cumin, preferably Moroccan

1 teaspoon ground coriander

¾ teaspoon ground Ceylon cinnamon

¼ teaspoon grated nutmeg

¼ teaspoon cayenne

Salt and freshly ground black pepper

2 tablespoons roughly chopped flat-leaf parsley

2 tablespoons roughly chopped cilantro

SAUCE

1 medium red onion, grated

2 tablespoons unsalted butter

¼ cup saffron water (see page 48)

1 teaspoon sweet paprika

½ teaspoon ground cumin, preferably Moroccan

¼ teaspoon ground ginger

¼ teaspoon freshly ground black pepper, or to taste

2 to 3 pinches cayenne

Pinch of ground turmeric

½ teaspoon salt, or to taste

1 cup chopped cilantro

2 tablespoons fresh lemon juice

1. To make the *kefta*: Combine all the ingredients in a food processor and blend until pasty. Form into 24 olive-size balls. Refrigerate until ready to poach in step 3.

2. To make the sauce: Set an 11- or 12-inch tagine or cazuela on a heat diffuser over medium-low heat. Add the grated onion, butter, saffron water, spices, salt, ³/₄ cup of the cilantro, and ¹/₂ cup hot water. Slowly raise the heat and bring to a boil, then reduce the heat to medium-low, cover, and simmer gently to blend the flavors, about 10 minutes.

3. Add the *kefta* and poach, covered, for 30 minutes, turning them over midway through.

4. Add the lemon juice and correct the seasoning with salt and pepper. Transfer the hot tagine to a wooden surface or a folded towel on a serving plate to prevent cracking. Garnish with the remaining ¹/₄ cup cilantro and serve directly from the tagine pot, with warm slices of toasted Moroccan bread for mopping up the sauce.

❊

KEFTA TAGINES

Here are two *kefta* tagine recipes: The tagine with herbs, spices, and lemon and the tagine with tomatoes and eggs are delicious variations on lamb dishes in which meatballs are substituted for cubes of meat.

KEFTA TAGINE WITH TOMATOES AND EGGS

Here is a delicious family-style dish, and one of my children's favorites.

——⊸ Serves 4 ⊷——

NOTES TO THE COOK

For information on choosing, preparing, seasoning, and cooking in a tagine, see pages 18–19.

KEFTA

1 pound lean ground lamb or beef

3 tablespoons crème fraîche or grated beef suet

2 tablespoons grated onion

2 garlic cloves

1½ teaspoons sweet paprika

1 teaspoon ground cumin, preferably Moroccan

¼ teaspoon ground Ceylon cinnamon

Pinch of ground ginger

Pinch of grated nutmeg or ground mace

Pinch of cayenne

1 teaspoon salt

1 packed tablespoon roughly chopped cilantro

TOMATO SAUCE

2 tablespoons extra virgin olive oil

1 small red onion, finely chopped

2 garlic cloves, crushed to a paste with 1 teaspoon salt

2 tablespoons Tomato Magic (page 41) or tomato paste

1½ pounds Roma (plum) tomatoes, halved and grated (2 cups)

1½ teaspoons paprika

¾ teaspoon ground cumin, preferably Moroccan

¼ teaspoon sugar

Salt and freshly ground pepper

4 large eggs

1 tablespoon chopped flat-leaf parsley, for garnish

1. To make the *kefta*: Combine all the ingredients in a food processor, add ¼ cup cold water, and blend until pasty. Form into 24 balls and refrigerate until ready to poach.

2. To make the sauce: Put the oil, onion, garlic, and ⅓ cup water in a 10- or 11-inch tagine or cazuela set on a heat diffuser over medium-low heat and cook gently until the water evaporates, about 10 minutes. Add the Tomato Magic or tomato paste to the sizzling oil and stir for an instant. Add the grated tomatoes, ⅓ cup warm water, the spices, sugar, and salt and pepper to taste. Slowly raise the heat and bring to a boil, then reduce the heat and simmer gently to blend the flavors, about 5 minutes.

3. Add the *kefta* to the sauce. Use a long-handled spoon to gently fold some of the sauce over each meatball, cover, and continue cooking for 25 minutes, turning them in the sauce midway through.

4. Uncover the tagine. Carefully crack the eggs and slip each one into the sauce. Cover and poach the eggs until the whites are set, 5 to 6 minutes. Remove the tagine from the heat to a wooden surface or a folded towel on a serving plate to prevent cracking. Let rest for 3 to 5 minutes, then sprinkle with salt and pepper and the parsley. Serve at once, directly from the tagine.

Variation:

Substitute the *kefta* from Kefta Brochettes (page 399).

TANGIA AND DAFINA, TWO ALL-NIGHT COOKED MEALS

The following story about the famous cooked-all-night meat specialty of Marrakech appeared in my earlier book. Rereading it and reliving the experience amused me so much, I decided to include it here more or less intact.

Some years back, I asked the Moroccan Ministry of Tourism to find a woman who could teach me to prepare *tangia*, one of the great meat specialties of Marrakech. When I arrived, the tourist office was in a state of pandemonium. The local director was frantically telephoning all over town, calling all the women he knew, sometimes using two phones at once. He was chain-smoking cigarettes, thrashing in his chair, buzzing his secretaries, and giving me embarrassed glances, because, as he finally explained, though everybody was quick to agree that *tangia* was the great Marrakech dish, nobody was prepared to teach me how to make it.

Then, finally, success. The director learned from one of his informants that *tangia* is a dish made by men—a dish of soldiers, sheepherders, and others separated from women. He pushed a button on his desk. His chauffeur appeared at the door.

"Do you know how to make *tangia*?"

"Of course I do, sir," said the chauffeur.

"Then take this American woman and teach her how to make it!"

I was dumbfounded, but I was also desperate and grateful. I had come a long way to learn to make *tangia* and had only a day for the task, and the hour was late.

The driver, Ahmed Labkar, was eager but somewhat stunned by his boss's request. We drove first to the medina so he could retrieve his precious *tangia* pot from his house. As soon as I saw it, my confidence was restored. It was shaped like a Grecian urn with a wide belly, a narrow neck, and handles on both sides, and it bore the patina of heavy use. Ahmed handled it with great care. A well-seasoned *tangia* pot, he told me, is one of the keys to the success of a good *tangia*. He further informed me that the best pots for this Marrakech specialty were to be bought in Rabat!

It was dark by the time we reached the Djemaa el Fna, the market-place, parked the car, and entered the *souks* to buy materials for the dish: 4½ pounds lamb shoulder, a small amount of saffron threads and ground cumin, a head of garlic (he used 8 cloves), a preserved lemon, a bottle of vegetable oil, and salt and pepper.

Our next stop was the kitchen of the Maison d'Accueil, directly beneath the Koutoubia Mosque, where Ahmed completed the entire preparation of the dish in less than ten minutes. Aside from crushing the garlic and rinsing the lemon, his only task was to stuff the ingredients into the pot and then cover the opening with parchment paper, tie it down with a string, and punch four holes in it with a pencil.

"*Voilà*, Madame! It is now ready to cook."

We next drove to a *hammam* (a public bathhouse), walked around to the back, and entered the furnace room area. Here a number of old men were lying around on piles of broken nutshells, smoking pipes and tending the furnace that heated the stones in the baths.

In exchange for one dirham (about 22 cents), our *tangia* pot was buried in hot ashes. Here it would cook, Ahmed explained, for a minimum of sixteen hours. As we parted for the evening, his final words were, "I'm sorry we didn't make it with camel meat—it makes a better *tangia*."

The next morning I received word that the Khalifa of Marrakesh was waiting for me in the hotel lobby. Somehow during the night, word of my mission had reached him.

Yes, he confirmed, indeed, *tangia* could only be made by a man, and it was also a dish that must be eaten outdoors. He had come to offer me the use of a pavilion in the Menara Gardens for the midday tasting.

Around noon, Ahmed and I fetched the *tangia* pot from the bathhouse furnace room. We took it to the beautiful Menara Gardens, closed to the public for the day to preserve my privacy, and ate it there while reclining upon an old Moroccan carpet sent over especially for our use.

How did it taste? Very good indeed.

In the years since this experience, I've had great success making *tangia* in a bean pot with veal, achieving a fine balance between the flavors of the meat, garlic, preserved lemons, spices, and *smen*. Basically everything is packed into the pot at the same time, the top is covered with paper, and then the dish is cooked very slowly. In a good *tangia* the meat juices become wonderfully savory due to the mixing of salt, steam, aromatics, and the special flavor imparted by the clay cooking vessel. Serve with warm bread.

Tagines.com now imports 4-quart true *tangia* pots; see Sources.

TANGIA

2 pounds boneless veal shoulder or 3 pounds bone-in veal shanks

4 garlic cloves

Coarse salt

1 tablespoon cumin seeds, preferably Moroccan

2 tablespoons saffron water (see page 48)

½ teaspoon *ras el hanout* (see page 36)

¼ teaspoon freshly ground black pepper

¼ teaspoon ground ginger

¼ teaspoon ground Ceylon cinnamon

¼ teaspoon grated nutmeg

2 tablespoons Smen or Oudi (page 159 or 161), or unsalted butter

1 preserved lemon (see page 21), pulp removed, rinsed, and quartered

1. Preheat the oven to 200°F.

2. Cut the veal into 4 roughly equal pieces. Crush the garlic with ¼ teaspoon coarse salt and the cumin seeds in a mortar. Loosen with the saffron water and stir in the spices. Toss with the meat.

3. Place the spiced meat in a *tangia* pot or bean pot, add all the other ingredients, use a wooden spoon to mix them gently, and then press them down into a compact mass. Cover with a small sheet of crumpled wet parchment and the lid. Bake for 10 hours.

4. Let the *tangia* cool; then pour into a bowl.

5. Skim off the fat. Pull out the bones from the meat. Reheat in a pot and serve in a warm serving bowl.

DAFINA

Another famous cooked-through-the-night dish is *dafina*, the Moroccan Jewish specialty alleged to be the mother of the Spanish or skhina, *olla podrida*, and first cousin to the Eastern European *cholent*.

Traditionally this dish of meat and eggs was prepared on Friday before sundown, the start of the Jewish Sabbath, then sent out to a community oven to bake all night, becoming meltingly tender and delicious in time for Saturday lunch.

Unfortunately, I wasn't able to work up a recipe good enough to include. They were all either too stodgy or too complicated even for me. I tried to duplicate the delicious version I had at the Riad Dar el Cigognes in Marrakech, made, among other things, with stuffed spleen. My best suggestion: go there, special order, and taste it yourself.

chapter eleven

BEAN
AND
VEGETABLE
DISHES

❊

"Allah gives beans to those who have no teeth."

—berber saying

❊

BEAN AND VEGETABLE DISHES

MARAK OF SWISS CHARD
{ page 415 }

MARAK OF OKRA AND TOMATOES
{ page 416 }

ARTICHOKE AND ORANGE COMPOTE
{ page 418 }

MARAK OF CAULIFLOWER WITH
TOMATOES AND OLIVES
{ page 419 }

LENTILS WITH SWISS CHARD, BUTTERNUT SQUASH,
AND MEAT CONFIT
{ page 421 }

WINTER SQUASH WITH
CARAMELIZED ONIONS (CASSOLITA)
{ page 422 }

EGGPLANT STUFFED WITH BRAINS
{ page 424 }

WHITE BEANS WITH SAFFRON AND MEAT CONFIT
{ page 425 }

EGGPLANT SMOTHERED WITH CHARMOULA
{ page 429 }

"THE BIRD THAT FLEW AWAY"
{ page 431 }

POTATO PANCAKES
{ page 432 }

POTATO TAGINE WITH OLIVES AND HARISSA
{ page 435 }

BERBER FAVA BEAN PUREE WITH OLIVE OIL (BYSSARA)
{ page 436 }

FAVA BEANS WITH MEAT CONFIT, CABBAGE,
AND PICKLED PEPPERS
{ page 437 }

BEAN AND
VEGETABLE DISHES

Most of the dishes in this chapter are vegetarian,
among them a good number of all-vegetable tagines, called *maraks,* that are a specialty of northern
Morocco.

One of the most interesting of the *maraks* is
a tagine of okra and tomatoes (see page 416),
which bears a resemblance to a warm salad. But
in Tetouan, this savory combination of tomatoes
adorned with a "necklace" of young okra is treated
as a main course. There are other *maraks* built
around vegetables such as cabbage (known as
a "*marak* of rags") and cauliflower flavored with
cumin and paprika (see page 419). And there is one
particularly savory, unorthodox *marak* made with
lentils, butternut squash, and meat confit cooked
with a whiff of paprika (see page 421).

MARAK OF SWISS CHARD

In Tetouan, this *marak* is often accompanied by a cup of boiled lentils.

———— ⌘ Serves 4 ⌘ ————

12 cups finely chopped Swiss
  chard stalks and leaves (about
  4 bunches)

1 cup chopped onion

½ cup extra virgin olive oil

½ cup chopped cilantro

1 teaspoon sweet paprika

Salt and freshly ground black
  pepper

¼ cup long-grain rice

1. Place the Swiss chard in a large casserole, add the onion, oil, cilantro,
   paprika, salt and pepper to taste, and ¼ cup water, and cook, covered,
   for 30 minutes over medium heat.

2. Add the rice and continue cooking, covered, until all the liquid has
   evaporated and the mixture has turned into a thick sauce slightly filmed
   with oil, about 20 minutes. (The lid of your casserole must be tight-
   fitting so that the rice will cook in the water released by the vegetables.
   If you are afraid the rice will burn, place a sheet of parchment paper
   directly over the rice and vegetables, tightly cover the casserole, and
   cook over medium heat.) Serve warm.

MARAK OF OKRA AND TOMATOES

In Tetouan, the cooks who prepare this dish need to stir the tomato sauce without breaking up the okra poaching in it. Moroccan ingenuity, as usual, has found a way: the okra is strung with a needle and threaded into a long "necklace." When the cook wants to stir the sauce, she pulls up the okra necklace, stirs, and then drops it back into the sauce to continue poaching.

Serves 4 to 6

8 ounces young, fresh okra

4½ pounds-fresh red-ripe tomatoes, peeled, halved, seeded, and chopped

2 tablespoons chopped flat-leaf parsley

1½ teaspoons sweet paprika

1 teaspoon chopped garlic

Salt

3 tablespoons extra virgin olive oil

1. Rub the okra with a towel to remove any fuzz, then rinse and pat dry. Carefully pare the cone tops of the okra pods and trim the tips if they are black, but do not cut into the pods. Place on a flat tray and string together with needle and thread into a "necklace."

2. Combine the tomatoes, parsley, paprika, garlic, salt to taste, and the olive oil in a deep wide casserole and cook over high heat, mashing the tomatoes down as they cook. After 10 minutes, lower the heat to medium, add the okra necklace, and poach it in the sauce for 20 minutes. From time to time, lift up the necklace and stir the sauce, then return the okra. When the okra is tender, remove and keep warm.

3. Continue to reduce the tomato sauce until all the water has evaporated, leaving the oil only. Fry the tomatoes in the oil, stirring continuously to avoid scorching.

4. Gently pull out the thread, then place the okra in the serving dish. Pour the sauce over. Serve hot or lukewarm.

ARTICHOKE AND ORANGE COMPOTE

A while back, Joan Nathan asked me to present a North African vegetable dish on her PBS show on Jewish cooking. I chose to prepare this compote, popular in Jewish communities throughout the Maghreb: Morocco, Algeria, and Tunisia. If you make it a day in advance and then serve it at room temperature, it is even better.

⊸ Serves 4 to 6 ⊶

1½ lemons

16 baby artichokes

2 tablespoons extra virgin olive oil, plus some for drizzling

2 garlic cloves, sliced

½ cup fresh orange juice

1 teaspoon salt, or to taste

½ teaspoon freshly ground black pepper, or to taste

2 navel oranges, peeled and sectioned

Pinch of ground coriander

1 tablespoon sugar, or to taste

4 mint sprigs

1. Place about 4 cups water and the juice of ½ lemon in a bowl. To clean the artichokes, one at a time, cut off the ends of the stems. Break off the outer leaves as far as they will snap, leaving only the yellow leaves. Using a vegetable peeler, trim the rough edges where the leaves were broken off. Cut off the thorny top about ¼ inch down. Rub with the remaining halved lemon, and drop into the lemon water as you go.

2. Heat the olive oil in a flameproof earthenware or shallow stainless steel saucepan. Add the garlic and sauté over low heat for 1 minute. Stir in ⅓ cup of the orange juice, the juice of the halved lemon, the salt, and pepper and cook, stirring with a wooden spoon, for an instant, then add the drained artichokes and ¼ cup water. Cover with a crumpled sheet of wet parchment paper and a tight-fitting lid and cook over the lowest heat for 20 to 25 minutes, or until the artichokes are tender.

3. Meanwhile, combine the orange sections, coriander, sugar, and the remaining orange juice in an 8-inch skillet and cook, stirring, over medium-low heat until the juice is reduced and syrupy, 10 to 15 minutes. Taste, and add extra sugar if bitter. With a slotted spoon, transfer the glazed orange sections to a serving dish.

4. Add the artichokes to the syrupy juices in the skillet (reserve the artichoke cooking liquid) and cook until glazed. Transfer the artichokes to the serving dish.

5. Add the artichoke cooking liquid to the skillet, raise the heat to medium-high, and quickly reduce to ⅓ cup. Correct the seasoning with salt, pepper, and a dash of olive oil, and pour over the artichokes and oranges. Let cool. Just before serving, scatter the mint sprigs on top.

MARAK OF CAULIFLOWER WITH TOMATOES AND OLIVES

Moroccans often steam or pan-roast vegetables such as sweet potatoes, eggplant, turnips, pumpkin, and cauliflower in order to preserve their sweet intense flavor and to endow them with a creamy texture. Here juicy bits of preserved lemon and ripe olives embellish pan-roasted cauliflower.

— Serves 4 —

¼ cup extra virgin olive oil

1 medium cauliflower, trimmed, halved, cored, divided into 1-inch florets, rinsed and drained (about 4 cups)

2 teaspoons sugar

2 ripe or canned tomatoes, peeled, halved, seeded, chopped, and drained

2 teaspoons sweet paprika

1½ teaspoons cumin seeds, preferably Moroccan

4 garlic cloves

1 teaspoon coarse salt

2 tablespoons chopped flat-leaf parsley

Juice of ½ lemon or to taste

½ preserved lemon (see page 21), pulp removed, rind rinsed and slivered

12 green-ripe, midway, or red olives, pitted

1. Heat the oil in a 10-inch straight-sided skillet over medium-low heat. Add the cauliflower and sugar, cover with a crumpled sheet of parchment paper and a tight-fitting lid, and cook gently for 10 minutes. Raise the heat to medium and continue cooking, uncovered, until the moisture in the pan has evaporated and the cauliflower turns pale golden brown.

2. Add the tomatoes and paprika and continue cooking, uncovered, for 5 more minutes.

3. Crush the cumin seeds and garlic to a paste with the salt in a mortar. Stir in ½ cup hot water and add to the skillet. Cook, uncovered, until all the moisture has evaporated and the cauliflower is soft and nicely coated in sauce, about 20 minutes.

4. Add the parsley and lemon juice, toss, and let stand at room temperature for at least 30 minutes before serving. Garnish with the slivered preserved lemon and olives.

LENTILS WITH SWISS CHARD, BUTTERNUT SQUASH, AND MEAT CONFIT

Serves 6

3 large chunks of "Express" Meat Confit (page 44), or Moroccan khlî (see Sources)

1½ cups brown lentils, preferably Pardina

1 large onion, thinly sliced

2 tablespoons extra virgin olive oil

2 tomatoes, peeled, halved, seeded, and finely chopped

2 garlic cloves, chopped

1 teaspoon sweet paprika

½ teaspoon ground cumin, preferably Moroccan

½ teaspoon ground black pepper

¼ teaspoon cayenne or red-hot peppers

3 large Swiss chard leaves, tender ribs and leaves rolled and finely shredded crosswise

1½ cups butternut squash or pumpkin, peeled and seeded and cut into 1 inch cubes

2 tablespoons chopped flat-leaf parsley

2 tablespoons chopped cilantro

A few drops of lemon juice (optional)

Salt

1. Remove the meat confit from the refrigerator and use a wooden or plastic utensil to remove 3 large chunks of meat, plus 2 tablespoons of the preserving fat. Let stand at room temperature.

2. Put the lentils in a saucepan, cover with water, and bring them slowly to a full boil and cook for 5 minutes. Drain the lentils.

3. Meanwhile, in a saucepan, toss the sliced onion in the oil with the tomatoes, garlic, and spices. Cook, stirring, over low heat for 5 minutes.

4. Spread the lentils over the onions; place the Swiss chard on top, add 3 cups water, and gently simmer over low heat for 20 minutes, skimming off any foam.

5. Add the meat confit, cover, and cook for 20 more minutes. Remove the confit; crush and shred finely.

6. Meanwhile, fill a saucepan with water and bring to a boil. Fasten on a colander or steamer; add the squash and steam, covered, for 20 minutes.

7. Add the squash, confit, preserved fat, and herbs to the lentils. Cook until the lentils are tender. Correct the seasoning with lemon juice and salt, if needed. Serve hot or warm.

NOTES TO THE COOK

You'll rarely find this juicy, earthy casserole of lentils and greens topped with cubed pumpkin and studded with shreds of meat confit in a Moroccan restaurant catering to tourists, although you might find it in a workingman's café, or sold off a stand on the street.

It's combined here with onions, tomatoes, and spices to provide a lush, meltingly rich sauce for the tender lentils.

The squash is steamed to protect its creamy texture and enhance its sweet earthy flavor.

As mentioned previously, meat confit is used throughout Morocco as a condiment. Taste the dish before salting—you probably won't need to use any.

WINTER SQUASH WITH CARAMELIZED ONIONS (CASSOLITA)

My friend Joan Nathan, who knows a great deal about Sephardic Moroccan cooking, kindly provided this recipe. You'll find more of them in her *Quiches, Kugels, and Couscous: My Search for Jewish Cooking in France.*

The word *cassolita* comes from the Spanish word *cassola* or *cazuela,* a word that can refer to both a round earthenware pot and the dishes that are cooked in it. This Sephardic *cassolita* from Tetouan is scented with cinnamon and caramelized onions and gets a nice crunch from fried almonds. It is typically served with lamb couscous, but it will go well with any hearty meat dish. It can be made ahead and then reheated before serving.

—— Serves 6 ——

2 pounds butternut, calabaza, or kabocha squash, halved lengthwise and seeded

3 tablespoons vegetable oil

½ cup slivered almonds

2 pounds onions, thinly sliced into rounds

Salt

⅓ cup finely chopped flat-leaf parsley

2 teaspoons sugar, plus (optional) 1 tablespoon

1 teaspoon ground Ceylon cinnamon

½ cup dark raisins

Freshly ground black pepper

1. Preheat the oven to 350°F.

2. Place the squash cut side down on a rimmed baking sheet. Add ¼ cup water, cover with aluminum foil, and bake until the squash is very soft, about 30 minutes. Remove from the oven, and, once cool enough to handle, scoop out the pulp into a large bowl.

3. Heat the oil in a large skillet. Toss in the almonds and cook until golden. With a slotted spoon, remove to a plate and set aside.

4. Sauté the onions in the same pan over medium heat until translucent. Add salt to taste, 2 tablespoons of the parsley, 2 teaspoons of the sugar, the cinnamon, and raisins and continue to cook, stirring occasionally, for about 30 more minutes, until the onions are caramelized.

5. Gently fold the onions into the squash. Season with pepper and more salt, if necessary, and sprinkle with the remaining parsley, the almonds, and, if you wish, the extra tablespoon of sugar. Serve warm.

EGGPLANT STUFFED
WITH BRAINS

—— ❧ Serves 4 to 6 ❧ ——

8 ounces lamb brains

2 or 3 small eggplant
(12 ounces total)

Salt

¼ cup extra virgin olive oil

2 red-ripe tomatoes, peeled,
cubed, and drained

2 whole garlic cloves

Freshly ground black pepper

1 tablespoon chopped flat-leaf
parsley

3 large eggs

1. Soak the brains in salted water to cover for 1 to 2 hours, changing the water at least three times. Drain and remove the membranes and any traces of blood.

2. Remove the eggplant stems. With a thin-bladed paring knife, remove thin vertical strips from each eggplant, leaving them striped. Halve lengthwise and carefully scoop out the center pulp, leaving a ¼-inch-thick wall of flesh in each half-shell. Cube the pulp.

3. Sprinkle each half-shell and the cubed eggplant with salt and let drain in a nonaluminum colander for at least 30 minutes. Squeeze gently, then rinse well under cold running water and pat dry.

4. Heat the oil in a medium skillet and fry the eggplant shells on both sides over low heat until soft. Remove and drain on paper towels. Remove and discard all but 1 tablespoon of the oil from the skillet.

5. Heat the oil remaining in the skillet. Add the tomatoes, eggplant cubes, garlic, salt and pepper to taste, and the chopped parsley and cook for a few minutes so that the flavors blend. Place the mixture in a bowl; discard the garlic cloves.

6. Simmer the brains in a small saucepan of salted water for about 10 minutes. Drain and cut into small cubes. Add to the tomato-eggplant mixture and mash together.

7. Preheat the oven to 350°F.

8. Stuff the eggplant shells with the brain-tomato-eggplant mixture. Place the shells in a lightly oiled ovenproof serving dish, packing them tightly so they don't fall over. Beat the eggs to a froth and pour over the stuffed eggplant. Sprinkle with salt and pepper.

9. Bake for 30 minutes. Serve directly from the dish, or loosen the edges of the firmly set eggs and then invert onto a serving platter. Cut into long slices and serve warm or at room temperature.

WHITE BEANS WITH SAFFRON AND MEAT CONFIT

In this recipe, the salty-spicy infused fat that surrounds meat confit provides the flavor for the beans.

———— ❧ Serves 4 ❧ ————

1 cup dried white beans (Great Northern, cannellini, navy, or white kidney)

1 medium onion, chopped

1 red bell pepper, cored, seeded, and chopped

2 tablespoons saffron water (see page 48)

1 cup crushed and shredded "Express" Meat Confit (page 44), with 2 tablespoons of the fat

1 tablespoon extra virgin olive oil

1 tablespoon Tomato Magic (page 41) or tomato paste

½ teaspoon sweet paprika

Pinch of cayenne

Salt and freshly ground black pepper

1. The day before: Pick over the beans to remove any grit. Rinse under cold water, then soak overnight in plenty of lightly salted water.

2. The following day: Drain the beans, reserving the soaking water. Place in a 2½- to 3-quart saucepan or bean pot, along with the onion, red pepper, saffron water, and 2 cups of the soaking water. Slowly bring to a boil, then cover and cook until the beans are tender, about 45 minutes.

3. Gently fry the meat confit shreds in the confit fat and the olive oil in a 10-inch skillet until crisp, about 3 minutes. Stir in the Tomato Magic or tomato paste and cook for 30 seconds. Add the paprika, cayenne, a pinch each of salt and pepper, and ¼ cup of the bean cooking liquid and bring to a boil.

4. Add the meat confit mixture to the beans, stir gently, cover, and cook over low heat for about 15 minutes to blend the flavors. Serve hot or warm.

EGGPLANT SMOTHERED
WITH CHARMOULA

Charmoula (made with mixed herbs, spices, oil, and vinegar or lemon juice) is most famous as a marinade and flavoring for fish, but it also makes an excellent sauce for vegetables such as cooked carrots, sweet potatoes, and eggplant. It's a good idea to make this dish in advance to allow the eggplant slices to absorb the flavor of the charmoula.

This recipe calls for two-step cooking. First you bake the eggplant slices, then fry them in oil. The initial baking keeps the eggplant from absorbing too much oil during frying.

———— Serves 4 ————

2 medium eggplant (about
   1½ pounds)

Coarse salt

CHARMOULA

1 large garlic clove, minced

1 teaspoon sweet paprika

Pinch of cayenne

¾ teaspoon ground cumin,
   preferably Moroccan

2 tablespoons finely chopped
   cilantro

2 tablespoons finely chopped
   flat-leaf parsley

3 tablespoons fresh lemon juice

6 tablespoons extra virgin olive oil

Salt

1. Slice the eggplant into ¾-inch-thick rounds and sprinkle lightly on both sides with salt. Place in a nonaluminum colander, cover with a paper towel or a cloth, and weight down with a heavy pot or cans. Let stand for 30 minutes, or until the eggplant exude their bitter juices.

2. Preheat the oven to 350°F.

3. To make the charmoula: Whisk together the garlic, paprika, cayenne, cumin, half of the cilantro and parsley, the lemon juice, 2 tablespoons of the olive oil, and salt to taste in a small bowl; set aside to mellow.

4. Pat the eggplant slices dry with paper towels and lightly brush each slice with olive oil. Spread them in a single layer on an oiled baking sheet and bake until tender and golden, about 25 to 30 minutes. Remove from the oven and set aside to cool completely.

5. Heat the remaining olive oil in a medium skillet over high heat. Add the eggplant slices one by one to the hot oil and fry until crisp and browned on both sides, about 30 seconds per side. Drain on paper towels and transfer to a shallow serving dish.

6. Whisk the charmoula once more and drizzle over the eggplant. Sprinkle the remaining cilantro and parsley on top. Let stand for 1 hour, then serve.

"THE BIRD THAT FLEW AWAY"

Fatema Hal is one of Morocco's most famous food personalities, author of several excellent cookbooks and owner of the restaurant Mansouria in Paris. When I spent some time with her in Marrakech, I enjoyed her great sense of humor and was dazzled by her deep knowledge of Moroccan cuisine.

Several years ago, she called to tell me she'd be attending a Culinary Institute of America food festival in nearby Napa Valley, and she asked if I'd interpret her recipes during her presentation. Included would be her famous "The Bird That Flew Away." The recipe title reflects Fatema's sense of humor—this is a *"plat de pauvre"* dish you make when you can't afford to buy a chicken.

Serves 6

2¼ cups dried chickpeas

1 medium red onion, grated (½ cup)

1 tablespoon finely chopped flat-leaf parsley

1 tablespoon finely chopped cilantro

¼ teaspoon sweet paprika

Pinch of hot paprika

¼ teaspoon ground turmeric

Salt and freshly ground black pepper

1 tablespoon Smen or Oudi (page 159 or 161), or clarified butter

1. One day ahead: Soak the chickpeas in water to cover generously.

2. The next day: Drain the chickpeas, and peel as directed on page 51. Place the chickpeas in a small casserole, cover with water, and bring to a boil. Skim off any remaining skins that rise to the surface. Add the grated onion, parsley, cilantro, paprika, turmeric, ½ teaspoon salt, a pinch of pepper, and the *smen*. Bring to a fast boil, then lower the heat, cover with a crumpled round of wet parchment paper directly on the chickpeas, and simmer for 45 minutes, or until the chickpeas are meltingly tender but not as soft as a puree.

3. Correct the seasoning and serve hot.

POTATO PANCAKES

In winter, these popular pancakes, called *maqqouda,* often accompany thick soups such as *harira,* while in summer they're likely to be served along with skewers of grilled lamb. They're also cooked and sold on the street in the form of a sandwich, packed between two thin slices of Moroccan bread and smeared with harissa or tomato sauce thinned with water and oil.

The flavor of the potato is important. I'm partial to Red Bliss potatoes, but any smooth one such as Yukon Gold will do. My old housekeeper, Fatima, would sometimes fold in small amounts of cooked vegetables from the previous day's couscous, or even some charmoula-flavored fried sardines, to enhance the flavor. Though most recipes call for vegetable oil, you'll get a better result using olive oil.

— Serves 6 —

2 pounds Red Bliss or Yukon Gold potatoes

3 garlic cloves

2 teaspoons coarse sea salt

2 teaspoons ground cumin, preferably Moroccan

2 tablespoons finely chopped cilantro

2 tablespoons finely chopped flat-leaf parsley

Pinch each of cayenne, ground turmeric, and freshly ground black or white pepper, mixed together

2 large eggs, whipped

Extra virgin olive oil

About ¼ cup all-purpose flour

1 or 2 lemons, quartered

1. Fill a saucepan with water; bring to a boil. Fasten on a colander or steamer, add the potatoes, cover, and steam for 30 minutes. Cool, peel, and crush the potatoes with a fork.

2. While the potatoes are cooling, mash the garlic, salt, and cumin to a paste in a mortar. Add the cilantro and parsley and mash to a puree, then stir in half the eggs.

3. When the potatoes are cool, add the spice mixture and blend. Shape into 12 small round cakes (about ¼ cup each), and flatten into 3-inch rounds.

4. Heat about 4 to 5 tablespoons olive oil in a medium skillet until hot. Loosen the remaining whipped egg with 1 teaspoon water. Working in batches, dip the potato cakes into the egg, and then into the flour, and gently slide into the hot olive oil. Fry for 1 to 2 minutes on each side, or until golden brown. Drain on paper towels. Serve at once, with the lemon quarters.

POTATO TAGINE WITH OLIVES AND HARISSA

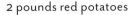

Serves 6

2 pounds red potatoes

4 tablespoons extra virgin olive oil

1 small red onion, grated and squeezed dry, plus 1 medium onion, halved and thinly sliced

⅓ cup tomato sauce or puree

½ teaspoon ground ginger

1 teaspoon sweet paprika

Pinch of ground cumin, preferably Moroccan

1 garlic clove, crushed

1 bay leaf

2 tablespoons saffron water (see page 48)

¼ fresh lemon

3 tablespoons chopped fresh parsley

3 tablespoons chopped fresh cilantro

Salt

2 dozen green-ripe olives, pitted

½ preserved lemon, rinsed and pulp removed

1 teaspoon Harissa Sauce (page 39)

NOTES TO THE COOK

This side dish adapted from a recipe by Fatema Hal integrates marvelous components: preserved lemons, juicy green-ripe olives, and harissa-flavored potatoes.

The dish can be prepared hours in advance and set aside at room temperature. Reheat in a preheated oven until the potatoes are heated through.

1. Peel the potatoes and cut into ½-inch-thick slices. Place in a bowl of cold water and set aside.

2. In a heavy casserole, heat 3 tablespoons of the olive oil over medium heat. Add the grated onion and cook until it starts to melt, 3 to 5 minutes. Add the tomato sauce, ginger, paprika, cumin, and garlic and cook, stirring, for an additional 2 to 3 minutes to toast the spices and reduce the tomato.

3. Drain the potatoes and add to the pot. Add the sliced onion, bay leaf, saffron water, fresh lemon quarter, parsley, and cilantro. Stir gently to mix the ingredients. Add 1½ cups hot water and a hefty pinch of salt, and bring to a boil. Reduce the heat to a simmer, cover, and cook until the potatoes are tender, about 40 minutes. Turn gently once or twice during cooking, being careful not to crush the potatoes.

4. When the potatoes are tender, use a slotted spoon to transfer them to a shallow baking dish. Discard the lemon quarter and bay leaf. Add the olives to the remaining cooking liquid and simmer, uncovered, until the liquid is reduced to a thick sauce. Taste to correct the seasoning. Pour the sauce over the potatoes and set the preserved lemon half in the center.

5. Thirty minutes before serving, place the potato casserole in a cold oven. Turn the heat to 350°F and bake for 20 minutes or until the potatoes are heated through. Toss the potatoes, olives, preserved lemon half, and onions to form an attractive heap. Mix the remaining olive oil with the harissa and dribble over the potatoes. Serve hot.

BERBER FAVA BEAN PUREE WITH OLIVE OIL (BYSSARA)

NOTES TO THE COOK

Dried fava beans are one of the oldest food staples in the Mediterranean. When peeled and cooked, they become luscious and smooth, delicate in flavor with a hint of piney resin.

This is a great dish for lovers of olive oil, as a goodly amount is swirled in at the end. It is especially delicious when the oil is green and freshly pressed. *Byssara* is usually eaten by scooping it up with pieces of flat bread, but it can also be thinned out with water and served as a soup (see page 180).

For an alternate presentation, heat 1 to 2 tablespoons olive oil in a small saucepan to a sizzle, then pour over the puree in overlapping swirls, being sure to cross the lines of cumin and paprika. You can also add a pinch of crushed oregano to the spicing.

This soupy, earthy dip is as popular in North Africa as hummus is in the Middle East. When cooked overnight in a clay pot over coals, it is revered by the Berbers of Northern Morocco as "better than meat!"

You can prepare the dip in advance, then reheat until warm. In Morocco, it is served spread out on a platter, decorated with dribbles of olive oil, a sprinkling of freshly ground cumin seed, and lines of sweet paprika and cayenne. Homemade bread, grilled sardines, and fresh oily black olives are often served with it, but some prefer to devour it with a spoon!

— Makes 3 cups —

2 cups (10 ounces) split dried fava beans (see Note on page 437)

3 large garlic cloves

6 tablespoons extra virgin olive oil

1 tablespoon cumin seeds, preferably Moroccan

Coarse sea salt

½ lemon, optional

1½ teaspoons sweet paprika

2 pinches of cayenne

Cruet of your best olive oil for garnish

1. The night before: Soak the fava beans in 3 to 4 times their volume of cold water. Discard any favas that float.

2. The following day: Bring 6 cups water to a boil. Wash and drain the fava beans. When the water is boiling, add the beans, reduce the heat to a simmer, and cook, uncovered, for 1 hour, skimming off any surface debris.

3. Add the garlic and 2 tablespoons of the olive oil to the beans and continue cooking them down to a nice thick consistency, about 2 more hours. (Timing depends upon the age and quality of the beans.) Remove from the heat and let cool.

4. Meanwhile, grind the cumin seeds with 1 teaspoon salt to a powder in a mortar. Stir half into the beans, and reserve the remaining cumin for garnish.

5. Press the beans through a fine sieve or strainer. Beat in the remaining ¼ cup olive oil and, if needed, a little hot water to create a truly smooth, thick dip. Correct the salt and add a few drops of lemon juice to taste, if desired.

6. Serve the puree on a shallow platter. Crisscross with thin lines of the reserved ground cumin and dot here and there with the paprika and cayenne. Serve with a cruet of olive oil on the side and toasted bread.

FAVA BEANS WITH MEAT CONFIT, CABBAGE, AND PICKLED PEPPERS

Here is a hearty nonpureed winter variation on the previous recipe.

——— Serves 6 ———

1½ cups split dried fava beans

Salt

½ cup crushed and shredded "Express" Meat Confit (page 44), plus 2 tablespoons fat

2 tablespoons extra virgin olive oil, plus more for drizzling

1 garlic clove, finely chopped

1 yellow onion, halved and sliced

⅓ red bell pepper, cored, seeded, and finely diced (⅓ cup)

½ teaspoon sweet paprika

1 teaspoon ground cumin, preferably Moroccan, or to taste

2 tablespoons chopped flat-leaf parsley

1 tablespoon chopped cilantro

¼ small white cabbage

Freshly ground black pepper

Commercial pickled hot red peppers for serving

1. Follow steps 1 and 2 in the previous recipe. Season the beans with salt and leave them in their cooking liquid until ready to reheat and serve. (Do not puree the beans.)

2. Place the meat confit and the fat in a 3-quart shallow casserole. Add the oil, garlic, onion, bell pepper, spices, and half the herbs and cook, stirring occasionally, over medium-low heat, until the onion turns golden, about 10 minutes.

3. Meanwhile, core the cabbage, and slice crosswise into ¼-inch-wide strips. Rinse in cool water and drain.

4. Add the cabbage to the casserole. Cover with the fava bean cooking liquid and cook until the cabbage is tender, 20 to 30 minutes.

5. Reheat the favas and use a slotted spoon to transfer them to the casserole. Add more cooking liquid if necessary to make the dish slightly soupy. Correct the seasoning with salt, pepper, cumin, and a fresh drizzle of olive oil. Serve directly from the casserole, with a sprinkling of the remaining herbs and the pickled red peppers on the side.

NOTE TO THE COOK

Split dried favas require only an overnight soak, but if you purchase unpeeled favas, allow 24 hours to soften. Change the water 2 or 3 times to avoid fermentation. If using unpeeled fava beans, salt at the end.

chapter twelve

DESSERTS

❖

"It's like trying to dunk a doughnut
by grabbing it by the ears."

—*berber saying*

❖

DESERTS

DESSERT COUSCOUS WITH ALMONDS,
WALNUTS, AND DATES
❧ page 443 ❧

HANDMADE DESSERT COUSCOUS
❧ page 444 ❧

DESSERT COUSCOUS WITH GOLDEN RAISINS
❧ page 446 ❧

DESSERT COUSCOUS WITH POMEGRANATES
❧ page 449 ❧

SWEET STEAMED RICE
❧ page 450 ❧

MOROCCAN RICE PUDDING
❧ page 451 ❧

MOROCCAN DESSERT "TRUFFLES" WITH DATES,
ALMONDS, AND APPLES (HAROSET)
❧ page 452 ❧

SESAME SEED, ALMOND,
AND HONEY CONE
❧ page 453 ❧

SEMOLINA YEAST PANCAKES WITH
HONEY AND BUTTER
❧ page 455 ❧

POACHED PEARS WITH PRUNES
❧ page 461 ❧

TARTE TATIN WITH APPLES, RAISINS,
AND ROSE WATER
❧ page 462 ❧

SEMOLINA ALMOND COOKIES
{ page 465 }

SEMOLINA COOKIES
{ page 466 }

DOUBLE-BAKED ANISE-FLAVORED COOKIES
{ page 467 }

"THE SNAKE" (M'HANNCHA)
{ page 470 }

GAZELLES' HORNS
{ page 473 }

SWEET BASTILA
WITH MILK AND ALMONDS
{ page 477 }

SWEET BASTILA
WITH PASTRY CREAM
{ page 478 }

FRIED PASTRY FROM SEFROU
{ page 479 }

FREE-FORM HONEY CAKES
(CHEBBAKIA)
{ page 482 }

HONEY-DIPPED PASTRIES STUFFED WITH
ALMOND PASTE (BRIWATS)
{ page 485 }

SHREDDED PASTRY WITH ALMONDS
(KTAIF)
{ page 486 }

DESSERTS

Moroccans are great connoisseurs of sweets. Two of their most famous are *kab el ghzal* (Gazelles' Horns, page 473), divine sugar-coated crescent-shaped pastries stuffed with almond paste, and *m'hanncha* ("The Snake," page 470), a sublime coil of browned almond-stuffed pastry. These, like the many cakes, cookies, and pastries sold in Moroccan confectionery shops, are usually eaten with tea, which can be served anytime, including before sitting down to a special-occasion feast, such as at a wedding. The traditional way to end a Moroccan dinner is with a bowl or platter of fresh fruits and nuts.

Other Moroccan sweets include the fried pastries dripping with honey that accompany the spicy *harira* soup served to break the fast at nightfall during the month of Ramadan, and my personal favorite, the sweet supper dishes made with steamed "dessert" couscous called *seffa*.

I call these sweet couscous dishes "supper dishes" because in various versions (couscous with raisins, couscous with pomegranates, couscous with ground almonds and dates), they are all popular evening meals, usually accompanied by a glass of the local buttermilk. Dessert couscous is different from regular couscous, being extremely fine and light. This fine grain is available by mail-order (see Sources) or at most Middle Eastern grocers. Or you can make it yourself, which is easy to do and a lot of fun (see page 444).

I've been teaching fine-couscous making for years to my students, confirming for them that it's a lot easier than making your own pasta or bread, yet delivers the same satisfaction: superior taste and a sense of wonder at the magic of it all.

DESSERT COUSCOUS
WITH ALMONDS,
WALNUTS, AND DATES

This dessert is traditionally served in a tall pyramid, decorated with lines of cinnamon shooting down from the top like rays of sunlight. Serve with glasses of ice-cold buttermilk.

—————◦❧ Serves 6 ❧◦—————

1 pound store-bought fine couscous (see Sources) or Homemade Dessert Couscous (page 444)

Oil or butter for greasing the colander or couscousier top and for raking the grains

8 tablespoons (1 stick) unsalted butter

½ cup blanched whole almonds

½ cup peeled walnuts

3 tablespoons superfine sugar

Salt

4 ounces Medjoul dates, pitted and sliced

Ground Ceylon cinnamon

Confectioners' sugar

1. Prepare the couscous as directed in steps 1 and 2 on pages 200–203 (or make the dessert couscous on page 444), noting the changes in the second step below.

2. Melt the butter in a small saucepan. Coarsely chop the nuts, then pulverize them with the superfine sugar in a blender or food processor. Mix with 2 tablespoons of the butter to make a crumbly nut paste. After the first steaming for store-bought couscous, or the second steaming for homemade, toss the drying couscous with the nut butter and salt to taste.

3. Steam the dates for 5 minutes. Then add the nut-buttered couscous to the dates in the steamer for the final steaming.

4. Dump the couscous onto a serving dish and toss with the remaining butter, then fluff. Decorate with lines of cinnamon and serve warm with confectioners' sugar in a small bowl.

HANDMADE DESSERT COUSCOUS

When making dessert couscous, you'll need two horsehair, wire, or plastic sieves of different calibers through which to shake the rolled beads of semolina. You'll also need a couscous cooker or a deep pot with a colander that will sit snugly on top. And, of course, you'll need some fresh coarse semolina purchased by mail-order (see Sources) or at a Middle Eastern grocery and some semolina (pasta) flour. With these items in hand, you'll be able to make fine-grain couscous to serve eight, and the entire process will take no longer than an hour.

Although it may seem counterintuitive to use coarse semolina to make fine couscous, it's necessary. The coarse semolina acts as a "magnet" to attract the fine semolina (pasta) flour. As for steaming dessert couscous, it must be steamed three times for about 15 minutes each time. This third steaming is necessary because the couscous has been freshly made (store-bought regular couscous only requires two steamings, because it has already been steamed once at the factory).

Once you have making dessert couscous in hand, try any of the three delightful supper recipes: with raisins, with pomegranate seeds, or with ground almonds and dates.

To serve a sweet supper couscous, present the dish on a beautiful round platter, decorate the couscous mound with lines of ground cinnamon, and spot here and there with dots of confectioners' sugar.

--- ❧ Makes 4½ to 5 cups cooked fine-grain couscous ❧ ---

1 cup coarse semolina	Oil or butter for greasing the colander or couscousier top
Fine sea salt	
⅔ cup pasta flour (semolina)	¼ cup milk
1 teaspoon extra virgin olive oil	1½ tablespoons melted butter

1. Spread the coarse semolina on a large round tray or in an unglazed flowerpot saucer. Sprinkle a few tablespoons of salted cold water over the semolina and, at the same time, rotate the palm and fingers of one hand in wide circles (in one direction only) to create tiny balls.

2. After 2 or 3 rotations, begin to sprinkle the pasta flour and about ¼ cup cold water alternately over the balls while continuing to rotate. As the balls absorb the flour and water, they will turn into tiny couscous "beads" more or less the same size. Allow to rest for 5 minutes.

3. Shake or lightly press the couscous "beads" through a coarse-mesh tamis or sieve (see Sources) to standardize their size. Place in a finer-mesh sieve and shake to remove excess flour. (You may discard the flour or use it, as Moroccans do, to start the next batch.) Makes about 3 cups uncooked fine couscous.

4. Meanwhile, bring plenty of water to a boil in a deep pot or the bottom of a couscousier cooker. Pile the freshly rolled couscous into a lightly oiled colander or the top steamer and fit onto the pot or bottom, checking for a tight seal (see page 199). Partially cover and steam for 15 minutes.

5. Dump the couscous onto the tray and break up lumps with a large fork or a whisk. Sprinkle with $\frac{1}{3}$ cup salted cold water and rake the grains to keep them separate. Gradually add another $\frac{1}{2}$ cup water and the olive oil while raking the couscous. When the couscous has absorbed all the water, steam for 15 minutes.

6. Dump the couscous onto the tray. Gradually work in the milk and $\frac{1}{4}$ cup cold water, and rake the grains to keep them separate. Allow to rest, covered, for 15 minutes.

7. Fluff up the couscous, toss with the melted butter, and cover loosely with a damp towel. The couscous can be prepared a few hours in advance up to this point. The third and final steaming takes place just before serving. At that time, you will add the raisins, pomegranate, etc., as described in the dessert couscous recipes.

DESSERT COUSCOUS
WITH GOLDEN RAISINS

Fine couscous is steamed, then tossed with fresh butter, mixed with plumped golden raisins, and sprinkled with ground cinnamon.

NOTE TO THE COOK

To prepare the almonds in a skillet, fry in 1 tablespoon olive oil until golden brown, then drain on a paper towel.

1 pound store-bought fine couscous (see Sources) or Handmade Dessert Couscous (page 444)

Oil or butter for greasing the colander or couscousier top and for raking the grains

1 cup golden raisins, soaked in hot water for 10 minutes and drained

2 tablespoons orange flower water

½ cup milk

6 tablespoons unsalted butter, melted

5 tablespoons superfine sugar

1 teaspoon salt

1 tablespoon extra virgin olive oil

⅓ cup blanched whole almonds, fried (see Note)

Ground Ceylon cinnamon

Confectioners' sugar

1. If using store-bought fine couscous, put the couscous in a fine sieve and rinse under cold running water. Turn into a bowl and let soak for a minute or two, then break up any clumps. Let stand for 5 minutes.

2. Steam store-bought couscous twice, or triple-steam freshly rolled couscous, as directed on page 202. Spread the raisins over the final steaming couscous.

3. Dump the couscous and raisins into a wide shallow serving dish. Mix in the orange flower water, milk, ¼ cup water, and the melted butter, then toss with the superfine sugar and salt. Use a long wire whisk to fluff the couscous and pile in a mound. Decorate with lines of fried almonds and cinnamon, dust the top with confectioners' sugar, and garnish with more fried almonds.

DESSERT COUSCOUS
WITH POMEGRANATES

⸺ Serves 6 ⸺

2 large very red pomegranates

2 tablespoons fresh orange
juice

1 tablespoon orange flower water

Salt and freshly ground white
pepper

Pinch of ground dried orange peel
(optional)

⅓ cup superfine sugar

1 pound store-bought
fine couscous (see Sources) or
Handmade Dessert Couscous
(page 444)

2 tablespoons extra virgin olive oil

5 tablespoons unsalted butter,
melted

Ground Ceylon cinnamon

2 tablespoons crushed peeled
pistachios or toasted pine nuts

Confectioners' sugar

1. Roll the pomegranates around on your kitchen counter to soften them, then break up in a bowl of water to keep the juice from spurting. Drain, place skin side up in the bowl, and give each section a good bang with the back of a heavy knife to loosen the seeds.

2. Combine the pomegranate seeds with the orange juice, orange flower water, salt and pepper to taste, the dried orange peel, if using, and superfine sugar in a bowl. Cover and refrigerate for at least 2 hours to soften the seeds.

3. Use the oil for greasing the colander or couscousier top and for raking the grains as described in Dessert Couscous with Golden Raisins (page 446).

4. Dump the couscous into a wide shallow serving dish. Add the melted butter and the pomegranate seeds with their soaking liquid. Gently fluff the couscous again and pile in a mound. Decorate with lines of pomegranate seeds, cinnamon, and the pistachios, and dust the top with confectioners' sugar.

SWEET STEAMED RICE

Rice can be steamed like couscous, decorated with cinnamon and sugar, and served with cold glasses of milk as an evening dish.

You can, of course, prepare steamed rice the regular way, which is easier and will give you an excellent result. But if you handle rice as you handle couscous, you will get absolutely separate grains, which will elevate the dish. It will come out light and airy and will look splendid piled high on a lovely platter, streaked with confectioners' sugar and ground cinnamon.

— Serves 12 —

3 cups white long-grain rice	Salt
Vegetable oil	Confectioners' sugar
4 tablespoons unsalted butter, melted	Ground Ceylon cinnamon

1. Toss the rice with oiled fingers until all the grains are lightly coated. Bring plenty of water to a boil in a deep pot or the bottom of a couscousier. Pile the rice into a lightly oiled colander or the top of the couscousier. Fit the perforated top onto the pot or bottom as for making couscous (see page 199), cover the top container tightly, and steam for 20 minutes.

2. Dump the rice into a shallow pan and sprinkle with water. Press the rice down with a spoon to break up lumps and enable the rice to absorb the water, then stir and smooth out again. Sprinkle with a little more water and let stand for 5 minutes.

3. Pile the rice back into the steamer and steam for 20 minutes, tightly covered.

4. Dump the rice out again and sprinkle with salted water, working it in as you would with couscous, and raking to keep it fluffy. Spread out to dry for 5 to 10 minutes.

5. Pile the rice back into the steamer and steam again for 10 minutes, then turn out and break up the lumps. Stir in the butter and salt to taste. Form into a huge mound on a serving plate and dust with confectioners' sugar and streaks of cinnamon.

MOROCCAN RICE PUDDING

The old way of preparing this excellent sweet supper dish was time-consuming and arduous, and for this reason it was seldom made. Present-day Moroccan cooks have blenders and thus can make this pudding as often as they like.

The decoration of this dish is very simple: the rice is presented in an enormous bowl spotted with 4 dabs of sweet butter just on the verge of melting. Each guest is given a large spoon, and the pudding is eaten communal-style.

——— ✑ Serves 12 ✑ ———

⅓ cup blanched whole almonds

2¼ cups medium- or short-grain rice

½ cup confectioners' sugar, or to taste

Two 3-inch cinnamon sticks

8 tablespoons (1 stick) unsalted butter

½ teaspoon salt

About 2 quarts milk

⅓ cup orange flower water

½ teaspoon pure almond extract

1. Coarsely chop the almonds, then liquefy in a blender with ½ cup very hot water. Press through a sieve into a saucepan. Return the almond pulp to the blender and add another ½ cup hot water. Whirl in the blender again, then strain into the saucepan once more; discard the pulp.

2. Add 2 cups water to the almond milk and bring to a boil. Sprinkle in the rice, confectioners' sugar, and cinnamon, then add half the butter, the salt, and 1 quart milk. Bring to a boil, then reduce the heat, cover, and simmer for 30 minutes, adding more milk if necessary.

3. Continue cooking the rice, adding the remaining 4 cups milk and stirring often, until the whole is thick and velvety yet still loose. As the milk becomes absorbed, add more; in all you will need about 1 quart milk. Add the orange flower water and almond extract and taste for sweetness. The dish should be barely sweet, but add more sugar if desired.

4. Continue cooking for 15 to 20 minutes, stirring continuously to prevent the rice from burning. Pour into a serving bowl and decorate with the remaining butter, in 4 dabs.

NOTES TO THE COOK

The cooking is long, but requires little attention if the burners on your stove can be set at a very low heat; otherwise, use a heat diffuser and stir often to avoid burning the rice.

This pudding is good cold and will keep for a few days in the refrigerator.

MOROCCAN DESSERT "TRUFFLES" WITH DATES, ALMONDS, AND APPLES (HAROSET)

Joan Nathan, my "go-to" person on everything to do with Sephardic cooking, shared this recipe with me. The recipe originated in Toledo, Spain, before the Inquisition, then found its way to Tetouan, an important refuge city for Spanish Jews near Tangier in northern Morocco. From Tetouan, it found its way to Paris, where it is served today.

Dates, normally the predominant fruit in Moroccan *haroset*, are mixed with apples, chopped, then rolled into little balls. Joan suggests rolling the balls in cinnamon and then serving them in little paper cups. Her description: "These balls look like chocolate truffles and taste like Passover petits fours!"

---- ❧ Makes 40 "Truffles" ❧ ----

1 pound blanched almonds

1 pound pitted dates

2 apples, peeled, cored, and quartered

1 teaspoon ground Ceylon cinnamon, plus ½ cup for rolling

¼ teaspoon ground ginger

1. The day before: Place the almonds in a food processor and pulse until finely ground. Add the dates, apples, the 1 teaspoon cinnamon, and the ginger and continue pulsing until the apples are chopped into tiny pieces and the mixture comes together. (You might have to do this in 2 batches.) Cover and refrigerate overnight.

2. The next day: Shape the mixture into balls the size of a large marble. Put the ½ cup cinnamon in a bowl and roll the balls in it.

SESAME SEED, ALMOND, AND HONEY CONE

Here's a charming Tetouanese confection, called *sfuf*, often served at weddings and eaten communally with demitasse spoons. It can be served with Moroccan mint tea.

⤙☙ Serves 12 ☙⤚

- 4½ cups (1 pound) all-purpose flour
- 1 cup sesame seeds, plus ¼ cup toasted sesame seeds
- 1½ cups blanched almonds, finely ground
- 1 teaspoon ground Ceylon cinnamon
- ½ teaspoon grated nutmeg
- 6 tablespoons unsalted butter, softened
- 3 tablespoons liquid honey
- Superfine sugar
- Confectioners' sugar

1. Toast the flour in a large skillet over medium-low heat, stirring it constantly until it turns a lovely light brown. Add the sesame seeds and continue stirring over medium heat until the sesame seeds turn golden and are well mixed with the flour. Add the almonds and spices and cook together for 2 to 3 minutes, stirring all the while. Remove from the heat.

2. Mix the butter and honey in a bowl and gradually, with the aid of a spatula, beat in the flour mixture. Add superfine sugar to taste. Place on a serving plate and form into a cone. Decorate with toasted sesame seeds and confectioners' sugar.

Variation:

ZOMMITA

Substitute barley flour for the all-purpose flour, and ginger for the cinnamon and nutmeg. Toast the almonds before grinding, and mix the butter when hot with 1 cup dark honey. Combine the mixture of almonds, sesame seeds, spices, and flour with butter and honey, then roll into fingers and serve as candy.

SEMOLINA YEAST PANCAKES WITH HONEY AND BUTTER

These wonderful very light and meltingly soft pancakes, called *beghrir,* are cooked on one side only until lightly tan. The uncooked side will have numerous tiny pinholes, popularly described on the Moroccan street as "a thousand holes."

Beghrir are traditionally served for breakfast during Aid el Seghrir, the so-called "little feast" near the end of Ramadan, the month of fasting. They're also sold on the streets of Marrakech, where the pancakes are made in advance, heated on order, and served with a drizzle of honeyed butter. You simply roll them up and eat them as you walk to wherever you're heading.

There are still women who hand-beat the batter for *beghrir* for up to 30 minutes, a procedure that can be duplicated in 60 seconds with a food processor or an electric blender. You want a smooth, velvety batter just a bit thicker than heavy cream, thick enough to lightly coat a spoon.

To make these very light yet thick pancakes, you need extra-fine stone-ground durum flour (sold as "durum" by King Arthur Flour; see Sources). Please do not substitute ordinary semolina pasta flour, which produces heavier pancakes that often taste undercooked.

When I lived in Morocco, women cooked these pancakes in unglazed earthenware pans. Nowadays they use Teflon skillets, which have some drawbacks compared to earthenware, in that they tend to overheat. Moroccan women get around this by quickly dipping the skillet into bowls of ice-cold water, then wiping it dry before making the next pancake. I have found that a heavy Anolon (or similar-quality) nonstick skillet can simulate an earthenware pan and keep the heat steady without this dipping-and-wiping step.

Though *beghrir* are often served right off the griddle, I allow them to cool side by side on kitchen towels. Once cooled, they can be stacked, wrapped, and refrigerated for a few days. Or, if you plan to freeze them, slip a round of wax paper between each pancake. Then, when ready to serve, I reheat them quickly in a hot dry skillet. Once they're hot, I smear them with dabs of honey butter, then roll them up just as they're served on the streets of Marrakech.

Cooks who specialize in *beghrir* seem to be quite superstitious. On my last trip to Marrakech, one of them told me, "If you stare at the crepe while it is forming its thousand holes, they will disappear!" Taking her advice to heart, I do check for holes, but try hard not to stare.

The following recipe is adapted from Rachida Amhaouche's *La Pâtisserie Marocaine.*

───◎ Serves 8 ◎───

½ cup milk, at room temperature

½ egg, beaten

1½ cups (8 ounces) extra-fine semolina flour ("durum"; see headnote above)

¼ cup all-purpose flour

2 teaspoons rapid-rise yeast

1 teaspoon salt

2 teaspoons double-acting baking powder

¼ cup clarified butter, melted

⅓ cup multifloral honey

1. Combine 2 cups water, the milk, and ½ egg in a blender or food processor. Pulse once, then add the two flours, the yeast, salt, and baking powder and blend for 1 minute. Pour into a 3- or 4-quart deep bowl, cover with a heavy cloth, and let stand in a warm place until doubled in volume, about 1 hour.

2. Whisk the batter until creamy. It should be just a little thicker than heavy cream. If it is too thick, add a tablespoon or two of warm water and let stand for a few minutes before continuing.

3. Slowly heat a small nonstick skillet, preferably Analon, over medium-high heat until hot. Immediately reduce the heat to medium and wipe down the skillet with a teaspoon of clarified butter. (You only do this before the first pancake.) Stir the batter, and ladle about ⅓ cup into the center of the pan. Immediately use the bottom of the ladle to spread the batter into a 5-inch round; or swirl the skillet so the batter evenly coats the bottom. Cook over medium heat until the top has lost its uncooked raw appearance and is completely covered with deep holes and the underside is colored pale golden, about 2 to 3 minutes. Use a spatula to remove the pancake, or shake the pan and slip the pancake, holes side up, onto a paper towel to cool. Repeat with the remaining batter; do not stack the pancakes until they are cool.

4. *To reheat one pancake:* Heat a nonstick skillet over medium-low heat, brush with butter, and gently fry the pancake, hole side up, until warm. Combine the melted butter, honey, and a little water in a small saucepan and bring to a boil, stirring. Dribble over the reheated pancake. Roll up to eat. *To reheat all the pancakes:* Preheat the oven to 350°F. Lightly brush 2 pancakes, holes side up, with melted butter and arrange side by side on an ovenproof dish. Place a second layer of pancakes, holes side up, over the first layer, without buttering. Continue alternating until all the pancakes are stacked. Loosely cover the dish with a sheet of foil and place in the oven for 10 to 15 minutes. Add the honey and a few tablespoons of water to the remaining butter, gently heat, and drizzle over the crepes just before serving.

KIF CANDY (MAJOUN)

This innocent-looking candy was made in my presence in Morocco. At the time, I didn't write down exactly what Mohammed Mrabet, a Moroccan writer and collaborator on numerous books with the writer Paul Bowles, did, as Fatima, my housekeeper, kept muttering disapproving remarks into my ear. Later, searching out the proper proportions, I came upon a recipe in *The Hashish Cookbook*, written by one "Panama Rose." A little bit of detective work among the "Tangier Mafia" in New York revealed the identity of "Panama Rose" (the deceased male American beatnik poet, Ira Cohen), leaving me to the conclusion "she" almost certainly learned to make *majoun* from Mrabet. "Her" recipe is very similar to his, except in the method of adding the *kif* (cannabis).

I deny, absolutely, that I have ever tested this recipe. On the other hand, let me tell you how it is made. Mrabet placed about a pound of clarified butter in a casserole with plenty of water and about 3 cups stalks, seeds, and leaves of *kif*. After bringing it to a boil, he let it simmer for 2 hours, then carefully strained it into a large deep roasting pan. He threw away the stalks, seeds, and leaves and let the butter cool and rise to the top in the refrigerator overnight.

Then he placed the butter in a casserole with 1 pound chopped dates, 1 pound chopped figs, ½ pound raisins, 1 teaspoon ground ginger, some ground cinnamon, 1 tablespoon aniseed, ½ cup heavy honey, and ½ cup each ground almonds and walnuts (these proportions are from *The Hashish Cookbook*). He cooked all this together until it became very thick and brown. Then he added some orange flower water and *ras el hanout* to taste and packed the *majoun* into clean jars.

My suggestion: Eat with care, never more than one tablespoon at a time.

POACHED PEARS
WITH PRUNES

This is my adaptation of a recipe given to me by Chef Fatima Mountassamin of the restaurant Le Tobsil in Marrakech. It's particularly good with Semolina Almond Cookies served on the side.

⟳ Serves 4 to 6 ⟲

1¼ cups sugar

½ navel orange, skin on, sliced
   ½ inch thick

One 3-inch Ceylon cinnamon stick

1 clove

1 small bay leaf

1 tablespoon fresh lemon juice

4 to 6 Bartlett or Bosc pears

12 pitted organic prunes

Semolina Almond Cookies
   (page 465)

1. Combine 8 cups water, the sugar, orange slices, cinnamon stick, clove, bay leaf, and lemon juice in a large saucepan and bring to a boil. Remove from the heat.

2. Meanwhile, using an apple corer or a long thin knife, remove the core from the bottom end of 1 pear. Peel the pear but do not remove the stem. Add to the saucepan, and repeat with the remaining pears. Return the pan to the stove and set over medium heat. Add the prunes and simmer until the pears are tender, about 20 minutes. Remove from the heat and allow to cool slightly.

3. Use a slotted spoon to transfer the pears and prunes to a bowl. Boil the poaching liquid over medium-high heat until reduced to 1½ cups, about 15 minutes. Strain the syrup over the pears and prunes. Cool, cover, and refrigerate for up to 4 days.

4. Return the pears to room temperature and serve with almond cookies alongside.

TARTE TATIN WITH APPLES, RAISINS, AND ROSE WATER

I've stayed clear in this book of "nouvelle cuisine Marocaine," the new style of merging European cooking with Moroccan. But for this recipe, I am making an exception. It is just so good!

I developed this tarte Tatin with a Moroccan touch (raisins, orange flower water or rose water) and serve it frequently to guests. With all due modesty, I have to agree with those who have told me it's the best they've ever eaten!

I do most of the preparation early on the day of a dinner party, peeling, coring, and partially cooking the apples, then leave them to absorb some of the caramel and firm up. About 2 hours before serving, I boil off the excess liquid and allow the caramel to darken to a lovely finish. Finally, I add a round of store-bought puff pastry and slip the dish into a hot oven to bake, then turn it out onto a flat platter and serve warm with crème fraîche.

—— ∞ Serves 6 to 8 ∞ ——

½ cup dark raisins

¼ cup rose water or orange flower water

8 tablespoons (1 stick) unsalted butter

½ cup sugar

10 Golden Delicious apples

Juice of 2 lemons

One 8-ounce frozen puff pastry sheet

Crème fraîche or vanilla ice cream

1. Soak the raisins in the flower water until ready to use.

2. Slowly melt the butter in a 12-inch shallow straight-sided ovenproof skillet or tart Tatin pan, preferably flameware (see Sources). Sprinkle the sugar evenly on top of the melted butter and cook over low heat for 5 minutes, without letting the sugar color. Remove from the heat and let the butter cool until solidified.

3. Meanwhile peel, halve, and core the apples; use a soft pastry brush to paint lemon juice over each apple half. Trim the stem end of each half and carefully arrange 12 of the apples halves cut side up in a slightly overlapping circle around the edge on top of the solid butter-sugar base, all facing the same direction. Place the remaining halves cut side up in the center to fill in the empty spaces.

4. Set the skillet over low heat, then slowly raise it to medium, and cook until the juices from the apples, along with the butter and sugar, begin to bubble and turn a dark yellowish-brown, about 40 minutes. (If the rings on your burner are small, move the skillet every ten minutes or so to ensure even cooking. Remove the skillet from the heat and let stand until cool. The dish can be prepared early in the day up to this point. Cover with foil and let stand in a cool place without disturbing the apples.)

Carefully arrange 12 of the apple halves cut side up in a slightly overlapping circle around the edge on top of the solid butter-sugar base, all facing the same direction. Place the remaining halves cut side up in the center to fill in the empty spaces.

5. About 2 hours before serving, set the skillet over medium-low heat and continue cooking the apples until the juices are caramel brown, about 45 minutes. (You do not need to baste the apples; they will cook in the steam.) Once or twice during cooking, gently shake the skillet to check that the apples aren't sticking. Remove the pan from the heat and use a flat spatula to gently press down on the apples, in one direction, so they fill in any empty spaces.

6. Preheat the oven to 400°F.

7. Drain the raisins. Scatter them evenly over the apples.

8. Roll out the pastry to a 13- to 14-inch circle and place on top of the apples. Carefully push the edges of the pastry down inside the skillet. Bake for 40 minutes, or until the pastry is golden brown.

9. Remove the tart from the oven and let it settle for a few minutes. Place a large round/rimmed platter upside down over the tart, then quickly and carefully invert the tart onto the platter. Gently tap on the bottom of the pan to help loosen any apples that have stuck. If any apples still stick to the pan, loosen with a thin spatula and set them back onto the tart. Wait for 10 to 20 minutes, then serve warm with crème fraîche.

Remove the pan from the heat and use a flat spatula to gently press down on the apples, in one direction, so they fill in any empty spaces.

Gently tap on the bottom of the pan to help loosen any apples that have stuck. If any apples still stick to the pan, loosen with a thin spatula and set them back onto the tart.

SEMOLINA ALMOND COOKIES

These terrific cookies are similar to my favorite Greek butter almond cookies. The main difference: Greeks cooks use ouzo, while Moroccan cooks use orange or rose flower water.

I urge you to make these cookies a few days in advance, as they improve with age.

— Makes about 3 dozen cookies —

2½ sticks (10 ounces) unsalted AA butter

1¾ cups pastry flour (8% protein)

1¼ teaspoons baking powder

¾ cup confectioners' sugar, plus extra for coating

1 large egg yolk

1 tablespoon orange flower water

½ teaspoon pure vanilla extract

¼ teaspoon pure almond extract

¾ cup finely ground almonds (almond meal; available at specialty food stores, or see Sources)

1. At least 2 to 3 days before you plan to serve the cookies, melt the butter in a saucepan over low heat without stirring. Lift off and discard the foamy top. Pour the clarified butter into a cup and refrigerate until well chilled, at least 3 hours.

2. Sift the pastry flour and baking powder together, and set aside.

3. Using an electric mixer, beat the chilled butter in a medium bowl at medium speed until very light and fluffy, at least 5 minutes (the more you beat, the lighter the cookie). Gradually beat in 7 tablespoons of the confectioners' sugar; beat for 2 minutes. Add the egg yolk and beat for 2 more minutes. Add the orange flower water, vanilla, and almond extract; beat for another minute. Carefully fold in the flour mixture with a rubber spatula, stirring always in the same direction, then gently fold in the almond meal. The dough will be quite soft. Refrigerate, wrapped in waxed paper, until the dough is cold enough to shape into small balls, about 45 minutes.

4. Preheat the oven to 350°F.

5. Shape the dough into small round cakes about 1 inch in diameter and ½ inch high. Place about ½ inch apart on an ungreased baking sheet. Bake for 12 to 15 minutes; the color should be pale, not brown. Place the baking sheet on a wire rack; immediately sift the remaining confectioners' sugar over the cookies. Cool for 5 minutes.

6. Remove the cookies from the baking sheet and roll in additional confectioners' sugar to coat them.

7. Store the cooled cookies in airtight tins for at least 2 days to mellow, or up to several weeks, before serving.

SEMOLINA COOKIES

NOTE TO THE COOK

The cookies will keep for at least a month in an airtight tin container.

These lovely light cookies, the size of half-dollars and sugar-dipped, are made with semolina flour, which endows them with a marvelous taste and texture.

When I was learning to make these cookies, I followed the lead of all the Moroccan ladies in their kitchen. Whatever they did, I followed, but when it came time to form the mounds, with their perfectly shaped domes, I just couldn't seem to get them right. No matter what I did, the dough kept sticking to my palms. The Moroccan cooks used a complicated rolling, clutching, squeezing, and back-and-forth motion that produced perfectly smooth balls and left their hands clean of dough. They then transferred the dough to their other palm, tapped the balls lightly, and produced one-inch disks with slightly raised domes that were smoother and much more celestial than mine. But in the end, mine tasted as good as theirs. I decided to think of them as a "rustic variation."

———— ❧ Makes 3½ dozen cookies ❧ ————

4 tablespoons unsalted butter, plus soft butter for greasing the baking sheets

¼ cup vegetable oil

2 large fresh free-range eggs

2 cups confectioners' sugar

2⅔ cups pasta flour (semolina)

1 teaspoon double-acting baking powder

⅛ teaspoon fine salt

½ teaspoon pure vanilla extract

1. Melt the butter in the oil in a small saucepan. Remove from the heat and set aside.

2. Using an electric mixer, beat the eggs and 1⅔ cups of the confectioners' sugar together in a large bowl until soft and fluffy. Add the butter-oil mixture and beat a few seconds longer. Using a spatula, fold in the pasta flour, baking powder, salt, and vanilla. Blend well.

3. Preheat the oven to 350°F.

4. Prepare the baking sheets by smearing them with dabs of butter. Place the remaining ⅓ cup confectioners' sugar in a flat dish. Form the cookies by pinching off walnut-sized balls of dough and rolling them between your palms until a perfect sphere is formed. (Since the dough is very sticky, it's a good idea to moisten your hands from time to time.) Flatten each sphere slightly, dip one side into the confectioners' sugar, and arrange on a buttered baking sheet.

5. Bake one sheet at a time on the middle shelf of the oven for 15 to 18 minutes. When they are done, the cookies will have expanded and crisscross breaks will have appeared on their tops. Allow to cool on a rack and crisp before storing.

DOUBLE-BAKED
ANISE-FLAVORED COOKIES

These little cookies are named for free-range chickens called *fekkas,* probably because although they are tough little things, they have an excellent flavor. They are very popular for tea dunking, in that they don't dissolve when dipped.

Traditional *fekkas* require two bakings, which in the 1970s meant sending trays of cookies twice to the community oven. If you lived far away, this made life difficult. In fact, when I made these cookies the traditional way in Morocco, I went to the house of a friend who lived near a community oven.

The recipe below is adapted for a modern American kitchen.

———❧ Makes enough cookies to fill a 1½ quart container ❧———

3 cups unbleached pastry flour

1½ teaspoons rapid-rise yeast

¼ teaspoon salt

1¼ cups confectioners' sugar plus
   extra for rolling

8 tablespoons (1 stick) unsalted
   butter, melted and cooled

1 scant tablespoon aniseed

1 scant tablespoon sesame seeds,
   toasted, if desired

¼ cup orange flower water

1. The day before: Combine the flour, yeast, salt, confectioners' sugar, butter, aniseed, sesame seeds, orange flower water, and enough lukewarm water to form a firm dough. Knead well until smooth, then turn out onto a board dusted with more confectioners' sugar.

2. Divide the dough into 4 portions and shape into balls. Shape 1 ball into a 1-inch-thick cylinder by rolling it back and forth under your palms with some force. The dough will be sticky at first, but after some strong, firm rolling it will start to stretch as you slide your palms toward the ends to lengthen the mass. Stretch and roll the dough until you have a 10- to 12-inch cylinder of even thickness. Repeat with the remaining balls. Place on two ungreased baking sheets, cover with towels, and let rise in a warm place for 1½ to 2 hours until doubled in volume.

3. Preheat the oven to 375°F.

4. Prick each cylinder with a fork to deflate it. Bake for 20 minutes, or until barely golden. They should not be cooked through. Remove from the oven and let cool on racks overnight.

5. The following day: Preheat the oven to 350°F.

6. Slice the cylinders crosswise into very thin cookies and arrange on ungreased baking sheets. Bake until pale golden brown and dry, about 10 minutes. Cool on racks, then store in airtight tins.

"THE SNAKE" (M'HANNCHA)

"The snake" is one of the best desserts in the Moroccan confectionery, a treat not to be missed. It is served most often after a special dinner, along with a glass of mint tea.

The cake is prepared in the form of a coiled snake, and guests are invited to break off pieces the size they desire. Some cooks have taken to remaking the dish by dividing the almond paste and paper-thin pastry into individual servings. I like it in a snake form and have opted to present it that way here.

You can halve the recipe to make a 6- or 7-inch round to serve 6 to 8, but I prefer a magnificent 10- to 12-inch presentation. The cake will keep for several days in an airtight tin stored in a cool place. You can decorate the top with chopped blanched almonds or dust with confectioners' sugar and lines of cinnamon.

The almond paste improves in flavor if made a few days in advance. The almonds are best ground when soft. Moroccan cooks boil them, then soak them in hot water for at least an hour before peeling in order to obtain the proper softness. I soften them by blanching them in a bowl of water set in the microwave for several minutes.

— Serves 12 —

ALMOND PASTE

1 pound (3 cups) unblanched whole almonds

2 small pieces gum arabic

2 tablespoons granulated sugar

1 scant cup (14 tablespoons) confectioners' sugar

2 tablespoons clarified butter, softened

2 tablespoons rose water or orange flower water, or more to taste

PASTRY

Sixteen 10-inch rounds Warqa leaves (page 130) or 8 fillo leaves

¼ cup melted clarified butter (optional)

1 egg yolk, lightly beaten

Ground Ceylon cinnamon

½ cup chopped blanched almonds (optional)

Confectioners' sugar (optional)

1. To make the almond paste: Blanch the almonds and peel (see headnote above).

2. Grind the gum arabic with 1 teaspoon of the granulated sugar to a powder in a mortar or blender. Dump into a bowl. Working in batches, grind the almonds with small amounts of the remaining granulated sugar in the blender until fine. Dump into the bowl with the gum arabic and confectioners' sugar, and mix well. Add the soft butter and fragrant water and mix well. Cover and chill.

3. Divide the chilled almond paste into 8 balls. Divide each one in half and roll each ball into a 5- or 6-inch pencil-thin cylinder.

4. Preheat the oven to 375°F.

5. Place 2 sheets of the pastry side by side, slightly overlapping (shiny side down if using *warqa*), on a large work surface. The width should be about 14 inches. Use a little beaten egg yolk to seal. If using fillo, lightly brush with melted butter; if using *warqa*, do not brush with butter. Place 2 of the cylinders of almond paste along the lower edges, about 1¼ inches from the bottom of the pastry, and roll up the leaves tightly, tucking in the ends. Shape into a coil and place in the center of a lightly buttered 10- to 12-inch ring mold set on a baking sheet. Repeat with the remaining pastry leaves and cylinders of almond paste, extending the coil in the shape of a coiled snake, to fill the ring. With the palm of your hand, gently flatten the snake to fill the ring.

6. Add ½ teaspoon ground cinnamon to the egg. Lightly brush the top and in between the coils with the egg mixture. Bake for 15 minutes, or until golden brown. Carefully invert, with the ring, onto another baking sheet. Scatter the chopped almonds on top, if using, and bake for 20 to 25 minutes. Carefully slide the pastry, with the ring, onto a wire rack and let cool.

7. Serve warm or lightly reheated. If you didn't use the chopped almonds, garnish the cake with a light dusting of confectioners' sugar and a dribbling of ground cinnamon in straight lines to form a lattice pattern.

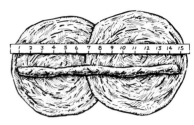

Place 2 of the cylinders of almond paste along the lower edges, about 1¼ inches from the bottom of the pastry.

Shape into a coil and place in the center of a lightly buttered 10- to 12-inch ring mold set on a baking sheet.

Repeat with the remaining pastry leaves and cylinders of almond paste, extending the coil in the shape of a coiled snake, to fill the ring.

GAZELLES' HORNS

Gazelles' horns, the famous crescent-shaped cakes of Morocco, show up everywhere, in all the sweet shops and bakeries, and they are of varying quality: sometimes too hard or brittle, sometimes too thick. This recipe produces the thinnest and most tender pastry, and, to my taste, a perfect not-too-sweet almond paste, made with confectioners' sugar.

My latest version is much easier to make than the version I published in my earlier cookbook, but the results are just as delicious. The food processor produces the proper dough in 40 seconds, instead of the 20-minute kneading traditionally required. Then you stretch the silky and elastic dough into paper-thin skins in which to wrap the almond paste.

Unlike most recipes for gazelles' horns, mine does not include an egg in the pastry, which I believe is the reason it is superior.

───── ❧ Makes 14 to 16 pastries ❧ ─────

1 cup plus 1 tablespoon (6 ounces) all-purpose flour

Pinch of fine salt

½ tablespoon clarified butter, melted, plus 3 tablespoons butter, at room temperature

8 ounces whole almonds

½ cup confectioners' sugar

Butter for greasing the baking sheet

Flour for dusting

1 tablespoon orange flower water or rose water

1. Combine the flour, salt, and melted butter in a food processor. With the machine on, add ½ cup lukewarm water and process for 20 seconds. Let the dough relax for 10 minutes, then cover and process again for 20 seconds.

2. Divide the dough in half and let rest for at least 30 minutes, while you prepare the almond filling.

3. Blanch, grind, and flavor the almonds as directed in the recipe for "The Snake" (page 470), using the confectioners' sugar and soft butter; omit the gum arabic and granulated sugar. Cover the almond paste and chill. (You can make this a few days in advance.)

4. Divide the almond paste in half, then divide one half into 7 or 8 equal parts. Roll 1 part between your palms to make a sausage shape 2 inches long, thicker in the center and tapered at the ends. Repeat with the remaining parts, then repeat with the remaining almond paste. Cover and keep chilled.

5. Preheat the oven to 325°F. Lightly butter a baking sheet.

6. On a lightly floured board, roll out one half the dough to a large thin rectangle (keep the other half under a kitchen towel). If the dough is sticky, roll out on parchment paper or waxed paper.

Roll out 1 circle of dough to a 4- or 5-inch-by-2-inch rectangle. Place an almond paste cylinder about 1 inch up from the bottom of the rectangle.

With a pastry wheel, cut around the mound. Repeat with the remaining dough and almond paste. Shape into a "horn."

Remove the paper, dip the cookie cutter into flour, and cut out 7 or 8 rounds, dipping in flour between each cutting.

7. Remove half the cylinders of almond paste from the refrigerator. Roll out 1 circle of dough to a 4- or 5-inch-by-2-inch rectangle. Place an almond paste cylinder about 1 inch up from the bottom of the rectangle. Stretch the piece of dough below the paste as thin as possible and fold it over the paste to cover it completely. Press the dough together to seal. With a pastry wheel, cut around the mound. Repeat with the remaining dough and almond paste.

8. Pick up each horn and, pressing lightly with the second and third finger and thumb of each hand, shape it into a crescent. Prick each horn twice with a needle, to prevent puffing and splitting, and place on the buttered baking sheet. Bake for 12 to 15 minutes, or until very pale gold in color. (Do not allow the crescents to brown, or they will harden. The crust should be rather soft; they will crisp slightly upon cooling.) Immediately brush each horn under and over with orange flower or rose water. Cool and serve piled high on a serving plate.

Variation:

Roll the horns in confectioners' sugar after brushing with the orange flower or rose water. If you plan to present them this way, reduce the sugar in the almond paste to 7 tablespoons.

SPONGE DOUGHNUTS

Fried doughnuts, called *sfinges*, are commonly eaten in the morning, along with a glass of mint tea or a cup of coffee. Just outside Tangier, in the village of Hayani, you'll find a number of light-blue-colored stalls (light blue being a symbol of good luck) where *sfinges* are prepared. I would often stop by these stalls to watch, fascinated, as the *sfinge* maker squeezed a piece of dough in his oiled hand, then allowed a round "crown" the size of a plum to emerge from between his forefinger and thumb. He'd pierce a hole through the center, twirl the dough into a ring, and toss it into boiling oil, where it immediately puffed up into a large, crisp, golden crown. He'd then fish it out with an iron hook and string it with others on a wire coat hanger to drain. I would choose a particularly well-formed lot, pay for them by weight, and rush home while they were still warm, to sprinkle them with confectioners' sugar and serve them to my children, along with hot chocolate.

SWEET BASTILA WITH MILK AND ALMONDS

Twenty 8-inch Warqa leaves (page 130) or 5 fillo sheets

Vegetable oil for frying

1 cup blanched whole almonds, plus 2 to 4 tablespoons ground blanched almonds

2 tablespoons confectioners' sugar

Ground Ceylon cinnamon

3½ tablespoons cornstarch

4⅓ cups milk

1 cup superfine sugar

Pinch of salt

2 tablespoons rose water or orange flower water

1. Early in the day: Separate the pastry leaves and cut into uniform 8-inch circles, about 4 circles from each fillo sheet. If working with fillo, keep the leaves you are not actually handling under a towel so they do not dry out. If using *warqa*, keep the shiny sides facing up.

2. Pour the oil into a large skillet to a depth of ⅛ inch and heat. Fry the pastry leaves (2 pressed together at a time) on both sides until pale golden and crisp, adjusting the heat to avoid browning in step 5. (If using warqa, press the dull sides together.) Drain on paper towels. (Leave the oil in the skillet.)

3. Brown the whole almonds in the oil remaining in the skillet. Drain and, when cool, coarsely chop or crush with a rolling pin. Mix with the confectioners' sugar and cinnamon to taste. Set aside.

4. Blend the cornstarch and ⅓ cup of the milk to a paste. Bring the remaining 4 cups milk, the superfine sugar, and the salt to a boil in a saucepan. Stirring constantly with a wooden spoon, add the cornstarch paste and cook until thickened; the sauce should coat the back of the spoon. Add the (nonbrowned) ground almonds and flower water and whisk until very smooth, then continue cooking for 1 minute. Remove from the heat and let cool. Chill if desired.

5. Just before serving, assemble the dish: Place 2 sets of leaves on a large platter and sprinkle with half the chopped browned almonds. Cover with 3 sets of leaves and spoon over 2 spoonfuls of milk sauce. Cover with another 2 sets of leaves and sprinkle with the remaining almonds. Cover with the remaining leaves and spoon over 1 or 2 spoonfuls of sauce. Serve the remaining sauce as described in the Note or pour around the assembly.

NOTES TO THE COOK

This specialty of Marrakech makes a regal ending to a meal of such importance that servings of fruit would be considered insufficient. Actually, it is both elegant and inelegant: the former when it is presented at table, the latter as the delicate creation is destroyed as it is portioned out.

The fried *warqa* leaves (you can substitute fillo) are piled high, sometimes as high as 16 inches, with browned almonds and a thickened almond-milk sauce spooned between layers. The presentation is splendid until you cut it with a knife or a pair of scissors. Immediately the frail tender leaves break into a million pieces and become soggy in the sauce, and five minutes later, you are facing a decimated and badly crumbled mass.

There is, however, another way! You can put just a tiny bit of sauce between the layers and serve the rest in small bowls as "dips" for your guests. With this method, the dish maintains a bit of dignity even while being consumed.

SWEET BASTILA WITH PASTRY CREAM

Many Moroccan cooks now make this dish with pastry cream instead of milk sauce in order to present a more compact dessert. The *warqa* or fillo is cut into 2-inch-by-3½-inch rectangles, lightly browned in the oven, and stacked individually with a medium-thick spread of pastry cream and a sprinkling of ground almonds between layers.

———— ❧ Makes 1½ cups ❧ ————

1 cup milk

1½ tablespoons superfine sugar

Pinch of salt

4 teaspoons cornstarch

3 large egg yolks

½ teaspoon pure vanilla extract

1 tablespoon unsalted butter

2 tablespoons heavy cream

2 tablespoons orange flower water

1. Bring the milk to a boil in a small saucepan. Cover and set aside.

2. Place the sugar, salt, cornstarch, and egg yolks in a medium bowl and beat until pale yellow and thick. Beat in the vanilla.

3. Gradually beat the hot milk into the egg yolk mixture. Pour into a clean saucepan and cook over medium heat, stirring constantly, until boiling. Reduce the heat to low and whisk vigorously until the custard is smooth, 1 to 2 minutes.

4. Remove from the heat and continue to beat vigorously for 30 seconds longer. Strain through a fine-mesh strainer into a bowl. Add the butter and stir until melted. Stir in the cream and orange flower water. Let stand until cool, stirring from time to time. Place a sheet of buttered waxed paper directly on the cream to inhibit the formation of a skin, cover, and refrigerate until chilled.

FRIED PASTRY FROM SEFROU

Sefrou is a charming town southeast of Fes, famous for its annual cherry festival and its historic and handsome mellah, a neighborhood that used to be home to a large Sephardic community.

These lovely honey-coated fritter strips were most likely brought to Sefrou from Spain by Jews expelled in 1492.

These strips keep for a few days in a cool place.

——— Makes about 2½ dozen pastries ———

3 cups all-purpose flour	1 large egg yolk
¼ cup confectioners' sugar, plus extra for dusting	About 2 tablespoons orange flower water
⅛ teaspoon salt	Vegetable oil for frying
2 large eggs	2 cups liquid honey

1. Mix the flour, confectioners' sugar, and salt in a bowl. Add the eggs, egg yolk, and enough orange flower water to make a rather soft dough. Turn out onto a board and knead well until smooth and elastic. Separate into 6 equal balls, coat with oil, and let stand for 30 minutes.

2. Heat 2 inches of oil in a deep fryer. Have a colander or draining rack ready.

3. Roll out 1 ball of dough by first flattening it with oiled hands and then rolling it into a large rectangle. Repeat with a second ball, place the rectangles on top of one another, and roll them together. Cut lengthwise into 2-inch strips.

4. Place one end of a strip in the oil, and as it swells and fries, slowly start to wrap the fried end around a long kitchen fork, while at the same time feeding more of the uncooked strip into the oil. Keep on turning and folding the strip until the strip is finished. (The oil should be maintained at a constant temperature so that the pastry does not brown too much, but comes out pale beige.) Remove to drain and continue until all the pastries have been rolled, fried, and drained.

5. Place a jar of honey, uncovered, in a saucepan filled with hot water. Heat until warm. Arrange the pastries on a platter, dribble the honey over them, and sprinkle with confectioners' sugar. Serve at room temperature.

FREE-FORM HONEY CAKES (CHEBBAKIA)

This is one version of the famous Moroccan honey cakes served with spicy *harira* soup during Ramadan, but they also make an excellent addition to the sweets tray for serving with afternoon tea. These cakes are very sweet: when you bite into them, you are biting into pure honey!

I've scaled down this somewhat difficult recipe in consideration of American tastes. In a Moroccan home, though, it wouldn't make sense to make fewer than five hundred cakes. Friends and neighbors help, and then everyone goes home with a large batch. Ramadan lasts a month, and the culinary frenzy at sundown when the fast is broken must be seen to be believed.

—◎ Serves 12 ◎—

10 tablespoons butter

3 large eggs

¼ teaspoon salt

2 tablespoons saffron water (see page 48)

1 teaspoon vanilla extract

2 tablespoons white vinegar

2 tablespoons orange flower water

1 packet (2½ teaspoons) rapid-rise yeast

1 teaspoon double-acting baking powder

8 cups (about 2 pounds) all-purpose flour

Pinch of pulverized saffron

1 quart orange blossom honey

Vegetable oil for deep-frying

⅓ cup sesame seeds, oven roasted

1. In an narrow saucepan, melt the butter slowly without stirring or browning. Remove foam as it appears on the surface. When the butter is golden and clear, remove it from the heat and allow to cool.

2. Beat the eggs, salt, saffron water, vanilla, vinegar, orange flower water, yeast, and baking powder in a bowl. Stir in the clarified butter.

3. Place the flour in a large bowl and make a well in the center. Slowly pour the egg mixture into the flour, stirring constantly with a wooden spoon until well combined. Add just enough water to work into a stiff dough. Knead well by pressing down and pushing forward with the heel of your hand and folding the dough over onto itself. Knead until smooth and elastic.

4. After the dough is made, blend 1 tablespoon butter with the pulverized saffron. Then blend into the dough until bright yellow. Separate the dough into 4 equal parts. Cover and let stand for 20 minutes.

5. Take 1 ball of dough and slap it around to flatten it out. Butter a rolling pin and start rolling the dough out until it is as thin as thick cardboard and about 10 inches round. Use a pastry wheel and cut

into pieces approximately 5 by 3 inches. Make 5 parallel incisions to form 6 strips within each piece. Loop every other strip in your fingers and then bring the lower opposite points together so that a pretzel shape is formed. Place on a buttered baking sheet, covered, while you prepare the rest of the dough. (The shape is really unimportant, as long as they look more or less like pretzels.)

6. Heat the honey in a large deep saucepan. (Honey tends to boil up rather high.) Pour the oil into a large deep skillet to a depth of at least 1¼ inches. Fry 6 or 7 cakes at a time on both sides until brown (not light, but not too dark). Immediately drop the cakes into the hot honey. As soon as the honey boils up, remove the cakes to a colander or rack to drain. Sprinkle at once with the sesame seeds. Let cool. Store in airtight tins; the cakes will keep for a month.

HONEY-DIPPED PASTRIES STUFFED WITH ALMOND PASTE (BRIWATS)

These are extremely rich pastries, and incredibly sweet. Happily, they will keep a long time when put up in airtight containers.

This is the traditional recipe as prepared in Fes, but you can make them a number of different ways: you can use plain almond paste, made according to the directions in the recipe for "The Snake" (page 470), or you can blend 4 ounces almond paste with 8 ounces dried pitted dates that have been pounded and mixed with a little orange flower water and butter. I have also heard of cooks who make the filling with dried figs.

———◎ Makes 2 dozen pastries ◎———

8 ounces blanched whole almonds

Vegetable oil for frying

8 tablespoons (1 stick) unsalted butter, melted and cooled (for fillo pastry only)

1½ teaspoons ground Ceylon cinnamon

Scant ½ teaspoon pure almond extract

2 to 3 tablespoons confectioners' sugar

5 tablespoons orange flower water

¼ pound fillo leaves or twenty-four 8-inch Warqa leaves (page 130)

2 cups honey, such as orange blossom honey

1. Fry the almonds in the oil in a skillet until golden. Drain on paper towels. Grind in a blender until smooth and pasty. (If you drained them too well, you will need to add a few tablespoons cooled melted butter.)

2. Transfer to a bowl and flavor with the cinnamon, almond extract, confectioners' sugar, and 1½ tablespoons of the orange flower water. Knead to a solid mass.

3. Preheat the oven to 350°F.

4. If using fillo, unroll one sheet at a time, keeping the others under a damp towel. Brush the sheet sparingly with melted butter. Cut lengthwise into 3 equal strips and place a nugget of almond paste at the bottom of each strip. Fold into a triangle according to the directions on page 144. If using *warqa* leaves, there is no need to brush with butter; place a nugget of almond paste on each sheet and fold into a triangle. Arrange shiny side out.

5. Meanwhile, heat the honey with the remaining 3½ tablespoons orange flower water in a large saucepan. (Avoid burning by continually controlling the heat.)

6. Bake the rolls for 30 minutes, or until puffed and golden brown on both sides. When the rolls are done, transfer immediately to the simmering honey, and allow the hot honey to penetrate the pastries for 2 to 3 minutes. Remove to a flat dish to dry and cool.

SHREDDED PASTRY WITH ALMONDS (KTAIF)

This Tetouanese pastry dessert was surely adapted from the Turkish *cadaif* (a honey-walnut concoction made with a type of paper-thin pastry similar to *warqa*, though differently prepared) when the Turks occupied Algeria in the sixteenth century. This recipe is adapted from Lord Bute's *Moorish Recipes*.

In the Middle East, the dough is pushed through a sieve onto a hot pan, and then removed before it is fully cooked. In Tetouan, there is a special instrument for making this pastry, a tin cup with two fine protruding open nozzles. The soft pastry dough is pushed through this gadget into a lattice pattern on a flat metal tray. The lattice is removed and another made, until all the batter is used up. These lattices, which look like shredded wheat, are then piled on top of each other and moistened with melted butter. In the Middle East, the lattices are baked in even layers and are quite attractive, while in Tetouan they are, in the words of Lord Bute, "by no means the most attractive to the eye."

You can buy the dough in Middle Eastern pastry shops, where it's called "cadaif pastry." (If frozen, defrost thoroughly before use.)

This pastry will keep for about 4 days. If broken up and piled onto a serving dish, it won't look too bad.

—— ∞ Serves 8 ∞ ——

5½ cups confectioners' sugar	Butter for frying
1 cinnamon stick	2 to 3 teaspoons ground Ceylon cinnamon
1 tablespoon fresh lemon juice	
¾ cup orange flower water	1 pound cadaif pastry threads
12 ounces blanched whole almonds	½ pound (2 sticks) unsalted butter, melted

1. To prepare the syrup: Cook 4 cups of the confectioners' sugar with 2 cups water, the cinnamon stick, and lemon juice in a heavy saucepan, uncovered, until it boils and thickens (about 220°F on a candy thermometer). Stir in ¼ cup of the orange flower water and continue cooking for a few minutes longer. Set aside to cool.

2. Meanwhile, prepare the filling: Fry the almonds in butter until lightly browned. Drain on paper towels. Pulverize in the blender, then mix with the cinnamon, the remaining 1½ cups confectioners' sugar, and enough of the remaining ½ cup orange flower water to moisten to a paste.

3. Place half the pastry strands in a large skillet and pour over half the melted butter. Cook without browning, by regulating the heat; after 10 minutes, there should only be a light golden crust on the bottom of the pastry. Turn the pastry over and gently fry the other side. (The strands will tend to stick together in one or two big clumps.) Transfer the strands to a plate and, using the remaining butter, cook the second

batch of pastry. Pour off any excess butter, and spread the almond mixture over the pastry in the skillet. Cover with the first batch of pastry.

4. Pour the syrup over the pastry and cook for about 15 minutes, basting the pastry with the syrup until well absorbed and turning the pastry over to as it crisps. Continue until all the strands are crisp and well moistened and the "whole is one shapeless mass." Leave in the pan to cool.

5. Break up into 1½-inch nuggets and serve at room temperature.

chapter thirteen

BEVERAGES

❈

"This garden here by the sea with its ceiling of grapes; the flat roofs of the Marrakesh cafés where the men sit at midnight waiting for a breath of cool air; the cave-like rooms in the mountain markets of the High Atlas, to which the customers must bring their own tea, sugar, and mint, the establishments furnishing only the fire, water, and teapot."

—paul bowles

❈

BEVERAGES

AVOCADO AND DATE MILK SHAKE
{ page 493 }

ALMOND MILK DRINK
{ page 494 }

APPLE MILK DRINK
{ page 494 }

COFFEE RAS EL HANOUT
{ page 495 }

MOROCCAN MINT TEA
{ page 497 }

THERAPEUTIC DRINK TO WARD OFF COLDS
{ page 498 }

BEVERAGES

You will see water sellers in souks throughout Morocco, wearing red robes, their chests crisscrossed with hooked straps, brass water cups hanging on the hooks. They portion out their penny's worth of liquid from a leather bag after elaborate exercises designed to convince the buyer that his cup has been hygienically rinsed.

While the poor traveler or day laborer may buy water by the cup, the rich may drink water that has been perfumed with gum arabic or the essence of orange blossoms. In Fes, I was once served deliciously refreshing water between the spicy courses of a lengthy meal. I was told that some grains of gum arabic had been thrown into a charcoal brazier and then an empty water jug inverted over the ascending fumes. Afterward, the jug was filled with water, which picked up the captured scent.

Fruit juices are popular in Morocco, where Islam forbids the consumption of alcohol. Moroccans drink orange juice, lemonade flavored with orange flower water, and sometimes, concoctions of pomegranate and lemon juice or grape juice flavored with cinnamon.

AVOCADO AND DATE MILK SHAKE

⸺ Serves 4 ⸺

4 Medjoul dates

Orange flower water

1 large ripe avocado, peeled and pitted

½ cup blanched almonds

1 quart goat's or cow's milk

1 tablespoon sugar, or more to taste

1. Wipe the dates with the orange flower water. Cut up and remove the pits.

2. Combine the dates, avocado, almonds, half the milk, and the sugar in a blender and puree until smooth. Pour through a strainer into a bowl, pressing down hard with the back of a wooden spoon to extract as much liquid as possible.

3. Stir in the remaining milk, 1 to 2 teaspoons orange flower water, and 1 cup cold water. Add more sugar to taste. Serve cold.

MILK DRINKS

Originally a *mahlaba* was a place to buy dairy products such as milk, cream, and cheese. Now the word is used in the major cities to describe a kind of snack bar, a place that sells not only milk products but also all sorts of fruit drinks and cakes that go well with them. A *mahlaba* isn't a café, where you sit and talk or you leisurely sip coffee or tea, but a place to grab something quick and nourishing on the run. *Mahlabas* are enormously popular, not unlike smoothie bars in our shopping centers. The difference lies in the flavorings: dates, almonds, orange flower water, and rose water.

ALMOND MILK DRINK

—— Serves 4 ——

8 ounces blanched whole almonds

½ cup sugar

Orange flower water or rose water

1 cup milk

1. Combine the almonds, sugar, a dash of flower water, and 1 cup water in a blender and blend until smooth. Pour through a strainer into a bowl, pressing down hard with the back of a wooden spoon to extract as much liquid as possible.

2. Stir in 1 more cup water and the milk. Chill, and serve in small glasses.

Note to the Cook:
If the flavor seems bland, add a dash of pure almond extract.

APPLE MILK DRINK

This very popular drink is a *sharbat*, rich, cool, and satisfying when served in the afternoon on hot days when dinner will be late and members of the household need sustenance.

—— Serves 2 ——

2 red apples, peeled, cored, and cubed

2 tablespoons sugar

2 scant teaspoons rose water or orange flower water

2 cups milk

Shaved ice (optional)

Place the apples in a blender with the sugar, flower water, and milk. Whirl at high speed for 15 seconds. Pour over the shaved ice, if desired. Serve chilled.

COFFEE RAS EL HANOUT

For those who love to play with spices, coffee with *ras el hanout* has got to be some kind of ne plus ultra. The mixture of peppery and sweet spices adds a flavor to coffee that is sweet and warm, mysterious and indefinable.

I have met Moroccans who dismiss this kind of coffee as "low class," but I also know others who drink it regularly, and even one family from Rabat whose members add ground grilled chickpeas to give their coffee an additionally strange smoky flavor.

Add ¼ teaspoon of the spice mixture to every ½ cup ground coffee before making coffee in your usual fashion. (It makes no difference whether you are using black Turkish-style coffee or American roast.)

——— Makes about ⅓ cup ———

2 whole nutmegs (or about 4 teaspoons ground nutmeg)

4 pieces cinnamon (or about 1 teaspoon ground Ceylon cinnamon)

6 to 8 dried rosebuds (see Sources)

12 cloves (or about ½ teaspoon ground cloves)

⅛ teaspoon mashed gum arabic

1 tablespoon ground ginger

2 pieces galingale (or about ½ teaspoon ground galingale) (see Sources)

2 allspice berries (or about ⅛ teaspoon ground allspice)

¾ teaspoon freshly ground white pepper

3 blades mace (or about ½ teaspoon ground mace)

15 white or green cardamom pods

1 teaspoon fennel seeds

1 teaspoon aniseed

1 tablespoon sesame seeds

Combine the spices in a spice grinder or blender. Sift, and store in a tightly sealed jar to preserve freshness.

Moroccans, along with the Chinese, Japanese, and British, make an enormous fuss over tea. Tea is often served before and always after a meal, is sipped for endless hours in Moorish cafés, and is prepared at any hour of day or night that a friend or stranger enters a Moroccan home.

Tea first came to Morocco in the 1800s, brought from the Far East by British traders who quickly found a limitless market. It is served in small glasses, into which it is poured from a silver-plated pot of the so-called Manchester shape. The pot is held high, allowing the tea to aerate and thus gain flavor as it falls into the glass.

I have always loved Moroccan tea, with its excessive sweetness and strong minty taste. (Spearmint is considered the herb of choice, but other varieties of mint have their admirers.) And there is something sublime about sitting in a familiar Moorish café. My favorite, Café Haffa, is perched high on a cliff in the Marshan of Tangier, overlooking the Strait of Gibraltar, where falcons hang in midair and then drop suddenly as they pursue their prey. My husband, Bill, and I used to spend hours there with our friend writer Paul Bowles, talking, sipping, and taking in the amazing view.

My friend Monika Sudakov titled her PhD thesis "Moroccan Tea Ritual: Religion, Gender, Socio-Economics, and Hospitality." Among her many interesting observations is the notion that Moroccan teahouses and tea cafés like Café Haffa are akin to pubs or sports bars—places where men gather and bond over a beverage. And since Morocco is a nonalcoholic society, tea plays the role of beer or ale.

Every Moroccan makes tea his own way, but there is a basic method. First, you should use green tea, preferably the type known as Gunpowder or Chun Mee. Second, the spearmint should be freshly cut. Third, the pot must be absolutely clean.

To make a 3-cup pot (enough for 6 small glasses): Rinse the pot with boiling water and then pour this water away. Put in 1 tablespoon tea, $^1/_3$ cup sugar, and a handful of fresh spearmint leaves. Cover with boiling water and allow the tea to steep for at least 3 minutes, stirring a little at the end, but not too much. After steeping, pour out a glass, look at it, taste it, and correct the sweetness if necessary before serving.

Traditionally you would drink three glasses (whether at a reception, at teatime, or after dinner) before taking your leave. Today this rule is rarely observed, and in a Moorish café, all rules are meaningless: You sip for hours, you talk, you read, you meditate, and you enjoy.

THERAPEUTIC DRINK TO WARD OFF COLDS

My friend Barbara Temsamani, who lives in Tangier, keeps this Moroccan formula for warding off colds and coughs taped to her refrigerator door. She taught her children to mix the spices and make the drink fresh three times a day for 1 to 2 days at the first sign of a cold. Drink hot, with honey added to taste.

———— ❧ Serves 1 ❧ ————

¼ dried ginger root or small piece, crushed

¼ lemon

½ teaspoon fenugreek seeds

1 scant teaspoon green aniseed

Honey

Heat 1½ cups water to a boil. Add all the ingredients, cover, and boil for 10 minutes. Strain and drink hot, with honey to taste.

SPECIAL HERBS AND FRUIT JUICES FOR WHAT AILS YOU

Moroccans are great believers in medicinal herbal teas and have assigned different herbs to different ailments as follows:

Lemon verbena calms the nerves, helps digestion, and gives comfort from the pain of menstruation.

Absinthe is the "winter tea of choice" for warmth and as an antispasmodic and digestive.

European pennyroyal (wild mint) is good for the digestion and colds.

Orange flower water mixed with milk and sugar helps children get to sleep.

Marjoram is an excellent remedy for a cold or stomachache.

Fruit juices are also used as curatives. In the Rif Mountains, they make a nonalcoholic "wine," called *samad*, from figs, peaches, bananas, grapes, and pears mixed with fenugreek and black caraway. On a recent trip, I asked Riffian-born chef Mohammed Belhaj, who has a great knowledge of Berber medicinal plants, what this drink is good for. His response: general good health and sexual problems, and if you catch a cold, drink it before sleeping and your cold will be gone by morning.

WINES

The Koran, of course, forbids the drinking of alcohol. Despite this prohibition, Morocco has a huge wine industry, producing decent wines for export. In my opinion, most wines do not go well with Moroccan food. But if you do want to drink wine with your tagines, I offer you the advice of the late Robert Mondavi, who pondered the question when I taught Moroccan cooking classes at his winery. "Probably the best wine to drink with this kind of food is a good California pinot noir or French burgundy," he said rather unenthusiastically.

ACKNOWLEDGMENTS

And now for my thanks:

... A huge thank-you to my editor and publisher, Daniel Halpern, for his wisdom, and to his associate editor, Libby Edelson, for her great source of strength and encouragement.

Enormous gratitude to Michelle Ishay-Cohen for the splendid design of the book, and to Quentin Bacon for taking so many wonderful photographs to choose from! Thank you to Mariana Velasquez for food styling.

Thanks to Mark Marthaler for his incredible how-to illustrations, and to Richard Bunk for his comprehensive culinary map of Morocco.

I offer very special thanks to Alison Saltzman, art director; Joyce Wong, production editor; Suet Chong, interior designer; Rachel Bressler, associate publisher; Michael McKenzie, publicist; and Judith Sutton, copy editor.

A very special thank-you to my agent, Sarah Jane Freymann; to Dana Cowin, editor in chief of *Food & Wine* magazine; and also to my editors there, Tina Ujlaki and Emily Kaiser. Also thanks to Barbara Wilde for her continued advice.

I especially want to thank Sara Baer Sinnot and the late Dun Gifford of Oldways for their friendship and support.

I am indebted to Carolyn Tillie; my son, Nicholas Wolfert; and to Sami Samir and Amanda Antara for their careful reading and comments.

For Moroccan recipe testing, I want to thank my daughter, Leila Wolfert; Kathy Gori; Shelly Larson Almasri; Lisa Lavagetto; Nancy Lang; Jane Ridolfi; Deanna Prichep; Patrick Jude; and Adam Balic. All of you gave me much good advice and kept me grounded.

I want to thank Fatima ben Larson Riffi for six years of wonderful cooking together.

I am grateful to Jamila and Nora Fitzgerald for their countless acts of kindness and hospitality.

Thanks to restaurant owners Mohamed Zhkiri of Yacout, Fatema Hal of Mansouria, Halima Chab of Al Fassia, and Christine Rios of Le Tobsil, for sharing their knowledge.

Thanks to the following chefs who were kind enough to share their knowledge: Mourad Lahlou, of the Restaurant Aziza in San Francisco; Mohammed Belhaj in Tangier; Rafih Benjelloun of Imperial Fez in Atlanta; Mohammed Boussaoud, former executive chef at the Mamounia in Marrakech; and Rachid and Fatiha of the Riad Dar Dmana in Fes.

I also want to thank Joan Nathan, Jill Elyse Grossvogek, Omar Kadir, Emily Swanter, Kit Williams, and Mana Samir in the States for their recipes. And in Morocco for sharing their recipes: Aicha of Beni Mellal; Zora Lahlimi Alami of Safi; Abselam Bennis of Rabat; Karima and Mina Kallamni of Marrakech; Fatima Drissiya of Tangier, Rakia Nadi of Oulmes; Zora Ouazzani of Tangier, and Khadija Ramouni from the valley of Imlil in the High Atlas.

Thank you to: Moroccan ambassador absalem Jaidi; Mustapha Haddouch, of Tangier and Seattle; Barbara Temsamani, of Tangier; Saad Hajouji, of Tangier; Abouchita Hajouji, of Fes; Khadija and Mehdi Bennouna, of Tetouan; Taleb Jouarhri, of Fes; Fama El Khatib, of Tetouan; Abdelhakim El Bahid, of Tinghrir; Alqoh M'hamed, of Itzer; M. Ben Gabrit, of Chaouen; Aziza Benchekroun, of Tetouan; Majoubi and Miriam Ahardan, of Oulmes and Rabat. Thank you to Eben Lender-King and his riads, Dar res Cigognes, Riad Kaiss, and le Nid, all in Marrakech.

My appreciation and gratitude to supportive friends Arsf Almasri and Shelly Larson of www.bramcookware; Tom Wirt and Betsy Price of www .claycoyote.com; Christine Benlafquih of www.moroccanfood.about.com; Eben Lenderking, owner of Dar Les Cigognes in Marrakech; Dana Bowen of *Saveur* magazine; Nathalie Herling of www.ancestralcookware.com; Janet Jaidi; Ami Paetzold; Joan Peterson; Freck and Vanessa Vreeland; and Hoppin' John Taylor. And a special thanks to the butchers and fishmongers at Sonoma Market: Scott Mcherney, Steve Franley, Frank Foiler, Eduardo Rosales, and Hector Contreras.

A special thanks to the snail wranglers of Sonoma and Napa: Kathleen Hill, Colleen McGlynn, Noel Gieleghem, and Laura Havlek. Good try—let's try it in Marrakech next time!

Finally, very special thanks to my beloved husband, Bill Bayer, for his love and support.

SOURCES

INGREDIENTS

Almonds, fuzzy green
www.greenalmonds.com

Almond meal
www.bobsredmill.com/almond-
meal-flour.html

Aniseed, green
www.chefshop.com
www.mustaphas.com

Argan oil
www.chefshop.com
www.mustaphas.com
www.zamourispices.com

Beans, heirloom
www.ranchogordo.com

Beans, split dried fava beans
www.kalustyans.com

Brik pastry
www.amazon.com

Capers, Moroccan
www.chefshop.com
www.mustaphas.com

Cheese (artisinal aged goat and
aged goat gouda)
www.igourmet.com
   (Cypress Grove Midnight
   Moon)
www.sheanadavis.com
   (aged goat cheese Bouchon)

Cinnamon sticks, Ceylon
www.kalustyans.com
www.thespicehouse.com

Cornmeal couscous
(coarse stone-ground corn grits)
www.bobsredmill.com/coarse
   -grind-cornmeal.html
www.hoppinjohns.net

Couscous, 100% semolina,
Moroccan hand-rolled, sun-dried
www.mustaphas.com

Couscous, 100% semolina,
fine-grain
www.kalustyans.com
www.shamra.com

Couscous, 100% semolina,
medium-grain
www.kalustyans.com
www.zamourispices.com

Couscous, *mhamsa*
www.musataphas.com
www.zingermans.com

Couscous, barley
www.bobsredmill.com/barley
   -grits-meal.html
www.kalustyans.com
www.sahadis.com

Cumin seeds, Moroccan
www.chefshop.com
www.mustaphas.com

Flour, coarse semolina
www.kalustyans.com

Flour, extra-fine semolina
http://www.kingarthurflour.com/
   shop/items/king-arthur-extra
   -fancy-durum-flour

Flour, high-gluten for *warqa*
giustos.com/home_baker/flours/
   bread-flours/organic-ultimate
   -performer-unbleached-white
   -flour.htm
www.kingarthurflour.com/shop/
   items/king-arthur-sir-lancelot
   -unbleached-hi-gluten-flour

Freekah (green wheat)
www.kalustyans.com

Gum arabic (mastic)
www.kalustyans.com

Herbs (plants), *Calamintha
nepeta* Pennyroyal (wild mint)
www.richters.com

Khliî—Moroccan beef confit
www.Moroccankhlii.com

Lemons, preserved
www.chefshop.com

Lamb
www.dartagnan.com
www.heritagefoodsusa.com
www.jamisonranch.com
www.preferredmeats.com

Lamb Merguez
www.dartagnan.com
www.jamisonranch.com

Olives, green-ripe, midway,
and red
www.chefshop.com
www.graberolives.com
www.lindsayolives.com
www.mustaphas.com

Orange flower water
www.kalustyans.com
www.mustaphas.com

Pepper, cubeb pepper
berries
www.kalustyans.com

Pepper paste, harissa
www.chefshop.com
www.mustaphas.com

Pepper paste, Turkish,
sweet or hot
www.kalustyans.com

Piment d'Espelette
www.spanishtable.com
www.thespicehouse.com
www.tienda.com

Plums, dried sour yellow
www.kalustyans.com

Poultry, chickens,
air-chilled
or organic and free range:
www.dartagnan.com
www.preferredmeats.com

Ras el hanout
www.chefshop.com
www.mustaphas.com
www.zamourispices.com

Rosebuds, dried
(for cooking)
www.kalustyans.com

Rose water
www.kalustyans.com
www.mustaphas.com

Saffron
www.mustaphas.com
www.spanishtable.com

Spice Mélange #2
www.chefshop.com
www.mustaphas.com

Thistle flowers, dried
www.tagines.com

Truffles, white, Aicha brand
www.israelikosher.com

KITCHEN ACCESSORIES

Earthenware and flameware
tagines
www.ancestralcookware.com
   (Columbian La Chamba)
www.barbotine.fr (contact@
   barbotine.fr for french stovetop
   tagines by master potter Philippe
   Beltrando)
www.bramcookware.com
   (Columbian and Egyptian)
www.claycoyote.com (American
   flameware)
www.mytoque.com (Columbian La
   Chamba)
www.surlatable.com (French
   flameware)
www.tagines.com (Moroccan)
www.toirokitchen.com (tagine-
   style Donabe; for gas stoves only)
www.williams-sonoma.com
   (French flameware)
www.pasquals.com (mica clay
   tagine signed by Felipe Ortega)

Moroccan *tangia* pot
www.tagines.com

Flameware tarte Tatin pans
www.claycoyote.com
www.surlatable.com
www.williams-sonoma.com

Ceramic pots and baking dishes
www.bramcookware.com
www.claycoyote.com
www.fantes.com
www.mytoque.com
www.surlatable.com
www.williams-sonoma.com

No-knead bread pans
www.claycoyote.com

Romertopf baker, 8- to 12-pound
capacity
www.surlatable.com
www.williams-sonoma.com

Ceramic chicken cookers and beer
can roasters
www.claycoyote.com
www.earlymorningpottery.com

Stoneware colander/steamer
www.claycoyote.com

Metal colanders and pasta pots
with steamer inserts
www.surlatable.com
www.williams-sonoma.com

Sieves for couscous (set of 5 sieves)
www.kalustyans.com

Silicone wrap for couscous cookers
www.France-Khafel.com

My sister, you are a stranger to this place.
Why be surprised that I know nothing?
My eyes have never seen the rose.
My eyes have never seen the orange.
They say there is plenty down there
In the good country
Where people and animals and plants are
    never cold.
My sister, stranger from the plains,
Don't laugh at a barefoot girl from the
    mountains
Who dresses in coarse wool.
In our fields and pastures
God hasn't made room for the rose,
God hasn't made room for the orange.
I have never left my village and its nut
    trees.
I know only the arbutus and red
    hawthorn berries,
And the leaves of green basil
That keep the mosquitoes away
When I fall asleep on the terrace
On a warm summer night.

—Mririda Nait Attik
courtesan of the High Atlas Mountains
translated by Daniel Hhalpern and Paula Paley

BIBLIOGRAPHY

Acharki, Choumicha. *Chi'hiwates*. Casablanca, Librairie Al Ouma, 2008.

Agourram, Touria. *La Cuisine Marocaine de Mère en Fille*. Paris, Albin Michel, 2000.

Amhaouche, Rachida. *La Cuisine Marocaine: Delices du Ramadan, Fêtes et Occasions*. Casablanca, Orientissime, 2006.

Bellakhdar, Jamal. *La Pharmacopée Marocaine Traditionnelle: Médecine Arabe Ancienne et Savoirs Populaires*. Paris, Ibis Press, 1997.

Bowles, Paul. *Their Heads Are Green and Their Hands Are Blue*. New York, Random House, 1963.

Bute, Fourth Marquis of (John). *Moorish Recipes*. London, Oliver and Boyd, 1954.

Dinia, Hayat. *La Cuisine Marocaine de Rabat*. Rabat, Ribat el Fath, 2000.

El Glaoui, Mina. *Ma Cuisine Marocaine*. Paris, Jean-Pierre Taillandier, 1987.

Field, Michael, and Frances Field. *A Quintet of Cuisines*. New York, Time-Life, 1970.

Guinaudeau-Franc, Zette. *Les Secrets des Cuisines en Terre Marocaine*. Paris, Jean-Pierre Taillandier, 1981.

Hal, Fatema. *Grand Livre de la Cuisine Marocaine*. Paris, Hachette, 2005.

Landry, Robert. *Les Soleils de la Cuisine*. Paris, Affont, 1966.

Lenderking, Eben Pierce. *Tanjia Marrakchia*. London, Bourbon & Pierce, 2007.

Meakin, Budgett. *The Moors*. London, Swan Sonnenschein & Co., 1902.

Mordelet, Alain. *Saveurs du Maroc*. Éditions de l'Aube, 2003.

Oufkir, Leila. *La Cuisine de Leila*. Ingersheim, France, Éditions SAEP, 2006.

Peterson, Joan. *Eat Smart in Morocco*. Madison, WI, 2002.

Sijelmassi, Abdelhaï. *Les Plantes Médicinales du Maroc*. Casablanca, Éditions Le Fennec, 1993.

Smires, Latifa Bennani. *La Cuisine Marocaine*. Casablanca, Éditions Al Madariss, 1991.

Sudakov, Monika. *Moroccan Tea Ritual: Religion, Gender, Socio-Economics and Hospitality*. Saarbrücken, Germany, Lambert Academic Publishing, 2010.

Westermarck, Edward. *Wit and Wisdom in Morocco*. New York, 1931.

Wharton, Edith. *In Morocco*. Hopewell, New Jersey, 1996.

Wolfert, Paula. *Couscous and Other Good Food from Morocco*. New York, Harper & Row, 1973. *Mediterranean Clay Pot Cooking*. New Jersey, John Wiley & Sons, 2009. *Mediterranean Cooking*. New York, 1975. *Mediterranean Grains and Greens*. New York, HarperCollins, 1998. *The Slow Mediterranean Kitchen*. New Jersey, John Wiley & Sons, 2003. *Paula Wolfert's World of Food*. New York, HarperCollins, 1988.

Wright, Clifford. *A Mediterranean Feast*. New York, William Morrow, 1999.

Yacoubi, Ahmed. *The Alchemist's Cookbook*. Tucson, Omen Press, 1972.

Zipprick, Jörg, and Marrakschi, Ben. *L'Authentique Cuisine Marocaine*. Aartselaar, Belgium, Éditions Chantecler, 2007.

INDEX

Note: Page references in *italics* indicate recipe photographs.

A

Allspice, 30
Almond(s)
  Amlou, 27, *27*
  Browned, Slow-Cooked Lamb
    Shoulder with, 350–51
  Chicken Kedra with, 324
  and Chickpeas, Chicken
    Kedra with, 324, *325*
  Couscous, and Raisins,
    Chicken Stuffed with, 333
  Dates, and Apples, Moroccan
    Dessert "Truffles" with
    (Haroset), 452
  Gazelles' Horns, *472*, 473–74
  and Milk, Sweet Bastila with,
    476, 477
  Milk Drink, 494
  Onions, and Hard-Cooked
    Eggs, Lamb with, 374–75,
    375
  Paste, Fish Baked with, 265
  Paste, Honey-Dipped Pastries
    Stuffed with (Briwats),
    484, 485
  and Prunes, Chicken Tagine
    with, in the Style of the Rif
    Mountains, 276, *277*
  and Prunes, Lamb Tagine
    with, 382–83
  Raisins, and Honey, Lamb
    Tagine with, 384
  and Raisins, Lamb Tagine
    with, Tiznit-Style, 372
  Rice, and Raisins, Chicken
    Stuffed with, *330*, 331–33
  and Rice, Chicken Kedra
    with, 326

Sautéed, Braised and Fried
  Game Hens with, 320–21
Sautéed, Honeyed Onions,
  and Spices, Crispy
  Chicken Fes-Style with,
  286–87
Semolina Cookies, *464*, 465
Sesame Seed, and Honey
  Cone, 453, *453*
Shredded Pastry with (Ktaif),
  486–87
"The Snake" (M'hanncha),
  468, 470–71
Walnuts, and Dates, Dessert
  Couscous with, 443
Zommita, 453
Amlou, 27, *27*
Aniseed, 30
  Bread with Sesame and Anise
    Seeds, 102–3
  Double-Baked Anise-Flavored
    Cookies, 467
Apple(s)
  Dates, and Almonds,
    Moroccan Dessert
    "Truffles" with (Haroset),
    452
  Green, or Pears, Lamb Tagine
    with, 385
  Milk Drink, 494
  and Prunes, Meat Tagine
    with, 373
  Raisins, and Rose Water,
    Tarte Tatin with, 462–63
Apricots
  Dried, and Pine Nuts,
    Chicken with, 282–83,
    283
  and Honey, Lamb Tagine
    with, 373

Argan oil, about, 26
Artichoke and Orange Compote,
  418
Avocado and Date Milk Shake,
  493, *493*

B

Barley
  for couscous, types of, 220
  Cracked, Berber Couscous
    with, 218–19
  grits, handling and steaming,
    for couscous, 221
  Grits Couscous with Beef and
    Leafy Greens, 222–23, *223*
  Grits Couscous with Fresh
    Fava Beans, 224
Bastila
  of Fes with Chicken or Quail,
    134, 135–37
  with Lemon, Tetouan-Style,
    138–39
  Meat, with Red Peppers,
    Raisins, and Olives, 140–41
  with Seafood, Spinach, and
    Noodles, 142–43
  Sweet, with Milk and
    Almonds, *476*, 477
  Sweet, with Pastry Cream,
    478
  warqa-wrapped, reheating,
    141
Bay leaves, 40
Bean(s). *See also* Chickpea(s);
  Lentils
  Fava, Fresh, Barley Grits
    Couscous with, 224
  Fava, Fresh, Salad, 80

Beans *(continued)*
  Fava, Puree, Berber, with
    Olive Oil (Byssara), 436
  Fava, Soup, Creamy, 180–81
  Fava, with Meat Confit,
    Cabbage, and Pickled
    Peppers, 437
  Riffian Split Pea Soup with
    Paprika Oil, 182, *183*
  White, with Saffron and Meat
    Confit, 425
Beef. *See also* Meat Confit;
  Veal
  Harira with Poached Eggs,
    175
  Kefta Brochettes, 399
  Kefta Tagine with Herbs,
    Spices, and Lemon, 401
  Kefta Tagine with Tomatoes
    and Eggs, 402–3
  khliî, about, 43
  and Leafy Greens, Barley
    Grits Couscous with,
    222–23, *223*
  Liver and Olive Salad, 94
  Marrakesh Flat Bread Stuffed
    with Meat, 106–7
  Meat Bastila with Red
    Peppers, Raisins, and
    Olives, 140–41
  Meat Tagine with Prunes and
    Apples, 373
  substituting for lamb, note
    about, 340
  Tagine with Roasted
    Cauliflower, 358–59, *359*
  Tangier-Style Harira, 174–75,
    175
Beet, Roasted, Salad with
  Cinnamon, 74, *75*
Beverages
  Almond Milk Drink, 494
  Apple Milk Drink, 494
  Avocado and Date Milk
    Shake, 493, *493*

Coffee Ras el Hanout, 495
  in Moroccan culture, 492
  Moroccan mint tea, about,
    497
  Therapeutic Drink to Ward
    Off Colds, 498, *498*
Brain(s)
  Eggplant Stuffed with, 424
  Salad, Spiced, with Preserved
    Lemons (Mokh), 95
  Salad with Tomatoes, 95
Breads, list of recipes, 98–99
Butter. *See also* Smen
  clarified, about, 158
  Clarified, Thyme-Scented
    (Oudi), 161
Buttermilk, Moroccan, 164

C

Cabbage and Trid, Chicken
  Wrapped with, 129
Cakes, Honey, Free-Form
  (Chebbakia), 482–83
Calamari
  Baby, Tagine of, with Red
    Pepper and Tomato, *256*,
    257
  Steamed, with Preserved
    Lemon and Argan Oil,
    262
  Stone-Ground Corn Grits
    Couscous with Shellfish,
    Caramelized Onions,
    and Glazed Turnips, *234*,
    235–37
Calamint, 40
Caper and Fresh Tomato Salad,
  58, *59*
Caraway, 30
Cardamom pods, 31
Cardoons, Lemon, and Olives,
  Lamb Tagine with, 360–61,
  361

Carrot(s)
  and Celery, Meat Tagine with,
    354–55
  Crushed Spiced, Salad, 78
  and Golden Raisin Salad, *76*,
    77
  Grated, and Orange Salad
    with Orange Flower Water,
    68
  Salad, Sweet, 78
  Salad with Cumin,
    Cinnamon, and Sweet
    Paprika, 79
Cauliflower
  Marak of, with Tomatoes and
    Olives, 419
  Roasted, Beef Tagine with,
    358–59, *359*
Cayenne, 30
Celery and Carrots, Meat Tagine
  with, 354–55
Charmoula
  Creamy Onion, Fish Tagine
    with, 254–55, *255*
  Eggplant Smothered with,
    428, 429
  for fish, 243
  Glaze, Broiled Fish with, 244
  Pepper Oil, Tagra of Fresh
    Sardines with, 248–49, *249*
  for seafood bastila, 142
Cheese
  aged goat, about (klila), 165
  Country, Quick Herb-
    Flavored, 167
  fresh Moroccan (jben), about,
    165
  Goat, and Honey Filling for
    Stuffed Pastries, 147
  or Meat, No-Knead Harcha
    Rounds Stuffed with, 119
Chicken
  Bastila with Lemon, Tetouan-
    Style, 138–39
  Berber Couscous, *216*, 217–18

Berber Couscous for Spring, 214–15, *215*
Berber Couscous with Cracked Barley, 218–19
buying, 275
with Caramelized Quinces and Toasted Walnuts, *278*, 279–80
Casserole-Roasted, with Preserved Lemon and Olives, 308–9
Cooked "Between Two Fires," 281
cooked with lemons and olives, in Morocco, 294
Couscous with Seven Vegetables in the Fes Manner, 209–10
Crispy, Fes-Style, with Spices, Honeyed Onions, and Sautéed Almonds, 286–87
Crispy, with Preserved Lemon and Olives Mqquali, 305
Double-Cooked Red, Marrakech-Style, 317
with Dried Apricots and Pine Nuts, 282–83, *283*
with Eggplant-Tomato Jam, 290–91
with Eggs, Preserved Lemon, and Olives, 304
Family Couscous, 204–5
with Fennel, Preserved Lemon, and Olives, 302, *303*
Fried, Tangier-Style, 322
Kedra with Almonds, 324
Kedra with Almonds and Chickpeas, 324, *325*
Kedra with Almonds and Rice, 326
Kedra with Chickpeas and Turnips, 323

with Lemon and Eggs, 310–11
Mechoui, *314*, 315
Msemmen / R'fissa, 127, *127*
or Lamb, Fine-Grain Couscous with, 226–27
or Quail, Bastila of Fes with, *134*, 135–37
with Preserved Lemon, Soft Black Olives, and Nigella Seeds, 298–99
with Preserved Lemon and Olives (M'chermel), 296–97, *297*
Rakia's Brilliant, Coated with Eggs, 312–13
Roast, on a Faux Spit with Lemon and Olives, 306–7, *307*
Smothered in Smen, 327
Smothered with Olives, 295
Smothered with Tomato Jam, 289
Steamed, 316
Steamed over a Bed of Onions, 284–85
steaming, for Moroccan recipes, 50
Stuffed with Couscous, Almonds, and Raisins, 333
Stuffed with Eggs, Onions, and Parsley, 328–29
Stuffed with Rice, Almonds, and Raisins, *330*, 331–33
tagines, notes about, 273–75
Tagine with Prunes and Almonds in the Style of the Rif Mountains, 276, *277*
Trid, 128–29
washing and seasoning, 127
Wrapped with Trid and Cabbage, 129
Chickpea(s)
and Almonds, Chicken Kedra with, 324, *325*

"The Bird That Flew Away," *430*, 431
Butternut Squash, and Ras el Hanout, Lamb Kedra with, 378–79
Couscous with Seven Vegetables in the Fes Manner, 209–10
Harira with Poached Eggs, 175
Lamb, Pumpkin, Carrots, and Raisins, Couscous with, *206*, 206–7
Meat Confit, and Pasta Soup, 184
peeling and cooking, 51
Tangier-Style Harira, 174–75, *175*
and Turnips, Chicken Kedra with, 323
Chiles. *See also* Harissa
cayenne, about, 30
Hot, Relish, Rabat-Style, 91
hot red pepper, about, 30
Cilantro, 40
Charmoula, 243
Charmoula (for seafood bastila), 142
Eggplant Smothered with Charmoula, *428*, 429
finely chopping, 49
Cinnamon, 29
Cloves, 31
Coffee Ras el Hanout, 495
Confit. *See* Meat Confit
Cookies
Anise-Flavored, Double-Baked, 467
Semolina, 466
Semolina Almond, *464*, 465
Coriander seeds, 31
Corn Grits
handling and steaming, for couscous, 232–33

Corn Grits *(continued)*
  Stone-Ground, Couscous
    with Shellfish,
    Caramelized Onions,
    and Glazed Turnips, *234,*
    235–37
Cornmeal
  No-Knead Harcha Made with,
    119
  porridge, about, 190
Couscous
  Almonds, and Raisins,
    Chicken Stuffed with,
    333
  artisanal sun-dried, buying,
    50
  barley, preparing, 220, 221
  Barley Grits, with Beef and
    Leafy Greens, 222–23,
    223
  Barley Grits, with Fresh Fava
    Beans, 224
  Berber, *216,* 217–18
  Berber, for Spring, 214–15,
    215
  Berber, with Cracked Barley,
    218–19
  commercially-made, buying,
    50
  corn grits, preparing, 232–33
  and Dates, Breast of Lamb
    Stuffed with, 346–47
  Dessert, Handmade, 444–45
  Dessert, with Almonds,
    Walnuts, and Dates, 443
  Dessert, with Golden Raisins,
    446, *447*
  Dessert, with Pomegranates,
    448, 449
  Eclectic, 212–13
  Family, 204–5
  Fine-Grain, with Chicken or
    Lamb, 226–27
  hand-rolled, sun-dried,
    buying, 200
  instant, buying, 200

  with Lamb, Pumpkin,
    Carrots, Chickpeas, and
    Raisins, *206,* 206–7
  with Lamb's Head and Seven
    Vegetables, 211
  large-grain (mhamsa), about,
    225
  with Meat Confit and Seven
    Vegetables, Mountain-
    Style, 211, *227*
  in Moroccan cuisine, 198–99
  semolina, steaming, 200–
    203
  serving methods, 198–99
  with Seven Vegetables in the
    Fes Manner, 209–10
  with Seven Vegetables in the
    Marrakech Manner, *208,*
    211
  Steamed Noodle (Chaariya
    Meftoun), *229,* 230–31
  steaming equipment for, 199
  steaming process, 198–99
  Stone-Ground Corn
    Grits, with Shellfish,
    Caramelized Onions,
    and Glazed Turnips, *234,*
    235–37
Cubeb pepper, 31
Cucumber(s)
  Armenian yard-long, buying,
    73
  Grated, Salad with Orange
    Flower Water, 73
  Grated, Salad with Oregano,
    72, 73
Cumin seeds, 29, 49

D

Date(s)
  Almonds, and Apples,
    Moroccan Dessert
    "Truffles" with (Haroset),
    452

  Almonds, and Walnuts,
    Dessert Couscous with,
    443
  and Avocado Milk Shake,
    493, *493*
  and Couscous, Breast of
    Lamb Stuffed with, 346–
    47
  Medjoul, Lamb Tagine with,
    387
  Orange, and Leafy Green
    Salad, 62
  Semolina Soup with Aniseed,
    190, *191*
Desserts, list of recipes, 440–41
Dips
  Amlou, 27, *27*
  Berber Fava Bean Puree with
    Olive Oil (Byssara), 436

E

Eggplant
  Smothered with Charmoula,
    428, 429
  Stuffed with Brains, 424
  and Tomatoes, Lamb Tagine
    with, 368–69, *369*
  -Tomato Jam, Chicken with,
    290–91
  Zaalouk, *92,* 93
Eggs
  Fried, with Meat Confit, 155
  Fried, with Meat Confit and
    Tomato-Onion Pancake,
    156, *157*
  Hard-Cooked, Onions, and
    Almonds, Lamb with,
    374–75, *375*
  Lamb, and Summer Leafy
    Greens, Harira with,
    176–77
  and Lemon, Chicken with,
    310–11
  in Moroccan cooking, 154

Onions, and Parsley, Chicken
    Stuffed with, 328–29
Poached, Harira with, 175
Preserved Lemon, and Olives,
    Chicken with, 304
Rakia's Brilliant Chicken
    Coated with, 312–13
and Tomatoes, Kefta Tagine
    with, 402–3
Tuna, and Capers, Brik with,
    149

F

Fennel, Preserved Lemon, and
    Olives, Chicken with, 302,
    303
Fenugreek, 31
Fish
    Baked with Almond Paste,
        265
    Bastila with Seafood,
        Spinach, and Noodles,
        142–43
    Brik with Tuna, Capers, and
        Eggs, 149
    Broiled, with Charmoula
        Glaze, 244
    Charmoula marinade for,
        243
    Fried Sardines, Tangier-Style,
        250, 251
    Grilled, Stuffed with Seafood,
        266–67, *267*
    Moroccan regional
        specialties, 263
    Moroccan varieties of, 242
    Smothered with Onion Jam,
        264
    tagines, preparing, 245
    Tagine with Creamy Onion
        Charmoula, 254–55, *255*
    Tagine with Tomatoes, Olives,
        and Preserved Lemon,
        246–47

Tagra of Fresh Sardines with
    Pepper Oil Charmoula,
    248–49, *249*
Trout with Preserved
    Lemons, Raisins, and Pine
    Nuts in Broth, *178,* 179
Flameware, cooking in, 18
Flour, semolina, about, 101
Fragrant waters, 42. *See also*
    Orange Flower Water; Rose
    Water
Fruit. *See also specific fruits*
    medicinal, 499
    steaming, for Moroccan
        recipes, 50

G

Game Hens, Braised and Fried,
    with Sautéed Almonds,
    320–21
Garlic
    in Moroccan cooking, 40
    Two-Day Pre-Ferment with,
        112
Gazelles' Horns, *472,* 473–74
Ginger, 29
Goat
    Mechoui, Marinated and
        Roasted, 345
    substituting for lamb, note
        about, 340
Grains. *See also* Barley; Corn
    Grits; Couscous; Rice
    steaming, for Moroccan
        recipes, 50
Greens
    Bastila with Seafood, Spinach,
        and Noodles, 142–43
    Berber Harira with Leafy
        Zegzaw, 173
    Blood Orange, Lettuce, and
        Toasted Almond Salad, 63
    Cooked "Wild Greens" Salad,
        81

Lamb Tagine with Baby
    Spinach, Lemon, and
    Olives, 364, *365*
Leafy, and Beef, Barley Grits
    Couscous with, 222–23,
    223
Lentils with Swiss Chard,
    Butternut Squash, and
    Meat Confit, *420,* 421
mallow, about, 40, 81
Marak of Swiss Chard, 415
Orange, Leafy Green, and
    Date Salad, 62
Orange, Romaine, and
    Walnut Salad, *60,* 61
purslane, about, 40
Purslane Jam, 84
Summer Leafy, Lamb, and
    Eggs, Harira with, 176–77
Guinea Hen and Spring Onions,
    Harcha with, 120–21
Gum arabic (or mastic), 31

H

Harissa
    Grilled Merguez Sausages
        with, *396,* 397
    Red Pepper Sauce, 211
    Sauce, *38,* 39
Herb(s). *See also specific herbs*
    -Flavored Country Cheese,
        Quick, 167
    medicinal, 499
    in Moroccan cooking, 40
Honey
    Amlou, 27, *27*
    and Butter, Semolina Yeast
        Pancakes with, *454,* 455–
        56
    Cakes, Free-Form
        (Chebbakia), 482–83
    -Dipped Pastries Stuffed with
        Almond Paste (Briwats),
        484, 485

Honey (continued)
  Fried Pastry from Sefrou, 479
  in Moroccan cooking, 42
  Raisins, and Almonds, Lamb
    Tagine with, 384
  Sesame Seed, and Almond
    Cone, 453, *453*
  Zommita, 453
Hot red pepper, 30

J

Jam
  Mixed Peppers and Tomato,
    90
  Purslane, 84
  Tomato, Sesame-Studded, 87,
    87

L

La Kama Spice Mixture, 37
Lamb. *See also* Meat Confit
  Berber Meat Tagine with
    Seven Vegetables, 356–57,
    357
  Breast of, Stuffed with
    Couscous and Dates,
    346–47
  Couscous with Lamb's Head
    and Seven Vegetables,
    211
  Couscous with Seven
    Vegetables in the Fes
    Manner, 209–10
  Couscous with Seven
    Vegetables in the
    Marrakech Manner, *208*,
    211
  Eclectic Couscous, 212–13
  Eggplant Stuffed with Brains,
    424
  Grilled Liver, Berber-Style,
    397

Grilled Merguez Sausages
    with Harissa, *396*, 397
gueddide, about, 43
Harira with Poached Eggs,
    175
Kebabs, Seared, Cooked in
    Butter, 394, *395*
Kedra with Chickpeas,
    Butternut Squash, and Ras
    el Hanout, 378–79
Kefta Brochettes, 399
Kefta Tagine with Herbs,
    Spices, and Lemon, 401
Kefta Tagine with Tomatoes
    and Eggs, 402–3
khlii, about, 43
Marrakesh Flat Bread Stuffed
    with Meat, 106–7
Meat Tagine with Carrots and
    Celery, 354–55
Meat Tagine with Prunes and
    Apples, 373
Mountain-Style Couscous
    with Meat Confit and
    Seven Vegetables, 211,
    227
with Onions, Almonds, and
    Hard-Cooked Eggs, 374–
    75, *375*
or Chicken, Fine-Grain
    Couscous with, 226–27
Pumpkin, Carrots, Chickpeas,
    and Raisins, Couscous
    with, *206*, 206–7
roasted whole (mechoui),
    about, 343
Roast Forequarter of, 344
Shoulder, Slow-Cooked, with
    Browned Almonds, 350–51
Shoulder, Steamed, with
    Baby Onions, 390–91
Skewered and Grilled, *392*,
    393
Steamed Noodle Couscous
    (Chaariya Meftoun), *229*,
    230–31

steaming, for Moroccan
    recipes, 50
Summer Leafy Greens, and
    Eggs, Harira with, 176–77
Tagine with Apricots and
    Honey, 373
Tagine with Baby Spinach,
    Lemon, and Olives, 364,
    365
Tagine with Cardoons,
    Lemon, and Olives, 360–
    61, *361*
Tagine with Globe Zucchini
    and Fresh Thyme, *366*, 367
Tagine with Honeyed Squash
    and Toasted Pine Nuts,
    376–77
Tagine with Layered Onions,
    380–81
Tagine with Layered
    Tomatoes and Onions, 381
Tagine with Medjoul Dates,
    387
Tagine with Pears or Green
    Apples, 385
Tagine with Prunes and
    Almonds, 382–83
Tagine with Quinces, 388–89,
    389
Tagine with Quinces and
    Okra, 370, *371*
Tagine with Raisins,
    Almonds, and Honey, 384
Tagine with Raisins and
    Almonds, Tiznit-Style, 372
Tagine with Rutabaga and
    Sesame Seeds, 362–63
Tagine with Tomatoes and
    Eggplant, 368–69, *369*
Tangier-Style Harira, 174–75,
    175
Tomato, Cinnamon, and
    Steamed Pasta Chorba,
    185
Lemon(s), 20. *See also* Preserved
  Lemon(s)

Lentils
  Harira with Lamb, Summer
    Leafy Greens, and Eggs,
    176–77
  Msemmen / R'fissa, 127, *127*
  with Swiss Chard, Butternut
    Squash, and Meat Confit,
    420, 421
Licorice, 31
Liver, Grilled, Berber-Style,
  397
Liver and Olive Salad, 94

M

Mace, 31
Mallow, about, 40, 81
Meat. *See also* Beef; Brain(s);
  Lamb; Meat Confit; Veal
  tagines, notes about,
    340–41
Meat Confit
  Cabbage, and Pickled
    Peppers, Fava Beans with,
    437
  Chickpea, and Pasta Soup,
    184
  "Express," 44–45
  Filling for Stuffed Pastries,
    148
  Fried Eggs with, 155
  gueddide, about, 43
  khliî, about, 43
  Marrakesh Flat Bread Stuffed
    with, 107
  No-Knead Harcha Rounds
    Stuffed with Cheese or
    Meat, 119
  preserved meat in Moroccan
    cooking, 43
  and Saffron, White Beans
    with, 425
  and Seven Vegetables,
    Mountain-Style Couscous
    with, 211, *227*

Swiss Chard, and Butternut
    Squash, Lentils with, *420*,
    421
  and Tomato-Onion Pancake,
    Fried Eggs with, 156, *157*
Mussels
  Fresh, Olives, Peppers, and
    Argan Oil, Tagine with,
    260, *261*
  Stone-Ground Corn Grits
    Couscous with Shellfish,
    Caramelized Onions,
    and Glazed Turnips, *234*,
    235–37

N

Nigella seeds, 31
Noodle(s)
  Seafood, and Spinach, Bastila
    with, 142–43
  Steamed, Couscous (Chaariya
    Meftoun), *229*, 230–31
Nutmeg, 31
Nuts. *See* Almond(s); Walnut(s)

O

Okra
  and Quinces, Lamb Tagine
    with, 370, *371*
  and Tomatoes, Marak of, 416,
    417
Olive(s)
  black, about, 23
  Chicken Smothered with,
    295
  choosing, for tagines, 294
  Crushed, Salad, 69
  Grated Cucumber Salad with
    Oregano, *72*, 73
  green Picholine, about, 22
  and Harissa, Potato Tagine
    with, *434*, 435

and Lemon, Roast Chicken
    on a Faux Spit with, 306–7,
    307
  in Moroccan cooking, 22–23
  and Orange Salad, *66*, 67
  Preserved Lemon, and Eggs,
    Chicken with, 304
  Preserved Lemon, and
    Fennel, Chicken with, 302,
    303
  and Preserved Lemon,
    Casserole-Roasted
    Chicken with, 308–9
  and Preserved Lemon,
    Chicken with (M'chermel),
    296–97, *297*
  and Preserved Lemon
    Mqquali, Crispy Chicken
    with, 305
  ripe or midway, about, 22–23
  Soft Black, Preserved
    Lemon, and Nigella Seeds,
    Chicken with, 298–99
  tasting and handling, 23
  Tomatoes, and Preserved
    Lemon, Fish Tagine with,
    246–47
Onion(s)
  Almonds, and Hard-Cooked
    Eggs, Lamb with, 374–75,
    375
  Baby, Steamed Lamb
    Shoulder with, 390–91
  a Bed of, Chicken Steamed
    over, 284–85
  Caramelized, Shellfish, and
    Glazed Turnips, Stone-
    Ground Corn Grits
    Couscous with, *234*, 235–37
  Caramelized, Winter Squash
    with (Cassolita), 422, *423*
  Creamy, Charmoula, Fish
    Tagine with, 254–55, *255*
  Eclectic Couscous, 212–13
  glazing, for tagines and
    soups, 48

Onion(s) *(continued)*
  grating, 48–49
  Honeyed, Spices, and Sautéed
    Almonds, Crispy Chicken
    Fes-Style with, 286–87
  Jam, Fish Smothered with,
    264
  Layered, Lamb Tagine with,
    380–81
  in Moroccan cooking, 40
  Spring, and Guinea Hen,
    Harcha with, 120–21
  and Tomatoes, Layered,
    Lamb Tagine with, 381
  -Tomato Pancake and Meat
    Confit, Fried Eggs with,
    156, *157*
Orange Flower Water
  about, 42
  Double-Baked Anise-Flavored
    Cookies, 467
  Grated Cucumber Salad with,
    73
  Moroccan Rice Pudding,
    451
  Orange and Grated Carrot
    Salad with, 68
  Orange and Grated Radish
    Salad with, 64, *65*
  Orange Salad with, 68
  Shredded Pastry with
    Almonds (Ktaif), 486–87
Orange(s)
  and Artichoke Compote,
    418
  Blood, Lettuce, and Toasted
    Almond Salad, 63
  and Grated Carrot Salad with
    Orange Flower Water, 68
  and Grated Radish Salad with
    Orange Flower Water, 64,
    65
  Leafy Green, and Date Salad,
    62
  and Olive Salad, *66, 67*

  peeling and sectioning, 62
  Romaine, and Walnut Salad,
    60, 61
  Salad with Rose or Orange
    Flower Water, 68

P

Pancakes
  Caid's Turban, about, 126
  M'laoui, 126
  Msemmen, *124*, 125
  Msemmen / R'fissa, 127, *127*
  Potato, 432, *433*
  rghaif, about, 125
  Semolina Yeast, with Honey
    and Butter, *454*, 455–56
Paprika
  Charmoula, 243
  Eggplant Smothered with
    Charmoula, *428*, 429
  in Moroccan cooking, 30
  Tagra of Fresh Sardines with
    Pepper Oil Charmoula,
    248–49, *249*
Parsley, 40
Pasta. *See also* Noodle(s)
  Meat Confit, and Chickpea
    Soup, 184
  Steamed, Lamb, Tomato, and
    Cinnamon Chorba, 185
  steaming, for Moroccan
    recipes, 50
Pastries
  Brik with Tuna, Capers, and
    Eggs, 149
  Chicken Wrapped with Trid
    and Cabbage, 129
  Fried Pastry from Sefrou,
    479
  Gazelles' Horns, *472*, 473–74
  Honey-Dipped, Stuffed with
    Almond Paste (Briwats),
    484, 485

  Shredded, with Almonds
    (Ktaif), 486–87
  "The Snake" (M'hanncha),
    468, 470–71
  Stuffed: Briwats and "Cigars,"
    144–45, *146*
  Trid, 128–29
  Warqa, 130–31, *132*
Pea, Split, Soup, Riffian, with
  Paprika Oil, 182, *183*
Pears
  or Green Apples, Lamb
    Tagine with, 385
  Poached, with Prunes, *460*,
    461
Peppercorns, fresh-ground, 30
Pepper(s). *See also* Chiles
  Green, and Tomato Salad, 91
  grilling and peeling, 86
  Late-Summer Salad, 57, *57*
  Mixed, and Tomato Jam, 90
  Red, and Tomato, Tagine of
    Baby Calamari with, *256*,
    257
  Red, Grilled, Salad, *88*, 89
  Red, Raisins, and Olives,
    Meat Bastila with,
    140–41
  Sweet Green, Relish, Fes-
    Style, 91
  Sweet Red, Tomatoes, and
    Preserved Lemons, 86
Pies. *See* Bastila
Pomegranates, Dessert
  Couscous with, *448*, 449
Potato(es)
  Fish Tagine with Creamy
    Onion Charmoula, 254–
    55, *255*
  Pancakes, 432, *433*
  Tagine with Olives and
    Harissa, *434*, 435
  Tagra of Fresh Sardines with
    Pepper Oil Charmoula,
    248–49, *249*

Poultry. *See also* Chicken
    Braised and Fried Game Hens
        with Sautéed Almonds,
        320–21
    Harcha with Guinea Hen and
        Spring Onions, 120–21
Preserved Lemon(s)
    Aziza Benchekoun's Five-Day,
        21
    Chicken with Lemon and
        Eggs, 310–11
    Eggs, and Olives, Chicken
        with, 304
    Fennel, and Olives, Chicken
        with, 302, *303*
    in Moroccan cooking, 20
    and Olives, Casserole-Roasted
        Chicken with, 308–9
    and Olives, Chicken with
        (M'chermel), 296–97, *297*
    and Olives Mqquali, Crispy
        Chicken with, 305
    recipe for, 21
    rinsing before using, 21
    Roast Chicken on a Faux Spit
        with Lemon and Olives,
        306–7, *307*
    Soft Black Olives, and Nigella
        Seeds, Chicken with,
        298–99
    storing, 21
Prunes
    and Almonds, Chicken
        Tagine with, in the Style
        of the Rif Mountains, 276,
        277
    and Almonds, Lamb Tagine
        with, 382–83
    and Apples, Meat Tagine
        with, 373
    Poached Pears with, *460*,
        461
Pudding, Rice, Moroccan, 451
Pumpkin, Lamb, Carrots,
    Chickpeas, and Raisins,

Couscous with, *206*, 206–7
Purslane, 40
Purslane Jam, 84

Q

Quail or Chicken, Bastila of Fes
    with, *134*, 135–37
Quinces
    Caramelized, and Toasted
        Walnuts, Chicken with,
        278, 279–80
    Lamb Tagine with, 388–89,
        389
    and Okra, Lamb Tagine with,
        370, *371*

R

Radish, Grated, and Orange
    Salad with Orange Flower
    Water, 64, *65*
Raisin(s)
    Almonds, and Couscous,
        Chicken Stuffed with, 333
    Almonds, and Honey, Lamb
        Tagine with, 384
    Almonds, and Rice, Chicken
        Stuffed with, *330*, 331–33
    and Almonds, Lamb Tagine
        with, Tiznit-Style, 372
    Apples, and Rose Water, Tarte
        Tatin with, 462–63
    Golden, and Carrot Salad,
        76, 77
    Golden, Dessert Couscous
        with, 446, *447*
    Lamb, Pumpkin, Carrots, and
        Chickpeas, Couscous with,
        206, 206–7
Ras el Hanout
    about, 32–33
    "Faux," #1, 36

"Faux," #2, 36
Relish
    Hot Chile, Rabat-Style, 91
    Sweet Green Pepper, Fes-
        Style, 91
Rice
    Almonds, and Raisins,
        Chicken Stuffed with, *330*,
        331–33
    and Almonds, Chicken Kedra
        with, 326
    Marak of Swiss Chard, 415
    Pudding, Moroccan, 451
    Sweet Steamed, 450
Rose Water
    about, 42
    Apples, and Raisins, Tarte
        Tatin with, 462–63
    Orange Salad with, 68
Rutabaga and Sesame Seeds,
    Lamb Tagine with, 362–63

S

Saffron, about, 29
Saffron water, preparing, 48
Salads, list of recipes, 54–55
Sardines
    Fresh, Tagra of, with Pepper
        Oil Charmoula, 248–49,
        249
    Fried, Tangier-Style, *250*,
        251
Sauce, Harissa, *38*, 39
Sauce, Red Pepper, 211
Sausages, Merguez, Grilled, with
    Harissa, *396*, 397
Semolina
    Almond Cookies, *464*, 465
    Cookies, 466
    flours, about, 101
    Soup with Aniseed, 190, *191*
    Yeast Pancakes with Honey
        and Butter, *454*, 455–56

Sesame Seed(s), 30
    Almond, and Honey Cone,
        453, *453*
    and Anise Seeds, Bread with,
        102–3
    Sesame-Studded Tomato Jam,
        87, *87*
    Zommita, 453
Shellfish. *See also* Shrimp
    Caramelized Onions, and
        Glazed Turnips, Stone-
        Ground Corn Grits
        Couscous with, *234*,
        235–37
    Moroccan varieties of, 242
    Steamed Calamari with
        Preserved Lemon and
        Argan Oil, 262
    Tagine of Baby Calamari with
        Red Pepper and Tomato,
        256, 257
    Tagine with Fresh Mussels,
        Olives, Peppers, and Argan
        Oil, 260, *261*
Shrimp
    Bastila with Seafood,
        Spinach, and Noodles,
        142–43
    Grilled Fish Stuffed with
        Seafood, 266–67, *267*
    Sautéed, Casa Pepe (Pil Pil),
        258, 259
    Stone-Ground Corn Grits
        Couscous with Shellfish,
        Caramelized Onions,
        and Glazed Turnips, *234*,
        235–37
Smen
    about, 158
    Chicken Smothered in, 327
    Homemade, 159, *160*
Soups, list of recipes, 171
Spice Mixtures
    "Faux" Ras el Hanout #1, 36
    "Faux" Ras el Hanout #2, 36

Harissa Sauce, *38*, 39
La Kama, 37
ras el hanout, about, 32–33
storing, 33
Spices. *See also* Spice Mixtures;
    specific spices
    Coffee Ras el Hanout, 495
    most frequently used, in
        Moroccan cooking, 29–30
    secondary, in Moroccan
        cooking, 30–31
    Therapeutic Drink to Ward
        Off Colds, 498, *498*
Spinach
    Baby, Lemon, and Olives,
        Lamb Tagine with, 364,
        365
    Seafood, and Noodles, Bastila
        with, 142–43
Split Pea Soup, Riffian, with
    Paprika Oil, 182, *183*
Squash. *See also* Zucchini
    Butternut, and Tomato Soup,
        188, 189
    Butternut, Chickpeas, and
        Ras el Hanout, Lamb
        Kedra with, 378–79
    Butternut, Swiss Chard, and
        Meat Confit, Lentils with,
        420, 421
    Couscous with Lamb,
        Pumpkin, Carrots,
        Chickpeas, and Raisins,
        206, 206–7
    Honeyed, and Toasted Pine
        Nuts, Lamb Tagine with,
        376–77
    Winter, with Caramelized
        Onions (Cassolita), 422,
        423
Swiss Chard
    Butternut Squash, and Meat
        Confit, Lentils with, *420*,
        421
    Marak of, 415

T

Tagines (earthenware)
    cooking in, 18, 273
    hot, handling, 18–19
    seasoning, 18
    substitutes for, 273
    washing, 19
Tangia, *408*, 409
Tarte Tatin with Apples, Raisins,
    and Rose Water, 462–63
Tea, Moroccan mint, about, 497
Tomato(es)
    Brain Salad with, 95
    and Butternut Squash Soup,
        188, 189
    Charmoula (for seafood
        bastila), 142
    Chicken Cooked "Between
        Two Fires," 281
    Eggplant Zaalouk, *92*, 93
    and Eggs, Kefta Tagine with,
        402–3
    Fresh, and Caper Salad, 58,
        59
    grating, 49
    and Green Pepper Salad, 91
    Jam, Chicken Smothered
        with, 289
    Jam, Sesame-Studded, 87, *87*
    Late-Summer Salad, 57, *57*
    Magic, 41, *41*
    and Mixed Peppers Jam, 90
    and Okra, Marak of, 416, *417*
    Olives, and Preserved Lemon,
        Fish Tagine with, 246–47
    -Onion Pancake and Meat
        Confit, Fried Eggs with,
        156, *157*
    and Onions, Layered, Lamb
        Tagine with, 381
    Oven-Roasted, with Toasted
        Pine Nuts, 85
    Preserved Lemons, and Sweet
        Red Peppers, 86

and Red Pepper, Tagine of
Baby Calamari with, *256,*
257
Trid, 128–29
Trid and Cabbage, Chicken
Wrapped with, 129
Trout with Preserved Lemons,
Raisins, and Pine Nuts in
Broth, *178,* 179
Tuna, Capers, and Eggs, Brik
with, 149
Turmeric, 29

V

Veal
substituting for lamb, note
about, 340
Tangia, *408,* 409
Vegetables. *See also specific*
vegetables
Berber Harira with Leafy
Zegzaw, 173

Seven, and Lamb's Head,
Couscous with, 211
Seven, and Meat Confit,
Mountain-Style Couscous
with, 211, *227*
Seven, Berber Meat Tagine
with, 356–57, *357*
Seven, Couscous with, in the
Fes Manner, 209–10
Seven, Couscous with, in the
Marrakech Manner, *208,*
211
steaming, for Moroccan
recipes, 50, 78

W

Walnut(s)
Almonds, and Dates, Dessert
Couscous with, 443
Orange, and Romaine Salad,
60, 61
Warqa, 130–31, *132*

Wine, pairing with Moroccan
food, 499

Y

Yogurt
Moroccan Buttermilk, 164
Moroccan (Raib), 164

Z

Za'atar, 40
Zucchini
Berber Couscous, *216,* 217–18
Berber Couscous for Spring,
214–15, *215*
Berber Couscous with
Cracked Barley, 218–19
Globe, and Fresh Thyme,
Lamb Tagine with, *366,*
367